The Legal Profession

in

The English-Speaking Caribbean

KAREN NUNEZ-TESHEIRA

THE CARIBBEAN LAW PUBLISHING COMPANY
KINGSTON

First published in Jamaica 2001 by
The Caribbean Law Publishing Company Ltd.
11 Cunningham Avenue, Box 686
Kingston 6

ISBN 976-8167-21-1
A catalogue of this book is available from the National Library of Jamaica

Typeset in 11/14pt Adobe Garamond
Cover and Book design by Pro-Design Ltd.
Printed and Bound in the USA

Contents

Table Of Cases

Table of Statutes

Anguilla

Eastern Caribbean Supreme Court (Anguilla) Ordinance 9/1982
Solicitors Act 1974, England
Solicitors Remuneration Act 1870, England
Solicitors Remuneration Act 1881, England

Antigua & Barbuda

Council of Legal Education Act Cap. 114
Eastern Caribbean Supreme Court (Antigua & Barbuda) Act Cap. 143
Legal Profession Act 9/1997
Solicitors Act 1974, England

Barbados

Council of Legal Education Act Cap. 366A
Legal Profession Act Cap. 370A

Dominica

Council of Legal Education Chap. 28:09
Eastern Caribbean Supreme Court (Dominica) Act Chap. 4:02
Solicitors Act 1974, England
Solicitors Remuneration Act 1870, England
Solicitors Remuneration Act 1881, England

Grenada

Council of Legal Education Act Cap. 71
Eastern Caribbean Supreme Court (Grenada) Act 19/1991
Solicitors Act 1974, England
Solicitors Remuneration Act 1870, England
Solicitors Remuneration Act 1881, England

Guyana

Council of Legal Education Act Cap. 4:04
Legal Practitioners Act Cap. 4:01
Legal Practitioners (Amendment) Act 3/1980
Legal Practitioners Ordinance 1897

Jamaica

Jamaica Nationality Act 8/1962
Jamaica Bar Regulations Law 3/1960
Legal Profession Act 1971
Legal Profession (Amendment) Act 1981
Legal Profession (Amendment) Act 1994
Solicitors Law Cap. 363

St. Christopher & Nevis

Eastern Caribbean Supreme Court (St. Christopher & Nevis) Act 1983
Solicitors Act 1974, England
Solicitors Remuneration Act 1870, England
Solicitors Remuneration Act 1881, England

St. Lucia

Eastern Caribbean Supreme Court (St. Lucia) Act 1969
Legal Profession Act 31/2000
Legal Practitioners Ordinance Ch. 116

St. Vincent & the Grenadines

Eastern Caribbean Supreme Court (St. Vincent & the Grenadines) Act Cap. 18
Solicitors Act 1974, England
Solicitors Remuneration Act 1870, England
Solicitors Remuneration Act 1881, England

The Bahamas

The Bahamas Bar Act Ch. 44
Legal Profession Act 26/1992
Supreme Court Act Ch. 41
Supreme Court Act Ch. 35

Trinidad & Tobago

Council of Legal Education Act Chap. 39:50
Legal Profession Act 21/1986
Legal Profession (Amendment) Act 16/1996
Legal Profession (Amendment) Act 76/2000
Solicitors Act Chap. 6:50

Table of Rules and Regulations

Antigua & Barbuda

- Code of Ethics, Fourth Schedule to the Legal Profession Act 9/1997
- Disciplinary Proceedings Rules Fifth Schedule to the Legal Profession Act 9/1997
- Solicitors Remuneration Act 1870, England
- Solicitors Remuneration Act 1881, England
- Eastern Caribbean Supreme Court Civil Procedure Rules, 2000

Barbados

- Disciplinary Proceedings Rules, Fifth Schedule to the Legal Profession Act Cap. 370A
- Legal Profession Code of Ethics 1988 S.I. 113/1988
- Legal Profession (Accounts) Rules 1973 S.I. 107/1973
- Legal Profession (Admission to) Rules 1999 S.I. 42/1999
- Legal Profession (Disciplinary Committee Reference to the Court of Appeal) Rules 1985 S.I.189/1985
- The Attorneys-at-Law Compensation Fund Rules1984 S.I.86/1984
- The Attorneys-at-Law (Remuneration for Non-Contentious Business) Rules 1997 S.I. 55/1997
- Rules of the Supreme Court 1982 S.I. 51/1982

Eastern Caribbean (save Antigua & Barbuda and St. Lucia)

- OECS Code of Ethics made and ratified by the OECS Bar Association effective 15 June, 1991.
- Solicitors' Practise Rules 1975
- Solicitors' Remuneration Order 1972 S.I. 1139/1972 England
- Solicitors' Remuneration (Non-Contentious Business) Order 1994 S.I. 2616/1994
- Eastern Caribbean Supreme Court Civil Procedure Rules, 2000

Guyana

- Disciplinary Proceedings Rules, First Schedule to the Legal Practitioners Act Cap 4:01
- Disciplinary Proceedings (Amendment) Rules 1980
- Rules of the High Court 1955

Jamaica

- Legal Profession (Canons of Professional Ethics) Rules 1978, S.I.168/1978
- Legal Profession Accounts Rules 1999
- Disciplinary Committee (Appeal) Rules 1972, S.I. 152/1972
- Enrolment and Practising Certificate Fees Rules 1971 S.I. 436/1971
- The Legal Profession (Disciplinary Proceedings) Rules, Fourth Schedule to the Legal Profession Act 1971
- General Rules and Orders of the Supreme Court of Judicature of Jamaica 1979
- Legal Profession (Enrolment and Practising Certificate Fees)(Amendment) Rules, 1999 S.I. 183A/1996

St. Lucia

- Code of Ethics Third Schedule to the Legal Profession Act 3/2000
- Disciplinary Proceedings Rules, Fifth Schedule to the Legal Profession Act 31/2000
- Eastern Caribbean Supreme Court Civil Procedure Rules, 2000

The Bahamas

- The Bahamas Bar (Code of Professional Conduct) Regulations S.I. 22/1991
- The Bar Articles (Period of Service) Regulations 1994 S.I. No. 86 of 1994
- Rules of the Supreme Court 1978

Trinidad & Tobago

- The Attorney-at-Law (Remuneration) (Non-Contentious Business) Rules 1997 LN 77/1997
- Code of Ethics, Third Schedule to the Legal Profession Act 21/1986
- Legal Profession (Disciplinary Proceedings) Rules, 1986, Fifth Schedule to the Legal Profession Act 21/1986
- Orders and Rules of the Supreme Court of Judicature of Trinidad & Tobago 1975

Table of Abbreviations

AC	Law Reports Appeal Cases
Ad & El	Adolphus and Ellis 's Reports, 1834-1842o
All ER Rep	All England Law Reports Reprint
All ER	All England Law Reports
App Cas	Law Reports Appeal Cases House of Lords, 1875-1890
Atk	Atkyn's Reports, 1736-1754
B&C	Barnewall and Cresswell's Reports, 1822-1830
B&S	Best and Smith's Reports, 1861-1870
Barb. L.R.	Barbados Law Reports
Beav.	Beavan's Reports, 1838-1866
B.G.A.J.	British Guiana Appeal Judgments
Bing.	Bingham's Reports, 1822-1834
CA	Civil Appeal
CPD	Law Reports Series, Common Pleas Division, 1875-1880
Ch D	Law Reports Chancery Division, 1875-1890
Ch.	Law Reports Series Chancery Division, 1891 and subsequently
Cl & Fin.	Clark and Finnelly's Reports, 1831-1846
Cox	Cox's Equity Cases, 1745-1797
Cr. App Cas	Criminal Appeal Cases
Curt	Curtis' Reports of Ecclesiastical Cases, 1833-1844
De GM & G	De Gex Macnaghten and Gordon's Reports, 1851-1857
Dougl	Douglas's Reports, 1778-1785
Dow	Dow's Reports of Appeals to the House of Lords, 1813-1849
Dow & Ry	Dow and Ryland's Reports
Dowl	Dowlings's Practice Reports, 1830-1841
Dr & War	Drury and Warren's Reports (Ireland), 1841-1843
E & E	Ellis's and Ellis's Reports, 1858-1861
E & B	Ellis and Blackburn's Reports, 1852-1858
East	East's Reports, 1800-1812
Eq Cas	Equity Cases

Exch	Exchequer Reports, 1847-1856
F & F	Foster and Finlason's Reports, 1847-1860
H.C.A.	High Court Action
H.L Cas	House of Lord Cases, 1847-1860
Hare	Hare's Reports, 1841-1860
J.L.R	Jamaican Law Reports
J.P.	Justice of the Peace Reports, 1837 and subsequently
Jur.	Jurist Reports, 1837-1854
Knapp	Knapp's Privy Council Cases
K & J	Kay and Johnson Reports, 1854-1858
KB	Law Reports Series Kings' Bench Division
Keen	Keen's Reports, 1836-1838
LJ	Law Journal Reports, 1831-1846
LRBG	Law Reports of British Guiana
LRG	Law Reports of Guyana
LT	Law Times Reports, New Series, 1859-1947
M & W	Meeson and Welsby's Reports 1836-1822
Mac & G	Mac Naghten and Gordon's 1849-1852
Moo & P	Moore and Payne's Reports 1827-1831
Moo PCC	Moore's Privy Council Cases 1836-1863
My & Cr	Mylne and Craig's Reports, 1835-1841
NZLR	New Zealand Law Reports
P	Law Reports, Probate Divorce and Admiralty, 1891 and subsequent
Pr	Prices' Reports, 1814-1824
QB	Queen's Bench Reports, 1841-1852
QBD	Law Reports Queen's Bench Division, 1891-1900 & since 1982
SCJB	Supreme Court Judgment Books
Sol Jo	Solicitor's Journal Newspaper 1856 and subsequently
Sim	Simon's Reports, 1826-1852
TLR	Times Law Reports, 1884-1952
Ves	Vesey Junior Reports, 1789-1817
W.I.R.	West Indian Reports
WLR	Weekly Law Reports
Wils	Wilson's Reports, 1830-1832

Preface

In my second effort at writing a legal text for law students and legal practitioners in the English-speaking Caribbean, the encouragement and support which I received in this regard only served to confirm for me that the publication of an indigenous textbook on legal ethics and responsibility would be both timely and welcomed.

Certainly the statutory regulation of the profession by the passage of legal profession legislation in many of the Caribbean territories and most recently in Antigua & Barbuda and St. Lucia bear testimony to the recognition by regional Governments and the legal fraternity for the need for a measure of legislative governance of the profession.

Indeed at the date of publication of this text, it is encouraging to report that the Governments of Dominica and of St. Vincent & the Grenadines are actively pursuing enacting for the first time, indigenous legislation specifically on the legal profession.

These salutary initiatives are especially welcomed at a time when the profession is growing at an unprecedented rate and when unfortunately complaints by the public against members of the profession have also grown at an alarming rate.

In this regard, it is significant to note that in an effort to address public concerns, that the Governments of Antigua & Barbuda, The Bahamas and St. Lucia have taken the laudable steps of making provision in their respective Legal Profession Acts, for the appointment of a non-attorney-at-law as a member of the Law Council in the case of Antigua & Barbuda, the Ethics Committee in the case of The Bahamas and the Ethics (Professional Misconduct) Commission in the case of St. Lucia.

And in Barbados, although there is no equivalent statutory provision, as a matter of practice, the Secretary of the Disciplinary Committee of the Bar Association has been, since 1995, a non-attorney-at-law.

All these initiatives, legislative and otherwise, can only bode well for the future of the legal profession, in the region, which in my view is still in a transitional stage. On this point, it is hoped that this text will in some measure contribute towards the development of the indigenous legal profession. And it is for this reason that emphasis was placed on topics such as professional misconduct and professional discipline.

In closing, I wish to thank my employer, the Council of Legal Education and in particular Madame Justice Annestine Sealey, the Principal of the Hugh Wooding Law School for their support in facilitating the writing and publication of this text.

And on a personal level, once again to my husband Russell and my parents, many thanks for their continued support.

Karen Nunez-Tesheira
June 2001

1. INTRODUCTION

SCOPE OF WORK

This book proposes to examine the law and practice as it pertains to the legal profession in the English-Speaking Caribbean territories hereunder listed: Anguilla; Antigua & Barbuda; Barbados; Dominica; Grenada; Guyana; Jamaica; St. Christopher & Nevis (also known as St. Kitts & Nevis); St. Lucia; St. Vincent & the Grenadines; The Bahamas; and Trinidad & Tobago.

APPLICABLE LAW AND RECEPTION PROVISIONS

Antigua & Barbuda, Barbados, Guyana, Jamaica, St. Lucia, The Bahamas, Trinidad & Tobago

The statutory law which regulates the law and practice in respect of the legal profession in the above territories is essentially provided for by the respective indigenous Legal Profession Acts of these territories.[1]

Eastern Caribbean (save St. Lucia and Antigua & Barbuda)

With the exception of Antigua & Barbuda and St. Lucia, none of the Eastern Caribbean territories has its own indigenous Legal Profession Act. However the respective Supreme Court Acts of these territories provide that:

> subject to local rules of court the law and practice relating to solicitors and the taxation and recovery of costs in force in England shall extend and be in force in (the respective territory) and shall apply to all persons lawfully practising therein as solicitors of the court.[2]

The extent to which the law and practice of England is received in the abovementioned Eastern Caribbean territories by virtue of this provision, was considered by Byron JA in the Kittitian Court of Appeal case of *Zuliani and Others v Veira.*[3]

In that case, the Court was called upon, *inter alia,* to determine whether the Solicitors Remuneration Order 1972, England was received in St. Kitts & Nevis.

Byron JA acknowledged that 'although there is a serious drawback to the practise of importing wholesale the law and practice on any given subject',[4] it was generally accepted that the above-mentioned reception provision 'was effective to enact in St. Kitts the law currently in force in England on this subject, being the Solicitors Act 1974 and the Solicitors' Remuneration Order 1972 S.I. 1972 No. 1139'.[5]

Indeed in the Privy Council decision in that case,[6] their Lordships concurred with Byron JA's interpretation. The Privy Council ruled that although certain practices in respect of solicitors in England were not applicable to St. Kitts (and in the words of Byron JA in the Court of Appeal judgment that 'England has institutions and traditions which support the law and practise relating to solicitors which do not exist in St. Kitts',[7]) that nevertheless the Solicitors' Act 1974, England and the Solicitors Remuneration Order 1972 were by the abovementioned reception provision incorporated into the laws of St. Kitts & Nevis.

It is to be noted that the Eastern Caribbean territories (including St. Lucia and Antigua & Barbuda) comprise one jurisdictional unit and that all these territories (save St. Lucia) have the identical ambulatory reception provision as St. Kitts. Accordingly, this provision (in the absence of any indigenous statutory and/or regulatory laws) has the effect of incorporating into these territories the current English law relating to solicitors. In this regard, it is to be noted, that the Solicitors' Remuneration Order 1972, England has been repealed and replaced by the Solicitors (Non Contentious Business) Remuneration Order 1994, England.

Antigua & Barbuda

The position with respect to Antigua & Barbuda is somewhat unclear. Section 77 of the Eastern Caribbean Supreme Court (Antigua & Barbuda) Act Cap 143 contains the identical reception provision in respect of solicitors as the other Eastern Caribbean territories (save St. Lucia). However the

Legal Profession Act 9/1997 has not expressly repealed this provision. Accordingly, it is submitted that the Legal Profession Act 9/1997 which is fairly comprehensive and similar in its contents to the Solicitors Act 1974, England, has in effect repealed the English law and practice in so far as this indigenous Act makes provision for the law and practice as it relates to the solicitor's branch of the profession.

St. Lucia

It is to be noted that, prior to the passage in November 2000, of the Legal Profession Act 31/2000 the law and practice in respect of legal practitioners (whether barristers or solicitors) was, unlike the other Eastern Caribbean territories governed by indigenous legislation – The Legal Practitioners Ordinance Ch. 116. However the Legal Practitioners Ordinance was expressly repealed by s.68 of the Legal Profession Act 31/2000.

CODE/CANON OF ETHICS

Antigua & Barbuda, Barbados, Eastern Caribbean (save Antigua & Barbuda and St. Lucia), Jamaica, St. Lucia, The Bahamas, Trinidad & Tobago

The ethical standards of the legal profession of the abovementioned territories are regulated *inter alia* by a Code/Canon of Ethics made under the respective Legal Profession Acts of these territories. The ethical rules contained therein essentially represent a codification of the common law principles which govern the norms and standards of the legal profession.

In the case of the Eastern Caribbean territories (save St. Lucia as of November 2000 and Antigua & Barbuda as of 1997) an Eastern Caribbean States Code of Ethics which came into effect on 15 June, 1991 (the contents of which are almost identical to the Code of Ethics of Antigua & Barbuda, Barbados, St. Lucia and Trinidad & Tobago,) has been ratified and accepted in principle by the respective Bar Associations of these territories. Although the Code does not have the force of law in any of these territories, it is adopted and followed in principle.

With respect to Guyana, there is no Code or Canon of Ethics prescribed by law. The ethics of the profession is governed *inter alia* by common law principles as enunciated in case law. These common law principles have been essentially codified in the Code/Canon of Ethics of the abovementioned territories. Accordingly, with respect to Guyana, the rules set out in the respective Code/Canon of Ethics may be deemed to be relevant to Guyana. However, it is to be noted that in May 2001, the Bar Council met with the Chancellor and the Chief Justice and the Council undertook to present copies of a draft Guyana Bar Association Code of Conduct for the perusal of the judges with a view to having it tabled before Parliament.

MEANING OF WORDS AND PHRASES

For the sake of clarity, given the number of jurisdictions considered in this text, the following terms and phrases should be noted. The term:

(a) attorney-at-law, unless otherwise stated, shall include attorney, barrister, solicitor, counsel, advocate and registered associate.
(b) English-speaking Caribbean, shall be a reference unless otherwise stated to the jurisdictions considered in this text.
(c) The Council of Legal Education (CLE), shall unless otherwise stated shall be a reference to the Council of Legal Education of the West Indies.
(d) The Code of Ethics shall be a reference:
    (i) with respect to the Eastern Caribbean (save St. Lucia and Antigua & Barbuda) to the Code of Ethics of the Eastern Caribbean States Bar Association.
    (ii) with respect to Trinidad & Tobago, to the Code of Ethics of The Council of the Law Association, made pursuant to s.35 of the Legal Profession Act 21/1986 as set out in the Third Schedule to the Act.
    (iii) with respect to Barbados, to the Legal Profession Code of Ethics of the Disciplinary Committee of the Bar Association, made pursuant to s.18 of the Legal Profession Act Cap. 370A.
    (iv) with respect to St. Lucia, to the Code of Ethics of the Council of the Bar Association made in accordance with s.35 of the Legal Profession Act 31/2000 as set out in the Third Schedule thereto.
    (v) with respect to Antigua & Barbuda, to the Code of Ethics of the Law Council of Antigua & Barbuda made under s.21 of the Legal Profession Act 9/1997, as set out in Fourth Schedule thereto.

(vi) with respect to The Bahamas, to the Bahamas Bar (Code of Professional Conduct) Regulations made under s.40 of the repealed Bahamas Bar Act Ch. 44.

(e) The Canon of Ethics shall be a reference with respect to Jamaica, to the Legal Profession (Canons of Professional Ethics) Rules prescribed by the General Legal Council, pursuant to s.12(7) of the Legal Profession Act of Jamaica.

ENDNOTES

1.	Antigua & Barbuda	-	Legal Profession Act 9/1997
	Barbados	-	Legal Profession Act Cap 370A
	Guyana	-	Legal Practitioners Act Cap 4:01 as amended by Legal Practitioners (Amendment) Act 3/1980
	Jamaica	-	Legal Profession Act 1971
	St. Lucia	-	Legal Profession Act 31/2000
	The Bahamas	-	Legal Profession Act 26/1992
	Trinidad & Tobago	-	Legal Profession Act 21/1986
2.	Anguilla	-	s.77 Eastern Caribbean Supreme Court (Anguilla) Ordinance 9/1982
	Dominica	-	s.78 Eastern Caribbean Supreme Court (Dominica) Act Chap. 4:02
	Grenada	-	s.84 Eastern Caribbean Supreme Court (Grenada) Act 19/1991
	St. Kitts & Nevis	-	s.78 Eastern Caribbean Supreme Court (St. Christopher & Nevis) Act 1983
	St. Vincent & the Grenadines		s.78 Eastern Caribbean Supreme Court (St. Vincent & the Grenadines) Act Cap. 18.

3. CA 5/1991 CA (Unreported)
4. *Ibid* at p.12.
5. *Ibid* at p.3.
6. *Zuliani and Others v Veira* (1994) 45 WIR 18
7. As per Byron JA in the Court of Appeal decision in *Zuliani v Veira, supra* at 13.

2. HISTORY AND FUSION OF THE LEGAL PROFESSION

Part I – Historical Background

Prior to 1970, when the Faculty of Law was established at Cave Hill Campus, University of the West Indies (UWI), Barbados, there was no organized system of legal education available in the West Indies, save for some part-time extra-mural coaching provided for in Barbados, Jamaica, and Trinidad & Tobago with the support of the University of the West Indies for those persons wishing to obtain an external LL.B. degree. However in 1956 a proposal was made for the establishment of a small institute of legal research with the intention of opening, in due course, a legal department or faculty of law. This idea was shelved until 1963 when the matter was reconsidered and, to this end, a decision taken by the Council of the University of the West Indies to appoint a Committee under the chairmanship of the late Sir Hugh Wooding the then Chief Justice of Trinidad & Tobago.[1]

THE STATUS QUO OF THE LEGAL PROFESSION IN 1963

Barristers

In order to be admitted to practise as a barrister locally one was required to attend one of the four Inns of Courts established by the British Council of Legal Education. Although the Inns provided professional training, academic qualifications were not a pre-requisite for entering the Inns of Court.

Indeed up to the late 1960s the policy of the Inns was to admit as students all persons of good character and of educational attainments who in the opinion of the British Council of Legal Education made it likely that with proper training they could become competent barristers.

In this regard, to be called to the Bar required the keeping of a certain number of dinners in Hall in each term (there were four terms a year); and the passing of the Bar examinations set by the Council of Legal Education.

With respect to the exams and the system of professional training in place at the time, L.C.B. Gower, the noted author and academic, remarked in an article entitled *English Legal Training*:

> There is no compulsory, theoretical training, practical apprenticeship or institutionalised attendance. The student is merely recommended to attend the Inns of Court Law School and read in Chambers. There is true a compulsory exam, but although it has been tightened in recent years it is still surprisingly easy.[2]

Solicitors

Unlike barristers, persons who wished to qualify as solicitors could qualify locally by sitting the examinations set by the Incorporated Law Society of England in their home territory. The local training was very similar to that which was available in England; a period of articles with a practising solicitor of at least five years standing and the sitting of preliminary, intermediate and final examinations. There were exemptions and reduced articles for graduates in law from United Kingdom universities. In addition, *bona fide* clerks who had completed ten years in the office of a legal practitioner were granted similar exemptions.[3]

There were however two major drawbacks to qualifying locally:

(1) the examinations were English exams; thus the student articled clerk's proficiency in local practice was to a large extent untested; and
(2) success was largely dependent on the quality of the firm to which the student was attached and the willingness of the more experienced solicitors to guide young trainees.[4]

These constraints or drawbacks were reflected in the shortage of solicitors in most of the territories and the high failure rate for those persons attempting the final solicitors' exams locally.

THE HUGH WOODING COMMITTEE

It was against this backdrop, that in 1963, the Wooding Committee had as its mandate *inter alia*:

> to consider and make recommendations to the Council as part of its service to the West Indian community and in light of its responsibilities for satisfying the intellectual and professional needs of the West Indies to provide for the training in the West Indies of legal practitioners – with a view to ensuring their admission to practise and right of audience before the Courts of the West Indies.

Other factors which acted as a catalyst for the establishment of an indigenous system of legal education included, the decision in 1967, by the British Council of Legal Education:

(i) to raise the entry requirements for overseas students to two (2) passes at GCE Advanced Level at Grade C or its equivalent where previously no academic qualifications were required; and
(ii) to cease to provide any training for Part 1 of the Bar Exams.[5]

ESTABLISHMENT OF THE COUNCIL OF LEGAL EDUCATION OF THE WEST INDIES

One of the recommendations which was made by the Wooding Committee in its report was the establishment of a Faculty of Law with a three year course leading to the Bachelor of Laws degree and in which the training would be wholly institutional.

In so far as the practical training was concerned, the Committee was of the opinion that it was manifestly impossible for all students to be apprenticed with equal advantage. As such the Committee recommended that the apprenticeship be supplemented by practical training.

To this end, the Committee recommended the establishment of The Council of Legal Education of the West Indies whose function it would be to oversee legal education and the qualifications for legal practice in the West Indies, very much along the lines of the British Council of Legal Education.

Emerging from the Wooding Committee report and two subsequent reports, the decision was taken after much debate in some quarters:

(i) to establish a Faculty of Law to serve the region and to be sited, after much haggling, at Cave Hill Campus, Barbados, where the student would obtain compulsory academic qualifications as a pre-requisite to professional legal training for lawyers;

(ii) to establish two professional law schools, one sited in Trinidad – the Hugh Wooding Law School and the other in Jamaica – the Norman Manley Law School. (As of 1998, a Law School was established in The Bahamas – the Eugene Dupuch Law School)

(iii) to establish Legal Aid training facilities to be operated by the Council of Legal Education, under the direction of a Director, responsible to the Principal for the policy of the Clinic.[6]

Implementation of Recommendations

Finally in July 1969, the Council of the University of the West Indies agreed to the introduction of an indigenous system of legal education in keeping with the recommendations made by the Wooding Committee. On March 25, 1971, the Council of Legal Education of the West Indies was established by a Treaty which was signed by the Governments of Barbados, Dominica, Grenada, Guyana, Jamaica, Trinidad & Tobago, The University of the West Indies and The University of Guyana. Since that date, the Governments of Anguilla, Antigua & Barbuda, St. Kitts & Nevis, Belize, Montserrat and The Bahamas have become signatories to the Treaty Agreement.

In addition, Antigua & Barbuda, Barbados, Dominica, Grenada, Guyana, Jamaica and Trinidad & Tobago have enacted a Council of Legal Education Act which Act *inter alia* gives the Treaty the force of law in these respective jurisdictions.[7] In the case of St. Lucia, although this territory is not a signatory to the agreement, in November 2000, the Legal Profession Act 31/2000 was enacted. In this regard, it is to be noted that the Act contains provisions equivalent to the Council of Legal Education Agreement.

Post-Script

Since the establishment of the Council of Legal Education and in particular the professional Law Schools in Jamaica, Trinidad & Tobago and more recently in The Bahamas, the programme of legal training offered by the Council has become increasingly practical in its focus and scope.

A combination of the courses offered in the two-year programme, the introduction of an Alternative Dispute Resolution and Negotiations component, and the overall enhancement and development of the Advocacy programme have all contributed to a training programme which has become more relevant and practical.

The Legal Aid Clinic

The Legal Aid Clinic of the respective Law Schools functions in a similar fashion to a small law firm. By way of illustration, the Legal Aid Clinic at the Hugh Wooding Law School is staffed by a team of four full-time attorneys, a secretarial support staff and a law clerk. The range of work which the Clinic undertakes (as envisaged by the Council) includes matrimonial, civil, criminal, conveyancing and probate matters. Although law students or student practitioners as they are otherwise called have no right of audience, in any of the courts in Trinidad & Tobago, (unlike other jurisdictions, most notably Canada), final year law students at the Hugh Wooding Law School have begun representing persons before the National Insurance Appeals Tribunal. And according to a newspaper report appearing in the Newsday on Wednesday April 5, 2000, 'the students gain experience and the appellants get proper representation'.

Part II – Fusion

INTRODUCTION

One of the terms of reference of the Wooding Committee was the issue of fusion, that is:

> whether there should continue to be any distinction between barristers and solicitors or whether the two branches of the profession should merge as obtains in most parts of the Commonwealth.

In this regard, the Committee noted the following points in support of fusion, *inter alia:*

(i) that qualification requirements for both branches of the law were substantially the same;

(ii) that there was a great deal in common between what a barrister did in everyday professional life and what a solicitor did in jurisdictions where there was no fusion;

(iii) that both branches of the law, in the course of their respective qualifying examinations, did many subjects in common, i.e. constitutional law, law of contract, law of tort, criminal law, land law, company law and family law; and

(iv) the comparatively low cost involved in training a merged profession as opposed to funding the cost for two separate training regimes for barristers and solicitors.

THE POSITION IN:

The Eastern Caribbean Territories (save Antigua & Barbuda and St. Lucia)

With the exception of Antigua & Barbuda as of 1997 and St. Lucia, as of 2000, the legal profession in the Eastern Caribbean territories is not a fused one. However with few exceptions, legal practitioners in these territories are admitted to practise as barristers.

This is the case because by law all persons enrolled as barristers, save and except Queen's Counsel, are entitled to practise as solicitors. However the converse is not the case. This is by virtue of the relevant provision contained in the respective Supreme Court Acts of these territories which in effect provides that every person enrolled as a barrister shall be entitled to practise also as a solicitor. [8]

Antigua & Barbuda

Until the passage in 1997 of the Legal Profession Act 9/1997, which Act fused the legal profession in Antigua, the position was the same as that which currently obtains in the other Eastern Caribbean territories (save St. Lucia) in that there was in Antigua & Barbuda *de facto* fusion of the two branches of the legal profession.[9]

St. Lucia

Prior to the passage of the Legal Profession Act 31/2000 in November, 2000, the position with respect to fusion was governed by The Legal Practitioners Ordinance Ch. 116. Pursuant to ss.2 and 4 of this Ordinance, the two branches of the profession were fully merged in that barristers (save and except for Queen's Counsel) could practise as solicitors *and* solicitors could also practise as barristers provided they had passed the intermediate and final exams set by the Law Society of England.

However, with the passage in November 2000 of The Legal Profession Act 31/2000 both branches have been formally fused so that qualified persons admitted to practise are admitted as attorneys-at-law and not as previously obtained, as barristers or solicitors.

The Bahamas

The legal profession in The Bahamas is a fused profession and has been fused as early as the nineteenth century. In this regard s.24 of the repealed Supreme Court Act Ch. 35, which Act became law in 1897 provided that every person admitted to practise in The Bahamas, shall be entitled to practise as counsel and attorney in any court in the colony. Section 2 thereof defines attorney to include solicitor. The provisions with respect to attorneys and counsel were repealed with the passage of the current Supreme Court Act Ch. 40, and included in Part III of The Bahamas Bar Act Ch. 44. The Bahamas Bar Act was subsequently repealed in 1992 and replaced by the Legal Profession Act. The relevant provision with respect to counsel and attorney is contained therein.[10]

Barbados, Guyana, Jamaica and Trinidad & Tobago

With respect to these territories, the two branches of the profession were kept separate but it was common to find barristers discharging functions normally undertaken by solicitors in England e.g. a barrister would appear in the Magistrate's Court without a solicitor or in a criminal case, would appear uninstructed. Indeed in Guyana, prior to the amendment in 1980 of the Legal Practitioners Act Cap. 4:01 (which amending Act fused the legal profession in Guyana) the respective functions of barristers and solicitors were codified in Part III of Legal Practitioners Act Cap. 4:01.

It is to be noted that with respect to Guyana, although the distinction between the two branches of the profession was generally maintained along the lines applicable to barristers called to the English Bar, one fundamental difference lay in the fact that, a British trained barrister, was entitled on admission at the local Bar to sue and recover his fees. Indeed, in the Guyanese case of *Sirikissun v Fernandes,*[11] the Court held that a barrister practising locally could sue for and recover fees from his client, even by way of a claim *quantum meruit.*

However with the passage of the respective Legal Profession Acts in these territories, both branches of the legal profession are now fused.

ENDNOTES

PART I

1. *Legal Education in the West Indies 1963-1972*, a publication of the Council of Legal Education.
2. 13 *Modern Law Review* 150 et seq
3. *Legal Education and the West Indian Lawyer, Past Present and Future*, at pp. 6-8. An Article by R. Michael Castagne.
4. *Ibid.*
5. Ch. IV *Legal Education in the West Indies 1963-1972*, a publication of the Council of Legal Education.
6. *Ibid.*
7.

Antigua & Barbuda	-	Council of Legal Education Act Cap. 114
Barbados	-	Council of Legal Education Act Cap. 366A
Dominica	-	Council of Legal Education Act Chap. 28:09
Grenada	-	Council of Legal Education Act Cap. 71
Guyana	-	Council of Legal Education Act Cap. 4:04
Jamaica	-	Council of Legal Education Act
Trinidad & Tobago	-	Council of Legal Education Act Chap. 39:50

PART II

8.

Anguilla	-	s. 70 Eastern Caribbean Supreme Court Anguilla Ordinance 9/1982
Dominica	-	s. 73 Eastern Caribbean Supreme Court (Dominica) Act, Chap 4:02
Grenada	-	s. 79 Eastern Caribbean Supreme Court (Grenada) Act 9/1991
St. Kitts & Nevis	-	s. 73 Eastern Caribbean Supreme Court (St. Christopher & Nevis) Act 1983
St. Vincent & the Grenadines		s. 73 Eastern Caribbean Supreme Court (St. Vincent & the Grenadines) Act Cap 18

9. Pursuant to s. 72 of the Eastern Caribbean Supreme Court (Antigua & Barbuda) Act. Cap 143.
10. See s. 18, Legal Profession Act 26/1992.
11. (1923) LR.B.G 1

3. QUALIFICATIONS

Part I – Qualifications for Admission to Law Schools of The Council of Legal Education

INTRODUCTION

Admission to the three Law Schools established by the Council of Legal Education is regulated by Article 3 of Council of Legal Education Agreement as amended by the Protocol to the Agreement establishing the Council of Legal Education[1] and by the Collaborative Legal Education Agreement entered into in 1999 by the University of the West Indies, the Council of Legal Education and the University of Guyana.

According to the amended Article 3 of the Council of Legal Education Agreement:

> Every person who holds a University of the West Indies LL.B. degree and having passed in such core subjects as may be prescribed in the Regulations shall be eligible for admission to the Law Schools. Every other holder of a University of the West Indies LL.B. degree as well as every person who holds a non-University of the West Indies LL.B. degree and has passed an examination conducted by the Council shall, subject to the availability of places, and to such conditions (if any) as the Council may impose, be eligible for admission to the Law Schools.

In addition, Article II, 2.1 of The Collaborative Legal Education Agreement provides that 'until such time as the quota arrangements are revisited by the Caribbean Heads of Government, no more than 25 Guyanese nationals shall be eligible for automatic entry into the course of training at the

Council of Legal Education in any academic year'. Article II, 2.2 further provides that 'during the continuation in force of this agreement the Council of Legal Education does not undertake to accept more than 25 graduates of the University of Guyana in any academic year who hold degrees, from 1998 and onwards'.

Both the Collaborative Agreement and the Caribbean Heads of Government Agreement have been co-jointly interpreted so as to limit the total number of Guyanese students eligible for automatic entry, whether as graduates of the University of West Indies or the University of Guyana, to 25 such students. Indeed, since the introduction of a full LL.B. degree programme at the University of Guyana, Guyanese nationals who are eligible for admission to the Law Schools of the Council of Legal Education are almost without exception holders of a University of Guyana, LL.B. degree.[2]

In any event, the cumulative effect of the amended Article 3 of the Council of Legal Education Agreement, and the above-mentioned Collaborative Agreement is that holders of the University of West Indies LL.B. degree and in addition, holders of the University of Guyana LL.B. degree, up to a maximum of 25 such persons, are guaranteed automatic admission to the respective Law Schools of the Council.

Those persons who hold what is referred to as an external LL.B. degree have no such guarantee of automatic admission and are admitted to the Law Schools of the Council based on the availability of space in accordance with Article 3, as amended by the Protocol to the Council of Legal Education Agreement.

This restriction or quota of external LL.B. degree holders to the Law Schools, in particular the Hugh Wooding Law School, has in recent years become an issue of great concern and not without its share of controversy. This is primarily because it is only within approximately the past seven years, that applications by holders of external LL.B. degrees have virtually mushroomed in Trinidad & Tobago, resulting in an unprecedented demand for admission to the Hugh Wooding Law School by such persons; a demand which continues to outstrip the current physical infrastructure and staff resources of the Law School.

The main reason for this significant increase in the number of external law degree graduates seeking admission to the Hugh Wooding Law School, is due to the fact that the external University of London LL.B. degree is offered by an increasing number of privately owned tertiary institutions in Trinidad.

In 1996, as a direct result of the increasing number of applications for admission by external LL.B. degree holders and the inability of the Council to admit all such applicants, a decision was taken by the Council to introduce an External Entrance Examination for external LL.B. degree holders. Article 3 of the Council of Legal Education Agreement as amended by the Protocol makes provision for the conduct of the entrance examination by the Council.

This examination is set and corrected, subject to the approval of the Council, by the academic staff of the Faculty of Law, University of the West Indies, Barbados, pursuant to an Agreement entered into between the Council and the Faculty of Law. An Admissions Board established by the Council under this Agreement, supervises the conduct of the exams and allocates a limited numbers of places to successful candidates. Admission is based on performance in this Entrance Exam.

Eligibility to the Law Schools, particularly the Hugh Wooding Law School, continues to be a source of great contention and concern, particularly among the external LL.B. graduates who have organised themselves into a lobby group called External Law Student Association (ELSA).

This issue of eligibility of admission to the respective Law Schools of the Council of Legal Education is of critical practical importance as persons wishing to be admitted to practise law in the territories which have enacted a Council of Legal Education Act are, with the exception of Trinidad & Tobago as of 2000, generally required to be holders of a Legal Education Certificate (LEC) awarded by the Council of Legal Education.

Legal Education Certificate

The Legal Education Certificate (LEC) awarded by the Council of Legal Education is granted in the following two cases:

(i) on completion of a two year course of training organised by the Council at one of the three Law Schools established by the Council. Persons who must complete the two years course are holders of either an LL.B. from UWI or a degree equivalent to the UWI LL.B. degree as recognized by the Council as being equivalent thereto; or

(ii) on completion of a six-month course of training organized by the Council for holders of qualifications obtained in a common law jurisdiction for admission to practise law in that jurisdiction, and which qualification is approved by the Council.

Current Position

Trinidad & Tobago

It is in response *inter alia* to this growing demand for admission to the Hugh Wooding Law School that the Legal Profession (Amendment) Act 76/2000 was enacted.[3] This amending Act has in effect varied the requirements for admission as prescribed by Arts. 5 and 6 of the Council of Legal Education Agreement, the provisions of which have been given the force of law by s.3 of the Council of Legal Education Act Chap 39:50. According to this amending Act, persons admitted to practise law in Trinidad & Tobago are no longer required to be holders of a Legal Education Certificate awarded by the Council of Legal Education. Once they attain the professional qualifications set out in the amending legislation they are as equally entitled without restriction or qualification as a holder of the LEC awarded by the Council of Legal Education to be admitted to practise law in Trinidad & Tobago

Part II – Professional Qualifications for Admission To Practise

INTRODUCTION

As a general rule, the professional qualifications necessary for admission to practise law in the various territories are governed by Arts. 5 and 6 of Council of Legal Education Agreement and by the respective Council of Legal Education Acts of the various territories, s.3 of which (in most jurisdictions) *inter alia* gives Arts. 5 and 6 of the Council of Legal Education Agreement the force of law. In this regard, Art. 5 of the Council of Legal Education Agreement was amended by a Protocol to the Agreement establishing the Council of Legal Education which was signed and entered into at the Council's twenty-sixth meeting held in Barbados on 12 and 13 September 1996. The original Art. 5 which must be read in conjunction with the new Art. 5 provides:

> The Government of each of the participating territories undertakes that it will recognise that any person holding a Legal Education Certificate fulfils the requirements for practice in its territory so far as institutional training and education are con-

> cerned and that (subject to the transitional provisions hereinafter contained and to any reciprocal arrangements that any of the said territories may hereafter make with any other country.

The new Art. 5 reads as follows:

> Notwithstanding Article 5, a participating territory may, in the interest of justice and after consultation with the Head of the Judiciary and, where practicable, the appropriate legal professional body in that territory, permit the admission to practice law in that jurisdiction of a person who is the holder of a qualification obtained in a Common Law jurisdiction for admission to practise law in that jurisdiction for the purpose of providing legal services or representation in a cause or matter, where there is no available attorney-at-law with the requisite specialty or experience in any of the participating territories.

Art. 6 provides:

1. The Government of each of the participating territories agrees that the following persons shall be recognized as professionally qualified for admission to practise in its territory, namely:
   (a) Any national who was on 1st October, 1972 qualified to be admitted to practise as a solicitor or a barrister in that territory;
   (b) Any national who, prior to 1st January, 1985, had undergone or is undergoing or has been accepted for a course of legal training leading to a qualification such as is referred to in paragraph 2(b)(I) of Article 4 of this Agreement and obtains that qualification.[4]

It is to be noted that the participating or signatory territories to the Council of Legal Education Agreement are Anguilla, Antigua & Barbuda, Barbados, Belize, Dominica, Grenada, Guyana, Jamaica, Montserrat, St. Kitts & Nevis, The Bahamas, and Trinidad & Tobago.

PROFESSIONAL QUALIFICATIONS

Antigua & Barbuda

Apart from the Council of Legal Education Act Cap 114, s.6(1)(c) of the Legal Profession Act 9/1997 provides that the professional qualifications for admission to practise as an attorney-at-law are in effect the professional qualifications prescribed by Arts. 5 and 6 of the Council of Legal Education Agreement prior to the amendments introduced by the Protocol to the Council of Legal Education Agreement. These professional qualifications apply to both citizens and non-citizens including non-citizens who are admitted to practise law under the reciprocal arrangement provision of s.7 of the Legal Profession Act.

However, it is to be noted, that in practice the qualifications prescribed by law as of 1996, are those set out in Arts. 5 and 6 of the Council of Legal Education Agreement as amended by the Protocol to the Agreement although these amendments have not been incorporated into the Legal Profession Act.

Barbados

The rules governing the qualifications for admission to practise law made under sections 7 and 17 of the Legal Profession Act Cap. 370A and contained in the Second Schedule thereto, are the identical professional qualifications provisions contained in Arts. 5 and 6 of the Council of Legal Education Agreement prior to the amendments made in 1996 by the Protocol to the Agreement.[5]

However, in this regard, the qualifications for admission are deemed as of 1996 to be amended to include the new Arts. 5 and 6 introduced by the Protocol to the Agreement. It is to be further noted that pursuant to the reciprocal admission provisions set out in s.6 of the Legal Profession Act, non-citizens who are not holders of the qualifications prescribed under Arts. 5 and 6 of the Agreement as amended by the Protocol may be admitted to practise law by order of the Minister after consultation with the Chief Justice provided *inter alia* that such legal practitioner possesses suitable qualifications and competency. In this regard, it is to be noted that the Act does not specify what constitutes suitable qualifications and competency.

Dominica

Pursuant to the Council of Legal Education Act Chap. 28:09, Arts. 5 and 6 of the Council of Legal Education Agreement have the force of law in Dominica. (In this regard the qualifications for admission to practise law are deemed to be amended so as to include the new Arts. 5 and 6 introduced by the Protocol to the Agreement).

In addition, by virtue of s.70(1)(a)(b) and (c) of the Eastern Caribbean Supreme Court (Dominica) Act, Chap. 4:02, the qualifications for admission to practise law in Dominica are effectively the same as those set out in Arts. 5 and 6 of the Council of Legal Education Agreement.

Further, s.70(1)(d) of the Supreme Court Act provides that a solicitor or barrister who has been admitted to practise by a Superior Court and to the Bar, respectively, in England, Northern Ireland and Scotland, may be admitted to practise in Dominica in circumstances where the Attorney General by order determines that in the interest of the public it is desirable, to waive the requirements, *inter alia* with respect to professional qualifications as set out in the Council of Legal Education Agreement.

Grenada

The provisions of s.77 of the Eastern Caribbean Supreme Court (Grenada) Act 19/1991 set out the requirements in respect of admission to practise law in Grenada.

Section 77(1) provides that a judge of the High Court may admit to practise:

(i) as a barrister, any member of the English Scottish, Northern Ireland or Canadian Bar;

(ii) as a solicitor or writer, any person who has been admitted in any of the Superior Courts of England, Scotland or Northern Ireland.

There are no cut-off dates prescribed for the admission of such persons to practise nor is any provision made in the Supreme Court Act for the admission to practise of holders of the LEC awarded by the Council of Legal Education. However in 1990, the Council of Legal Education Act was enacted. Pursuant to s.4 thereof, Arts. 5 and 6 of the Council of Legal Education Agreement as amended by the Protocol have the force of law in Grenada.

Guyana

Pursuant to s.4(1)(d) of the Legal Practitioners (Amendment) Act 3/1980, a person is qualified to practise law if he holds a LEC or is professionally qualified for admission in accordance with Arts. 5 and 6 of the Council of Legal Education Agreement. The Council of Legal Education Act Cap. 4:04 as amended by LN 21/1986 also provides for Arts. 5 and 6 of the Council of

Legal Education Agreement to have the force of law in Guyana. In this regard it is to be noted that the professional qualifications for admission, are as of 1996, those set out in the new Arts. 5 and 6 as amended by the Protocol to the Agreement.

In addition, s.4A of the Legal Practitioners (Amendment) Act makes provision for reciprocal admission (along the same lines as are applicable to Trinidad & Tobago) for legal practitioners of any country not being a participating country within the meaning of Art. 6 of the Council of Legal Education Agreement[6] and who to the satisfaction of the Minister after consultation with the Chancellor *inter alia* possesses suitable qualifications and competence.

Such person, in accordance with s.4A(2) is also required to have attained the age of 21 years and satisfy the court of his qualifications and good character.

Jamaica

Apart from the Council of Legal Education Act, which effectively gives Arts. 5 and 6 as amended by the Protocol to the Agreement the force of law, the professional qualifications for admission to practise as an attorney in Jamaica are governed by sections 6 and 9 of the Legal Profession Act 1971.

According to s.6(1), a person is qualified for enrolment if *inter alia* he holds the qualifying certificate issued by the General Legal Council pursuant to s.9 of the Legal Profession Act.

According to s.9(3) of the Act, the General Legal Council through the Legal Education Authority (constituted under the General Legal Council), is the body responsible for issuing the qualifying certificate. In this regard, the qualifying certificate is issued by the Authority to any person who has satisfied the Authority that he has:

(a) obtained adequate practical experience in law; and
(b) is otherwise qualified to practise law.

Section 6(2)(b) provides that a person is qualified for enrolment if he satisfies the Council that he is qualified to practise law in any country having a sufficiently analogous system of law and that his qualifications are such as to render him suitable for enrolment.

In practice to date, persons who are qualified for enrolment under s.6(1) are holders of the LEC awarded by the Council of Legal Education; it is only persons who are retained by the Government of Jamaica in respect of matters of national interest who are deemed to be qualified for enrolment under s.6(2)(b).

St. Kitts & Nevis

Although the Government of St. Kitts & Nevis is a signatory to the Council of Legal Education Agreement, to date this territory has not enacted a Council of Legal Education Act. However s.71(2) and s.71(3) of the Eastern Caribbean Supreme Court (St. Christopher and Nevis) Act 1983 give effect in part to Arts. 5 and 6 of the Council of Legal Education Agreement. According to s.71(2) of the Supreme Court Act, in order to be admitted to as a barrister or solicitor in St. Kitts/Nevis, the applicant must be the holder of the LEC issued by the Council of Legal Education. This is save and except for the provisions of s.71(3) which provision is equivalent to the transitional provision contained in Art. 6 of the Council of Legal Education Agreement. In this regard it is to be noted that Arts. 5 and 6 have been amended by the Protocol to the Agreement, so that persons qualified to practise law under the Agreement include such persons provided for by the new Arts. 5 and 6.

Further, in accordance with s.71(6) of the Supreme Court Act, the Chief Justice may, by Order, admit a barrister or solicitor from a Commonwealth territory outside of the participating territories (of the Council of Legal Education Agreement) who *inter alia* possesses, to his satisfaction, proper qualifications and competency.

St. Lucia

According to s.15(1) of the Legal Profession Act 31/2000 a person is qualified to be admitted to practise law in St. Lucia if *inter alia* he holds the 'qualifications prescribed by law'. In this regard s.2(2) of the Legal Profession Act provides that the 'qualifications prescribed by law' are:

(a) the qualifications as required under the Legal Practitioners Ordinance Ch. 116 if the qualifications are obtained before 1st January, 2006,

(b) qualifications for admission to practise law as set out in the (Council of Legal Education) Agreement which are obtained on or after 1st January, 2006.

With respect to (a) above, the following are the persons qualified as barristers under the repealed Legal Practitioners Ordinance Ch. 116:

(i) Any English or Irish barrister at law or a Scottish advocate;

(ii) Any barrister or advocate of any of the Superior Courts of any British Possession where similar privileges are accorded to barristers of the Supreme Court;

(iii) Any solicitor of the United Kingdom or law agent admitted to practise in Scotland;

(iv) Any person who being of full age and otherwise qualified shall have passed the intermediate and final examination of the Law Society of England.[7]

In so far as (b) above is concerned, although St. Lucia is not a signatory to the Council of Legal Education Agreement nor has the Council of Legal Education Act been enacted, nevertheless, the Seventh Schedule to the Legal Profession Act 31/2000, contains the provisions of the Council of Legal Education Agreement.

However, pursuant to s.2(2) of the Legal Profession Act, the provisions of the Council of Legal Education Agreement as contained in the Seventh Schedule to the Act do not come into effect until January 2006, in so far as the professional qualifications for admission to practise law in St. Lucia are concerned. Further, it is to be noted that in respect of the transitional provisions, Art. 6 provides that the cut off date in respect of persons who are undergoing or had been accepted for a course of legal training for St. Lucia is on or before December 31, 1980 and not June 1, 1985, as is the case with the other territories.

St. Vincent & the Grenadines and Anguilla

In the case of Anguilla and St. Vincent & the Grenadines, these territories have not enacted a Council of Legal Education Act. In addition, the Government of St. Vincent & the Grenadines is not a signatory to the Council of Legal Education Agreement. The requirements for admission to practise as a barrister or solicitor are governed by the provisions of the respective Supreme Court Acts of these territories and in addition in the case of Anguilla, by Arts. 5 and 6 of the Council of Legal Agreement as amended by the Protocol to the Agreement. According to the provisions of the respective Supreme Court Acts of St. Vincent & the Grenadines and Anguilla, the following persons may be allowed to practise law in these territories:

(i) any person who has been admitted as a barrister to the English, Scottish, or Northern Irish Bar;
(ii) any person who has been awarded the Legal Education Certificate from the Council of Legal Education of the West Indies;
(iii) any person who has been admitted as a solicitor or law agent by a Superior Court in England, Scotland or Northern Ireland;
(iv) any person who being of full age and otherwise qualified should have passed the intermediate and final examination of the Law Society of England.[8]

The Bahamas

Although the Government of The Bahamas is a signatory to the Council of Legal Education Agreement, it has not to date enacted a Council of Legal Education Act. In this regard, the Agreement contains a Protocol which allows the Bahamian Government, to be able to admit to practise in The Bahamas, persons holding qualifications other than the LEC awarded by the Council of Legal Education. However, the Protocol also provides that 'the Government of the Bahamas undertakes to review the position within five years of the coming into force of the Agreement with a view to implementing fully the provisions of Art. 5 of the Council of Legal Education Agreement'. To date the position remains the same as it was at the date of signing the agreement in 1971.

In this regard the professional qualifications for admission to practise law in The Bahamas are set out in the First Schedule to the Legal Profession Act 26/1992. According to the First Schedule, a person is qualified to practise law in The Bahamas if:

(a) he has been admitted to practise as a barrister to the Bar of England, Scotland, Eire and Northern Ireland or of such country within the Commonwealth or not as may be prescribed;
(b) he has been admitted to practise as a solicitor by the Supreme Court of England, Scotland, Eire and Northern Ireland or any country within the Commonwealth or not as may be prescribed;
(c) he has been awarded the Legal Education Certificate from the Council of Legal Education of West Indies either on completion of the six month or two year course of training organized by the Council.

In addition, the First Schedule also provides that a person is qualified if *inter alia* he has completed a period of articleship with a counsel and attorney in practice in The Bahamas.[9]

Trinidad & Tobago

Apart from the Council of Legal Education Act Ch. 39:50 which effectively gives Arts. 5 and 6 of the Council of Legal Education Agreement as amended by the Protocol to the Agreement the force of law in Trinidad & Tobago, s.15(1)(c) of Legal Profession Act 21/1986 provides that a person who makes an application to the High Court and satisfies the court that *inter alia* he holds the qualifications prescribed by law shall be eligible to practise as an attorney-at-law in Trinidad & Tobago.

Section 15(5) thereof provides that the qualifications prescribed by law means the qualifications for admission to practise as set out in the Council of Legal Education Agreement.

In addition by Act No.16 of 1996, the Legal Profession Act was amended by the inclusion of s.15A thereof. Section 15A provides in effect, that pursuant to the Order of the Minister of Legal Affairs after consultation with the Chief Justice, persons who are the holders of qualifications prescribed by law may be admitted to practise in Trinidad & Tobago provided that such person is a Commonwealth citizen who has been admitted to practise in a Commonwealth Court for at least ten years.

However, as of 12 November, 2000, the Legal Profession (Amendment) Act 76/2000 has further expanded the class of persons who may be admitted to practise law in Trinidad & Tobago.

Such person who may be admitted is a person who:

(a) has passed the Bar Finals or the Bar Vocational Course at an institution validated by the General Council of the Bar of England and Wales, has been called to the Bar of England and Wales and has completed pupilage of at least 6 months and is certified as such;

(b) has passed the Law Society Finals or the Legal Practise Course at an institution validated by the Law Society of England and Wales and having undertaken articles or a training contract in accordance with the Training Regulations of the Law Society of England and Wales, has been admitted to the roll of solicitors of the Supreme Court of England and Wales;

(c) has passed the Bar Vocational Course at an institution validated by the General Council of the Bar of England and Wales; or
(d) has passed the LPC at an institution validated by the Society of England and Wales; and
(e) in the case of persons referred to in (c) and (d) above, has obtained a certificate from the head of Chambers of an attorney of not less than ten years standing practising in Trinidad & Tobago to the effect that the national has undergone an attachment at those Chambers for a continuous period of not less than six months doing work relating to the practice of law.

In this regard it is to be noted that although the new Art. 5 to the Council of Legal Education Agreement has in effect expanded the categories of persons who may be admitted to practise law in Trinidad & Tobago so as to include persons who are not holders of the LEC, such admission is subject to clearly defined qualifications and circumstances.

Certainly the scope of persons admitted to practise law in Trinidad & Tobago under the Legal Profession (Amendment) Act 76/2000 is far wider than that which is provided for or contemplated by the new Art. 5. This is of particular concern as the definition of qualifications prescribed by law under s.15(5) of the principal Act has neither been repealed nor amended.

Part III – Citizenship Qualifications

INTRODUCTION

There are significant jurisdictional variations in respect of the citizenship requirements for admission to practise law in the respective territories. Accordingly, the requirements in respect of these territories will be considered separately, where necessary.

Antigua & Barbuda

Pursuant to s.6 of the Legal Profession Act 9/1997, a person is qualified to be admitted to practise as an attorney at law in Antigua & Barbuda if he is:

(i) a citizen of Antigua & Barbuda;
(ii) a citizen of country specified in the Second Schedule in which there is a law in force conferring the status of citizenship of that country; or
(iii) regarded as belonging to a country specified in the Second Schedule under any law in force in that country.[10]

In addition, s.7 of the Act contains the identical reciprocal arrangement provision as contained in s.16 of the Legal Profession Act of Trinidad & Tobago.[11] It should be noted that in addition, the non-citizen must have obtained the qualifications prescribed by law i.e. he or she must be the holder of the LEC awarded by the Council of Legal Education subject to the amendments(s) made by the new Art. 5 of the Council of Legal Education Agreement as contained in the Protocol to the Agreement.

Barbados

Section 5(1)(a) of Legal Profession Act Cap. 370A, provides that a person is qualified to practise law in Barbados if he is:

(i) a citizen of Barbados;
(ii) a citizen of a country specified in the First Schedule in which there is a law in force conferring the status of citizen of the country; or
(iii) regarded as belonging to a country specified in the First Schedule, under any law in force in that country.

The countries specified in the First Schedule are the same as those specified in the Second Schedule in respect of Antigua & Barbuda.[12]

However, s.6 of the Legal Profession Act which is in effect a reciprocal admission provision, specifies that persons other than citizens of Barbados may be admitted to practise law in Barbados upon Order of the Minister of Legal Affairs after consultation with the Chief Justice. Persons admitted under s.6 are not required to be the holders of the LEC but must possess to the satisfaction of the Chief Justice, suitable qualifications and competency.

Section 7 also provides for the eligibility of non-citizens to be admitted to practise law in Barbados, pursuant to an Order of the Minister of Legal Affairs after consultation with the Chief Justice. However persons admitted to practise under s.7 are required to have obtained the qualifications prescribed in Appendix I to the Second Schedule to the Legal Profession Act. Appendix 1 to the Second Schedule provides that a person is qualified to practise law in Barbados if he is the holder of LEC or other form of recognition awarded by the Council of Legal Education. (It is to be noted that the qualifications to practise law in Barbados have been effectively amended, as of 1996, by the New Arts. 5 and 6 introduced by the Protocol to the Agreement).

The Order made under s.6 and s.7 is made by the Minister if he is satisfied that the terms and conditions specified in ss.6 and 7 are complied with. These terms and conditions are essentially the same as those specified in s.16 of the Legal Profession Act of Trinidad & Tobago.[13]

Dominica

Pursuant to s.70 of Supreme Court (Dominica) Act Chap. 4:02, a person is eligible to be admitted to practise law in Dominica whether as a barrister or solicitor, if he or she is a national of Dominica.

However, pursuant to s.70(1)(d) the nationality requirement may be waived, in circumstances where the Attorney General by Order declares that in the interest of the public service it is desirable to waive such requirement. However it is to be noted that this provision applies in the case of a barrister, to a barrister who has been admitted to the English, Scottish or Northern Ireland Bar; in the case of a solicitor, to a solicitor who has been admitted to practise by a Superior Court in England, Scotland or Northern Ireland and in the case of a law agent, to a law agent admitted to practise in Scotland.

Grenada and Anguilla

The Eastern Caribbean Supreme Court (Grenada) Act 19/1991 and the Eastern Caribbean Supreme Court (Anguilla) Ordinance 9/1982, contain no provisions with respect to citizenship or nationality requirements for admission to practise law in either of these territories. The position is therefore governed by the general citizenship requirements of the citizen/nationality Acts of Grenada and Anguilla, respectively.

Guyana

In so far as citizenship requirements are concerned, pursuant to s.4(1) of the Legal Practitioners (Amendment) Act 3/1980, a person admitted to practise law in Guyana is required to be a national.

A national is defined as having the same meaning as Article 6(2) of the Council of Legal Education Agreement. According to Article 6(2) thereof, a national is a person who is a citizen of any participating territory, which in this regard are the following territories: Anguilla, Antigua & Barbuda, Barbados, Belize, Dominica, Grenada, Guyana, Jamaica, Montserrat, St. Kitts & Nevis, St. Lucia, St. Vincent & the Grenadines, The Bahamas, The Cayman Islands, Turks & Caicos Island, Trinidad & Tobago.

In addition, pursuant to s.4B of the Legal Practitioners (Amendment) Act 3/1980, persons who are not citizens or nationals of participating territories (as defined above) and who hold a LEC shall be eligible for admission to practise if the Minister after consultation with the Chancellor, is satisfied that the country to which the non-citizen or non-national belongs has in effect reciprocal arrangements. In this regard, these arrangements are effectively the same as those which are applicable to Trinidad & Tobago.[14]

Further, s.4A of the Act also contains a similar reciprocal arrangement provision as s.4B save that the provision is in respect of non-nationals, as defined in s.4B, who do not possess the LEC but possess suitable competency and qualifications.

Jamaica

In so far as citizenship requirements are concerned, s.6 of the Legal Profession Act simply provides that a person is not qualified for admission if he is an alien.

Section 2(1) of Legal Profession Act defines alien as having the meaning assigned to it in the repealed Jamaica Nationality Act. According to s.2(1) of the Jamaica Nationality Act, alien means a person who is not a Commonwealth citizen, a British protected person or a citizen of the Republic of Ireland.

Unlike the other territories, there is no reciprocal arrangement provisions contained in the Legal Profession Act. An attorney-at-law who is qualified to be enrolled in Jamaica whether under s.6(1) or s.6(2) must satisfy the General Legal Council, the body responsible for issuing the qualifying certificate to practise law in Jamaica, that he or she is not an alien.

St. Kitts & Nevis

Pursuant to s.71(1)(3) of the Eastern Caribbean Supreme Court (St. Christopher & Nevis) Act 17/1975, persons admitted to practise as barristers or solicitors in St. Kitts & Nevis are required to be nationals of St. Kitts & Nevis.

However s.71(6) contains a reciprocal arrangement provision which empowers the Chief Justice by Order to admit non-nationals to practise law in St. Kitts & Nevis. The reciprocal provision is similar to that which is applicable to Trinidad & Tobago.[15] It is to be noted that persons admitted under this section are not required to be holders of the LEC awarded by the Council of Legal Education but must to the satisfaction of the Chief Justice possess proper qualifications and competency.

St. Lucia

Pursuant to s.15(1)(a) of Legal Profession Act 31/2000, a person who makes an application to the High Court to practise as an attorney-at-law in St. Lucia must satisfy the court that he is a citizen of St. Lucia.

In addition, s.16 contains effectively the same reciprocal arrangement provision as is applicable to Trinidad & Tobago[16] save that the Order for admission is made by the Attorney General after consultation with the Chief Justice. It must be noted that persons admitted under the reciprocal arrangement provision of this section are required to satisfy the identical professional requirements for admission as a citizen of St. Lucia.[17]

St. Vincent & the Grenadines

There are no specific nationality or citizenship requirements stipulated in the Eastern Caribbean Supreme Court (St. Vincent & the Grenadines) Act Cap. 18, save that s.70(2)(b) thereof provides 'that legal officers of the courts of the territories mentioned in s.70(3) who possess qualifications entitling them to serve and who have actually served in the legal services of the Government shall be deemed to be entitled to practise as a barrister in St. Vincent so long as he continues to be a legal officer of the Government of St. Vincent'. The states and territories mentioned in s.70(3) are the same territories mentioned in the Second Schedule to the Legal Profession Act of Antigua & Barbuda.[18]

The Bahamas

Section 10(2)(c) Legal Profession Act 26/1992 sets out in the negative the citizenship requirements for admission to practise. Section 10(2)(c) provides that 'a person shall be disqualified for admission to practise, save in the case of a person appointed to a legal public office or of a person applying for special admission, if he is not a citizen of The Bahamas'.

Special admissions are governed by s.11 of the Legal Profession Act. According to s.11, 'the Bar Council upon being satisfied that the interests of justice so require may determine that any person qualified in accordance with the First Schedule shall be specially admitted to practice for the purpose of conducting the particular proceedings specified'.[19]

Trinidad & Tobago

Pursuant to s.15(1) of the Legal Profession Act 21/1996, a Commonwealth citizen is eligible to practise as an attorney at law in Trinidad & Tobago.

In addition, s.16 which is in effect a reciprocal arrangement provision, provides that non-citizens may be admitted by Order of the Minister after consultation with the Chief Justice, upon the Minister being satisfied that *inter alia*:

(i) the non citizen has obtained the qualification prescribed by law to practise in Trinidad & Tobago; and

(ii) a citizen of Trinidad & Tobago who had satisfied the qualifications for admission to practise law in the country to which the non-citizen belongs, would be so admitted to practise law in a superior court of jurisdiction in that country and upon as equally favourable terms as those which the non-citizen or non-national would be or become entitled to if an Order were made admitting such person to practise as an attorney-at-law in Trinidad & Tobago.

ADDITIONAL QUALIFICATIONS FOR ADMISSION

Antigua & Barbuda, Barbados, Jamaica, St. Kitts & Nevis, St. Lucia, The Bahamas, Trinidad & Tobago

Apart from the professional and citizenship qualifications already considered, the respective Legal Profession Acts of Antigua & Barbuda, Barbados, Jamaica, St. Lucia, St. Kitts & Nevis, The Bahamas and Trinidad & Tobago contain additional qualifications for admission to practise law in these territories.

In this regard, all the abovementioned territories require that the applicant whether he is a citizen or non-citizen, be a person of good character.[20]

In the case of Antigua & Barbuda, Barbados, Guyana and Jamaica, the relevant provision of the respective Legal Profession Acts of these territories further requires that the applicant attain the age of 21 years.[21] In addition, with respect to St. Lucia, s.15(1) of Legal Profession Act requires that the applicant not have a criminal record except if it is for a minor traffic offence, and further that he has not been declared by a court to be bankrupt.

Part IV – Unqualified Persons

With the exception of The Bahamas, although there is no specific statutory definition of unqualified persons, unqualified persons are deemed to be persons who are not enrolled on the Roll of the Court and accordingly are persons who are not entitled to act or practise as an attorney-at-law.[22]

The Bahamas

In the case of The Bahamas, an unqualified person is defined by s.2 of the Legal Profession Act 9/1997 as *inter alia,* 'either a person whose name does not for the time being appear on the Roll or counsel and attorney whose name is on the Roll but who is for the time being suspended from practice'.

STATUTORY PENALTIES FOR UNQUALIFIED PERSON PRACTISING LAW

1. Wilfully Pretending to be an Attorney, etc.

All jurisdictions (save Guyana)
A person who is unqualified in that his name is not enrolled but who practises law, and wilfully pretends to be an attorney-at-law or who makes use of the name, title or description implying that he is entitled to be recognised or act as an attorney-at-law is liable on summary conviction to a fine and/or a term of imprisonment.[23]

In addition, any person not being entitled to act as an attorney and who acts in any respect as an attorney in any action or matter or in any court in the name or through the agency of an attorney is liable on summary conviction to a fine or to a prescribed term of imprisonment.[24]

Anguilla

In addition in Anguilla, by virtue of s.68(3) and 68(4) of the Eastern Caribbean Supreme Court (Anguilla) Ordinance 9/1982, such unqualified person is also guilty of contempt of court and may be punished accordingly.

Anguilla, Antigua & Barbuda, Barbados, Jamaica and The Bahamas

Apart from the abovementioned provisions, the respective Legal Profession Acts of Anguilla, Antigua & Barbuda, Barbados, Jamaica and The Bahamas specifically provide that no fees in respect of anything done by a person who is not enrolled or not entitled to practice law shall be recoverable in any action suit or matter by any person whomsoever.[25]

2. Valid Practising Certificate

Antigua & Barbuda, Barbados, Jamaica, St. Lucia, Trinidad & Tobago

In the abovementioned territories, a person is also deemed to be unqualified in that he cannot sue for and recover his legal fees, in respect of any legal business done by him in the course of such practice, if he is not the holder of a valid practising certificate.[26] In addition, the relevant Code of Ethics of the various territories provides that an attorney-at-law shall not practise unless he has been issued a practising certificate. Practising law without a practising certificate constitutes a mandatory disciplinary offence.[27] In this regard a practising certificate is issued in the above territories on an annual basis to attorneys-at-law whose names are enrolled on the Roll of the Court. [28]

The Position in Eastern Caribbean territories (save Antigua & Barbuda and St. Lucia) Guyana and The Bahamas

In the Eastern Caribbean territories (save Antigua & Barbuda and St. Lucia,*)* the Solicitor's Act 1974 England, is deemed to extend to and be in force in these territories by virtue of the reception provision contained in their respective Supreme Court Acts.[29] According to s.1 of the Solicitor's Act 1974 one of the requirements for practice as a solicitor is that a solicitor is required to have in force a valid practising certificate. This certificate is issued in England on an annual basis by the Law Society. However in so far as the Eastern Caribbean territories (save St. Lucia and Antigua & Barbuda) are concerned there is no equivalent requirement for a practising certificate, as upon admission to practise, the solicitor or barrister is issued a certificate of enrolment on a once and for all basis.[30]

This is also the case in Guyana and The Bahamas in that the certificate of enrolment entitles an attorney to practise law without time restrictions.

3. Drawing and Preparation of Legal Documents by Unqualified Persons

All Jurisdictions (save Antigua & Barbuda, Barbados, St. Lucia and Trinidad & Tobago)

In respect of the drawing and preparation of legal documents including probate papers, the relevant provision of the Legal Profession/Supreme Court Acts of the various territories provides *inter alia* that an unqualified person who prepares or draws legal documents is liable on summary conviction to fine of a prescribed amount.[31]

Jamaica

In addition, in Jamaica, pursuant to s.32(1) of the Legal Profession Act, any agreement to pay, fee or reward an unqualified person in consideration of his drawing or preparing any legal document is null and void. However, pursuant to s.32(2) any person who has paid any fee to such person may sue for whatever the amount of the fee or reward from the person to whom paid.

4. Attorney-at-Law Acting as Agent For/Holding Out Unqualified Person, etc.

Anguilla, Eastern Caribbean (save Anguilla and St. Lucia), Jamaica, St. Lucia, Trinidad & Tobago

In the abovementioned territories, statute provides that an attorney-at-law is guilty of professional misconduct and liable to have his name struck off the Roll of the Court if he acts as agent *inter alia* in any action or matter for any unqualified person, permits his name to be made use of in any action upon the account or for the profit of any unqualified person, or does any act enabling an unqualified person to appear, act or practise in any respect as an attorney-at-law in any such action or matter.[32]

In addition, the mandatory provisions of the Code of Ethics of the respective jurisdictions (save Jamaica and The Bahamas) provide that an attorney-at-law:

(a) shall not permit his professional services or his name to be used in any way which would make it possible for persons who are not legally authorised to do so, to practise law;[33]
(b) shall not delegate to a person not legally qualified and not in his employment or under his control, any functions which are only to be performed by a qualified attorney-at-law;[34]and in all jurisdictions (save The Bahamas)
(c) shall not hold out any person not qualified to as a lawyer, partner, consultant, an attorney-at-law or associate;[35]and
(d) shall not enter into a partnership or fee sharing arrangement concerning the practice of law with non professional bodies or persons.[36]

Part V – Disqualified Persons

STATUTORY PENALTIES FOR DISQUALIFIED PERSON PRACTISING LAW

1. Practising as an Attorney-at-Law

All jurisdictions (save Jamaica and The Bahamas)
Statute provides that an attorney who has been suspended from practice or whose name has been struck off the Roll of the Court is guilty of an offence and is liable on summary conviction to a fine of a prescribed amount and a term of imprisonment of a specified period if:

(a) he practises law;
(b) he pretends to be entitled to practise law; or
(c) he wilfully implies that he is entitled to be recognised as an attorney-at-law.[37]

2. Disqualified Persons Seeking Employment

Antigua & Barbuda, Barbados, Jamaica, St. Lucia, Trinidad & Tobago
An attorney-at-law, while suspended from practising law or whose name has been removed from the Roll, who seeks or accepts employment from another attorney-at-law without informing him in writing of his suspension or removal from the Roll is liable on summary conviction to a fine and a term of imprisonment of a prescribed period.[38]

3. Attorney Employing Disqualified Person

Antigua & Barbuda, Barbados, Jamaica, St. Lucia, The Bahamas, Trinidad & Tobago.
Where an attorney employs any person who to his knowledge is disqualified in that such person's name has been removed from the Roll of the Court or has been suspended from practice, statute provides that he shall be guilty of professional misconduct.[39]

Granting of Permission

Antigua & Barbuda, Barbados, Jamaica and Trinidad & Tobago
However an attorney may, with the written permission of the Disciplinary Committee (or its equivalent) in the abovementioned territories, employ or remunerate a person who has been suspended from practice or whose name has been removed from the Roll and he may do so for such period and subject to such conditions as the Committee deems fit. However where this written permission is not obtained, the attorney who employs such disqualified person shall be guilty of professional misconduct.[40]

Part VI – Attorney in Prison

1. Acting Whilst In Prison

Eastern Caribbean territories (save St. Lucia), St. Lucia and Trinidad & Tobago
Pursuant to the relevant statutory provision of the above territories, an attorney whilst in prison is prohibited from commencing or defending, in his own name, any action or any matter in bankruptcy. And if he does, he shall be incapable of maintaining any action for recovery of any costs in respect of any business done whilst in prison.[41]

2. Attorney Permitting Attorney in Prison To Act

Eastern Caribbean (save St. Lucia), St. Lucia and Trinidad & Tobago
In the above territories, statute also provides that an attorney who permits a fellow attorney who is in prison to commence, prosecute or defend proceedings in his name, shall be guilty of professional misconduct.[42]

ENDNOTES

1. The Protocol to the Agreement establishing the Council of Legal Education was entered into at the Council's Twenty-sixth Meeting in Barbados on 12 and 13 September 1996.
2. Pursuant to Art. II of the Collaborative Legal Education Agreement, the LL.B. degree awarded by the University of Guyana is subject to direct input and scrutiny by the Faculty of Law, UWI, e.g. the examination papers set by the University of Guyana are sent to UWI moderators for advice and comments and the second markers of all exams are UWI appointed moderators and most significantly, Art. II provides that in the final assessment, the independent judgment of the UWI appointed moderator shall prevail over that of the other markers in the papers for which he is responsible.
3. See pp. 25 & 26 post in respect of professional qualifications for admission to practise law in Trinidad & Tobago.
4. Article 4 of the Council of Legal Education has been amended by the 1996 Protocol to the Agreement to the Council of Legal Education. According to the Protocol, the new Art. 4 (2)(b)(1) provides that 'the holder of a qualification which had it been obtained prior to the 1st October 1972 would have been recognized by all the participating territories as a qualification to be admitted to practise as a barrister or solicitor in those territories shall be awarded the Legal Education Certificate'.
5. See The Legal Profession (Qualification for Admission to Practise Law) Rules 1985 S.I. 1985 No. 24, The Legal Profession Admission to) Rule 1999 S.I. 1999 No. 42
6. Article 6 of CLEA does not identify the territories which are not participating territories nor does it specifically identify those which are participating territories. However in accordance with the Annex A to CLEA, those territories set out in Annex Aare deemed to be the participating territories.
7. Pursuant to s.5 of the Legal Practitioners Ordinance Ch 116
8. Anguilla - s.68 Eastern Caribbean Supreme Court (Anguilla) Ordinance 9/1982

   St. Vincent & the Grenadines s.71 Eastern Caribbean Supreme Court (St. Vincent & the Grenadines) Act Cap 18
9. Pursuant to the Legal Profession (Amendment) Act 9/1997, Part C of the First Schedule to the Legal Profession Act 26/1992 is amended by deleting paragraph (d)
10. The countries specified in the Second Schedule are Anguilla, Antigua & Barbuda, Bermuda, British Honduras, Dominica, Grenada, Guyana, Jamaica, Montserrat, St. Kitts & Nevis, St. Lucia, St. Vincent & the Grenadines, The Bahamas, The British Virgin Islands, Trinidad & Tobago,Turks and Caicos Islands.
11. See 31 post
12. See Endnote 10, *supra*
13. See 31 post
14. *Ibid.*
15. *Ibid.*
16. *Ibid.*
17. See on this pp. 31 & 32 post
18. See endnote 10. *supra*
19. See pp. 24 & 25 ante
20. Antigua & Barbuda - s.6(1)(d) Legal Profession Act 9/1997

    Barbados - s.5(1)(d) Legal Profession Act Cap. 370A

    Jamaica - s.6 (1) Legal Profession Act 1971

Guyana	-	s.4(1)(c) Legal Practitioners (Amendment) Act 3/1980
St. Kitts & Nevis	-	s.71(5) Eastern Caribbean Supreme Court (St. Christopher & Nevis) Act 1983
St. Lucia	-	s.15(1)(b) Legal Profession Act 31/2000
The Bahamas	-	s.10(b) Legal Profession Act 26/1992
Trinidad & Tobago	-	s.15(1)(a) Legal Profession Act 21/1986
21. Antigua & Barbuda	-	s.6(1)(b) Legal Profession Act 9/1997
Barbados	-	s.5(1)(b) Legal Profession Act cap 370 A
Guyana	-	s.4(1)(b) Legal Practitioners (Amendment) Act 3/1980
Jamaica	-	s.6(1) Legal Profession Act 1971
22. Antigua & Barbuda	-	ss.10 and 15(1) Legal Profession Act 9/1997
Barbados	-	s.10 Legal Profession Act Cap. 370A
Eastern Caribbean (save Antigua & Barbuda and St. Lucia)	-	s.1 Solicitors Act 1974, England
Jamaica	-	ss. 6 and 8 Legal Profession Act 1971
Guyana	-	s.5 Legal Practitioners Act cap 4:01
St. Lucia	-	ss.2 and 20 Legal Profession Act 31/2000
Trinidad & Tobago	-	ss.2 and 20 Legal Profession Act 21/1986
23. Anguilla	-	s.58(5) Eastern Caribbean Supreme Court (Anguilla) Ordinance 9/1982
Antigua & Barbuda	-	s.15(1) Legal Profession Act 9/1997
Barbados	-	s.12(1) Legal Profession Act cap 370A
Eastern Caribbean (save Anguilla, St. Lucia and Antigua & Barbuda)	-	s.21 Solicitors Act 1974, England. See also s.22 and s.23 1974, England
Jamaica	-	s.8(1) and (2) Legal Profession Act 1971
St. Lucia	-	s.47(1) Legal Profession Act 31/2000
The Bahamas	-	s.21. See also s.22 Legal Profession Act 26/1992. See also Code of Professional Conduct, Rule XV, Commentary 4
Trinidad & Tobago	-	s.47(1) Legal Profession Act 21/1986
24. Anguilla	-	s.68(3) Eastern Caribbean Supreme Court (Anguilla) Ordinance 9/1982
Antigua & Barbuda	-	s.15(2) Legal Profession Act 9/1997
Barbados	-	s.12(2) Legal Profession Act cap 370A
Eastern Caribbean (save St. Lucia and Antigua & Barbuda)	-	s.20 Solicitor's Act 1974, England
Jamaica	-	s.8(3) Legal Profession Act 1971
St. Lucia	-	s.47(2) Legal Profession Act 31/2000
Bahamas	-	s.20 Legal Profession Act 26/1992
Trinidad & Tobago	-	s.47(2) Legal Profession Act 21/1986
25. Anguilla	-	s.68(3)(b) Eastern Caribbean Supreme Court (Anguilla) Ordinance 9/1982
Antigua & Barbuda	-	s.15(3) Legal Profession Act 9/1997
Barbados	-	s.12(2) Legal Profession Act cap 370A
Jamaica	-	s.8(4) Legal Profession Act 1971
The Bahamas	-	s.24 Legal Profession Act 26/1992
26. Antigua & Barbuda	-	s.11(1) and (2) Legal Profession Act 9/1997

Barbados	-	s.9(1) and (2) Legal Profession Act Cap 370 A
Jamaica	-	s.5(2) and (3) Legal Profession Act 1971
St. Lucia	-	s.21(1) and (2) Legal Profession Act 31/2000
Trinidad & Tobago	-	s.15(2) and (3) Legal Profession Act 21/1986

27. Antigua & Barbuda - Code of EthicsPart B r.1
    Barbados - Code of Ethics Part VIII r.1
    Jamaica - Canon of Ethics Canon II(i)
    St. Lucia - Code of Ethics Part B r.1
    Trinidad & Tobago - Code of Ethics Part B r.1
28. See chapter 5 pp. 63 & 64 post
29. See chapter 1 pp. 1 & 2 ante
30. See chapter 5 pp. 63 & 64 post
31. Anguilla - s.74 Supreme Court Anguilla Ordinance 9/1982
    Dominica - s.77 Eastern Caribbean Supreme Court (Dominica) Act Chap 4:02
    Grenada - s.83 Eastern Caribbean Supreme court (Grenada) Act 19/1991
    Jamaica - s.31 Legal Profession Act 1971
    Bahamas - s.22 Legal Profession Act 26/1992
    St. Kitts & Nevis - s.77 Eastern Caribbean Supreme Court (St. Christopher & Nevis) Act 1983
    St. Vincent & the Grenadines s.77 Eastern Caribbean Supreme Court (St. Vincent & the Grenadines) Act. Cap 18
32. Anguilla - s.75(1) Eastern Caribbean Supreme Court Legal Profession Act
    Eastern Caribbean (save Anguilla and St. Lucia) - s.39 Solicitors Act 1974
    Jamaica - s.20(4) Legal Profession Act
    St. Lucia - s.43 Legal Profession Act 31/2000
    Trinidad & Tobago - s.43 Legal Profession Act 21/1986
    In the case of Antigua & Barbuda it is submitted that s.39 of Solicitor Act 1974 applies to Antigua & Barbuda as *inter alia*, the reception provision contained in s.74 of the Supreme Court (Antigua & Barbuda) Act Cap. 143 was not repealed by the Legal Profession Act 9/1997 or any other Act. As the Legal Profession Act contains no equivalent provision, it is submitted that s.39 of the Solicitor's Act 1974 is deemed to be incorporated into the laws of Antigua & Barbuda.
33. Antigua & Barbuda - Code of Ethics Part B r.16
    Barbados - Code of Ethics Part VIII r.72
    Eastern Caribbean (save Antigua & Barbuda and St. Lucia) - OECS Code of Ethics Part B r.16
    St. Lucia - Code of Ethics Part B r.19
    Trinidad & Tobago - Code of Ethics Part B rr.16
34. Antigua & Barbuda - Code of Ethics Part B r.17
    Barbados - Code of Ethics Part VIII r.73
    Eastern Caribbean (save Antigua & Barbuda and St. Lucia) - OECS Code of Ethics Part B r.17
    St. Lucia - Code of Ethics Part B r.19
    Trinidad & Tobago - Code of Ethics Part B r.17

35. Antigua & Barbuda - Code of Ethics Part B r.3
Barbados - Code of Ethics Part VIII r.59
Eastern Caribbean (save Antigua & Barbuda and St. Lucia)
- OECS Code of Ethics Part B r.3
Jamaica - Canon of Ethics, Canon II (a)
St. Lucia - Code of Ethics Part B r.3
Trinidad & Tobago - Code of Ethics Part B r.3
36. Antigua & Barbuda - Code of Ethics Part B r.9(1)
Barbados - Code of Ethics Part VIII r.65
Eastern Caribbean (save Antigua & Barbuda and St. Lucia)
- OECS Code of Ethics Part B r.9(1)
Jamaica - Canon of Ethics, Canon IV (a)
St. Lucia - Code of Ethics Part B r.12(1)
Trinidad & Tobago - Code of Ethics Part B r.9(1)
37. Antigua & Barbuda - s.31(1) Legal Profession Act 9/1997
Barbados - s.28(1) Legal Profession Act Cap 370 A
Eastern Caribbean (save Antigua & Barbuda and St. Lucia)
- See s.21Solicitors Act 1974, England
St. Lucia - s.47(1) Legal Profession Act 31/2000
Trinidad & Tobago - s.47(1) Legal Profession Act 21/1986
38. Antigua & Barbuda - s.31(2) Legal Profession Act 9/1997
Barbados - s.28(2) Legal Profession Act Cap. 370A
Jamaica - s.20(3) Legal Profession Act 1971
St. Lucia - s.48 Legal Profession Act 31/2000
Trinidad & Tobago - s.48 Legal Profession Act. 21/1986
39. Antigua & Barbuda - s.31(3) Legal Profession Act 9/1997
Barbados - s.28(3) Legal Profession Act cap 370A
Jamaica - s.20(1) Legal Profession Act 1971
St. Lucia - s.45(1) Legal Profession Act 31/2000
The Bahamas - Code of Professional Conduct, Rule XV, Commentary 2
Trinidad & Tobago - s.45(1) Legal Profession Act 21/1986
40. Antigua & Barbuda - s.31 Legal Profession Act 9/1997
Barbados - s.28(3) Legal Profession Act Cap. 370 A
Jamaica - s.20(1) and (2) Legal Profession Act 1971
Trinidad & Tobago - s.45 (1) Legal Profession Act 21/1986
41. Eastern Caribbean (save Antigua & Barbuda and St. Lucia)
- s.41, Solicitors Act 1974, England
St. Lucia - s.44 Legal Profession Act 31/2000
Trinidad & Tobago - s.44 Legal Profession Act 21/1986
In the case of Antigua & Barbuda, it is submitted that s.41 of Solicitors Act 1974, England applies to attorneys-at-law in Antigua & Barbuda as the reception provision contained in s.74 of the Eastern Caribbean Supreme Court (Antigua & Barbuda) Act Cap. 143 was not repealed. Accordingly as the Legal Profession Act 9/1997 does not contain an equivalent provision, it is submitted that s.41 of Solicitors Act 1974, England is incorporated into the laws of Antigua & Barbuda in so far as solicitors are concerned.
42. Eastern Caribbean (save St. Lucia)
- s.40(2)(b) Solicitors Act 1974, England

St. Lucia	-	s.44(2) Legal Profession Act Cap. 143 31/2000
Trinidad & Tobago	-	s.44(2) Legal Profession Act 21/1986
Antigua & Barbuda	-	s.40(2) Solicitors Act 1974, England is deemed to apply to Antigua & Barbuda by virtue of the reception provision contained in s.74 of the Eastern Caribbean Supreme Court (Antigua & Barbuda) Act Cap 143

4. RETAINER

Part I – Mode, Nature and Termination of Retainer

INTRODUCTION

A retainer is a contract of employment, whereby in return for a client's offer of employment, an attorney agrees to render the legal services specified therein. The retainer, when given, puts into operation, the normal terms of a contractual relationship; to safeguard the client's interest and carry out his instructions in the matter to which the retainer relates by all proper means.[1] It is the foundation upon which the relationship of attorney and client rests.

In this regard it is to be noted that there is no general relationship of attorney and client of a standing and permanent character.[2] As James LJ observed in *Saffron Walden Second Benefit Building Society v Rayner:*

> A man has no more a solicitor than he has an accountant or a baker or a butcher. A person is a man's accountant or baker or butcher when that man chooses to employ or deal with him and the solicitor is his solicitor when he chooses to employ him and in the matter in which he is so employed. Beyond that, the relationship of solicitorship does not extend.[3]

However, once an attorney is retained the relationship is essentially one of principal and agent for the retainer gives the attorney his authority to act for and bind the client not only as between the client and himself but also third persons, with whom the attorney deals, within scope of the authority conferred upon him under the retainer.

MODE OF RETAINER

1. Oral Retainer

With the exception of St. Lucia and the qualified exception of Guyana and Jamaica, a retainer need not be in writing unless the general law of contract, the terms of the retainer or the disability of a party makes writing requisite. However, it is always advisable for an attorney to have the retainer reduced to writing for, if there is no evidence except a statement by the attorney which the client contradicts, the court will treat the attorney as having acted without authority from his client.[4]

The rationale for the court's approach in such instances, was considered by Denning LJ in *Griffiths v Evans.* Denning LJ observed:

> On this question of retainer I would observe where there is a difference between a solicitor and client on it, the courts have said for the last 100 years or more, that the word of the client is to be preferred to that of the solicitor, or at any rate more weight is to be given to it. It is because the client is ignorant and the solicitor is or should be learned. If the solicitor does not take the precaution of getting a written retainer he has only himself to thank for being at variance with his client on it and he must take the consequences.[5]

Indeed in the case of *Allen v Bone,*[6] a solicitor's bill of costs was dismissed with costs to be paid by the solicitor on the ground that the suit in question had been instituted without the authority of the client. It was admitted by the solicitor that no authority in writing had been given to him. As the Master of the Rolls noted, where the client disputes the authority of the solicitor 'there is nothing but assertion against assertion, the court will treat him (the solicitor) as unauthorised and he must abide by the consequences of his neglect'.[7]

2. Written Retainer

Generally the form of writing is immaterial provided there is a note or memorandum signed by the party to be charged or some other person lawfully authorised by him.

However, it is to be noted that in Guyana and Jamaica an attorney who commences proceedings on behalf of a client is required to obtain the signed written authority of his client and produce this authority to the Registrar at the time of filing the proceedings or as soon afterwards as the Registrar may allow.[8] In the Guyanese case of *Georgetown Coconut Estate Ltd v Argosy Co Ltd and J Carrington,*[9] a writ issued on behalf of the plaintiff company was set aside on the ground *inter alia* that the attorney had no written authority to issue the writ.

With respect to St. Lucia, a written authority is required in all instances where an attorney is retained. In this regard, r.39 Part B of the Code of Ethics provides that 'an attorney-at-law shall not act on behalf of any person unless the attorney-at-law is authorised in a document evidenced by the signature or mark of that person to act on that person's behalf'.

In the other jurisdictions, with respect to proceedings in court, an attorney should obtain the written authority of his client and in the appropriate case the Registrar can require him to furnish proof of that authority.

3. By Implication

Even where there is no written authority or express retainer, the court may imply the existence of a retainer from the acts of the parties. Instances of an implied retainer include:

(a) Acquiescence

Acquiescence arises where a client ratifies and adopts proceedings which were in the first instance, commenced without his authority. In *Danish Mercantile Co Ltd v Beaumont,*[10] a solicitor instituted proceedings in the name of a company without verifying whether he had proper authority to do so. The court held that when the company went into liquidation the actions of the liquidator in instructing the solicitor to continue proceedings on behalf of the company amounted to a ratification of the solicitor's authority to act and brought into effect an implied retainer.

It is to be noted that if the required authority is not obtained, this is so fundamental a flaw as to make the proceedings a nullity and in such instances the defendant is entitled to have the proceedings set aside *ex debito justitiae.*[11] However, in accordance with the ordinary law of agency and the equitable doctrine of ratification, it is open to the plaintiff to adopt the proceedings, and thereby cure the original defect in the proceedings by the subsequent filing of such authority.[12]

(b) Estoppel

Estoppel arises where the client is estopped by his conduct from denying the authority of the solicitor. In *Blyth v Fladgate,*[13] it was held that although there was no express retainer, the relationship of client and solicitor might be inferred from the acts of the parties and the benefits conferred.

(c) Doctrine of Past Performance

This arises where a client by his conduct has performed part of the contract of employment. In *Parrott v Echells*[14] the defendant called at the solicitor's office and left notes and other papers and subsequently expressed an intention for the solicitor 'to get to the bottom of the matter' and this was held to bring an implied retainer into existence.

(d) Consolidation Order

Where the client consents to a consolidation order, the litigation operates to bring a joint retainer into effect.

JOINT AND SEVERAL RETAINERS

Where an attorney is retained by more than one litigant, an issue which may arise is whether the retainer is joint or several. Generally speaking where an attorney is employed by joint litigants there is a presumption that the retainer is joint unless the contrary is shown.

The case of *Re Allen, Davies v Chatwood*[15] is instructive on this point. In that case the court held that though there was joint employment of the solicitor, the rights and grounds of defence of the litigants were different. The court accordingly held that the retainer was joint only to the extent that all the parties to the joint employment agreed to pay the amount of the attorney's charges but not joint in so far as liability to pay the costs thereby incurred.

The distinction between a joint and several retainer is important for a number of reasons, *inter alia:*

i) if a retainer is several the parties to the retainer are liable only for their share of the costs;[16]

ii) if joint, the attorney can receive his whole demand (i.e. his costs) from all or one of the parties. However the disadvantage of this is that a judgment obtained against one party is a bar to any subsequent action against the other;[17]

RETAINER BY PERSONS WITH DIFFERENT INTERESTS

An attorney-at-law may represent multiple clients only if he can adequately represent the interest of each and if each consents to such representation after full disclosure of the possible effects of multiple representation. If the interests of the clients are likely to conflict or the attorney's independent professional judgment is likely to be impaired, an attorney is under a duty not to accept or continue his retainer in such circumstances.[18] For the purposes of determining whether an attorney can properly represent persons with different interests, the following provide some guidelines:

In Contentious Business:

(i) where no conflict exists among parties the attorney may act for all;
(ii) where a compromise of a minor's interest is concerned, the minor should be separately represented;
(iii) in a trust matter, the attorney cannot act for one defendant against the other.

In Non-Contentious Business

In non-contentious business, the most common instances of which are conveyancing and mortgage transactions, an attorney may properly represent both or multiple parties transaction provided no conflict of interest arises or is likely to arise although as Dankwerts J observed in *Goody v Baring*:

> It seems practically impossible for a solicitor to do his duty to each client properly where he has to act for both vendor and purchaser.[19]

NATURE OF RETAINER

1. Entire Contract

The contract of an attorney upon a retainer accepted by him to carry on or defend a suit or do any other business is, in general, an entire contract to carry the suit or defence or other business to its termination, subject however to the condition of his being paid by his client upon request made by him for such reasonable funds as will be necessary to carry on the proceedings and a reasonable time allowed for compliance with it.[20] (As to what is deemed reasonable funds, that is sufficient funds necessary for the attorney to take the next step in the business for which he is engaged, including out of pocket expenses).

What this means is that in the absence of a fee arrangement with the client in which the client agrees to pay the attorney for his professional services as the matter proceeds and benefits are conferred on him, an attorney is not entitled to be paid or alternatively to sue for his costs until the completion of the business for which he was retained. More particularly, he is not entitled to abandon a matter at any stage of it as he may think fit and insist upon payment of his bill up to that period.[21]

As Lord Esher MR observed in *Underwood, Son and Piper v Lewis*:

> When a man goes to a solicitor and instructs him for the purpose of bringing or defending an action, he does not mean to employ the solicitor to take one step and then give fresh instructions to take another and so on...; the retainer is that the solicitor carry on the action. It necessarily follows that the contract of a solicitor is an entire contract – a contract to take all the steps which are necessary to bring the action to a conclusion.[22]

It is to be noted that the doctrine of entire contract is a creature of the common law. Common law suits were regarded at the time, as relatively inexpensive and simple and quickly disposed of. Accordingly, it was deemed reasonable and fair for the attorney to be paid his professional charges upon completion of the business for which he was engaged unless there was an agreement to the contrary.[23]

2. Non-Entire Contract

A non-entire contract applies to legal work for which there is an agreement to employ an attorney in work of a certain class which would entitle the attorney to deliver and receive payment on a bill of costs as the matter proceeds and as the client obtains the benefit from the completion of each item of work.[24]

TERMINATION OF ENTIRE CONTRACT RETAINER

1. Common Law

In accordance with the common law, an entire contract retainer can only be terminated by the attorney without breach before completion, only for good reason and on reasonable notice.

Examples of good reason includes the failure of the client to provide the necessary funds for disbursements; discovery that the action cannot properly be maintained; the attorney being called upon to take any step which is dishonourable or unlawful[25] but in any event, the attorney must also give notice to the client.

This point was made in *Vandasau v Brown*[26] where although there was good cause for termination, no notice was given to the client. It was held that the retainer had not come to an end.

2. Equity

Although the doctrine of entire contract is applicable to suits in equity, the courts have long recognised that because of the protracted and relatively complicated nature of many equity matters such as the administration of trust property, it was, in many instances, inappropriate to insist, that in the absence of an agreement, that a solicitor could only deliver and demand payment on a bill of costs when the matter for which he was retained was completed.[27]

As Lord Esher MR remarked in the case of *Underwood, Son and Piper v Lewis* when referring to the entire contract doctrine:

> It would be unjust to apply the rule in the case of chancery suits where the proceedings might be of a very long and complicated character and be divided into several stages and the solicitor might be unable to recover anything for work he had been doing for a long period of years.[28]

As a consequence, the natural break doctrine or rule was formulated. In effect it permits an attorney, in the absence of an agreement with his client, to divide proceedings into stages, divisions or breaks and to treat each such natural break as independent litigation for the purposes of entitling an attorney to deliver to his client, a bill of costs for business done up to the occurrence of such break and demand payment of his bill of costs whenever these natural breaks are deemed to occur.[29]

It is to be noted that although the natural break doctrine developed in equity it is also applicable to common law suits which are of a protracted nature and which can also be divided into stages for the purposes *inter alia* of payment of costs.[30]

TERMINATION OF NON-ENTIRE CONTRACT

A non-entire contract may be terminated without breach for a number of reasons including the bankruptcy, death or insanity of the client, effluxion of time and for good cause upon reasonable notice.[31]

TERMINATION OF ENTIRE/NON ENTIRE CONTRACT RETAINER

In General

Irrespective of whether the retainer is an entire or a non-entire contract retainer, an attorney may, pursuant to the relevant rules contained in the Code/Canon of Ethics of the various territories,[32] withdraw from employment *inter alia* for the following reasons:

(a) where the client fails, refuses or neglects to carry out an agreement with, or his obligation to, the attorney-at-law as regards the expenses or fees payable by the client;
(b) where his inability to work with colleagues indicates that the best interest of the client is likely to be served by his withdrawal;
(c) where his client freely assents to the termination of his employment;
(d) where by reason of his mental and physical condition or other compelling reason it is difficult for him to carry out his employment effectively;
(e) in cases of conflict.

With respect to The Bahamas, Rule XI Commentary 5 of the Code of Professional Conduct, specifically prescribes that 'where there has been a serious loss of confidence between the attorney and client and the loss of confidence goes to the very basis of the relationship, the attorney will have a justified cause for withdrawal'.

In all the above instances the attorney is required in accordance with the relevant rule of the Code/Canon of Ethics of the respective territories to take reasonable steps to avoid prejudice or injury to the possible rights of his clients.[33]

Accordingly an attorney is required to, *inter alia:*

(a) give due notice of withdrawal to his client.
(b) allow time for employment of another attorney-at-law.
(c) deliver to the client all documents and property to which he is entitled subject to any lien which the attorney-at-law may have over the same.
(d) comply with such laws, rules or practice as may be applicable.
(e) where appropriate, obtain the permission of the court when the hearing of the matter has commenced.

In addition the attorney is required to promptly refund such part of the fees, if any, which have already been paid by the client, as may be fair and reasonable to all the circumstances.[34]

In Contentious Proceedings

All jurisdictions (save The Bahamas)

In respect of contentious proceedings, the Code/Canon of Ethics[35] of the various territories (save The Bahamas), expressly prescribes the circumstances in which an attorney may withdraw forthwith from employment (i.e. without being required to give notice to the client) in respect of matters pending before the Court or other tribunal. These reasons include:

(a) where the client insists upon him representing a claim or defence that he cannot conscientiously advance;
(b) where the client seeks to pursue a course of conduct which is illegal or which will result in deliberately deceiving the Court;
(c) where the client has in the course of the proceedings perpetrated a fraud upon a person or tribunal and on request by the attorney-at-law has refused or is unable to rectify the same;
(d) where his continued employment will involve him in the violation of the law or a disciplinary rule;
(e) where the client by any other conduct renders it unreasonably difficult for the attorney-at-law to carry out his employment as such

effectively, or in accordance with the judgment and advice of the attorney-at-law or the rules of law or professional ethics;
(f) where for any good and compelling reason it is difficult for him to carry out his employment effectively.

Guyana
As stated in chapter one, Guyana has no Code of Ethics to date. Accordingly, the guidelines in respect of termination of retainer as set out in the relevant Code/Canon of Ethics of the various territories are presumed to be relevant in the absence of provisions regulatory or otherwise to the contrary.

EFFECT OF TERMINATION OF RETAINER

Where a retainer is terminated without breach on the part of the attorney, the attorney is entitled to recover costs for his work done on a *quantum meruit* basis. If however the retainer is unjustifiably terminated by the attorney, then the client is not liable for any work done.

Where the client discharges the attorney in the course of contentious business, the court can direct taxation on the matter and can order payment as if work had been fully performed. However regard will be given to:

(i) the circumstances under which the discharge took place;
(ii) the terms of the attorney's retainer; and/or
(iii) whether the attorney's default or negligence led to the discharge.

If the client has discharged the retainer unjustifiably, in addition to liability for the costs of the action, the attorney has a lien on the client's documents. On this issue, the question of whether the attorney has discharged himself or was discharged by the client is a critical factor.[36]

CHANGE OF ATTORNEY

In litigation, in accordance with the relevant rules of court the name of the new attorney must be noted on the court record as having been terminated for so long as the attorney's name remains on the record, his authority is deemed to continue.

In this regard, the respective Rules of the Supreme Court of the various Caribbean territories[37] provide that a party to any cause or matter suing or defending by an attorney shall be at liberty to change his attorney without an order but until notice of change is filed and the copies of notice are served, the authority of the attorney is deemed to continue until the final determination of the cause or matter.

Part II – Authority Under Retainer

INTRODUCTION

As stated previously, the retainer forms the basis of an attorney's authority to act on behalf of his client and subject to any special agreement, the scope of an attorney's authority whether express or implied is limited to the particular matter for which he is engaged[38] and in the absence of an express retainer to the contrary, an attorney is deemed to have the implied authority to take any steps within the scope of his authority.

By way of illustration, in *Wright v Pepin*,[39] it was held that although the solicitor was not expressly authorised to do so, the language of the retainer being one to put the client's affairs in order, the attorney had the implied authority to acknowledge a debt owed by his client. In the Jamaican Court of Appeal case of *Thompson v Alexander*[40] an attorney was given instructions to accept an offer for the sale of land and complete the sale. It was held that this included an implied authority to do whatever was reasonably necessary to bring the sale to conclusion and that the attorney successfully obtaining a waiver from the purchaser, was binding on the client, although he did not consult his client before doing so. And in the Trinidad & Tobago case of *Walker v Beckles*,[41] the Court of Appeal held that counsel had not exceeded the scope of his implied authority in failing to consult the appellant before submitting to judgment as no authority was withdrawn from him.

SPECIAL AUTHORITY

1. Unusual Expenses

With respect to incurring unusual expenses or charges, it is essential that an attorney obtain special authority from his client for if he fails to do so, he will be unable to recover the costs thereby incurred.[42]

In the case of litigation, where an unusual expense is about to be incurred in the course of an action such as the taking of shorthand notes,[43] and procuring the attendance of scientific or expert witnesses, it is the duty of the attorney to inform his client fully on it and further to point out to him that such expense will or may not be allowed on a taxation between party and party, and might therefore have to be borne by the client whatever may be the outcome of the trial. If the attorney omits to do so, he will not be allowed these expenses on a taxation as between attorney and client.

This is known as the Rule in *Blyth v Fanshawe*,[44] a case in which a solicitor was authorised to employ a shorthand typist, but failed to point out to his client that this expense might not be allowed on a party and party taxation. On taxation, the solicitor was not allowed to recover against his client the costs of the shorthand notes.

Journeys

In the absence of special instructions an attorney has, as a general rule, no authority to undertake long journeys whether locally or abroad at his client's expense.[45] However, if whilst abroad and in the locality, the attorney does work for his client and this is accepted by the client, he is entitled to be paid.[46] In *Re Snell*[47] a case on point, it was held that although the solicitor had no special authority, he was nevertheless, in the special circumstances of the case, entitled to charge for his professional services rendered in America and also for his professional services and expenses incurred in respect of three journeys to Paris for the purpose of conducting negotiations for a compromise on behalf of the client company, although in both instances, he acted without special instructions from his client.

2. Notices

In the absence of special authority an attorney has no authority to receive notices on behalf of his client.[48]

3. Commencing Proceedings

A special authority is essential to entitle an attorney either to commence proceedings in his client's name or to appear for and represent a client in an action or taxation.[49] In Guyana, Jamaica and St. Lucia, the attorney's authority to act for his client in respect of contentious proceedings is required to be in writing and signed by the client.[50]

The issue of an attorney's want of special authority was raised in *Enviro Farms Ltd v Caribbean Food Corp*[51] a case in which the defendant company applied for the dismissal of the proceedings brought against it on the grounds that the attorney had no authority to institute the action. However the court found on the facts of the case that the attorney had the authority to institute the proceedings.

4. Embarking on New Litigation

In litigation the attorney's authority comes to an end upon execution of the judgment. When execution has been levied, the attorney has done all that he was employed to do under his retainer. Accordingly, an attorney has no authority to embark on second litigation even if for technical purposes it is regarded as part of the original action.[52] As Wills J observed in *James v Ricknell* with reference to the attorney's client:

> As a reasonable man, he may well decide to give way and refuse to stake the cost and anxiety of a second litigation against the chance of success.[53]

5. Sale and Purchase of Land

An attorney has no general authority to bind his client in respect of the sale or purchase of land, unless the authority was conferred expressly or by necessary implication.[54]

IMPLIED AUTHORITY

1. In Contentious Business

An attorney has an implied authority *inter alia*:

(i) To make Admissions

Admissions by an attorney (or by his clerk having management of the action) made after the start of an action are binding and admissible as evidence against the client and fall within the scope of his implied authority.[55] However before commencement, this is not the case. Such admissions must be made with the client's express authority. Unless fraudulent, formal admissions as to the facts made by attorney are binding. However formal admissions can always be withdrawn by the client unless the other party has acted upon them to his detriment.[56]

(ii) To Compromise an Action

An attorney has a general authority to compromise an action on behalf of his client provided he acts *bona fide* and not in defiance of his client's direct and positive instructions.[57] However before action, an attorney has no implied authority to effect a compromise with a third party in respect of a claim against the client. Quite apart from the attorney's implied authority, the attorney also has the ostensible or apparent authority, *vis-a-vis* the opposing litigant, to bind his client to a compromise of an action without prior reference to his client for his consent and even where he in fact has no implied authority from his client, provided it does not involve any matter collateral to the action.[58] The opposing litigant is entitled to rely on the apparent or ostensible authority of the attorney without having, for his own protection, to scrutinise the authority of the attorney of the other side or *inter alia* to demand that the other side sign the terms of the compromise.[59]

(iii) To recover debts

As a general rule, an attorney can recover payment of a debt or damages or costs except where the client is under a disability.[60]

(iv) To Accept Service

An attorney on record may accept service on behalf of his client and even on behalf of the client who has changed attorneys provided the client has not given notice of such change. The attorney also has authority to accept substituted service.[61]

2. In Non-Contentious Business

An attorney has an implied authority *inter alia*:

(i) To have custody of his client's deeds;
(ii) To receive consideration on sale of a client's property, provided the attorney produces the duly endorsed deed;[62]
(iii) To receive deposits on the sale of land.

AUTHORITY OVER DOCUMENTS AFTER TERMINATION OF RETAINER

Documents which have come into existence during the course of the retainer and are either prepared by the attorney for the benefit of the client, or received by the attorney on behalf of his client, belong to the client. This rule is based on the principal/agent relationship.[63]

The above situation must however be distinguished from the position in respect of documents prepared by a professional man for his client, where the rule of law, subject to any express proviso to the contrary, is that these documents are the professional man's property irrespective of who has paid for them.[64]

Documents prepared by the attorney for his own protection or benefit and in addition letters written by the client to the attorney belong to the attorney.[65]

Documents prepared by a third party during the course of the retainer and sent to the attorney which are not prepared at the attorney's expense belong to the client.[66]

EFFECT OF WANT OF AUTHORITY

1. In Litigation

(i) Stay of Proceedings

Where an attorney acts or continues to act without proper authority from his client, the practice is to direct a stay of proceedings in the name of the person wrongly named as a party and to have the name of the attorney struck out for the purposes of future proceedings.[67] It makes no difference that the attorney commenced the proceedings in ignorance of the client's incapacity. In *Yonge v Toynbee,*[68] a case on point, the solicitors in ignorance of the unsoundness of mind of their client and the client having been so certified, entered an appearance for him in an action. The court struck out the proceedings and held *inter alia* that the solicitors were liable personally to pay the plaintiff's costs in the action.

It is to be noted that if the court becomes aware that the plaintiff is incapable of giving a retainer whether because of minority, mental or other incapacity, it will strike out the action at the trial without formal application.[69]

(ii) Costs

Additionally the attorney will, as a general rule, be ordered by the court to pay all costs as between the attorney and the person wrongly named by him as a party to the action, as well as the costs of the other side on a party to party basis.[70] Such costs include the cost of the application for dismissal.[71] (This is of course, subject to any ratification by the person found without authority).[72]

However, the fact that an attorney is not authorised to institute proceedings, whether because of a client's disability or otherwise cannot be raised by the defendants, at the trial. This point was made in the case of *Richmond v Branson & Son,*[73] a case in which the defendant raised at the trial, the issue of want of authority of the plaintiff's solicitor. The court held that the trial was not the place to do so. According to Warmington J:

> The proper course in such cases is for a substantive application to be made for the action to be stayed on the ground of want of authority.[74]

In making an order as to costs, on the grounds of an attorney's want of authority, the court bases much of its inherent jurisdiction to do so on the reliance which it places on attorneys, as officers of the court. As Swinfen Eady J noted in *Yonge v Toynbee:*

> The court places much reliance upon solicitors, who are its officers. It issues writs at their instance and accepts appearances for defendants which they enter as a matter of course without the court questioning their authority; the other parties to the litigation also act upon the same footing... Much confusion and uncertainty would be introduced if a solicitor were not to be under any liability . . .[75]

(iii) Action for Breach of Warranty of Authority

Where an attorney wrongly represents that he has the authority to do a particular act and another person is misled to his prejudice, the ground upon which the attorney is held liable in damages is that there is an implied contract or warranty that he had the authority which he professed to have.[76]

This liability extends not only to cases where he has acted fraudulently but also to cases where he innocently misrepresents that he has the authority which he either never had or which he has ceased to have by reason of facts of which he had no knowledge or means of knowledge.[77]

In practice, the court may order the attorney to personally pay the costs of the party on the other side in order to save the expense of an action for breach of warranty of authority or negligence.[78]

(iv) Disciplinary Proceedings

An attorney who acts without authority is also liable to disciplinary sanctions for professional misconduct. In such instances the court may summarily punish an attorney for wilfully bringing an action without authority.[79] Alternatively, the attorney may be suspended[80] or struck off the Roll. In *Wheatley v Bastow*,[81] a solicitor was struck off the Roll of the Court for instructing counsel without authority from his client, to consent to the disposal of certain funds in court, which resulted in a loss to the client.

2. Out of Court

An attorney who enters into a contract on behalf of a client is liable for any damages which may directly flow as a result of any breach with respect thereto.[82] This liability is not limited to the bare case of contract, but extends to every transaction of business into which a third party is induced to enter, by the representations of the attorney.

Where an attorney enters into a contract as agent for a named principal but in fact he has no such authority, he is deemed to be contracting on his own behalf, but he may nevertheless obtain specific performance of the contract unless his misrepresentation induced the other party to enter the contract.

RATIFICATION AND SCOPE OF RATIFICATION OF AUTHORITY

As previously stated, where proceedings are started in the name of plaintiff without proper authority, it is open to the purported plaintiff to ratify the act of the attorney who started the action and to thereby adopt the proceedings.[83]

Although the client may ratify the unauthorised acts of the attorney, there are limits to the extent to which he may do so. In this regard, an unauthorised act may be ratified only if the act of ratification was done at a time and in circumstances in which the ratifying party could have lawfully done the act ratified.[84] Secondly, if a time was fixed for doing a particular act, whether by statute or by agreement, the doctrine of ratification does not apply if it has the effect of extending that time.[85] This is also the case if ratification by a putative principle of the acts of an assumed agent would adversely affect the rights to property, including intellectual property which had arisen in favour of a third party or others since the unauthorised act of the assumed agent.[86]

ENDNOTES

PART I

1. *Groom v Crocker* [1938] 2 All ER 394 at 413; [1939] 1 KB 194 at 222 CA. See also *Hepburn v Fawkes* (1971-76) LRG 287.
2. *Saffron Walden Second Benefit Building Society v Rayner* (1880) 14 Ch D 406 CA.
3. *Ibid* at p.409.
4. *Allen v Bone* (1841) 4 Beav. 493, *Griffiths v Evans* [1953] 2 All ER 1364 at p. 1369 CA. See also *Bramson v Carrington and Sealy* (1979) 14 Barb. L.R. 180 at p. 183.
5. *Ibid.*
6. (1841) 4 Beav. 491.
7. *Ibid* at p.494.
8. *Re Petition by Shafi Janali* (1974) 21 WIR 172. See also *Georgetown Coconut Estate Ltd v Argosy Co Ltd and J Carrington* (1917-18) LRBG 78
9. (1917-18) LRBG 78
10. [1951] 1 Ch. 680 CA; See also *Reynolds v Howell* (1873) LR 8 QB 398. Contrast with *Re Beckett, Purnell v Paine* [1918] 2 Ch. 72.
11. See *Heeralall v Shivcharran* (1959) 1 WIR 28 at p.30
12. *Danish Mercantile Co. Ltd and Others v Beaumont, supra*; *Re Beckett, Purnell v Paine, supra* contrast with *Reynolds v Howell, supra*
13. [1891] 1 Ch. 337, 7 TLR 29
14. (1839) 3 J.P.771.
15. (1879) 11 Ch D 244, 40 LT 187
16. *Ibid.*
17. *Ibid.*
18. See chapter 8 pp. 141-144 post
19. [1956] 2 All ER 11 at p.12 See for further discussion on this issue chapter 8 pp. 141-144 post
20. *White v Bell* (1881) 3 SCJB 77
21. *Underwood, Son and Piper v Lewis* [1897] 2 QB 306 at p.310 CA
22. *Ibid* at p.310.
23. *Ibid* at p.312.
24. *JH Milner & Sons v Percy Bilton Ltd* [1966] 2 All ER pp.894 at pp.899, 900
25. *Underwood, Son and Piper v Lewis* [1894] 2 QB 306 at p.314 CA
26. 9 Bing 402.
27. *Re Romer and Haslam* [1893] 2 QB 286 CA; See also *White v Bell* (1881) 3 SC JB 77.
28. *Supra* at p.312
29. *Re Romer and Haslam* [1893] 2 QB 286 CA.
30. *Re Hall and Barker* (1878) 9 Ch D 538
31. See on this *Cordery on Solicitors* 8th ed. Chap. 3 pp. 72-74.
32. Antigua & Barbuda - Code of Ethics Part A r. 34
    Barbados - Code of Ethics Part A r. 34
    Eastern Caribbean (save Antigua & Barbuda and St. Lucia) - OECS Code of Ethics Part A r. 34

St. Lucia - Code of Ethics Part A r. 33
Trinidad & Tobago - Code of Ethics Part 34
33. Antigua & Barbuda - Code of Ethics Part B r. 12(1)
Barbados - Code of Ethics Part V111 r. 68(1)
Eastern Caribbean (save Antigua & Barbuda and St. Lucia)
 - OECS Code of Ethics Part B r. 12 (1)
The Bahamas - Code of Professional Conduct Rule X1, Commentaries 2 and 7
Jamaica - Canon of Ethics, Canon (IV)(o)
St. Lucia - Code of Ethics Part B r.15(1)
Trinidad & Tobago - Code of Ethics Part B r. 12 (1)
34. Antigua & Barbuda - Code of Ethics Part B r. 12(2)
Barbados - Code of Ethics Part V111 r. 68(2)
Eastern Caribbean (save Antigua & Barbuda and St. Lucia)
 - OECS Code of Ethics Part B r. 12(2)
Jamaica - Canon of Ethics, Canon IV(0)
St. Lucia - Code of Ethics Part B r. 15(2)
The Bahamas - Code of Professional Conduct Rule XI, Commentaries 7 and 8
Trinidad & Tobago - Code of Ethics Part B r. 12(2)
35. Antigua & Barbuda - Code of Ethics Part B r. 13
Barbados - Code of Ethics Part VIII r. 69
Eastern Caribbean (save Antigua & Barbuda and St. Lucia)
 - OECS Code of Ethics Part B r. 13
Jamaica - Canon of Ethics Canon IV(q)
St. Lucia - Code of Ethics Part B r. 16
Trinidad & Tobago - Code of Ethics Part B r. 13
36. *Gamlen Chemical Co. (UK) Ltd v Rochem Ltd* [1980] 1 All ER 1049, [1980] 1 WLR 614 CA
37. Barbados - RSC O.67 Rules of the Supreme Court of Judicature 1982
Guyana - RSC O.6, Rules of the Supreme Court 1955
Eastern Caribbean - Part 63 Eastern Caribbean Supreme Court Civil Procedure Rules 2000
The Bahamas - RSC O.63 Rules of the Supreme Court 1978
Trinidad & Tobago - RSC O.67 Orders and Rules of the Supreme Court of Judicature 1975

PART II

38. *Hepburn v Fawkes* (1971-76) LRG 287
39. [1954] 2 All ER 52
40. (1964) 6 WIR 538
41. CA 16/1964 Trinidad & Tobago(Unreported)
42. See *Cocks v Bruce Searl and Good* (1904) 21 TLR 62
43. *Ibid.*
44. (1882) 10 QBD 207. See also *Re Broad and Broad* (1885) 15 QBD 420 and *Cocks v Bruce, Searl and Good* (1904) 21 TLR 62.
45. *Re Storer* (1884) 26 Ch D 189.

46. *Re Snell* (1877) 5 Ch. D 815 CA.
47. *Ibid.*
48. *Singer v Trustee of the Property of Munro (bankrupt)* [1981] 3 All ER 215 at p.218. See also *Saffron Walden Second Benefit Building Society v Rayner* (1880) 14 Ch D 406 CA.
49. *James v Ricknell* (1887) 20 QBD 164 *Newbiggen-By-The-Sea v Armstrong* (1879) 13 Ch D 310, 41 LT 637 CA
50. See endnote 8 *supra* and pp. 43 & 44 *ante*
51. HCA 258/1987 Trinidad & Tobago (Unreported)
52. *James v Ricknell* (1887) 20 QBD 164.
53. *Ibid* at p.166.
54. *Gavaghan v Edwards* [1961] 2 QB 220, (1961)2 AII ER477, *North v Loomes* [1919], 1 Ch 378, [1918-1919] All ER Rep 936
55. *H Clarke (Doncaster) Ltd v Wilkinson* (1965) Ch 694, [1965] 1 All ER 934 CA.
56. *Ibid* at p. 703.
57. *Little v Spreadbury* [1910] 2 KB 658; *Shepherd v Robinson* [1919] 1 KB 474 CA.
58. *Waugh v HB Clifford & Sons Ltd* [1982] 1 All ER 1095 CA. See also *Hillocks Agencies v Saunders Int Sales* (1993) 46 WIR 111.
59. *Shepherd v Robinson, supra.*
60. *James v Ricknell* (1887) 20 QBD 164; *Habil Kadir v Demerara Mutual Life Assurance Society Ltd* (1968) LRG. 312
61. *Jay v Budd* (1898) 1 QB 12 CA.
62. *Day v Woolwich Equitable Bldg Society* (1888) 40 Ch D 491. See also *Habil Kadir v Demerara Mutual Life Assurance Society Ltd* (1968) LRBG 312 at pp.320, 321.
63. *Re Ellis and Ellis* (1908) 25 TLR 38.
64. *Leicestershire County Council v Michael Farraday and Partners Ltd* [1941] 2 KB 205; *Chantrey Martin (a firm) v Martin* [1953] 2 QB 286; *Gibbon v Pease* [1905] 1 KB 810.
65. *Re Thomson* (1855) 20 Beav. 545; *Re Wheatcroft* (1877) 6 Ch D 97.
66. *Re Thomson* (1855) *Supra*
67. *Fricker v Van Grutten* [1896] 2 Ch 649 CA; *Reynolds v Howell* (1873) LR8QB 398. Contrast with *Re Becket, Purnell v Paine* [1918] 2 Ch. 77; *Nurse v Durnford* (1879) 13 Ch D 764.
68. [1910] 1 KB 215. See also *Geilinger v Gibbs* [1897] 1 Ch 479; *Newbiggin-By-The-Sea Gas Company v Armstrong* (1879) 13 Ch D 310, 41 LT 637 CA.
69. *Daimler Co Ltd v Continental Tyre & Rubber Co (Great Britain) Ltd* [1916] 2 AC 307; [1916-17] All ER Rep. 191 HL. See also *Selangor United Rubber v Craddock* [1969] 3 All ER 965 CA.
70. *Newbiggen-By-The-Sea Gas Company v Armstrong, supra; Fricker v Van Grutten* (1896) 2 Ch 649 CA, *Yonge v Toynbee, supra.*
71. *Ibid.*
72. *Danish Mercantile Co Ltd v Beaumont* [1951] Ch 680, [1951] 1 All ER 925 CA
73. [1914] 1 Ch 968.
74. *Ibid* at p. 974. See also *Daimler Co Ltd v Continental Tyre & Rubber Co (Great Britain) Ltd* [1916] 2 AC 307; [1916-17] All ER Rep. 191 HL.
75. (1910) 1 KB 215 at p. 233
76. *Yonge v Toynbee* [1910] 1 KB 215, [1908-10] All ER Rep. 204 CA.
77. *Ibid.*
78. *Myers v Elman* [1940] AC 282 at p.319 per Lord Wright HL.
79. *Ex p Stuckey* (1791) 2 Cox Eq. Cas. 283.

80. *Re James Gray (a solicitor)* (1869) 20 LT 728.
81. (1855) 7 De GM & G 558, [1843-60] All ER Rep. 644.
82. *Collen v Wright* (1857) 7 E&B 34, on appeal 8 E&B 647.
83. *Danish Mercantile Co Ltd v Beaumont* [1951] Ch 680, [1951] 1 All ER 925 CA
84. *Presentaciones Musicales SA v Secunda and Another* [1994] 2 All ER 737 CA.
85. *Ibid*
86. *Ibid*

5. REMUNERATION OF AN ATTORNEY-AT-LAW

Part I – Restrictions on Right To Charge Remuneration

INTRODUCTION

Once it is settled that an attorney has been retained, then according to Atkin LJ in *Adams v London Improved Motor Coach Builders* Ltd:

> The ordinary terms applicable to a person who employs a professional man to do professional work on his behalf – namely that he shall remunerate him[1] come into effect.

This according to the learned judge is 'the prima facie obligation which at once emerges when the employment is proved'.[2]

RESTRICTIONS ON CHARGING REMUNERATION

There are however restrictions on an attorney-at-law charging remuneration in the following instances:

1. where the work is done by an attorney who is not the holder of a current practising certificate;
2. where the attorney is acting for himself; and
3. where the attorney is under a disability imposed by law

1. PRACTISING CERTIFICATE

Antigua & Barbuda, Barbados, Jamaica, St. Lucia and Trinidad & Tobago

Pursuant to the relevant statutory provision contained in the respective Legal Profession Acts of the above territories, no person is qualified to practise law unless he has been admitted as an attorney-at-law (as evidenced by a certificate of enrolment), his name is on the Roll of the Court and in addition he has been issued a practising certificate.[3]

If an attorney is not the holder of a valid practising certificate which is issued on an annual basis, upon payment of the prescribed fees, he is according to the relevant provision, an unqualified person in that he is incapable of bringing an action to recover his fees in respect of anything done by him whilst acting in the course of such practice.[4]

In addition, in Trinidad & Tobago, pursuant to s.23(2) of the Legal Profession Act 21/1986 and in Barbados pursuant to s.49 of the Legal Profession Act Cap. 370A, an attorney-at-law is required to pay an annual contribution to the Compensation Fund as a pre-condition for the issuance of the practising certificate.[5]

However the following are exceptions to this general rule:

(a) if the work is done by the attorney in a non-professional capacity, the statutory provision does not apply e.g. work done as a clerk to a Commissioner at a fixed rate salary;[6] and
(b) in accordance with the relevant statutory provision of the above territories, an attorney-at-law who holds office in the Judicial and Legal Services of the Government, so long as he remains a law officer, he shall be deemed to be holder of a valid practising certificate.[7]

Anguilla, Dominica, Grenada, Guyana, St. Kitts & Nevis, St. Vincent & the Grenadines, The Bahamas

It is to be noted that in the abovementioned territories, upon issuance of the certificate of enrolment, an attorney can practise unrestrictedly. More specifically, there is no provision in these territories for the issuance of a practising certificate on an annual basis or otherwise. [8]

2. ATTORNEY-AT-LAW ACTING FOR HIMSELF

Where an attorney-at-law brings or defends an action in person he is entitled to all the costs of conducting the litigation of which he is a party as if he had employed another attorney to act for him. He is however not entitled to charge for such items as instructions from and attendances upon himself or perusal of his own documents.[9]

The reasons for these restrictions according to Brett MR in *London Scottish Benefit Society v Chorley* ' are because such costs do not exist'.[10]

3. DISABILITY IMPOSED BY LAW – ATTORNEY/TRUSTEE

No person in whom fiduciary duties are vested shall make a profit of them by employing himself because in so doing, he cannot perform one part of his trust, namely that of ensuring that no improper charges are made.[11] This is in keeping with the age-old adage that a trustee ought not to make his office a source of personal emolument.

Accordingly, an attorney-at-law who acts as a trustee is prohibited from making a charge against the trust estate other than for out-of-pocket expenses; that is the rule as regards work *done out of court* by a trustee whether acting for himself or for other trustees as well.[12] He is to charge nothing for his time and trouble. If the rule were otherwise, according to Chitty J in *Re Barber Burgess v Vinicome:*

> A trust estate might be heavily burdened by reason of business done by a trustee employing himself as commission agent for the estate. The difficulty would be in saying, in each particular case, that the business was not required to be done.[13]

Exceptions

The following are exceptions to the general rule than an attorney acting in the dual capacity of attorney and trustee cannot charge for his professional services:

(a) Charging Clauses

Where the trust instrument such as a will provides for remuneration of an attorney by way of a charging clause, the attorney/trustee is entitled to make the usual professional charges and receive the same pecuniary emoluments for all business done by him in respect of the trust as if he, himself not being the trustee, were so employed by the trustee. However he is not entitled to charge for everything which he does of whatever kind which is not of a strictly professional character and which may be performed in person by a trustee who is himself not an attorney-at-law, unless there is a clause in the trust instruments to this effect. For these non-professional charges to be enforceable, the charging clause must be distinct and its terms and its effect explained to the client. The case of *Re Chapple Newton v Chapman*[14] is instructive on this point.

In *Re Chapple Newton v Chapman* a testatrix, by her will, appointed her solicitor one of two executors and trustees. The will made provisions for the solicitor *inter alia* to be paid for his *usual professional charges*. The solicitor included in his bill of costs, charges in respect of all business done by him whether such business was strictly professional or not or could have been performed by a lay person. Much reliance was placed by the solicitor, on the wording of the charging clause which further provided that the solicitor be entitled to receive 'the same pecuniary emoluments and remuneration for all business done by him in all attendances, time and trouble given and bestowed by him in or about the execution of the trust and power of the will and the management and administration of the trust estate real or personal as if he, not being himself a trustee or executor were employed by the trustee or executor'. Kay LJ held that only items of a strictly professional nature would be allowed as the charging clause did not specifically provide that the solicitor could charge for business which was not strictly professional.

(b) In Litigation - The Rule in Craddock v Piper[15]

The general rule is that an attorney/trustee, in the absence of a charging clause, is not entitled to charge costs except out-of-pocket expenses. However, this rule applies to cases where a trustee is acting as attorney for himself alone but does not extend to proceedings in court where there are other trustees and they come to employ him though this employment may arise out of his being a co-trustee.

In such instances in accordance with what is referred to as the Rule in *Craddock v Piper* first enunciated by L.Cottenham, in the case by that name,[16] and considered by Stirling J in *Re Doody, Fisher v Doody,* whenever a solicitor or his firm appears in a suit or action on behalf of himself and co-trustee(s) and the cost of the suit has not thereby been increased, the attorney or his firm, as the case may be, is entitled to their usual profit costs.[17]

It is to be noted that the Rule in *Craddock v Piper* does not apply to out of court work, but it does extend to any proceedings in court whether with respect to friendly or hostile proceedings such as an application for maintenance of an infant.[18]

(c) Cestui que Trust

An attorney-at-law/trustee is entitled to charge the trust estate, profit costs when he acts as attorney-at-law for the *cestui que trust* in an action for as Chitty J observed in *Re Barber Burgess v Vinicome*, 'that is not part of the business of the trust properly so called'.[19]

(d) Agent for Attorney/Trustee

Where an attorney/trustee employs another attorney as agent for the purposes of conducting business in respect of the trust estate, the attorney/trustee is not permitted to make a profit out of the business.[20] As the Vice-Chancellor noted in *Re Burge v Brutton*:

> the reason for the rule is that the solicitor/trustee is bound to exercise control over the solicitor he employs to watch the proceedings and see that they are proper; and the Court guards the performance of that duty by excluding him from any pecuniary interest in the steps taken.[21]

However the attorney/trustee may pay the agent, as out of pocket expenses, the usual profit costs for conducting the trust business for which he was so employed as agent.

(e) Partners of Attorney/Trustee

An attorney/trustee may employ his partner(s) as attorney(s) for himself and his co-trustee(s) in reference to trust affairs and may pay the partner(s) the usual charges provided:

(1) it has been expressly agreed that the attorney/trustee shall not participate in the profits or derive any benefits from the charges even if all the business is transacted by the attorney/trustee himself;[22]or

(2) there is a definite agreement in existence before the work is undertaken, proof of which may be evidenced either in the partnership agreement or a letter or memorandum written by the attorney/trustee to his partner(s).[23]

Part II – Agreements For Remuneration

INTRODUCTION

Before examining agreements for remuneration in any detail it is important at the outset to draw a distinction between contentious and non-contentious business agreements not only because the distinction between the two directly impacts on the validity and enforceability of these agreements, but also because the method of ascertaining costs, in the absence or unenforceability of such agreements, is also dependent on whether the business for which remuneration is being charged is contentious or non-contentious in nature.

Meaning of Contentious/Non-Contentious Business

Contentious business means business done as an attorney-at-law in or for the purpose of proceedings begun before a court or before an arbitrator, not being non-contentious/common form business.[24]

Non-contentious business or common form business includes out of court work such as preparation of pleadings, conveyances, common form probate papers and the preparation of leases.

It is to be noted that business which is done for the purpose of any action or proceedings contemplated but not instituted is non-contentious so that the business of advising whether or not proceedings should be started is non-contentious and only becomes contentious if proceedings are in fact commenced.[25]

CONTENTIOUS BUSINESS AGREEMENTS

With the exception of St. Lucia and The Bahamas, contentious business agreements for remuneration, depending on the jurisdiction, are governed by:

1. the common law; or
2. by statute; or
3. by the common law and statute.

1. By The Common Law Only

Antigua & Barbuda

In the case of Antigua & Barbuda, prior to the passage in 1997 of the Legal Profession Act 9/1997, the statutory provisions contained in the Solicitors Act 1974, England were deemed to be incorporated *inter alia* into the laws of Antigua & Barbuda.[26] However when the Legal Profession Act 9/1997 was enacted, provisions in respect of contentious business agreements were not included. Accordingly, the common law position is deemed to apply to Antigua & Barbuda.

Trinidad & Tobago

Prior to the passage of the Legal Profession Act 21/1986 the law with respect to solicitors was governed by the Solicitors Act Chap 6:50. The Act contained statutory provisions with respect to contentious business agreements,[27] which were equivalent to the current statutory provisions in respect of contentious business agreements contained in the Solicitors Act 1974, England. However when the Solicitors Act was repealed and replaced by the Legal Profession Act 21/1986, these provisions were not included in the new Act. Accordingly, the common law position in respect of contentious business agreements is currently applicable to Trinidad & Tobago.

2. By Statute Only

Barbados

Section 36(1) of the Legal Profession Act Cap. 370A provides that a client may make an agreement as to amount and manner of payment of remuneration for the whole or part of any legal business done or to be done by the attorney-at-law.

Guyana

Section 21 of the Legal Practitioners Act Cap. 4:01 provides in effect that a special agreement for remuneration otherwise valid in law shall not be good and valid unless it is in writing.[28] A special agreement is not defined by the Act. However in *Farnum v Serrao*,[29] the court construed the meaning of special agreement as contained in s.13 of the Legal Practitioners Ordinance 1897, British Guiana, the equivalent of which provision is contained in s.21 of the current Legal Practitioners Act.

According to Smith CJ in *Farnum v Serrao* the term special agreement as used in s.13 of the 1897 Ordinance, 'must have some reference to some business to be transacted in the court or offices of the court in connection with some proceeding or matter whether of a contentious or non-contentious business'.[30]

Most significantly Smith CJ noted that the word *business* as used in respect of such special agreements 'did not include work done or services rendered by a solicitor for his client in the other matters e.g. negotiating the purchase or sale or arranging a transport of a property or preparing documents not intended for use in Court'.[31]

Accordingly, the Court held that since the business for which the barrister was retained was with respect to the drawing up of a petition to the Governor

General; it was not business to be transacted in the Court or the offices of the Court and accordingly was not a special agreement within the meaning of the Ordinance and it was not therefore essential that it be in writing.

It is to be noted that the decision in *Farnum v Serrao* was approved and adopted in the later case of *Thierens v Fernandes*[32] and more particularly, the meaning assigned to special agreements as provided for in the Legal Practitioners Ordinance.

In *Thierren v Fernandes* a barrister entered into an oral agreement with respect to the settlement of proceedings pending in Court. The Court held *inter alia* that the agreement not being in writing it could not be enforced.[33]

Jamaica

Agreements for remuneration are governed by s.21 of the Legal Profession Act. In this regard no distinction is made between contentious and non-contentious business agreements.

3. By the Common Law and Statute

Eastern Caribbean territories (save St. Lucia and Antigua & Barbuda)

Pursuant to the current English provision contained in s.59(1) of the Solicitors Act 1974, which provision is deemed to be incorporated into the laws of the Eastern Caribbean territories (save St. Lucia and Antigua & Barbuda),[34] agreements for remuneration in respect of contentious business agreements are governed by the common law and by statute.

St. Lucia

Contentious business agreements in St. Lucia are neither governed by statute nor the English common law and in that sense St. Lucia is in a unique position *vis-à-vis* the other territories. Unlike the other Eastern Caribbean territories, the Supreme Court Act of St. Lucia makes no provision for the reception of English law with respect *inter alia* to attorneys' costs. Indeed prior to the passage of the current Legal Profession Act 31/2000 St. Lucia had its own indigenous legislation on the legal profession - The Legal Practitioners Ordinance Ch 116.

However neither the repealed Legal Practitioners Ordinance nor the current Legal Profession Act contain any provisions with respect to contentious business agreements.

In addition, St. Lucia, unlike the other English-speaking Caribbean territories does not receive English common law unless statute expressly so provides (as in the case of wills).

Accordingly, neither the common law nor statutory position applies to St. Lucia. As such contentious business agreements are governed by custom and convention. According to the custom and convention to date, practitioners are free to enter into contentious business agreements for remuneration and such agreements are both valid and enforceable provided the fees charged thereunder are fair and reasonable.

The Bahamas

There are no statutory provisions in the Legal Profession Act 26/1992 with respect to agreements for remuneration, whether in respect of contentious or non-contentious business.

Although in the absence of indigenous statutory provision the common law position should be applicable to The Bahamas, that is not the case.

Agreements for remuneration are in practice governed by local custom and convention. Accordingly, such agreements may be in writing or oral and are valid and enforceable provided the fees chargeable thereunder are fair and reasonable.

A. The Common Law Position

Antigua & Barbuda and Trinidad & Tobago

In accordance with the common law, contentious business agreements are both valid and enforceable whether made orally or in writing provided they are fair and reasonable. However in so far as the enforceability as opposed to the validity of these agreements are concerned, a distinction must be drawn between agreements which are favourable to the client and those which are favourable to the attorney.

In accordance with the common law position such agreements while valid, are not as a general rule, enforceable against the client if they are not favourable to the client. This is so because as Kay LJ noted in *Re Baylis,* 'the court must consider the great influence which a solicitor has over his client'.[35]

Fletcher Moulton LJ explained the common law position in England in the case of *Clare v Joseph.*[36] He noted that while such agreements were not necessarily unenforceable, they were however viewed with great jealousy by the Courts because they were reached between a man and his legal advisers as to the terms of the latter's remuneration.

As Buckley LJ observed in *Clare v Joseph,*

> the solicitor could not charge his client more than the amount of his bill of costs when taxed and it was his duty to advise his client that it was contrary to his interests to pay more. There was so great an opportunity for the exercise of undue influence that the courts were very slow to enforce these agreements unless they were satisfied that they were made under circumstances that precluded any improper attempt on the solicitor's part to benefit himself at the client's expense.[37]

These agreements Fletcher Moulton LJ remarked in *Gundry v Sainsbury* were of 'imperfect validity in the hands of the solicitor'.[38]

However it is to be noted that where such agreements are favourable to the client such as agreements not to charge any fees or to charge less than what would be recovered as costs by way of taxation, such agreements are held by the court not only to be valid but also enforceable for 'there was no ground in equity why they should be suspicious of a bargain of that kind'.[39]

By way of illustration, in *Jennings v Johnson*[40] an oral agreement by a solicitor with his client to charge nothing if the client lost his action or if successful to take nothing out of any monies awarded in such an action was held valid and enforceable. It is to be further noted that under the common law, that the agreement for remuneration is not so binding on the client so as to preclude the delivery and taxation of a bill of costs.

B. The Statutory Position

Barbados and Guyana

In accordance with the statutory position contentious business agreements must be in writing and signed by the party to be charged in order to be valid and enforceable. However once in writing, the attorney can enter into a valid and enforceable agreement with his client to charge more or less than that to which he would otherwise be entitled to be remunerated,[41] bearing in mind that the fees chargeable by an attorney-at-law are required to be fair and reasonable.

Such agreements (subject to certain exceptions) are not subject to taxation or the provisions relating to the delivery or signing of an attorney's bill of costs. In Barbados, statute provides that such exceptions include where the agreement has been set aside by the court on the grounds that it is unfair and unreasonable, and where the contentious business agreement is made by the client as the guardian or committee of or as a trustee under the deed or will of any person whose property will be chargeable with the whole or part of the amount payable thereunder.[42]

Jamaica

With respect to Jamaica there is no requirement that a contentious business agreement for remuneration must be in writing to be valid and enforceable. Although the position is governed by statute, it differs from the position in Barbados and Guyana in that such agreements in Jamaica are equally valid and enforceable by the attorney whether in writing or oral, provided that the fees charged by the attorney are fair and reasonable. It is to be noted that although the wording of s.21 of the Legal Profession Act is similar to the wording of s.59(1) of the Solicitors Act, 1974 England, the English common law position in respect of remuneration for contentious business, is not received in Jamaica, as contentious business agreements are specifically governed by this indigenous statutory provision.

C. The Common Law and Statutory Position

Eastern Caribbean (save Antigua & Barbuda and St. Lucia)

The common law position is not affected by the statutory position as contained in s.59 of the Solicitors Act 1974, England, in that the rights conferred by s.59 do not displace or replace the common law. It merely provides in effect that in order to enjoy the rights and protection conferred by statute the contentious business agreement must be:

(1) in writing; and
(2) signed at least by the person to be bound or his agent on his behalf.[43]

According to the English statutory position, which is deemed to be received in these territories, the agreement may provide for the attorney to be remunerated *inter alia* at a higher or lower rate than that at which he would otherwise be entitled (which was previously not the case under the common law).

In this regard, it is to be noted that when the statutory provision was first enacted in England, (by s.4 of the Solicitors Act, 1870 England), it was contended that the common law position was thereby displaced and the effect of the statute was to render unenforceable, oral agreements in respect of an attorney's remuneration.

This point was raised by the solicitor in *Clare v Joseph,*[44] a case in which the client sought to rely on an oral agreement entered into with the solicitor and which was favourable to him. The solicitor argued that the agreement was unenforceable because of the passage of the Solicitors Act 1870 which Act introduced statutory provisions with respect to contentious business agreements.

However, the judgment of Fletcher Moulton LJ in *Clare v Joseph* made it quite clear that s.4 of the 1870 Act was an enabling not a disabling provision and did not thereby displace the common law.[45] Accordingly, once a contentious business agreement is oral the common law position applies. Once it is in writing and duly signed it is governed by statute.

ENFORCEMENT OF CONTENTIOUS BUSINESS AGREEMENTS

Pursuant to the Legal Profession Acts of Barbados and Jamaica and the Solicitors Act 1974, England, which Act is deemed to be incorporated into the laws of the Eastern Caribbean territories (save St. Lucia and Antigua & Barbuda),[46] an agreement for remuneration in respect of contentious business may be sued and recovered on or set aside on the like grounds as an agreement not relating to the remuneration of an attorney-at-law (i.e. by writ or other equivalent originating summons proceedings in these territories).

It is submitted that in the absence of statutory provision that the same holds true for the other jurisdictions.

IN GENERAL

Fees Chargeable Under A Contentious Business Agreement

All jurisdictions (save The Bahamas and Jamaica)

The Code of Ethics of the various territories provides that an attorney shall not charge fees that are unfair and unreasonable.[47] Guidelines for determining the fairness and reasonableness of the fees charged are also set out in the relevant rule of ethics. In addition, the Code of Ethics of these territories provides that:

> An attorney shall not enter into an agreement for or charge a fee in contravention of these Rules or any other law.[48]

Accordingly, whether the common law and or statutory position, the fees chargeable under agreements for remuneration must comply with the guidelines prescribed by the Code of Ethics. Breach of these guidelines, which have the force of law, having been made under the respective of Legal Profession Acts of the various territories, not only renders such agreements unenforceable but may also constitute professional misconduct on the part of the attorney.

The Barbadian case of *Re Eastmond*[49] is instructive. In that case, an attorney-at-law was suspended from practice for six months. The court held that although the attorney was entitled to enter into an agreement for remuneration in respect of contentious business, (including charging fees at a higher or lesser rate than that to which he would be entitled), the fees chargeable thereunder were unreasonable having contravened the Legal Profession Code of Ethics rule 65(2) which provides that no agreement as to fees may contravene the Code, and rule 66(1) which provides that fees may not be unfair and unreasonable.

It is submitted that even with respect to Guyana which does not have a Code of Ethics and in the Eastern Caribbean territories (save St. Lucia and Antigua & Barbuda) where the OECS Code of Ethics is not legally binding, having not been made under any Act, that nevertheless pursuant to the guidelines set out in the OECS Code of Ethics and in the case of Guyana, the RSC O.49 r.7 Rules of the High Court Cap. 3:02, that breach of these respective guidelines will not only render such agreements unenforceable, but may also constitute, in the appropriate case, professional misconduct.

Jamaica

The Canon of Ethics also sets out general guidelines in respect of charging fees, similar to those applicable to Trinidad & Tobago, Barbados and the Eastern Caribbean.[50]

However the Canon of Ethics does not specifically provide that an attorney-at-law shall not charge a fee in contravention of the guidelines set out in Rules of the Canon, nor does breach thereof automatically constitute professional misconduct. Nonetheless s.21 of the Legal Profession Act empowers the court to reduce the amount agreed to be payable under an agreement for remuneration, if it appears in the court's opinion to be unfair and unreasonable.

The Bahamas

In the case of The Bahamas, although the Code of Professional Conduct also sets out guidelines in respect of charging fair and reasonable fees[51] neither the Code nor the Legal Profession Act prescribe any penalty for breach of the guidelines in respect of charging fees whether in respect of contentious or non-contentious business.

Costs Payable to Third Party in Respect of Contentious Business Agreements

With respect to the recovery of costs from any other person under any order for the payment of costs to which a contentious business agreement relates, whether under the common law and/or statutory position, the client is not entitled to recover more than the amount payable by him to his attorney-at-law in respect thereof under such agreement.

Accordingly, as in the case of *Gundry v Sainsbury*[52] where an attorney entered into an oral agreement with the plaintiff to charge nothing in respect of his costs and judgment was entered for the plaintiff client, the client was not entitled to recover any costs from the defendant more than that which he was liable to pay to his solicitor under the oral agreement.

Form of Contentious Business Agreement

Although the respective Legal Profession Acts of Antigua & Barbuda, St. Lucia, The Bahamas and Trinidad & Tobago make no provision with respect to contentious business agreements, the respective Legal Profession Acts of Barbados, Jamaica and The Solicitors Act 1974, England, which Act is deemed to be incorporated into the laws of the Eastern Caribbean territories (save St. Lucia and Antigua & Barbuda)provide that contentious business agreements may take the form of a gross sum, retainer or otherwise.[53]

In so far as the form that the agreement may take, it is submitted that in absence of any provision to the contrary, in the other jurisdictions, remuneration in respect of contentious business agreements in all the jurisdictions may take the form *inter alia* of a gross sum retainer.

NON-CONTENTIOUS BUSINESS AGREEMENTS

Introduction

Position in England

Prior to the enactment in 1870 of the Solicitors Remuneration Act in England in particular s.4 thereof, the position in respect of the validity and enforceability of non-contentious business agreements was the same as that which was applicable to contentious business agreements i.e. such agreements whether oral or in writing were valid and enforceable if favourable to the client, but as a general rule, they were not enforceable if favourable to the solicitor.

The Solicitors Remuneration Act, 1870, as stated previously, in effect balanced the scales between solicitor and client by making no distinction between contentious and non-contentious business agreements. As such, the provisions of that Act applied to both types of agreement in that there was no requirement that such agreements be made in writing. However in 1881, when the Solicitors Remuneration Act became law it enacted a separate set of provisions for non-contentious business agreements, in particular s.8 of the Act expressly excluded the Solicitors Remuneration Act 1870 as to all business to which the new Act applied and provided that non-contentious agreements shall be in writing and signed by the party to be charged. [54]

It is to be noted that the equivalent provision contained in the Solicitors Remuneration Act 1881, was subsequently re-enacted and is currently contained in s.57 of the Solicitors Act 1974, England.

All jurisdictions (save Guyana, Jamaica and The Bahamas)

In accordance with the respective statutory provisions (which is equivalent to the current s.57 of the Solicitors Act 1974, England) non-contentious business agreements must be in writing and signed by the person to be bound or his agent so authorised in writing.[55] The decision in *Re A Solicitor* [1956][56] is instructive on this point. In that case the court held that an oral agreement between a solicitor and client which provided for the solicitor to charge nothing or less than the scale charges for conveyancing business was not effective as the agreement was not in writing as required by statute. Accordingly, the solicitor's application for taxation of a bill of costs on the prescribed scale for the conveyancing business was allowed to stand.

Guyana

Pursuant to RSC O.60 rr. 2, 3 and 4 of the Rules of the High Court, Cap. 3:02 the provisions of which are identical to the original English statutory provisions with respect to agreements for remuneration for contentious business, an agreement for remuneration in respect of non-contentious business may be in writing or may be oral. However where statutory protection is sought the agreement must be in writing to be valid.

Jamaica

As stated previously, the Legal Profession Act makes no distinction between agreements in respect of contentious and non-contentious business. Indeed s.21 provides that agreements in respect of fees may be in writing. Accordingly, non-contentious business agreements for remuneration need not be in writing to be valid and enforceable.

The Bahamas

In the case of The Bahamas, there is no provision in the Legal Profession Act or otherwise prescribing that such agreements be in writing. Accordingly, as is the case with respect to Jamaica, non-contentious agreements may be oral or in writing.

Provision for Remuneration

All Jurisdictions (save The Bahamas)

Although there may be some variation in the wording, statute provides that non-contentious business agreements may provide for the remuneration of the attorney by gross sum or by commission or percentage or by salary or otherwise and may be made on such terms that the amount of remuneration therein stipulated shall not include any disbursements made by the attorney.[57]

Enforcement of Non-Contentious Business Agreements

An agreement for remuneration in respect of non-contentious business may be sued and recovered on or set aside in the same manner as an agreement not relating to the remuneration of an attorney. In other words by writ proceedings or other equivalent originating process.[58]

It is to be noted that non-contentious business agreements are not exempt from taxation but the right of a client to taxation is not unqualified but is limited to instances where the client can furnish *prima facie* evidence that the agreement is unreasonable.

Accordingly, the client is not automatically entitled to impugn or go behind the agreement and to require the attorney to deliver an itemised bill of cost and have the bill taxed. Indeed, the court will not order the delivery of a bill of costs and taxation of the bill unless it is satisfied, on the evidence, that there are grounds to investigate whether the agreement is fair and reasonable. As Lord Evershed MR observed in *Rutter v Sheridan-Young* with respect to the Court's power to order the delivery and taxation of a bill of costs:

> Such a power in the Court will not be exercised merely because the client asks for it or because his counsel thinks of some argument for suggesting it would be a good thing.[59]

However once the court is of the opinion that there are *prima facie* grounds for inquiry, it will order the delivery and taxation of a bill of costs.

MIXED AGREEMENTS

Eastern Caribbean (save St. Lucia), Trinidad & Tobago

Mixed agreements, with respect to contentious and non-contentious business are severable for the purpose of enforcement of any part thereof. Accordingly, where in the case of *Electrical Trades Union v Tarlo*[60] an oral agreement was made in respect of non-contentious and contentious business, the court held that the client was entitled to enforce the part of the oral agreement relating to contentious business. This was so notwithstanding that the part of the agreement dealing with non-contentious business was not in writing as required by statute and therefore unenforceable.

Part III – Quantum of Costs

QUANTUM CHARGEABLE IN RESPECT OF NON-CONTENTIOUS BUSINESS

The quantum of fees chargeable by an attorney-at-law, whether in respect of contentious or non-contentious business, is required by law to be fair and reasonable. In determining what is fair and reasonable, general guidelines have been laid down and in certain instances, a scale of fees has been prescribed or recommended.

RULE-MAKING BODIES

The relevant rule making body of the following territories has been empowered by statute to regulate and prescribe an attorney's remuneration in respect of non-contentious business:

Barbados – The Bar Association with approval of the Judicial Advisory Council pursuant to s.35 of the Legal Profession Act, Cap. 370A.

Guyana – The Rules Committee comprising the Chancellor, Chief Justice, a puisne judge and four practising attorneys pursuant to s.29 of the Legal Practitioners Act, Cap. 4:01 as amended by The Legal Practitioners (Amendment) Act 3/1980 and s.67 of the High Court Act Cap. 3:02.

Trinidad & Tobago – The Law Association with the approval of the Chief Justice and Minister of Legal Affairs pursuant to s.52 of the Legal Profession Act 21/1986.

Antigua & Barbuda – The Law Council with the approval of the Minister of Legal Affairs pursuant to s.39 of the Legal Profession Act 9/1997.

St. Lucia – The Bar Association with the approval of the Chief Justice pursuant to s.52 of the Legal Profession Act 31/2000.

Eastern Caribbean (save Antigua & Barbuda and St. Lucia) – For the purpose of making and prescribing rules with respect to remuneration, none of these territories has a local rule making body. However, by virtue of the relevant reception provision contained in the respective Supreme Court Acts of these territories, the Rules and Orders made by the Rules Committee in England pursuant, *inter alia* to s.56 of the Solicitors Act, 1974 are deemed to be incorporated into the laws of these territories.[61]

The respective 'reception' provision provides:

> Subject to the rules of court, the law and practise relating to solicitors and the taxation and recovery of costs in force in England shall extend to and be in force in (name of State) and apply to all persons lawfully practising therein as solicitors of the court.[62]

In this regard, in the case of *Zuliani et al v Viera,*[63] the Eastern Caribbean Court of Appeal was called upon to address the issue of reception in St. Kitts & Nevis of the Solicitors Remuneration Order 1972, England, which Order was made by the Rules Committee in England pursuant to s.56 of the repealed Solicitors Act 1957, England. According to r.3(1) of the Order, a client may, prior to taxation of a bill of costs, require a solicitor to obtain a certificate from the Law Society stating that in the Society's opinion the solicitor's charges were fair and reasonable. Although Byron JA observed 'that the law cannot blind itself to the real and practical situation that exists locally', he nevertheless held that the Solicitors Act 1974, England and the Rules and Order made thereunder including the Solicitors Remuneration Order 1972 made under the repealed Solicitors Act 1957, England formed part of the law of St. Kitts & Nevis, a decision which was affirmed by the Privy Council.[64]

It is to be noted, that since the Privy Council decision in *Zuliani v Veira*, the Solicitors' Remuneration Order 1972 has been repealed and replaced by the Solicitors (Non-Contentious Business) Remuneration Order 1994. Accordingly, the 1994 Remuneration Order is deemed to be incorporated into the laws of the Eastern Caribbean territories (save Antigua & Barbuda and St. Lucia).

Jamaica

Although the Legal Profession Act confers on the General Legal Council the power to prescribe standards of professional etiquette and professional conduct for attorneys,[65] the Council, unlike the case in Antigua & Barbuda, Barbados, St. Lucia and Trinidad & Tobago, has no specific or express power to make rules with respect to the charging of remuneration in respect of non-contentious business.

The Bahamas

In the case of The Bahamas, there is no rule making body to whom the responsibility has been delegated to prescribe fees. Indeed s.28 of the Legal Profession Act 26/1992 specifically prohibits the Bar Association from imposing or sanctioning a minimum scale of fees.

STATUTORY GUIDELINES IN MAKING RULES

Antigua & Barbuda, Barbados, Eastern Caribbean (save Antigua & Barbuda and St. Lucia), St. Lucia and Trinidad & Tobago

In making rules governing remuneration for non-contentious business the relevant provision of the respective Legal Profession Acts of Antigua & Barbuda, Barbados, St. Lucia and Trinidad & Tobago[66] requires that in prescribing any scale of fees the Law Association or its equivalent body shall take the following into account:

(a) the position of the person for whom the attorney is concerned in the business i.e. whether as vendor or purchaser; lessor or lessee; mortgagor or mortgagee; or the like;
(b) the place where and the circumstances in which business or any other part of it is transacted;
(c) the amount of capital, money or rent to which the business relates;
(d) the skill and labour and responsibility involved in the business on the part of the attorney;
(e) the number and importance of the documents prepared and perused without regard to length.

REGULATORY GUIDELINES

Code/Canon of Ethics - Antigua & Barbuda, Barbados, Eastern Caribbean (save Antigua & Barbuda and St. Lucia), Jamaica, The Bahamas, St. Lucia and Trinidad & Tobago

The relevant rule of the Code/Canon of Ethics of the above territories prescribes that in charging fees an attorney at law shall not charge fees that are unfair and unreasonable.[67]

In determining the fairness and reasonableness of fees, the following factors as a general rule, are required to be taken into account:

(a) the time and labour required, the novelty and difficulty of the questions involved and the skill required to perform the legal service properly;
(b) the likelihood that the acceptance of the particular employment will preclude other employment by the attorney-at-law;
(c) the fee customarily charged in the locality for similar legal services;

(d) the amount, if any involved;
(e) the time limitations imposed by the client or by the circumstances;
(f) the nature and length of the professional relationship with the client;
(g) the experience, reputation and ability of the attorney-at-law concerned;
(h) any scale of fees or recommended guide as to charges prescribed by law or by the Judicial Advisory Council/Law Association/Bar Association, General Legal Council, Law Council as the case may be.

OTHER REGULATORY GUIDELINES

Trinidad & Tobago

The Solicitors (Remuneration Professional Charges) Order made under s.55 of the repealed Solicitors Act Chap. 6:50 but deemed to have been saved by s.52(4) of the Legal Profession Act also sets out regulatory guidelines. In this regard, the Solicitors (Remuneration Professional Charges) Order contains essentially the same guidelines as provided for by Part B r.10 of the Code of Ethics.

Guyana

Order 60 Part V Appendix V of the Rules of the High Court Cap. 3:02 sets out the matters to be taken into account by an attorney-at-law in charging fees with respect to non-contentious matters. These guidelines are essentially the same as those set out in the Code of Ethics of Barbados and Trinidad & Tobago and include *inter alia*:

(a) the complexity of the matter or the difficulty or novelty of the questions raised;
(b) the skill, labour, specialised knowledge and responsibility involved on the part of the attorney-at-law; and
(c) the number and importance of the documents prepared or perused, without regard to length.

Eastern Caribbean (save Antigua & Barbuda and St. Lucia)

The general guidelines contained in the Solicitors Remuneration Order 1994 England made by the Rules Committee under s.56 of the Solicitors Act 1974 and the guidelines set out in the Rules of the Supreme Court

(Non-Contentious Probate) Costs 1956 England and made by the Rules Committee under the Solicitors Act 1932 are deemed to be part of the law of these territories for the purposes of determining the fees chargeable in respect of non-contentious business.[68] These guidelines are similar to those set out in r.10 of the Organisation of Eastern Caribbean States (OECS) Code of Ethics.

SCALE OF FEES

Recommended or Prescribed

Apart from the general guidelines set out in the rules and/or legislation of the various territories, a scale of fees either recommended or prescribed is also used by practitioners for the purposes of determining the fees chargeable in respect of non-contentious business. In this regard, the position in the various territories is considered below.

Barbados and Trinidad & Tobago

With respect to the exercise of the powers conferred by statute on the rule-making bodies of these territories, the Bar and Law Associations of Barbados and Trinidad & Tobago, respectively, have made rules regulating remuneration in respect of certain non-contentious business. In the case of Barbados, these rules are the Legal Profession (The Attorneys-at-Law) (Remuneration for Non-Contentious Business) Rules 1997 made under s.35 of the Legal Profession Act. These Rules which replaced the Legal Profession (The Attorneys-at-Law) (Remuneration Non-Contentious Business) Rules 1983 prescribe the *minimum* fees which may be charged by an attorney in respect of non-contentious business. In this regard it is to be noted that where an attorney wishes to charge less than the prescribed fee he is required to refer the matter to the Costs Committee of the Bar Association. However where an attorney agrees to waive his entire fees he may do so without any reference to the Costs Committee.[69]

In the case of Trinidad & Tobago, The Attorneys-at-Law (Remuneration) (Non-Contentious Business) Rules 1997, made under s.52 of the Legal Profession Act prescribe the *maximum* fees which may be charged by an attorney-at-law in respect of the non-contentious business to which the Rules apply.

Eastern Caribbean (save Antigua & Barbuda and St. Lucia)

Although there are no prescribed or mandatory scale fees in these territories, it is the custom, convention and practice for the local Bar Association to publish a recommended scale of fees in respect of certain contentious and non-contentious business.

The respective Bar Associations of these territories are incorporated societies with no statutory powers. However the recommended scale of fees published by the Association is followed to the extent that in taxing bills of costs, the Taxing Master applies the Bar Association's scale of fees as a guide in determining the appropriate fees to be charged in a matter.

In addition, a scale of fees is provided for in the Schedule to certain Acts, in particular the Companies Act and Title by Registration Acts of these territories. According to the Kittitian case of *Wade v Daniel*, 'where an Act provides for a scale of fees with respect to non-contentious business, any arrangements made to charge fees which are more than those prescribed by the Act is unlawful'.[70]

St. Lucia and Antigua & Barbuda

With respect to St. Lucia and Antigua & Barbuda, although the respective Legal Profession Acts of these territories,[71] make provisions for the Bar Association/Law Council to make rules with respect to the fees chargeable in non-contentious business, to date this has not been done.

Guyana

By Legal Notice 5/1986, Appendices R, U, V and W, to the Rules of the High Court Cap. 3:02 have been repealed and replaced by a new scale of prescribed fees. These new Appendices make provisions *inter alia* for the fees to be charged in respect of non-contentious business, including conveyancing and non-contentious probate matters, and admiralty cases. However in practice the new scale of fees has not been followed primarily because it is acknowledged that the prescribed fees chargeable particularly in respect of transports and other conveyancing transactions and non-contentious probate matters are financially prohibitive to the majority of persons in Guyana.

Jamaica

Until recently, the General Legal Council of the Bar Association published a recommended scale of fees in respect of certain contentious and non-contentious business. The scale of fees recommended by the Bar Association was published pursuant to Canon IV(f)(ix) of the Legal Profession (Canon of Professional Ethics) Rules made under s.12(7) of the Legal Profession Act.

In this regard, Canon IV(f)(ix) provides that in determining the fairness and reasonableness of fees, an attorney-at-law *may* take into account (*emphasis added*) any fees or recommended guides as to the charges by the Bar Association or any other body approved by the General Legal Council for the purposes of prescribing fees.

Apart from the above rule, no express statutory authority is conferred on the General Legal Council to prescribe a scale of fees, in respect of any legal business done by attorneys-at-law in Jamaica.

However, until recently, legal practitioners applied the scale of fees published by the Bar Association of the General Legal Council. This continued to be the practice until the passage of the Fair Competition Act, 1993, when a question arose as to whether the provisions of the Legal Profession Act and the rules made thereunder, in so far as they related to services by the legal profession, were governed by the Fair Competition Act.

In this regard, in November, 1994 the Chairman of the Fair Trading Commission (which Commission was established under the Fair Competition Act), wrote to the President of the General Legal Council of the Bar Association to the effect that some of the Canons of the Legal Professional Ethics Rules (Canon of Ethics) were inconsistent with the provision of s.35 of the Fair Competition Act as amounting to a conspiracy between the Government of Jamaica and the General Legal Council, for the purposes of restraining or injuring competition unduly. (The specific Canon to which the letter alluded was Canon IV(f)).

As a consequence, the Council filed originating summons proceedings (*General Legal Council v The Fair Trading Commission E 55/1985)* seeking several declarations, including a declaration that the Legal Profession Act was not governed by the Fair Competition Act.

On November 14, 1995, in a landmark decision, Orr J declared on behalf of the Court, that the Legal Profession (Canons of Professional Rules) and/or Statutory rules made under the Legal Profession Act were not governed by the Fair Competition Act and that in performing its statutory duties and functions under the Legal Profession Act, the General Legal Council established by the Legal Profession Act, was not amenable or subject to the jurisdiction of the Fair Trading Commission.

Since that decision was handed down by the Court, it is the practice for attorneys to charge in accordance with their own fee structure, taking into account the guidelines for charging fees as set out in Canon IV(f).

The Bahamas

Section 28 of the Legal Profession Act 26/1992 provides that:

> Nothing in this Act shall be construed as or have the effect of authorising the imposition or sanction by the Bar Association or the Bar Council of a minimum scale of fees rendered by a counsel and attorney.

Although the Bar Association has no authority to prescribe a scale of fees, nevertheless in practice a recommended scale of fees published by the Bar Association in 1984 and adjusted for inflation, is used by practitioners for the purposes of determining the fees to be charged in respect of certain contentious and non-contentious business.

This recommended scale of fees, is followed by practitioners to the extent that in taxing bills of costs, the Taxing Master applies the Bar Association's recommended scale as a guideline.

QUANTUM OF COSTS CHARGEABLE IN CONTENTIOUS BUSINESS

GENERAL GUIDELINES IN RESPECT OF CONTENTIOUS BUSINESS

The Rules of the Supreme Court of most of the territories provide guidelines for quantifying an attorney's charges in respect of contentious business in the absence of a scale of fees.[72] The guidelines set out in the relevant Rule(s) of the Supreme Court, are essentially the same factors prescribed in the respective Code of Ethics of these territories. Although these guidelines have been formulated for the guidance of the Taxing Master for the purposes of taxation of a bill of costs, they are nevertheless taken into account by an attorney in charging fees.

CODE/CANON OF ETHICS

The general guidelines set out in the Code/Canon of Ethics of the various territories in respect of charging fees which are fair and reasonable, are also applicable to contentious business.[73]

SCALE OF FEES

Eastern Caribbean territories, Barbados, Guyana, Trinidad & Tobago
To a limited extent the relevant Appendices to the Rules of the Supreme Court of the above territories, set out the costs to be charged by an attorney in respect of certain contentious business.[74] In the case of Eastern Caribbean these provisions are quite extensive.

Eastern Caribbean territories (save Antigua & Barbuda and St. Lucia), The Bahamas
In addition, the recommended scale of fees which is published by the respective Bar Associations of these territories, is also followed in practice, although it is of no binding legal effect.

METHOD OF CALCULATING/ASCERTAINING FEES

Where no scale of fees is prescribed a formula or method has been devised for the purposes of calculating fees in respect of contentious and non-contentious business, although it should be pointed out that the method lends itself more readily to contentious business. According to this method, fees are calculated in two stages; stage one is referred to as the Expense Factor, Hourly Rate or A Factor and stage two is referred to as the General Care and Conduct or Uplift/Profit Factor.[75]

It is to be noted that in applying this method of calculating fees the object of the exercise as Donaldson J observed in *Property and Reversionary Investment Corporation Ltd v Secretary of State for the Environment*, 'is to arrive at a sum which is fair and reasonable, having regard to all the circumstances of the case. It is an exercise in assessment, an exercise in balanced judgment – not an arithmetical calculation'. [76]

In applying this method Donaldson J concluded, 'that it follows that different people may reach different conclusions as to what is fair and reasonable although all should fall within a bracket which in the vast majority of cases will be narrow'.[77]

Stage 1 - Expense Factor/Hourly Rate or Factor A

The Hourly Rate or Expense Factor is in effect, the time spent on the client's business or any aspect thereof either by the attorney, his partner, or employee excluding time spent on a part of the case for which there is already a fixed charge prescribed by statute or the Rules of Court. It is generally calculated at an hourly rate having regard to a reasonable estimation of the overhead expenses of the firm. If the time spent is that of an employee the reasonable salary of the employee or if that of a partner, a notional salary.

The Expense Factor is the logical starting point in the absence of an approved scale. It is the only figure which is readily calculable and if calculated correctly it informs an attorney of the minimum he might charge if he is not to suffer loss in a transaction. In addition it gives the attorney a good idea of the relationship of overhead to the transaction and profits accruing to him – the longer the time spent justifies larger profits.[78]

In this regard not all the time spent on a transaction can necessarily be recorded although the fullest records are kept for as Walton J noted in *Maltby v D J Freeman & Co*, 'no matter how meticulously time records are kept this will always, save in the plainest of all possible cases, represent an undercharge'.

Walton J continued:

> no professional man stops thinking about the days' problem the minute he lifts his coat and umbrella from the stand and sets out on his journey home. Ideas, often very valuable, occurs to him in the train, or car or at home in the bath or even whilst watching television which can never adequately be reflected by time spent.

The other shortcomings in applying the Expense Factor are that it may not sufficiently take into account inflation and in addition different firms have different methods of apportioning expenses.[79]

Stage 2 - Factor B/General Care and Conduct Uplift/Profit Cost

Factor B represents in effect all the factors except time spent, which an attorney is required to take into account in determining whether the amount charged is fair and reasonable. These are basically the same factors or guidelines outlined *inter alia* in r.10 Part B of the Code of Ethics.[80]

Duplication in Charges

It is to be noted that no duplication in charges is permissible. The effect of the various guidelines set out in Factor A and B are intended to be cumulative in effect; there must be no overlap in charges eg. if the matter has been sufficiently taken care of by the charges under the ***nature and value*** headings, there is nothing to be added under the *complexity* heading.[81]

ACTION FOR RECOVERY OF COSTS

In accordance with the relevant provision of the various territories, an attorney-at-law may not commence suit for the recovery of the amount of any bill of costs for any legal business done by him unless a bill of costs in respect of the legal business is taxed and the taxed bill served on the client within the time prescribed[82](in most cases either fifteen days or one month depending on jurisdiction) prior to the filing of the suit.

Exceptions

However, prior to the expiration of the time prescribed, an attorney may with leave of the High Court commence an action for recovery of his fees and for an order for taxation where there is probable cause to believe that the party chargeable with the fees:

(i) is about to leave the jurisdiction of the court;

(ii) is about to become bankrupt; or

(iii) is about to do any other act which would tend to prevent or delay the attorney-at-law from obtaining payment.[83]

Part IV – Bill of Costs

INTRODUCTION

In the absence, unenforceability, invalidity or setting aside of an agreement for remuneration between an attorney and his client, whether in respect of contentious or non contentious business, statute and/or the rules of court require that any charge by an attorney for his professional services must be evidenced by a bill of costs properly drawn and delivered.

In addition, bills of costs are usually drawn where the court orders, at the conclusion of legal proceedings, that the unsuccessful litigant to proceedings pay the costs of the other side and further orders that these costs be taxed.

A bill of costs is also drawn as a preliminary step by an attorney to recover costs by action. In this regard, the relevant statutory provision provides that no action may be brought to recover costs due to the attorney until he delivers a taxed bill of costs to the party chargeable.[84]

DRAWING AND DELIVERY

It is to be noted that the drawing and delivery of a bill of costs are distinct from taxation as not all bills are taxed. An application must be made for taxation, even in instances where the court, at the conclusion of legal proceedings, makes an order for costs in the proceedings to be taxed, as in many such instances, the parties to the proceedings arrive at an out of court settlement.

WHAT IS TAXATION?

Taxation is in effect a judicial scrutiny of an attorney's costs for the purposes of determining whether the sums charged are fair and proper in all the circumstances of the case. It is to be noted that the jurisdiction of the court to tax bills of costs is unlimited and extends to both contentious and non-contentious business.

PURPOSE OF BILL OF COSTS

One of the primary purposes of a bill of costs is to furnish the party chargeable, and also the court, in the event of taxation of the bill, with full particulars to enable a fair opinion to be formed as to the reasonableness of the legal costs contained therein.

FORM AND CONTENT OF BILL OF COSTS

Bills, both with respect to contentious or non-contentious business, may take the form of a gross sum bill or a detailed bill. However in practice, attorneys in many instances, prepare and deliver a detailed bill, whether in respect of contentious or non-contentious business as:

(a) the client is entitled, in any event, to demand the delivery of a detailed bill and to apply for taxation of the bill;[85] and further

(b) on an application for taxation of a gross sum bill, the court may, on such taxation, direct the attorney to give details of the bill.

Although there is no prescribed form, a bill of costs is usually cast in vertical columns; the first column usually sets out the amount taxed off, if any, by the Taxing Master in event that the bill is taxed. The second column sets out item numbers to be taxed in chronological order. The third column sets out particulars of each item. In this regard the particulars of items charged must be given in sufficient detail so that the attorney and the party to be charged can identify the various claims made. A bill must therefore disclose on its face, sufficient information as to the nature of the charges,[86] but if a party to be charged wants more information he may demand it.

In respect of contentious business, the nature of the action should be specified.[87] Where a bill is brought in for taxation and does not contain adequate information to enable the Taxing Master reasonably to exercise his discretion, the bill must be amended and thereafter reviewed by the Taxing Master.[88]

Importance of Clarity – In addition, where items are inextricably mixed up so that it is impossible to determine what is charged or what sum should be allowed in respect of items chargeable, the proper course for the Taxing Officer to adopt is to reject the bill and require the attorney to remodel the bill.[89]

However, notwithstanding the need for clarity and adequacy of information, precise exactness of form will not be insisted upon in order to defeat *bona fide* claims. As the Court noted in *Haigh v Ousey,* the 'degree of detail should not be such as to enable a fraudulent client to defeat just claims upon a pretense of a defect of form'.[90]

CLASSIFICATION OF COSTS

Costs fall into two categories; professional charges and disbursements. In this regard, in a bill of costs the instructing attorney/solicitor's professional charges and disbursements must be entered in separate columns and every column must be cast before the bill is submitted for taxation.[91] Professional charges are in essence the attorney's fees and in the case of contentious business, professional charges are instructing attorney or solicitor's general care and conduct of the proceedings. With respect to disbursements these are of two types: professional disbursements and non-professional disbursements or cash accounts.

Professional Disbursements

Professional disbursements are included in a bill of costs and constitute all payments made by an attorney in the performance of his professional duties which he has undertaken in that capacity on behalf of the party to be charged. Such disbursements include stationer's charges, photocopying, the cost of service of documents and in the case of litigation, court fees advocate/counsel's fees.

Non-Professional/Cash Accounts

These are not included in the bill and these are expenses paid by an attorney on behalf of his client which he is not bound to make either by law or custom (e.g. the cost of registering a company) but which are nevertheless paid by the attorney on behalf of his client, as a matter of convenience. Such payments may be regarded as advances and loans to the client.

They must be included in a separate cash account and delivered with the bill of costs. It should give details of receipts and payments for and on behalf of the client.

FORMALITIES

Signature

The bill must be signed by the attorney and if costs are due to a firm, the bill must be signed by one of its members or alternatively it may be enclosed with or accompanied by a letter which is duly signed referring to the bill. [92] Signature by a clerk is insufficient unless the attorney ratifies it. In addition, in the absence of some incapacity, the use of a rubber stamp to sign a bill of costs or to accompany it is not desirable as it lacks the authenticity of a written signature.[93]

In respect of an unsigned bill, an attorney who delivers an unsigned bill is bound by it and it may be taxed;[94] but the client may treat it as a nullity or waive the want of signature and adopt it. Once he adopts it by e.g. negotiating a reduction or by applying to have it taxed, he cannot thereafter treat the bill as a nullity.

DELIVERY OF BILL

Delivery may be effected personally or by post or by leaving it for the client at his place of business, dwelling house or last known address. Delivery to an agent appointed for the purpose is however sufficient, or delivery to a servant at the client's residence is *prima facie* sufficient evidence of delivery.[95] Once the bill is properly delivered, it is immaterial that it is thereafter misdirected[96] and where several persons are jointly liable, the delivery of the bill to one of them is sufficient to maintain an action for recovery of costs against the others.[97]

DELIVERY OF SUCCESSIVE BILLS

Where an attorney delivers more than one bill of costs for payment, it is a question of fact whether each is a final bill or an interim bill, i.e. a portion of one entire bill. The distinction between the two is important because in the absence of an express agreement to the contrary or circumstances entitling the retainer to be terminated by either party without breach, the attorney or client's right to taxation of a bill comes into effect only upon the delivery of a final as opposed to interim bill.

However, where successive bills of costs are delivered in respect of a protracted matter such as the administration of a trust, each bill delivered is treated as a separate and final bill for the purposes of taxation.[98] Accordingly, in such instances time begins to run for the purposes of an application for taxation upon delivery of each successive bill.[99]

Upon delivery of the final bill, the attorney and client have twelve calendar months or other period prescribed for referring the matter to taxation. Thereafter, the bill is not liable to be taxed except in special circumstances.

Special Circumstances

In special circumstances, the court, in the exercise of its inherent jurisdiction will allow taxation of a bill after it has been paid whether by the client or a third party or where the time for applying for taxation has elapsed. Such special circumstances are not confined to pressure,[100] gross overcharge,[101] fraud, dishonest practice or extortion but include any special circumstance of an exceptional nature in which a judge in exercise of his judicial discretion may consider justifies such taxation.

Part V – Contingency Fee Arrangements

INTRODUCTION

The essence of contingency fee arrangements, often referred to as 'no win no fee arrangements' is that an attorney's right to receive payment for his professional services is made contingent or dependant on his client receiving an award by way of settlement or judgment. In other words, if the client loses his case, the attorney receives no payment (no win no fee); if the client wins he will be paid in some instances, a percentage of the amount received.

GENERAL GROUNDS OF OBJECTION

Contingency fee arrangements have long been criticized as unethical. One of the main arguments against their use is that such fee arrangements could result in a conflict of interest between the attorney and client in that the attorney would have a direct financial interest in the outcome of litigation, which interest could affect his ability to render impartial advice to his client. In addition, the attorney's anxiety to ensure or enhance his client's chances of success could lead to improper practices on his part including solicitation of business, bribery of jurors and coaching of witnesses.

POSITION IN ENGLAND

In England, contingency fee arrangements have historically been regarded as contrary to public policy or otherwise illegal for maintenance or champetry.

In this regard, maintenance is defined by Lord Denning MR in *Re Trepca Mines Ltd* as 'improperly stirring up litigation and strife by giving aid to one party to bring or defend a claim without just cause or excuse'[102] and champetry, according to Scrutton LJ in *Ellis v Torrington* 'is where a person who maintains, takes as a reward, a share in the property received'.[103]

However, there have been two major developments in the law in England which have impacted on the validity in England of contingency fee arrangements. These are:

(i) the passage of the Court and Legal Services Act 1990, in particular, s.58 thereof which provides in effect that conditional fee arrangements (as they are referred to in the Act) are valid and enforceable, with effect from July 23 1993, provided they fall within the scope of the proceedings specified therein; and
(ii) the passage of the Criminal Law Act 1967, in particular s.14(2) thereof which provides in effect that maintenance and champetry are no longer criminal or tortious.

Nevertheless, in spite of these developments, it is to be noted that the Criminal Law Act 1967 has preserved the rule of common law that contingency fee arrangements are invalid and unenforceable on the grounds of public policy or illegal for champetry or maintenance.

Reasons for Preservation of Common Law Rule

As Denning L J explained, in *Re Trepca Mines,* 'the reason why the common law has preserved champetry is because of the abuses to it may give rise to'. In this regard, Denning L J went on to explain:

> The common law fears that a champetor's maintainer might be tempted for his own personal gains, to inflame the damages to suppress the evidence or even to suborn witnesses.[104]

Another reason for the preservation of the common law rule, was advanced by Buckley L J in *Wallersteiner v Moir.*[105] Buckley L J noted:

> Under a contingency fee arrangement, the remuneration payable by the client to his lawyer in the event of his success must be higher than it would be if the lawyer was entitled to be remunerated, win or lose... .[106]

He concluded that ' it would be unfair to the opponent of a contingency fee litigant if he were at risk to being ordered to pay higher costs to his opponent in the event of the latter's success in the action'.[107]

Changing Attitudes and Current Challenges

Although contingency fee arrangements which are outside the scope of the Court and Legal Services Act 1990 are unlawful or void on grounds of public policy, the passage of this Act in particular s.58 thereof, clearly signals a trend towards a relaxing and rethinking of the public policy objections to such fee arrangements. As Sir Richard Scott VC acknowledged in *Bevan Ashford v Yeandle Ltd:*

> Notions of public policy change with the passage of time and arrangement of agreements held in the past to be champetrous and consequently void need not be so held today. [108]

In this regard, the factors which have influenced this trend in England towards an incremental though limited acceptance of contingency fee agreements and which are also relevant to the Caribbean are:

(i) the cost of litigation without legal aid has become increasingly prohibitive.[109]

(ii) the cost to Government of providing legal aid and advice is escalating and becoming unmanageable.[110]

(iii) Changing attitudes toward litigation. As Schiemann LJ noted in *Awwad v Geraghty & Co* (a firm): Access to justice is regarded as a fundamental right which ought to be readily available to others in today's world but in an earlier age litigation was regarded as an evil, and recourse to the law was discouraged.[111]

(iv) The redefining and narrowing of the scope of maintenance and champetry, with the result that since 1967 in England neither champetry or maintenance (which form the main basis of the objection to contingency fee arrangements), are either criminal or tortious.[112]

This changing approach is reflected in the decision in *Thai Trading Co (a firm) v Taylor and Another.*[113] Although the decision in *Thai Trading* was not followed in later cases, it is nevertheless instructive in that it clearly signals a changing attitude at least on the part of some members of the judiciary, towards the acceptance of contingency fee arrangements.

In *Thai Trading,* the court held that it was not now contrary to public policy for a solicitor acting for a party in litigation to agree to forego all or part of his fee if he lost, provided he did not seek to recover more than his residuary profit costs and disbursements.

In arriving at its decision the court was careful to draw a distinction between what it referred to as contingency normal fee arrangements as articulated by Millet LJ in the *Thai Trading* case and a contingency fee arrangement which entitles the solicitor to a reward over and above his ordinary profits if he wins. According to Millet LJ, in his leading judgment, 'the latter fee arrangements should be condemned as tending to corrupt the administration of justice'.[114]

In arriving at his decision that contingency normal fee arrangements were lawful, Millet LJ expressed the view that s.59(2) of the Solicitors Act 1974, did not prohibit contingent fees. According to Millet LJ:

> Although the provision did not legitimize such arrangements, if they are otherwise unlawful, neither does it make them unlawful, if they were otherwise lawful.[115]

Millet LJ further concluded that r.8 of Solicitors Practice Rules 1987 which rule was made by the Law Society pursuant to s.31 of the Solicitors Act 1974 was merely 'a professional rule which did not make such arrangements contrary to law'.[116] (According to r. 8, a solicitor is prohibited from entering into a contingency agreement in respect of contentious proceedings.)

Arguments in Favour of Contingency Normal Fee Arrangements

Most recently in the case of *Awwad v Geraghty & Co (a firm)*[117]Schiemann LJ identified several reasons in support of contingency normal fee arrangements as opposed to contingency fees arrangements. Schiemann LJ noted in reference to such arrangements:

(i) They do not in fact increase the potential liability for costs of the client's litigant's opponent should he be ordered to pay the cost of the litigation;
(ii) Such agreements do not allow for division of spoils;
(iii) They facilitate access to court by members of the public;
(iv) If the lawyer's client has no assets, a contingency normal fee arrangement merely gives form to what is a practical reality – the lawyer only gets paid if his client wins.

Current Position

Nevertheless in spite of the many attractive and compelling arguments advanced in support of contingency normal fee arrangements the *Thai Trading* decision was not followed in the later case of *Hughes v Kingston Upon Hull City Council*[118] and was expressly disapproved of in *Awwad v Geraghty & Co (a firm).*[119]

Indeed in the *Hughes* case, the court held that the decision in the *Thai Trading* case was *per incuriam* by reason of the non-citation of the House of Lord's decision in *Swain v Law Society.*[120] In *Swain v Law Society* the Court of Appeal held that the Solicitor Practise Rules which were made under the Solicitors Act 1974, England were delegated or subordinate legislation having been made under s.31 of the Act.

The Court therefore concluded in *Hughes* that (contrary to Millet LJ's conclusions in the *Thai Trading* case), r.8 was not merely a professional rule but was in effect subsidiary legislation and had the force of law, thereby making contingency fee arrangements unenforceable.

Accordingly in England, contingency fees arrangements including contingency normal fee arrangements, are invalid and unenforceable as being against public policy, save and except conditional fee arrangements made pursuant to s.58 of the Court and Legal Services Act, and the Contingent Fee Agreement Order 1995 and the Regulations made thereunder.[121]

POSITION IN ENGLISH-SPEAKING CARRIBBEAN

Antigua & Barbuda, Barbados, St. Lucia, Trinidad & Tobago

The respective Legal Profession Acts of the above mentioned territories contain no provision(s) with respect to contingency fee arrangements. However the Code of Ethics of these territories, provides that:

> an attorney-at-law shall not charge a contingency fee except reasonable commissions on collection of liquidated claims with the prior agreement of the client.[122]

Although the above provision is contained in the Code of Ethics, it is deemed to be subsidiary or delegated legislation having been made under or pursuant to the respective Legal Profession Acts of these territories and accordingly has the force of statute law in these territories.

Eastern Caribbean (save St. Lucia and Antigua & Barbuda)

Rule 10(3) of Part B of the OECS Code of Ethics provides:

> An attorney-at-law may, with the prior agreement of the client, charge a contingency fee not exceeding twenty percent and reasonable commissions on collection of liquidated claims.

It is assumed that the twenty percent is referable to contingency fee arrangements in general and the reasonable commission is referable to liquidated claims only. Accordingly in these territories, contingency fee arrangements may be entered into within the guidelines provided for by r.10(3) of the Code.

However the difficulty with the application of this rule is that the OECS Code of Ethics is not made under or pursuant to any Act as indeed none of these territories, to date, has an indigenous Legal Profession Act. Although the Code has been ratified and accepted in principle, the Code, unlike the position in Antigua & Barbuda, St. Lucia and Trinidad & Tobago, is not delegated or subsidiary legislation and therefore has no statutory force.

What complicates the matter further, is that the Solicitors Act 1974 England and the Rules and Orders made thereunder are deemed to be part of the laws of these territories in accordance with the respective reception provisions contained in the Supreme Court Acts of these territories.[123]

Accordingly, the Solicitors' Practise Rules 1990 of England, in particular, r.8 thereof and s.58 of the Court and Legal Services Act 1990, England (being legislation relating to solicitors) should be valid and enforceable within the specified circumstances provided for by r.8 and s.58.

However it is submitted that in practice, the OECS Code of Ethics is applicable in these circumstances, so that contingency fee arrangements are valid and enforceable in these territories; within the guidelines prescribed by Rule 10(3).

Barbados

Neither the Legal Profession Act nor The Legal Profession Code of Ethics made thereunder contain any provision with respect to contingency fee arrangements.

However, r.65(2) of Part VIII of the Code of Ethics provides that:

> An attorney shall not enter into an arrangement for or charge or collect a fee in contravention of this Code *or any other law* (*emphasis added*)

It is therefore submitted that in the absence of statutory or regulatory provisions to the contrary, the common law position applies to Barbados and accordingly, contingency fee arrangements are invalid and unenforceable on public policy grounds.

The Bahamas

The Legal Profession Act 26/1992 contains no provision with respect to contingency fee arrangements. However Rule X of the Code of Professional Conduct of The Bahamas provides *inter alia* that:

> The attorney should not enter into any arrangements or stipulate payments only in the event of success in any suit, action or other contentious proceedings for which he is retained or employed to prosecute.

As such in accordance with the above ethical rule, contingency fee arrangements are invalid and unenforceable in The Bahamas.

Guyana

To date, a Code of Ethics has not been introduced in Guyana. Accordingly, it is submitted that, in the absence of any provisions, statutory or regulatory, contingency fee arrangements are in accordance with the English common law, void on grounds of public policy.

Jamaica

Although the Legal Profession Act of Jamaica contains no provision(s) with respect to contingency fee arrangements, Canon IV(f)(x) of the Legal Profession (Canon of Ethics) Rules made pursuant to s.12(7) of the Legal Profession Act, provides that in determining whether the fees charged by an attorney are fair and reasonable, the attorney shall take into account whether the fees payable are contingent or not. Accordingly, although neither the Act nor the rules made thereunder, expressly provide that contingency fees arrangements are lawful and enforceable, the effect of the rule which has the force of statute law, (having been made under s.12(7) of the Legal Profession

Act), is that contingency fee arrangements are lawful and enforceable in Jamaica. However, unlike England or the United States of America there are no ethical or statutory restrictions or guidelines imposed with respect to their application.

POSTSCRIPT

In practice, as the courts have long recognized, clients often enter into credit arrangements with their attorneys in respect of the payment of their attorney's fees. These arrangements in effect operate as contingency fee arrangements. In this regard, there has been a call in recent times in some of the Caribbean territories, most notably Trinidad & Tobago, for the formal acceptance of contingency fee arrangements within appropriate guidelines and regulatory restrictions.

Indeed in the United States of America since 1858, contingency fee arrangements have been recognised as valid by the Supreme Court. Such arrangements are usually entered into by the plaintiff's lawyer in speculative pecuniary claims, whether tortious or contractual including personal injury cases, where the potential award is the highest.[124] However it is to be noted that in the United States of America the use of these arrangements is regulated by Disciplinary Rules contained in the Code of Professional Responsibility which rules prohibit their use in criminal cases, similar to the current position in England. The Ethical Considerations of the Code of Professional Responsibility further advises that their use in domestic cases is also inappropriate.

ENDNOTES

PART 1

1. [1921] 1 KB 495; at p.503 [1920] All ER Rep. 340 at 344 CA.
2. *Ibid.*
3. Antigua & Barbuda - ss.10,11 Legal Profession Act 9/1997. See also Code of Ethics Part B r.1

   Barbados - s.10(1) & (2), 11 Legal Profession Act Cap. 370A. See also Code of Ethics, Part VIII r.57

   Jamaica - s.5(1) & (2) Legal Profession Act. See also Canon of Ethics, Canon II(i)

   St. Lucia - s.21 Legal Profession Act 31/2000. See also Code of Ethics Part B r.1

   Trinidad & Tobago - s.20(1)and (2) Legal Profession Act. See also Code of Ethics, Part B r.1

4. Antigua & Barbuda - s.11 (1) and (2) Legal Profession Act 9/1997
   Barbados - s.10(2) and (3) Legal Profession Act Cap 370A
   Jamaica - s.5(2) and (3) Legal Profession Act 1971
   St. Lucia - s.21(1) and (2) Legal Profession Act 31/2000
   Trinidad & Tobago - s.20 (2) and (3) Legal Profession Act 21/1986
5. See chapter 13 post with respect to the Compensation Fund
6. *Re Shilson, Coode & Co* (1904) 1Ch. 837; 90 LT 641, 20 TLR 418
7. Antigua & Barbuda - s.16 Legal Profession Act 9/1997
   Barbados - See s.44(5) Legal Profession Act Cap 370A
   Jamaica - s.7 The Legal Profession Act
   St. Lucia - ss.26, 27 Legal Profession Act 31/2000
   Trinidad & Tobago - ss.26, 27 Legal Profession Act 21/1986
8. Anguilla - ss. 26, 27 Eastern Caribbean Supreme Ordinance 9/1982
   Dominica - ss.72,73 Eastern Caribbean Supreme Court (Dominica) Chap. 4:02
   Grenada - ss.78, 79 Eastern Caribbean Supreme Court (Grenada) Act 19/1991
   Guyana - ss.8, 9 Legal Profession Act Cap 4:04 as amended by s. 8 and 9 Legal Profession (Amendment) Act 3/1980
   St. Kitts & Nevis - ss.72,73 Eastern Caribbean Supreme Court 17/1975
   St. Vincent & the Grenadines ss.72, 73 Eastern Caribbean Supreme Court (St.Vincent & the Grenadines) Act Cap. 18
   The Bahamas - ss.14, and 17 Legal Profession Act 26/1992
9. *The London Scottish Benefit Society v Chorley* (1884) 13 QBD 872 CA. See also *H Tolputt & Co Ltd v Mole* (1911) 1 KB 836 CA: *Re Doody, Fisher v Doody* [1893] 1 Ch. 129 at p. 134 CA
10. *Ibid* at pp. 875, 876, CA. See also *Reed v Gray* [1952] Ch. 337 [1952] 1 All ER 241.
11. *Re Doody, Fisher v Doody* [1893] 1 Ch. 129 at p.134 CA.
12. *Re Corsellis, Lawton v Elwes* (1887) 34 Ch D 675 CA; *Re Doody, Fisher v Doody* [1893] 1 Ch. 129; *Broughton v Broughton* 5 De GM & G 160.
13. [1886] 34 Ch. D 77 at p. 81.
14. (1884) 27 Ch. D. 584, 51 LT 748, See also *Clarkson v Robinson* [1900] 2 Ch. 722, 83 LT. 164.
15. (1850) 1 Mac & G 664.
16. *Ibid.*
17. [1893] 1 Ch 129
18. See *Re Corsellis Lawton v Elwes*, (1887) 34 Ch D 675
19. [1886] 34 Ch D 77 at p. 81
20. *Re Burge v Brutton* (1843) 2 Hare 373; See also *Re Taylor* 23 LT Ch. 857.
21. *Ibid* at pp. 377, 378
22. *Re Doody, Fisher v Doody* [1893] 1 Ch 129 at p. 134
23. *Re Gates Arnold v Gates* [1933] Ch. 913 [1933] All ER Rep. 546.

PART II

24. For meaning of Contentious and Non-Contentious Business, see s.87 Solicitors Act 1974, England and with respect to Guyana – See RSC O.60 r.1 High Court Act Cap. 3:02.

25. *Re Simpkin v Marshall* [1959] 1 Ch. 229 at pp. 235, 236
26. See s.77 Eastern Caribbean Supreme Court (Antigua & Barbuda) Act Cap. 143.
27. See ss.58, 59 of the repealed Solicitors Act Chap 6:50
28. See *Dinzey v Barcellos* (1923-24) LRBG 65
29. (1898) LRBG 19
30. *Ibid* at p.20
31. *Ibid.*
32. (1926) LRBG 71. See also *Dinzey v Barcella, supra*
33. See also *Dukhni v Adams* (1965) LRBG 52
34. See Chapter 1 pp. 1 & 2 ante
35. [1895-9] All ER Rep 599 at p.603 CA
36. [1907] 2 KB 369, [1904-7] All ER 508 CA
37. [1907] 2 KB 369 at p.378, [1904-7] All ER 508 at p.511 CA
38. [1910] 1 KB 645 at p.650 CA.
39. *Clare v Joseph* [1907] 2 KB 369 at p.376, [1904-7] 508 at p.511 CA per Fletcher Moulton LJ.
40. (1873) LR 8 CP 425. See also *Gundry v Sainsbury* [1910] 1 KB 99 CA
41. Barbados - See s.36(3) Legal Profession Act Cap. 370A.
42. Barbados - See s.37 Legal Profession Act Cap 370 A
43. See *Re Baylis* (1896) 2 Ch 107 (1895-9) All ER Rep 599 CA
44. [1907] 2 KB 369 at 376 [1904] All ER Rep 508 at p.511 CA.
45. *Ibid.*
46. See Chapter 1 pp. 1 & 2 ante
47. See pp. 82 & 83
48. Antigua & Barbuda - Code of Ethics, Part B r.9(2)
    Barbados - Code of Ethics, Part VIII r.65(2)
    Eastern Caribbean (save Antigua & Barbuda and St. Lucia)
    - OECS, Code of Ethics, Part B r.9(2)
    St. Lucia - Code of Ethics, Part B r.12(2)
    Trinidad & Tobago - Code of Ethics, Part B r.9(2)
49. (1995) 50 WIR 76
50. See Canon IV (f).
51. See Rule X, Commentary 1.
52. [1910] 1 KB 99 CA
53. Barbados - s.36(3) Legal Profession Act Cap 370 A
    Jamaica - s.21 (1) Legal Profession Act 1971
    Eastern Caribbean (save St. Lucia and Antigua & Barbuda)
    - s.59 Solicitors Act 1974, Engla
54. See *Re A Solicitor* [1956] 3 All ER 516, (1956) 1 WLR 1312. See also *Clare v Joseph* [1907] 2 KB 369, [1904-7] All ER Rep 508, *Gundry v Sainsbury* [1910] 1 KB 99 CA
55. Antigua & Barbuda - s.40(3) Legal Profession Act 9/1997
    Eastern Caribbean (save St. Lucia and Antigua & Barbuda)
    - s.57(2) Solicitors Act, 1974 England
    St. Lucia - s.53(2) Legal Profession Act 31/2000
    Trinidad & Tobago - s.53(2) Legal Profession Act 21/1986
56. [1956] 3 All ER 516, [1956] 1 WLR 1312
57. Antigua & Barbuda - s.40(2) Legal Profession Act 9/1997
    Barbados - s.36(2) Legal Profession Act Cap 370A

Eastern Caribbean (save St. Lucia and Antigua & Barbuda)
- s.57(2) Solicitors Act 1974, England

Jamaica - s.21(1) Legal Profession Act
St. Lucia - s.53(2) Legal Profession Act 31/2000
Trinidad & Tobago - s.53(2) Legal Profession Act 21/1986
Guyana - R.S.C. O.60 r.3 Rules of the Supreme Court Cap 3:02

58. Antigua & Barbuda - s.40 Legal Profession Act 9/1997
Barbados - s.36(6) Legal Profession Act Cap 370A
Eastern Caribbean (save Antigua & Barbuda and St. Lucia)
- s.57(4) Solicitors Act 1974, England
Jamaica - s.21(1) Legal Profession Act 1971
St. Lucia - s.53(4) Legal Profession Act 31/2000
Trinidad & Tobago - s.53(4) Legal Profession Act 21/1986

59. [1958] 2 All ER 13 at p.19 CA. See also *Re Palmer* (1890) 45 Ch D 291, *Re Frape ex p Perrett* [1893] 2 Ch 284
60. (1964) Ch 720

PART III

61. See Chapter 1 pp. 1 & 2 ante
62. Anguilla - s.77 Eastern Caribbean Supreme Court (Anguil
Dominica - s.78 Eastern Caribbean Supreme Court (Dominica) Act
C
Grenada - s.84 Eastern Caribbean Supreme Court (Grenada) Act
19/1991
St. Kitts & Nevis - s.78 Eastern Caribbean Supreme Court (St. Christopher & Nev
St. Vincent & the Grenadines s.78 Eastern Caribbean Supreme Court (St. Vincent & the Grenadines) Act Cap. 18.
63. CA 5/1991 St. Christopher and Nevis (unreported).
64. [1994] 45 WIR 188
65. Pursuant to s.12(7) Legal Profession Act 1971
66. Antigua & Barbuda - s.39(2) Legal Profession Act 9/1997
Barbados - s.35(2) Legal Profession Act Cap 370A
Eastern Caribbean (save Antigua & Barbuda and St. Lucia)
- s.56(5) Solicitors Act 1974, England
St. Lucia - s.52(2) Legal Profession Act 31/2000
Trinidad & Tobago - s.52(2) Legal Profession Act 21/1986
67. Antigua & Barbuda - Code of Ethics, Part B r.10(1)
Barbados - Code of Ethics Part VIII r.66(1) and (2)
Eastern Caribbean (save Antigua & Barbuda and St. Lucia)
- OECS Code of Ethics Part B r.10(1)
Jamaica - Canon of Ethics Canon IV (f)
St. Lucia - Code of Ethics Part B r.13(1)
The Bahamas - Code of Professional Conduct Rule, Rule X; Commentary 1
Trinidad & Tobago - Code of Ethics, Part B r.10(1).
68. See pp. 79-81 ante
69. See r.6(2) Legal Profession (Attorneys-at-Law) (Remuneration for Non-Contentious Business) Rules 1997

70. HCA 4/1995 at p.22-23 St. Christopher & Nevis (unreported).
71. Antigua & Barbuda - s.39 Legal Profession Act 9/1997
St. Lucia - s.52 Legal Profession Act 31/2000.
72. Barbados - RSC O.62 r.7 Rules of the Supreme Court 1982 and Appendix 1 thereto
Eastern Caribbean States - Part 65 of the Eastern Caribbean Supreme Court Civil Procedure Rules 2000, and Appendices A, B, and C thereto
Guyana - RSC O.49 r.7 Rules of the High Court Cap.3:02 and Appendix IXV thereto
Guyana - RSC O.62 r.32 Orders and Rules of the Supreme Court of Judicature of T&T, 1975. See also Appendices 1 and 28 thereto.
73. See pp. 82-83 ante re guidelines set out in Code/Canon of Ethics.
74. *Supra* at endnote 72
75. See *Treasury Solicitor v Register and Another* [1978] 2 All ER 920 at p.924; *Maltby v D.J. Freeman & Co (a firm)* [1978] 2 All ER 913 at p.916.
76. [1975] 2 All ER 436 at p.441.
77. *Ibid.*
78. *Treasury Solicitor v Register* [1978] 2 All ER 920 at pp.924-925.
79. *Ibid.*
80. *Ibid.*
81. *Maltby v DJ Freeman & Co, supra* at p.916.
82. Antigua & Barbuda - s.38(1) Legal Profession Act 9/1997
Barbados - s.34(1) Legal Profession Act Cap 370A
Eastern Caribbean (save Antigua & Barbuda and St. Lucia)
- s.69(1) Solicitor's Act 1974, England
Guyana - RSC O.60 r.24, Rules of the High Court Cap. 3:02
Jamaica - s.22(1) Legal Profession Act
St. Lucia - s.51(1) Legal Profession Act 31/2000
Trinidad & Tobago - s.51(1) Legal Profession Act 21/1986
See also *Ewing v Stafford* (1934-36) LRBG 344
83. Antigua & Barbuda - s.38(2) Legal Profession Act
Barbados - s.34(2) Legal Profession Act Cap 370A
Eastern Caribbean (save Antigua & Barbuda and St. Lucia)
- s.70 Solicitors' Act 1974, England
St. Lucia - s.51(2) Legal Profession Act 31/2000
Trinidad & Tobago - s.51(2) Legal Profession Act 21/1986
Jamaica - s.22(1) Legal Profession Act 1971
See also *Ewing v Stafford* (1934-36) LRBG 344

PART IV

84. See p.89 ante. See also *Ewing v Stafford* (1934-1936) LRBG 344.
85. See *Re Wells, Wells v Wells* [1962] 2 All ER 826 at p.827; CA, *Re Newman* 30 Beav. 195 *Re Taxation of Costs* [1942] 2 All ER Rep. 499 CA.
86. *Slingsby v AG* [1918] P 236 at p.237 CA
87. *Haigh v Ousey* (1857) 7 E & B 578.
88. *Slingsby v AG Supra;* See also *Cobbett v Wood* [1908] 2 KB 420 CA.

89. *Haigh v Ousey* (1857) 7 E & B 578.
90. *Ibid.*
91. Barbados - RSC O.62 r.18 Rules of the Supreme Court 1982
    Guyana - O.60 r.7; O.49 r.51 Rules of the High Court 1955
    The Bahamas - RSC O.59 r.23 Rules of the Supreme Court 1978
    Trinidad & Tobago - RSC O.62 r.25 Orders & Rules of the Supreme Court of Judicature 1975
92. Antigua & Barbuda - s.38(4) Legal Profession Act 9/1997
    Barbados - s.34(4) Legal Profession Act Cap 370A
    Eastern Caribbean (save Antigua & Barbuda and St. Lucia)
    - s.69(2) Solicitors' Act 1974, England
    Guyana - O.60 r.25 Rules of the High Court 1955
    Jamaica - s.22 Legal Profession Act 1971
    St. Lucia - s.51(4) Legal Profession Act 31/2000
    Trinidad & Tobago - s.51(4) Legal Profession Act 21/1986
93. *Goodman v J Eban Ltd* [1954] 1 QB 550; [1954] 1 All ER 763 CA.
94. *Re Sutton and Elliott.* See also *Ewing v Stafford* [1934-36] LRBG 344 [1883] 11 QBD 377, CA
95. *Mac Gregor v Keily* (1849) 3 ExCh. 794
96. *Welsh v Silwell* (1847) 11 Jur. 471.
97. *Oxenham v Lemon* (1823) 2 Dow & Ry KB 461
98. *Re Romer and Haslam* [1893] 2 QB 286 CA; See also *Re Hall and Barker* [1878] 9 Ch. D 538
99. *Ibid.*
100. *Blunt v Heslop*[1838] 8 Ad & E 577; *Re a Solicitor* [1961] 1 Ch. 491, [1961]2 All ER 321; *Hirst and Capes v Fox* [1908] 1 KB 982, CA *Re Bennett* (1845) 8 Beav 467, *Re Newman* (1867) 2 Ch Ap 707.
101. *Sanders v Isaacs* [1971] 1 All ER 755; *Re Norman* (1886) 16 QBD 673 CA; *Watson v Rodwell* (1878) 7 Ch. D 625; aff'd (1879) 11 Ch D 150 CA.

PART V

102. [1962] 3 All ER at 355 (1963) Ch. 199 at p. 219 CA
103. [1918-19] All ER Re 1132 at p. 1138 CA
104. [1962] 3 All ER 351 at p. 355, [1963] Ch 199 at p. 219 CA
105. [1975] 1 All ER 849 at p. 867, [1975] QB 373 CA.
106. [1975] 1 All ER 849 at p. 867, [1975] QB 373 at p. 402 CA
107. *Ibid*
108. [1998] 3 All ER 239 at p. 247
109. See *Awwad v Geraghty & Co (a firm)* [2000] 1 All ER 608 at p. 623 CA
110. *Ibid.*
111. *Ibid* at p. 614 CA.
112. *Ibid* at p. 623 CA.
113. [1998] 3 All ER 65, [1998] QB 781 CA.
114. [1998] 3 All ER 65 at p. 71, [1998] QB 781 at p. 788 CA.
115. [1998] 3 All ER 65 at p. 68; [1998] QB 781 at p. 785 CA.
116. [1998] 3 All ER 65 at pp. 68-69; [1998] QB 781 at pp. 786 CA.
117. [2000] 1 All ER 608 at p. 623.
118. [1999] 2 All ER 49

119. [2000] 1 All ER 608
120. [1982] 2 All ER 827
121. Pursuant to s.58 of the Court and Legal Services Act proceedings in respect of which contingent fee arrangements are unenforceable include:
(i) arbitration proceedings,
(ii) proceedings *inter alia* under the Matrimonial Causes Act, Adoption Act, Domestic Violence and Matrimonial Proceedings Act and
(iii) proceedings taken pursuant to a contentious business agreement.
122. Antigua & Barbuda - Code of Ethics Part B r.10(3)
St. Lucia - Code of Ethics Part B r.10(4)
Trinidad & Tobago - Code of Ethics Part B r.10(3)
123. See Chapter 1 pp. 1 & 2 ante in respect of the reception provision.
124. See *Bevan Ashford (a firm) v Geoff Yeandle Ltd* [1998] 3 All ER 238

6. LIENS

INTRODUCTION

Where an attorney's right to recover costs from his client is in question, he is entitled to exercise a lien at common law. The common law lien falls into two categories – general retaining liens and particular liens. Additionally, in Barbados and the Eastern Caribbean territories (save St. Lucia and Antigua & Barbuda), an attorney is entitled to a statutory lien or charging order. Both the common law liens and the statutory lien are exercisable over certain prescribed property belonging to the attorney's client and operate as an effective security for costs due and owing to the attorney.[1]

SCOPE OF LIENS IN GENERAL

1. Whether the lien is a common law or statutory lien, it attaches only to the attorney's taxable costs i.e. charges and expenses incurred by virtue of acting as attorney for the client; most particularly, it does not extend to general debts but only to those owed to the attorney when acting as attorney. For example, it does not extend to cases where the attorney was acting as a land agent.[2] In addition the lien only attaches to costs which are due, not to future costs or costs to be incurred.[3]
2. A lien does not extend to costs incurred by the client at any time when the attorney was not qualified to act in his professional capacity, eg. where the attorney was suspended from practice.

1. COMMON LAW LIENS

(a) General Retaining Liens

A general retaining or possessory lien is exercisable by the retention of the client's documents, trust deeds and papers including money, insurance policies or other personal chattels which came into the attorney's possession in the course of his professional employment. [4] This right to a retaining or possessory lien is merely passive and cannot be enforced by suit. As Sir Raymond Evershed M.R. noted in *Barratt v Gough-Thomas*:

> It has not the character of an encumbrance or equitable charge. It is merely possessory, that is to say the solicitor has no right of actively enforcing it but it confers on himself the right to withhold possession of the documents or other personal property of his client.[5]

In the words of Sir Sugden in *Blunden v Desart*, 'to lock them in his box, to put the key in his pocket until his client satisfies the amount of the demand'.[6]

However it is to be noted that even when an attorney parts with physical possession of the documents or other personal property of the client, he does not lose his lien if the circumstances show that the lien was expressly or impliedly reserved[7] nor is the lien lost by an attorney applying for an order for his costs. However, a condition precedent to an attorney claiming a lien over his client's documents is that his possession of them must be referable, at the date of demand, to the relationship of attorney and client between himself and the claimant.[8]

Position where Attorney Discharges Himself

Subject to exceptional circumstances, where an attorney discharges himself, even for good cause (usually the failure of the client to keep him in funds), he acquires only a qualified lien over documents in his possession i.e. he must hand over his client's papers to his client's new attorney against an undertaking by the successor attorney to preserve his lien on the papers for costs and to redeliver the papers to him at the end of the litigation. The reason for this rule as explained in *Robins v Goldingham*[9] is to ensure that the attorney not be allowed to exert his lien so as to interfere with the course of justice. In this regard it is to be noted that copying of every document sent to the new attorney on record, and the sending of copies of all those documents to the client is, in the absence of any agreement to the contrary, breach of the attorney's lien.[10] As Roch LJ observed in *Bentley v Gaisford*, 'if the new attorney could copy and distribute to the client the documents which are subject to the lien, the undertaking that they be held to his solicitor on order or his account would in practice disappear'.[11]

Exceptional Circumstances

The exceptional circumstances in which an attorney may be permitted to exercise his retaining lien include cases where the papers are valueless after litigation is ended and the client accepts that he is indebted to the original attorney for an agreed sum and has no counter claim or the client accepts that the attorney has admittedly paid out reasonable and proper disbursements for which he must be repaid. In such cases the court may make an order providing that the client pay the original attorney a sum fixed by the court representing in whole or in part the monies due from the client to the original attorney.[12]

But as Templeman LJ noted in *Gamlen Chemical Co (UK) Ltd v Rochem Ltd*:

> Much would depend on the nature of the case, the stage at which litigation had reached, the conduct of the client and the solicitor and the balance of hardship which might result from the order the court is asked to make.[13]

The case of *A v B*[14] provides an excellent illustration of exceptional circumstances in which the court ordered a solicitor's retaining lien to stand. In that case the solicitor discharged himself in the course of proceedings for non-payment of costs by the plaintiff clients. The solicitor then obtained a default judgment for the amount of the unpaid costs which was equivalent to an admission by the clients that they owed the costs claimed. The plaintiff clients thereafter applied for an order that the papers in the action be handed over to their new solicitor.

The court held that while it is the usual practice that where a solicitor discharges himself, to order the former solicitor to hand over to the new solicitor the papers which he had, even if the lien is thereby rendered useless, the court would not exercise this power automatically, the matter being equitable and therefore one of discretion. Accordingly, the court in that case took into account *inter alia* the conduct of the solicitor who in their view acted impeccably and that of the plaintiffs who, without any excuse, had not paid that which was the subject of the default judgment against them and accordingly dismissed the plaintiffs' application.

Another case which is instructive on this point is *Ismail v Richards Butler (a firm).*[15] In that case the defendant solicitors refused to continue to act because of the plaintiff clients' failure to pay outstanding costs. Although the court ordered the solicitor to deliver the papers required for the pending litigation to the plaintiffs' new solicitors, the plaintiffs were required to provide security in the sum of £450,000 for the defendants' claim by way of payment into court, or bank guarantee. In making its order the court took into account the nature of the case, the stage at which litigation had reached, the conduct of the parties, the interests of justice and the fact that the value of the defendants' lien would be considerably diminished if the papers were handed over.

Position where Client Discharges Attorney

Where the client discharges the attorney with or without just cause the lien endures and the court has no right or title to call for the client's documents to be handed over to the new attorney on record. The lien is unqualified even where the papers in question concern pending litigation.

However as was stated in *Robins v Goldingham,*[16] even in cases where the client discharges the attorney the court recognises that the retaining lien presents obvious difficulties for the client and new attorney. The new attorney will need the documents to protect the client's interest in the continuing action and in addition the former attorney's bill may be disputed and taxation may take some time. In this regard, guidelines have been developed by the Law Society in England that:

> where a solicitor is properly exercising a lien in respect of unpaid costs following his or her discharge by his client the society recommends that the solicitor's papers should be released to the successor solicitor, subject to a satisfactory undertaking as to the outstanding costs being given in lieu of the lien. There is however no duty on the original solicitor to accept an undertaking.[17]

Further, according to the Rule XI, Commentary 10 of the Bahamas Bar Code of Professional Conduct :

> Generally speaking the attorney should not enforce his lien if the result would be to materially prejudice the client's position in any uncompleted matter.

Exceptions

It is to be noted that where the attorney acts in a representative capacity the court may order him to hand over the documents subject to the lien.[18] In addition an attorney's right to possession of the client's documents and other personal property ceases, i.e. he cannot refuse to deliver them up where a third party claims an interest in them.[19]

(b) Particular Liens

With respect to proceedings in court, including arbitration proceedings, where there is a probability of a client depriving an attorney of his costs, the attorney is entitled to claim as security for the payment of his costs, a lien on property recovered or preserved through his professional exertions, including the fruits of any judgment obtained by him on behalf of his client.[20] The right of lien also extends to the costs of proceedings taken by the attorney in order to establish the existence of his retainer.[21]

This right to claim a particular lien is grounded on the basic principle that it is not right and just that the client should get the benefit of the attorney's labour without paying for it.[22]

The particular lien differs from the possessory lien in that it is actively enforced by the attorney making an application to the court, effectively asking the court to charge the client's property in his favour. Until this application is made the attorney has no right to the money.[23]

In that sense the term lien is really a misnomer[24] for as Cockburn J noted in *Mercer v Graves:*

> There is no such thing as a lien except upon something of which you have possession; although we talk of a solicitor having a lien upon a judgment it is in fact only a claim or right to ask for the intervention of the court's protection.[25]

It is to be noted that the granting of a particular lien does not operate as an equitable assignment but is rather an exercise of the court's equitable jurisdiction for the protection of attorneys in the proper cases.[26]

Although the particular lien does not extend to real property, it covers other property including money received by way of compromise where the money is in substance the fruits of an action.[27] However, the lien does not attach to property received by way of negotiation where there is no litigation attendant thereto.[28]

It is to be noted that an attorney will not be deprived of his lien for costs incurred:

(i) where the court orders that the other side pay the attorney's client personally[29]
(ii) where there is collusion or connivance of the client with the other party to proceedings for the purpose of defeating the attorney's lien.[30]
(iii) in the case of the bankruptcy of the client.[31]

Set Off

As a general rule, in the absence of fraud or collusion between the parties, the court will allow a set-off, notwithstanding a client's attorney's lien. The right to claim a lien is a right which exists between the attorney and his client.[32] And as Sir George Jessel observed in *Pringle v Gloag:*

> It would be a monstrous extension of the rights of a solicitor against the parties to an action to say that he should have the right to make the party who may have been successful in the ultimate results pay the losing party's costs.[33]

However in independent proceedings which are not cross-related, a set off claimed in any such proceedings will not be allowed to defeat or prevail over a client's attorney's lien.

2. STATUTORY LIEN/CHARGING ORDER

Barbados, Eastern Caribbean territories (save St. Lucia and Antigua & Barbuda)[34]

The statutory lien extends to real and personal property recovered or preserved through the attorney's instrumentality in the prosecution or defence of any suit, matter or proceedings in any court. The attorney in such instances can actively enforce this lien by applying to the court for a charging order i.e. for a declaration that the attorney is entitled to a charge for his taxed costs over the property which is the subject matter of the suit and which has been recovered or preserved by his instrumentality and further for an order for taxation of these costs and for raising money to pay these costs out of the said property including out of any funds in court.[35] The statutory lien in effect operates like an injunction.

It is to be noted:

(i) that all conveyances and acts done to defeat or which operate to defeat that charge, save with respect to a *bona fide* purchaser for value without notice, shall be void against the attorney; and
(ii) an attorney's right to enforce the lien will be defeated where the debt is statute-barred.

ENDNOTES

1. *Barratt v Gough-Thomas* [1951] Ch. 242, [1950] 2 All ER 1048. See also *Espeut v Bourke* (1855) Eq. J.B. Vol. 1 p. 193
2. *Re Walker, Meredith v Walker* [1891-4] All ER Rep. 324, (1893) 68 LT 517; *Pelley v Wathen* (1849) 7 Hare 351
3. *Re Birmingham, Savage v Stannard* [1959] Ch. 230 CA.
4. *Barratt v Gough-Thomas, supra.*
5. [1951] Ch. 242 at p.250; [1950] 2 All ER 1048 at p.1053 CA.
6. 2 Dr & War 418.
7. *Caldwell v Sumpters (a firm) and another* [1972] 1 All ER 567 CA.
8. *Barratt v Gough-Thomas, supra.*
9. (1872) LR 13 Eq 440. See also *Re Rapid Road Transit Co* [1909] 1 Ch. 96, *Hughes v Hughes* [1958] 3 All ER 179 CA; *Heslop v Metcalfe* (1837) 3 My & Cr 183
10. [1997] 1 All ER 842 at p.856 CA.
11. *Ibid.*
12. *Gamlen Chemicals Co (UK) Ltd v Rochem Ltd* [1980] 1 All ER 1049 at pp.1058, 1059 CA.
13. *Ibid* at p.1059.
14. [1984] 1 All ER 265. Contrast with *Bentley v Gaisford* [1997] 1 All ER 842 CA.
15. [1996] 2 All ER 506.
16. (1872) LR 13 Eq. 440.
17. See *The Guide to the Professional Conduct of Solicitors* 6th edn. 1993 para. 12:18.
18. *Clifford v Turrill* (1848) 2 De G & Sm. 1
19. *Hughes v Hughes* [1958] 3 All ER 179 CA.
20. *Re Meter Cabs Ltd* [1911] 2 Ch 557.
21. *Re Hill, A Solicitor* (1886) 33 Ch D 266. See also *Re Meter Cabs Ltd, supra.*
22. *Re Meter Cabs Ltd, Ibid* at p.560. See also *Bibby (James) Ltd v Wood and Howard* [1949] 2 All ER 1.
23. *Re Hill, A Solicitor, Ibid.*
24. *Bibby (James) Ltd v Wood and Howard supra* at p. 3
25. (1872) LR 7 QB 499 at p.503.
26. *Re Fuld's Estate* [1967] 2 All ER 649 [1967] 3 WLR 314. See also Re *Sullivan v Pearson*

ex p. Morrison (1868) LR 4 QB 153, 19 LT 430

27. *Ross v Buxton* (1889) 42 Ch D 190, 60 LT 630.

28. *Megeurditchian v Lightbound and Others* [1917] 2 KB 298 CA.

29. *Re Fuld's Estate, supra* at p.654, *Campbell v Campbell and Lewis* [1941] 1 All ER 274, *Re Bryant* (1815) 1 Madd. 49.

30. *Hall v Hall* [1891] P.300, *Omerod v Tate* (1801) 1 East 464.

31. *Jones v Turnbull ex p. Lovett* 2 M&W 601, *Emden v Carte* 19 CH D 311.

32. *Puddephatt v Leith (No. 2)* [1916] 2 Ch 168

33. (1879) 10 Ch D 676, at 680.

34. Barbados - s.41 Legal Profession Act Cap. 370A

Eastern Caribbean (save Antigua & Barbuda and St. Lucia) - s.73(1) and (2) of Solicitors Act 1974, England. Section 73 is deemed to be applicable to the Eastern Caribbean (save Antigua & Barbuda and St. Lucia) by virtue of the reception provision contained in the respective Supreme Court Act of these territories. See also Chapter 1 ante. See *also Re Cockrell's Estate* [1911] 2 Ch. 318.

35. *Kay v Lovell* [1940] Ch. 650, [1940] 3 All ER 89. See also *Re Clayton Collins v Clayton and Others* [1940] Ch. 539, [1940] 2 All ER 233.

7. RIGHTS AND PRIVILEGES OF AN ATTORNEY

IN GENERAL

In order to be accorded the status of an attorney-at-law and to practise as such, with all the rights and privileges attendant thereto, an attorney-at-law must be the holder of a valid practising certificate whether issued on an annual basis or otherwise.[1]

Once an attorney is the holder of such a certificate he is entitled as an officer of the court: *inter alia*:

1. to a right of audience before any court;[2]
2. to practise law and sue for and recover his fees in respect thereof;[3]
3. to enter any court except a juvenile court;
4. to immunity from an action in negligence, when engaged in any action as an advocate or counsel in any court, with respect to the conduct of such proceedings.[4]
5. to exemption from performing any public service which might interfere with his professional duties e.g. jury service.
6. to wear robes. In this regard it is to be noted that an attorney does not wear robes in Chamber court, the Registrar's Court, the Magistrate's Court or before an arbitration tribunal nor when appearing as a witness or as a party to an action. Robes are worn in open court. Queen's Counsel/Senior Counsel wear silk except when the court is in mourning.

With respect to general attire, the respective Code/Canon of Ethics of Trinidad & Tobago, Antigua & Barbuda, St. Lucia, the Eastern Caribbean and Jamaica provides in general terms that an attorney is required to dress in a manner appropriate to and compatible with the status of the profession and as may befit the dignity of the court.[5]

With respect to Barbados, Part II r.16 of the Barbados Legal Profession Code of Ethics is more specific on this matter of appropriate attire. Rule 16 provides *inter alia* that:

(i) the dress of an attorney-at-law appearing in court should be unobtrusive and compatible with the wearing of robes;
(ii) suits and dresses should be dark in colour ;
(iii) no conspicuous jewellery or ornaments should be worn;
(iv) dresses or blouses should be long-sleeved and compatible with the wearing of bands and collarettes;
(v) shirts and blouses should be predominantly white or some other unemphatic colour; and
(vi) collars should be white and shoes dark.

It is to be noted that with respect to St. Lucia that prior to the repeal in November, 2000 of the Legal Practitioners Ordinance Ch. 116, s.5 thereof provided that:

> Counsel appearing before the Supreme Court or Court of Appeal have no right of audience unless they are clad in dark clothes and wear robes and bands proper to their calling.

PRIVILEGED COMMUNICATIONS

With respect to the law of evidence and the law of defamation, communications whether oral or in writing passing between an attorney and his client including the client's predecessors in title, and in certain circumstances, between the attorney and third parties are afforded legal protection by the court, i.e. they are treated as privileged communications. More specifically in the law of evidence, such communications are protected in the first instance from disclosure, whether by production of documents or in oral evidence. However, if the client chooses to lift the veil, i.e. waive the privilege afforded to these communications, they are then available as evidence.

Once the communications have been admitted in evidence, the second limited protection comes into force in that in respect of an action for defamation only, the communications are privileged.[6]

THE LAW OF EVIDENCE – PRIVILEGE FROM DISCLOSURE

Communications In General

Pursuant to the relevant rule of the Code/Canon of Ethics of the various territories, an attorney-at-law is prohibited from disclosing, unless lawfully ordered to do so by the Court or required by statute, what has been communicated to him by his client in his capacity as an attorney-at-law and this extends to his partners or attorneys-at-law assisting him and to his employees.[7]

The reason that such communications are afforded this protection from disclosure was explained by Lord Lyndhurst LC in *Holmes v Baddely*[8] and quoted with approval by Lord Taylor of Gosforth in *Regina v Derby's Magistrates Court ex parte B.*[9] Lord Lyndhurst observed:

> The principle upon which the rule is established in that communications between a party and his professional advisers.... should be unfettered and they should not be restrained by the apprehension of such communications being afterwards divulged and made use of to his prejudice. The necessary confidence will be destroyed if it be known that the communication can be revealed at any time.[10]

An Absolute Privilege

This privilege from disclosure is absolute not qualified in the sense that once the claim of privilege comes within the rule, the communications are absolutely inadmissible in evidence whether oral or documentary.

The absolute nature of the privilege was confirmed by the House of Lords in *Regina v Derby Magistrates' Court ex parte B*,[11] the facts of which are instructive. In that case, the applicant was arrested for the murder of a 16 year old girl and at the time of his arrest, he made a statement to the police admitting sole responsibility for the murder. Shortly before his trial he retracted that statement and alleged that his step-father had killed the girl. At his trial he was acquitted and the step-father was subsequently charged with the girl's murder. At committal proceedings, counsel for the step-father in cross-examining the applicant, asked about instructions he had initially given his solicitor when admitting the murder. The applicant declined on the grounds of legal professional privilege.

An application was thereafter made pursuant to s.97 of the Magistrates' Courts Act 1980, England, for a witness summons to be issued directing the applicant's solicitor to produce notes and proofs of evidence disclosing the relevant instructions.

At the hearing of the application the Magistrate held that the applicant's instructions were *likely to be material evidence* within s.97 and having weighed the public interest in securing that all relevant evidence was available to the defence, ordered that the summons be issued. A second summons was issued to the applicant himself, by which summons the applicant applied for judicial review of the Magistrate's decision.

The divisional court dismissed his application and he thereafter appealed to the House of Lords. The House of Lords held that the production in court of documents which were subject to legal professional privilege which had not been waived by the client could not be ordered as the predominant public interest in such instances was the preservation of the legal professional privilege and not the securing that all relevant evidence was made available to the defence. This was so even where there was no recognisable or continuing interest in preserving the confidentiality of the communications. Lord Taylor of Gosforth summed up the position succinctly:

> The refusal of the client to waive his privilege, for whatever reason, or no reason, cannot be questioned or investigated by the court.[12]

The absolute and unqualified nature of this privilege was considered in a recent unreported Jamaican case involving no less an eminent jurist than the Chief Justice of Jamaica. According to the facts of the case, Terrence Williams, the attorney-at-law for the accused, was cross-examining a witness in a carnal abuse case, when in the presence of the jury, the Chief Justice demanded to see the instructions given to him, Williams, by his client.

After perusing the instructions, the Chief Justice showed it to the prosecution despite the strong objections of defense counsel. Subsequently, the Council of the Jamaican Bar Association issued a statement on December 16, 1996 to the effect that the Chief Justice's actions 'strikes at the very foundation of lawyers and the confidentiality of the communications with their clients'. The statement continued in part:

> The principle that all communications written or oral passing between a client and his lawyer are privileged is a rule of very

long standing throughout the Commonwealth... It is a fundamental condition on which the administration of justice as a whole rests.

It is to be noted that this privilege from disclosure as Atkin LJ noted in *Minter v Priest*, 'being part of the law of evidence bears no direct relation to the question whether the communications itself constitutes a cause of action'[13] Accordingly, neither the attorney-at-law nor the client need be a party to the action in which the question of evidence arises in order to claim this privilege.

(ii) Privilege of the Client

It is the duty of the attorney to claim privilege from disclosure for the benefit of his client if called upon to disclose such communication in evidence yet the privilege is the privilege of the client.[14] It exists for the benefit of the client. Accordingly the client alone may, if he wishes, waive this privilege. However it is to be noted that the mere fact that a client waives the professional privilege which exists between himself and the attorney, does not also result in the waiver of the further privilege which protects documents brought into existence for the purpose of litigation.[15]

Joint Retainer

With respect to a joint retainer, the waiver of privilege which is implied at the outset is limited so as to exclude communications made after the emergence of a conflict.

Once notice of the conflict is brought to the attention of the respective parties, they may continue or terminate the retainer. If the joint retainer is continued then a further waiver of privilege is implied.[16]

(iii) Scope of Privilege From Disclosure

With respect to the ambit or scope of privilege from disclosure, whether in respect of oral or written communications, the following should be noted:

(i) the death of the client does not destroy the privilege.[17]

(ii) privilege from disclosure continues indefinitely, i.e. it survives the retainer.[18]

(iii) confidences or secrets may be revealed by an attorney if it becomes necessary for him to do so in order to establish and collect his fees or defend himself or his employees against an accusation of wrongful conduct.[19]

(iv) communications which enable either party to commit a crime, fraud or other illegal act are not privileged.[20] As Dillon LJ noted in *Finers v Miro (a firm) and others,* 'It is well established that privilege is lost by the criminal or fraudulent intent of the client.[21]

However an allegation of wrongful conduct is not sufficient to displace the claim of privilege. A *prima facie* case of fraud or other illegal act must be made out in fact.[22]

WRITTEN COMMUNICATIONS IN PARTICULAR

(i) Between Attorney and client

An attorney will not be compelled to produce confidential correspondence passing between himself or his clients and his client's predecessors in title although no litigation was contemplated or pending at the time when the communications were made or came into existence.[23] Both the attorney and client may act through an agent and therefore communications to or through an agent are within the privilege.[24]

(ii) Between Attorney and Non-Professional Agent or Third Party

However, communications between an attorney and a non-professional agent or third party are privileged from disclosure only when litigation was pending or contemplated and the anticipated or pending litigation was the dominant purpose for which the documents came into existence e.g. a surveyor's report obtained by the attorney with a view to giving the client legal advice.[25]

(iii) Copies of Privileged Documents

At common law, legal professional privilege extends only to original documents not to copies however improperly obtained. This rule of evidence is referred to as The Rule in *Calcraft v Guest.*[26] According to the rule, where a litigant wishes to prove a particular document which by reason of privilege or some other circumstance he cannot furnish, he may produce a copy as secondary evidence although the document has been obtained by improper clandestine or even criminal means.[27]

However in such instances, the courts of equity in the proper case, will intervene and restrain publication or disclosure of the copies by granting an injunction, not only to prevent copies which have been made from being further copied, but also to restrain persons into whose possession such information has come, from themselves divulging it whether by oral evidence or otherwise.

Basis of Court's Jurisdiction

Prior to *Derby & Co Ltd and Others v Weldon and Others (No. 8)* the decision by the Court as to whether or not to grant injunctive relief with respect to copies of privileged documents, was based essentially on preserving the confidentiality of the documents in question. Accordingly, the court in exercising its discretion in favour of either party weighed the two competing interests; the interest of the public that the truth should be ascertained against the legitimate interest of the party seeking to keep confidential information from being disclosed. In balancing these two interests, the court took into account the circumstances in which the information came into the hands of the defendant i.e. whether by stealth, deceit or inadvertence, the relevance of the documents and the privileged nature of the documents themselves.[28]

However in the *Derby* case, the court held that it was not required to exercise its discretion by balancing conflicting public policy considerations; that the basis of its equitable jurisdiction was not the preservation of the confidential nature of the documents but rather the preservation of the legal profession privilege and accordingly it would only refuse to grant an injunction in aid of the privilege on general principles affecting the grant of any discretionary remedy such as inordinate delay by the party seeking such relief.[29]

As Nourse LJ succinctly observed in *Goddard v Nationwide Building Society* and quoted with approval by Vinelott J in *Derby*:

> If an injunction is sought in aid of legal professional privilege, no balancing act is called for[30].

Accordingly, once the documents in respect of which an injunction is sought, are documents to which a claim of legal professional privilege properly attaches, the issue which the court is thereafter required to address is whether there has been an implied waiver of the privilege.[31]

In this regard the circumstances under which the documents got into the hands of the other side is relevant for the purposes of determining whether there has been an implied waiver by the client of the legal professional privilege. Accordingly, where the copies of documents to which legal professional privilege properly attaches, are obtained by trickery, stealth, and deceit or even by obvious mistake or inadvertence, there can be no implied waiver of the privilege.

It is to be noted that the court has the power, in accordance with the exercise of its equitable jurisdiction, to intervene and grant an injunction after disclosure of confidential information, even after the documents have been inspected.[32]

Oral Communications in Particular

For oral communications to be privileged from disclosure it is not necessary that the relationship should have reached the definite status of attorney and client. It is sufficient only that the contemplated relationship is that of attorney and client so that oral communications passing between an attorney and a potential client with a view to such person retaining the attorney on a professional basis is privileged from disclosure even if the attorney does not accept the retainer.[33] However, any conversation passing between them must be fairly referable to that professional relationship,[34] whether contemplated or otherwise. More particularly, the communications passing between the attorney and (potential) client must be for the purpose of giving and or receiving legal advice but as Buckmaster L J noted in *Minter v Priest,* 'such conversation will be interpreted within a very wide and generous ambit of interpretation'. [35] In this regard, the facts of *Minter v Priest* are instructive. In that case the court held that a conversation between a solicitor and his client relating to the business of obtaining a loan for the deposit on the purchase of real estate was privileged from disclosure as the business was professional business i.e. within the ordinary scope of a solicitor's employment.

PRIVILEGE FROM AN ACTION FOR DEFAMATION

When the right to claim privilege from disclosure has been waived by the client it is at this stage that the second limb of privilege comes into effect – i.e. the defence of privilege in an action for defamation. This privilege exists for the benefit of both the client and the attorney-at-law.[36]

However it is not settled whether this privilege is a qualified or absolute one; qualified in the sense that the claim of privilege will be upheld only if express malice is not proved;[37] or absolute in that once the claim of privilege is referable or relevant to the communication, it is not actionable whether the words published or spoken were motivated by express malice.[38]

In this regard, although it was held that in *More v Weaver* that such communications are absolutely privileged from an action for defamation, Scrutton LJ acknowledged that there was some difference of opinion in the reported cases on the question of whether the privilege is absolute or qualified.[39] Indeed in *Minter v Priest*[40] the House of Lords preferred to leave the question open.

Nevertheless it appears that even where the court is of the view that the defence of privilege in an action for defamation can only afford a qualified defence, it seems that the court is very slow to hold that the words spoken or published were actuated by malice. As Sir Robert Collens observed in the Privy Council decision in *Laughton v Bishop of Sodor and Man*[41] (which was quoted with approval by Lord Atkinson in *Adam v Ward*)[42]:

> To submit the language of privileged communications to strict scrutiny, and to hold all excess beyond the absolute exigency of the occasion, to be evidence of malice, would in effect greatly limit, if not altogether, defeat the protection which the law throws over privileged communications.

Privilege from an Action for Defamation in Judicial Proceedings

Statements made in the course of judicial proceedings are absolute privileged from action for defamation. This is even where the words were uttered by the advocate maliciously and not with the object of supporting his client's case (This privilege extends to judges, witnesses and parties to the action). The rationale for this privilege was eloquently explained by Brett MR in *Munster v Lamb*. Brett MR observed:

> To my mind it is illogical to argue that the protection of privilege ought not to exist for a counsel who deliberately and maliciously slanders another person. The reason of the rule is, that counsel, who is not malicious and who is acting very bona fided may be in danger of having actions brought against him. If the rule of law were otherwise, the most innocent of counsel might be unrighteously harassed with suits, and therefore it is better to make the rule of law so large that an innocent counsel shall never be troubled.[43]

But as Brett MR acknowledged that by making 'the rule so large counsel are included who have been guilty of malice and misconduct'.[44]

It is to be noted that this absolute privilege extends to defamatory statements, in an attorney's bill of costs provided it is relevant and germane to the occasion and necessary for the client to know that for which he is being charged.

Ambit of Proceedings Covered

According to the authority of *Lincoln v Daniels*[45] the absolute privilege from an action for defamation action covers proceedings in or before a court of justice and can be divided into three categories:

1) matters that are done *coram judice* i.e. everything that is said in the course of proceedings by judges, parties, counsel and witnesses including contents of documents put in evidence;
2) everything done from the inception of the proceedings onwards and extends to all pleadings and other documents brought into existence for the purpose of the proceedings and starting with the writ or other documents which institute proceedings;[46] and
3) statements to *coram judice* made by witnesses to the client and the attorney in preparing the proof for trial.[47]

PRIVILEGE FROM ARREST

An attorney who is proceeding to the court to attend his professional business there pending, including an appointment at the office of the court, is privileged from arrest. This privilege also extends to an attorney, proceeding from court, provided in so doing there is no unreasonable delay or deviation on his part.[48]

The case of *AG v Skinners' Co ex p Watkins*[49] is instructive on this point. In that case a solicitor stopped to speak to some friends he met on his way home from attending court. Being much exhausted by his long attendance in the House of Lords he went into a public house in order to procure some refreshments whereupon he was arrested for non-payment of cost in a Chancery suit. It was held the deviation from course was not unreasonable. According to the Vice Chancellor, stopping to speak to some person on the way home from court or his deviating a yard or two from his course to procure the refreshment of which he stood in need are not sufficient grounds for depriving him of the benefit of this privilege.[50]

This privilege from arrest enjoyed by attorneys-at-law is not the privilege of the person attending the court, but of the court which he attends so that there should be a proper administration of justice. For that purpose, persons properly in court, including parties and witnesses are not to be interfered with by being arrested and thereby prevented from assisting the court or carrying on their business in court.

However, it is be noted that an attorney is not immune from arrest if the arrest is made in pursuance of an order of the court whether in respect of a civil or criminal contempt.[51]

ENDNOTES

1. See chapter 5
2. Antigua - s.10(1) Legal Profession Act 9/1997
   Barbados - s.10(1) Legal Profession Act 370A
   Eastern Caribbean (save Antigua & Barbuda and St. Lucia) - s.19(1) Solicitors Act, 1974 England
   St. Lucia - s.20(1) Legal Profession Act 31/2000
   Trindad & Tobago - s.20(1) Legal Profession Act 21/1986
3. Anguilla - s.70 Eastern Caribbean Supreme Court (Anguilla) Ordinance 9/1982
   Antigua - s.10(1) Legal Profession Act 9/1997
   Barbados - s.10(1) Legal Profession Act 370A
   Dominica - s.73 Eastern Caribbean Supreme Court (Dominica) Act Chap. 4:02
   Eastern Caribbean (save Antigua & Barbuda and St. Lucia) - s.19(1) Solicitors Act, 1974 England
   Guyana - s.9 Legal Practitioners (Amendment) Act 3/1980
   Jamaica - s.5(1) Legal Profession Act 1971
   St. Lucia - s.20(1) Legal Profession Act 31/2000
   St. Kitts & Nevis - s.72 (2) and (3) Eastern Caribbean Supreme Court (St. Christopher & Nevis) Act 1983
   Trindad & Tobago - s.20(1) Legal Profession Act 21/1986
4. See chapter 11 post
5. Antigua - Code of Ethics Part A r.40
   Eastern Caribbean (save Antigua & Barbuda and St. Lucia) - OECS Code of Ethics Part A r.40
   Jamaica - Canon of Ethics Canon (r)
   St. Lucia - Code of Ethics Part A r.39
   Trindad & Tobago - Code of Ethics Part A r.40
6. *Minter v Priest* [1930] AC 558 at pp.579-580 HL per Atkin LJ
7. Antigua - Code of Ethics Part B r.15
   Barbados - Code of Ethics Part VIII r.71
   Eastern Caribbean (save Antigua & Barbuda and St. Lucia) - OECS Code of Ethics Part Br.15
   Jamaica - Canon of Ethics Canon IV (t)
   St. Lucia - Code of Ethics Part B r.18
   Trindad & Tobago - Code of Ethics Part B r.15

8. (1844) 1 Ph 476 at pp.480 & 481
9. [1996] AC 487 HL
10. (1844) 1 Ph 476 at pp.480 and 481
11. [1996] AC 487 HL.
12. *Ibid* at p.503
13. *Minter v Priest* [1930] AC 558 at 579 HL. See also *R v Bowden* [1999] 4 All ER 43
14. *Waugh v British Railway Board* [1980] AC 521 HL, *Minet v Morgan* (1873) 8 Ch App 361, *Reg v Cox and Railton* (1884) 14 QBD 153
15. *Doland (George) Ltd. v Blackburn Robson Coates and Co* [1972] 3 All ER 959, [1972] 1 WLR 1338
16. *TSB Bank plc v Robert Irving & Burns* [2000] 2 All ER 826
17. *Bullivant v AG for Victoria* [1901] AC 196, [1900-3] All ER Rep 812 HL
18. *Allison v Clayhills* (1907) 97 LT 709 [1904-7] All ER Rep 500
19. Antigua - Code of Ethics Part B r.15
    Barbados - Code of Ethics Part VIII r.77
    Eastern Caribbean (save Antigua & Barbuda and St. Lucia) - OECS Code of Ethics Part B r.15
    Jamaica - Canon of Ethics Canon IV (t)
    St. Lucia - Code of Ethics Part B r.18
    The Bahamas - Code of Professional Conduct, Rule IV, Commentary 10
    Trindad & Tobago - Code of Ethics Part B r.15
20. *O'Rourke v Darbishire* [1920] AC 581 HL, *Reg v Cox and Railton* (1884) 14 QBD 153, *Butler v The Board of Trade* [1971] 1 Ch 680, *Reg v Bullivant* [1900] 2 QB 163 HL
21. [1991] 1 All ER 186 at p.186 CA, See also *Reg v Cox and Railton* supra
22. *O'Rourke v Darbishire* supra See also *Dubai Aluminium v Al Alawi* [1999] 1 All ER 703
23. *Minet v Morgan* (1873) 8 Ch App Cas 361CA. See also *Reg v Bullivant* [1900] 2 QB163 at pp.167 and 168 CA
24. *Jones v Great Railway Co.* [1910] AC 4 at p.6 HL.
25. *Waugh v British Railways Board* [1980] AC 521 [1979] 2 All ER 1169, [1979] 3 WLR 150 HL
26. (1898) 1 QB 759, [1895-9] All ER Rep 346 CA. See also *Ashburton (Lord) v Pope* [1913] Ch 469 at p.473 CA, *Guineas Peat Properties Ltd. v Fitzroy Robinson Partnership (a firm)* [1987] 2 All ER 716, [1987] 1 WLR 1027 CA, *Webster v Chapman & Co. (a firm)* [1989] 3 All ER 939
27. *Ibid.*
28. [1990] 3 All ER 762 CA. See also *ITC Film Distributors v Video Exchange Ltd.* [1982]1 Ch 431
29. *Ibid.*
30. [1956] 3 All ER 264, [1987] QB 670 at p.722 of *Derby & Co Ltd. v Weldon* [1990] 3 All ER 762 CA
31. *Derby & Co Ltd v Weldon* [1990] 3 All ER 762 at pp.772-775 CA
32. *Ibid.*
33. *Minter v Priest* [1930] AC 558 HL
34. *Ibid.*
35. *Ibid* at p.568
36. *Baker v Carrick* [1894] 1 QB 838
37. *Minter v Priest, supra* at p.580. See also *Egger v Viscount Chelmsford & Others* [1964] 3 All ER 406 [1965] 1 QB 248 CA

38. *More v Weaver* [1928] 2 KB 520
39. *Ibid* at p.523
40. [1923] AC 558 HL
41. (1872) LR 4PC 495.
42. [1917] AC 309 at p.337 PC
43. (1883) 11 QB 588 at p.605
44. *Ibid.*
45. [1962] 1 QB 237 at pp.257, 258 CA
46. *Ibid.*
47. *Lincoln v Daniels, supra.* See also *Watson v M'Ewan* [1905] AC 480 HL, [1904-7] All ER Rep 1, *Marrinan v Vibart* [1963] 1 QB 528, [1962] 3 All ER 380, *Roy v Prior* [1971] AC 470, [1970] 2 All ER 729 HL
48. *Re Hunt* [1959] 1 QB 378. See also *Stourton v Stourton* [1963] P 232, [1963] 1 All ER 606
49. (1837) 8 Sim 377
50. *Ibid* at pp.382, 383
51. *Re Hunt, supra.* See also *Stourton v Stourton, supra*

8. DISABILITIES

The disabilities which attach to an attorney in his dealings or transactions with his client and in some instances, former client, arise as a consequence of the fiduciary nature of the client/attorney relationship.

The basis of the specific disabilities arising therefrom may be conveniently classified into three main categories:

(1) Disabilities based on undue influence.
(2) Disabilities based on confidentiality.
(3) Disabilities based on conflict, more specifically, conflict of duty and conflict of interests.

Part I – Disabilities Based on Undue Influence

INTRODUCTION

In accordance with the rule of equity which is based on public policy considerations, any transaction in which one of the parties is under a fiduciary duty to the other, as is the case with respect to the attorney/client relationship, such a transaction shall be presumed to have been procured by undue influence, unless the contrary is shown. As Slade LJ explained in the Court of Appeal decision in *National Westminster Bank plc v Morgan*, 'the purpose of the court applying the presumption as a matter of public policy, is to mitigate the risk of a particular relationship existing between the two parties and the influence arising therefrom from being abused'.[1]

ELEMENTS OF A FIDUCIARY RELATIONSHIP WHICH RAISE PRESUMPTION

Although the *National Westminster Bank v Morgan* case concerns the banker/customer relationship, it is nevertheless instructive in identifying the elements which raise the presumption of undue influence. These elements are:

1) Reliance on the guidance or advice of another party who is not only aware of that reliance but also stands to benefit from the transaction or had some other interest in it being concluded.
2) The existence of an element of confidentiality between the parties that goes beyond that which might be present between persons dealing with each other at arm's length.[2] In this regard Dunn LJ noted:

> Confidentiality is intended to convey that extra quality in the relevant confidence that is implicit in the phrase confidential relationship:[3]

Once the presumption of undue influence is raised the Court will set aside the transaction in question, unless the party who gave the advice or guidance can rebut the presumption by showing that he has discharged his fiduciary duty for as Slade LJ observed in *National Westminster Bank v Morgan*:

> It is still possible that the relationship and influence arising therefrom has been abused even though the transaction is on the face of it, one which in commercial terms, provides equal benefits to both parties.[4]

That is not to say that an attorney cannot in any circumstances, enter into a valid and binding business transaction with his client in which he may directly or indirectly profit, merely because the relationship of attorney/client exists. In this regard Cairns' LJ comments in *McPherson v Watt*[5] are instructive. Cairns LJ observed, in reference to the solicitor's power to purchase property from his client:

> A solicitor is not affected by the absolute disability to purchase which attaches to a trustee.[6]

Rebutting the Presumption

In order to rebut the presumption of undue influence, judicial guidelines have been formulated. In this regard, the Privy Council decision in the Guyanese case of *Demerara Bauxite Co v Hubbard,*[7] is particularly instructive. According to the *Demerara Bauxite* case, to rebut the presumption of undue influence:

1) the attorney must act with complete faithfulness and fairness;
2) he must be prepared to show that he has concealed nothing;
3) he must have afforded the client the opportunity of obtaining competent independent advice; and
4) where relevant, must have paid an adequate price.

DURATION OF DISABILITY

The disabilities which arise as a result of the presumption of undue influence in respect of the attorney/client relationship, may outlast that relationship in its strict sense. Indeed in the case of *McMaster v Byrne,*[8] it was held that although the solicitor was not acting as solicitor for the client in relation to the particular transaction in question, that nevertheless in the circumstances, the confidence arising from the relationship of solicitor and client which had previously existed between them must be taken to have continued to exist at the date on which the transaction in question was entered into.

Factors taken into Account

The factors which the court takes into account in determining whether the disabilities arising from the attorney/client relationship are still operable were considered in the case of *Allison v Clayhills.*[9] In that case the defendant solicitor had taken a lease of a public house with an option to purchase from the owner, Allison, who from time to time employed him as his solicitor. After Allison's death his widow brought an action to have the lease set aside on the grounds *inter alia* that the solicitor had acted as solicitor for both parties in the lease transaction and that her deceased husband had had no independent advice at the time of entering into the lease transaction.

Although the court held that the granting of lease to the solicitor was valid because at the time of the lease transaction the solicitor had no personal influence over his former client and therefore was not acting as his solicitor, the court nevertheless noted:

(1) that a solicitor may by virtue of his employment acquire a personal ascendancy over a client and this ascendancy could last long after the employment has ceased; and
(2) that a solicitor by virtue of his employment may acquire special knowledge and such knowledge may put upon him a duty of making full and proper disclosure long after the relationship of solicitor and client in its strict sense has ceased to exist.[10]

It is to be noted that for the presumption of undue influence to arise the fiduciary relationship must have existed at the time of the purchase, sale or other transaction. If it comes into existence afterwards and there was no fraud and all parties to the transaction were fully aware of the relevant facts of the case, the sale or purchase will not be set aside. *Masons' Hall Tavern Co v Nokes*[11] is a case on point. In that case a firm of solicitors purchased certain leasehold property and soon afterwards formed a company (of which they were solicitors) to take over the property which they sold to the company at a price greatly in excess of what they had paid for it. The court held that the sale would not be opened and the solicitors were not accountable for the profit made on the transaction as no fiduciary relationship existed between the parties at the time when the solicitors purchased the property.

PARTICULAR INSTANCES OF UNDUE INFLUENCE

Purchases by Attorney from Client

The case of *Demerara Bauxite Co v Hubbard*[12] is illustrative of the court's position in cases where an attorney purchases property from his client. In that case, the court set aside a sale of property by the plaintiff client to her solicitor and held that a purchase by an attorney from his client or where a similar confidential relationship exists, and where the vendor client has not had independent advice, cannot be upheld unless it is proved affirmatively that the attorney disclosed without reservation all the information in his possession and that the transaction was fair in all the circumstances.

The adequacy of the price paid as indicated above, is also an important factor in determining the fairness of the transaction in question. As the court observed in *Lowther v Lowther*,[13] the adequacy of the price paid will be subject to the scrutiny of the court where a purchaser appears to have stood in a confidential relationship with regard to his vendor.

In determining the adequacy of the price paid, the circumstances affecting the value of the property will be considered. However, the mere fact that the price of the property has considerably increased since purchase, is not of itself sufficient to render the transaction void and unenforceable.

It is to be noted that with respect to the purchases of property from a client, the respective Code/Canon of Ethics of the respective territories (save Jamaica and the Bahamas) specifically provides that, 'an attorney shall not acquire directly or indirectly by purchase or otherwise a financial or other interest in the subject matter of a case which he is conducting'.[14]

Indeed in the Jamaican case of *Knowles v Francis*,[15] an agreement by a client to sell land to his solicitor was set aside on the ground *inter alia* that at the time when the agreement was made, the solicitor had been retained to represent the client in a civil suit and the agreement for sale involved the subject matter of that litigation.

Sale by Attorney to Client

As is the case with purchases from the client, there is no absolute rule or disability that an attorney-at-law cannot sell property to his client; but if challenged, he must establish that the client exercised his free will. Independent advice, though not strictly requisite, would also be advisable.

Loans, Mortgages to or from Client

Commentary 7 of Rule V of Code of Professional Conduct of The Bahamas is particularly instructive on this point. Commentary 7 provides *inter alia* that 'save in exceptional circumstances the attorney should not borrow money from a client who is not in the business of lending money and it is undesirable that he lend money to his client except by way of advancing necessary expenses in a legal matter which he is handling for that client'.

Accordingly, when entering into a loan or mortgage agreement with a client, an attorney is bound to take care that the client has the same protection as if he had employed an independent attorney for that purpose. If that is not done, he must preserve evidence that the terms and conditions of the loan or mortgage agreement were explained to the client. As Jessel MR observed in *Cockburn v Edwards:*

> A solicitor who lends money or mortgages property to his client on any but the strictly usual terms would be wise if he also required the intervention of another solicitor.[16]

Gifts to Attorney by Client

The rules as to gifts from client to attorney are far more stringent and more absolute than those with respect to commercial transactions. In this regard, a gift from a client to his attorney or the spouse or child of the attorney is presumed to have been procured by undue influence and it will be difficult for an attorney to retain the gift particularly where it is of substantial value.[17]

Devises and Bequest to Attorney by Client

An attorney can take a benefit under a will prepared by him for his client but in the case of large benefits the burden of proof is on the attorney to show that:

(1) the testator was capable of making the will;
(2) he knew and approved of the contents of the will;
(3) there was nothing in the way of undue advice or influence by the attorney; and in that regard that
(4) the testator received proper and independent advice.[18]

Part II – Disabilities Based on Confidentiality

ATTORNEY ACTING AGAINST FORMER CLIENT

There is no general rule that an attorney or a firm who has at one time acted for a client cannot subsequently act against that client. In such cases the court balances the two competing interests:

(i) the entitlement of the client to the fullest confidence of his solicitor and in particular that there shall be no risk or perception of risk that confidential information will be disclosed to anyone else; and
(ii) the freedom of an attorney to obtain instructions from any member of the public and of all members of the public to instruct such attorney.[19]

ATTORNEY ACTING AGAINST FORMER CLIENT IN SAME OR CONNECTED MATTER

According to the Court of Appeal decision in *Rakusen v Ellis, Munday & Clarke*[20] there is no general rule that an attorney who has acted for some person either before or after litigation began can in no case act for the opposite side in the same or connected matter. The court in such instances, must examine the facts of each case and must be satisfied that mischief and real prejudice would result from the attorney so acting. Indeed in the Jamaican case of *Johnson v Williams*[21] the court held that an attorney who had acted for one party in an action should not be restrained from acting for the opposite party but must undertake not to communicate secrets. In the 1962 Guyanese case of *Allen v Allen*[22] the court held that there was no objection to the solicitors who had acted for the defendant in preparation of documents for advertisement of a mortgage, acting in the opposition proceedings relating to the passing of the second mortgage as it was not suggested that any confidence reposed in the solicitors in respect of the mortgage transaction had been or was likely to be violated. Further, in the court's opinion no conflict of interest or duty arose in the solicitors so acting.

It is however submitted that *Allen v Allen* which was decided in 1962 and *Johnson v Williams* which was decided in 1895 and more significantly the 1962 case of *Rakusen v Ellis Munday & Clarke* are not representative of the current position on this issue, particularly in light of the 1999 House of Lords decision in *Prince Jefri Bolkiah v KPMG (a firm).*[23]

Indeed it is submitted that the *ratio decidendi* in *Rakusen* is an overstatement of the law and a more accurate and current representation of the law on this issue is that a firm of attorneys is disabled from acting against a former client in the same or connected litigation unless the firm can satisfy the court:

i) that the attorney currently acting against the former client is not the same attorney in the firm who formerly acted for and was retained by that client in the same or connected litigation; and
ii) that there is no real risk of leakage of information from the former attorney to the new attorney.

In this regard the facts of *Rakusen* clearly do not support the expansive *ratio decendi* of that case. In *Rakusen* there were only two partners in the firm named EM&C. It was established that both parties were in the habit of conducting their business separately and without knowledge of each other's clients. More particularly, when the plaintiff consulted with Maundy, one of the two partners of the firm, with a view to bringing an action for wrongful dismissal against his former employer, the other partner, Clarke, (who eventually acted for the plaintiff's former employer) knew nothing of this prior consultation and in fact was away at the time when it took place. The court was satisfied that in the *special circumstances* (*emphasis added*)of that case that it was not necessary for it to intervene by granting an injunction to prevent the defendant firm from acting against the plaintiff in the pending arbitration proceedings.

Basis of Court's Intervention – Confidentiality or Conflict of Interest?

The basis of the court's intervention with respect to granting or not granting an injunction, was considered in the House of Lords decision in the case of *Prince Jeffri Bolkiah v KPMG (a firm)*.[24] In that case a distinction was drawn between the position with respect to a former client and an existing client and the basis of the court's intervention in such instances. Although the case concerned a firm of accountants, Lord Hope of Craighead observed, 'the court is required to exercise the same jurisdiction to intervene on behalf of a former client of the firm as it exercises in the case of a solicitor'.[25]

Existing Client

Where an existing client is concerned, the court's intervention is based on the inescapable conflict of interest which is inherent in the situation. Millet LJ summed up the position succinctly when he observed:

> A fiduciary cannot act at the same time for and against the same client and his firm is in no better position . . . His disqualification has nothing to do with the confidentiality of the client's information.[26]

Former Client

With respect to a former client, Millet LJ opined:

> Where the court's intervention is sought against a former client the court's jurisdiction is not based on any conflict of interest real or perceived for there is none. The fiduciary relationship which subsists between solicitor and client comes to an end with

> the termination of the retainer. The only duty which survives, is a continuing duty to preserve the confidentiality of information imparted during its subsistence.[27]

It is clear from the House of Lords decision in *Prince Jefri Bolkiah* that the court's jurisdiction to intervene, is based not on a conflict of interest but on the preservation of a former client's confidential information, to the disclosure of which he has not consented.

Evidential Burden

Where the plaintiff seeks to restrain his former attorney from acting for another client in the same or connected litigation, the burden of proof is on him to show that the attorney is in possession of confidential information, the disclosure of which he has not given consent and which disclosure is adverse to his interest.

Once the former client has established to the court's satisfaction that the attorney and/or his firm is in possession of such information, the evidential burden shifts to the attorney to show that there is no risk that the information will come into the possession of those in the firm now acting against the former client.[28]

Degree of Risk

According to the authority of *Prince Jefri Bolkiah v KPMG*, it seems that once there is some risk of disclosure of confidential information, though not a substantial one, the court will, in such instances, intervene and grant an injunction.[29]

The earlier cases generally required that there be a real risk, an appreciable risk,[30] or a reasonable probability of real mischief as in *Rakusen*. However, as the Court observed in *Prince Jefri Bolkiah*, the clear trend of the authorities seems to be towards a stricter approach. Indeed Millet LJ in his judgment opined that 'the criticisms which have been made of the test supposed to have been laid down in Rakusen's case are well founded. It imposes an unfair burden on the former client, exposes him to a potential and avoidable risk to which he has not consented and fails to give him a sufficient assurance that his confidence will be respected. It is in any event difficult to discern any justification in principle for a rule which exposes a former client without his consent to any avoidable risk however slight'.[31]

Effectiveness of 'Chinese Wall'

The measures to prevent the leakage of confidential information by creating a so called chinese wall were considered in the case of *Re a firm of Solicitors* [1992],[32] where a proposal was made by the firm of solicitors who had acted in connected litigatation against a former client for the erection of such a wall or information barrier. These measures included providing a different team to act against the former client, locating the team in a different department and a different building.

However, the Court of Appeal, while acknowledging that the former solicitors of the client 'proposed measures to erect what reads like a formidable chinese wall to prevent leakage of information within the firm',[33] the court was nevertheless of the opinion, that this was insufficient to guard against inadvertent leakage of information. However, in *Prince Jefri Bolkiah*, the House of Lords was prepared to accept that a chinese wall which was an established part of the organisational structure of a firm and not created ad hoc could be an effective barrier against the leakage of confidential information.[34]

However in order for such walls to be effective and considered acceptable by the Court, Lord Millet noted that the following measures would need to be implemented:

(a) physical separation of departments to insulate them from each other;
(b) an education programme emphasizing the importance of not improperly or inadvertently divulging confidential information;
(c) monitoring by compliance officers;
(d) disciplinary sanctions in cases of breach; and
(e) strict and carefully defined procedures.

In *Re a Solicitor* [1992], there was no such information barrier or chinese wall in existence or integrated into the institutional framework of the firm. The firm of solicitors in that case proposed the erection of an information barrier *after* an injunction was granted restraining them from acting against the former client.

The Current Position

It seems based on current trends, as expressed in the House of Lords decision in *Prince Jefri Bolkiah,* that once there is some risk of disclosure (and this of course will depend, on the facts of each case) even though the risk of disclosure of confidential information is not a substantial one, a firm who has acted for a former client will be restrained from acting against that client in the same or connected litigation, unless the firm can satisfy the court that it has a chinese wall in place along the lines, laid out by Millet LJ in *Prince Jefri Bolkiah* or otherwise comes within the exceptional circumstances of *Rakusen.* It is for that very reason that a sole practitioner would not in any circumstances, be allowed to act against a former client in the same or connected litigation.

The Bahamas

It is to be noted that Rule V, Commentary 11 of the Code of Professional Conduct of The Bahamas provides guidelines with respect to an attorney acting against a former client. Rule V Commentary 11 provides that:

> an attorney who has acted for a client in a matter should not thereafter act against him (or against persons who were involved in or associated with him in that matter) in the same or any related matter, or place himself in a position where he might be tempted or appear to be tempted to breach the Rule relating to Confidential Information.

The Commentary further states that:

> it is not, however, improper for the attorney to act against a former client in a fresh and independent matter wholly unrelated to any work he has previously done for that person.

Instances Where Attorney Not Permitted to Act

- In Criminal Proceedings
  In no circumstances would it be proper for an attorney who acted for one defendant to act for a co-defendant where there is a cut-throat defence between them.[35]

- Judicial Disability
  An attorney-at-law shall not accept private employment in a matter upon the results of which he previously acted in a judicial capacity or for which he had substantial responsibility while he was in public employment.[36]

Part III – Disabilities Based on Conflict

1. CONFLICT OF DUTY – ATTORNEY ACTING FOR MORE THAN ONE PARTY

An attorney who acts for more than one party in a transaction faces a potential conflict of duty in that he must safeguard the adverse interest of each of his clients. As Scrutton LJ observed in *Moody v Cox and Hatt,*

> 'it may be that a solicitor who tries to act for both parties puts himself in such a position that he must be liable to one or the other whatever he does... It will be his fault for mixing up himself up with transactions in which he has two entirely inconsistent interests and solicitors who try to act for both vendors and purchasers must appreciate that they run a very serious risk of liability to one or the other, owing to the duties and obligations which such curious relation puts upon them'.[37]

This is not to say that an attorney-at-law may not represent multiple clients. He may, if he can adequately represent the interest of each, and if each client consents to such representation after full disclosure of the possible effects of multiple representations.[38]

However in cases where conflict arises or the attorney's independent judgment is likely to be impaired, he should determine the brief on behalf of one or both of them. [39]

Informed Consent

Even where a conflict of interest may arise, there is no general rule that an attorney should not act for both parties in the transaction. This is provided that he obtains the informed consent of both parties.

The case of *Clark Boyce v Mouat*[40] is instructive on the meaning of informed consent. According to *Clark Boyce v Mouat,* informed consent means consent given in the knowledge that there is a conflict of interest between the parties and that as a result the attorney might be disabled from disclosing to each party the full knowledge which he possesses of the transaction or might be disabled from giving advice to the party which conflicts with the interest of the other. If the parties are content to proceed on that basis, the attorney can properly act for both. He should however obtain their written consent or record their separate consent in a separate letter to each.[41]

In determining whether informed consent has been obtained the following must be established *inter alia*:

(a) the particular services required; and
(b) whether the client is in full command of his faculties.

In *Clark Boyce v Mouat*, the respondent's son wished to borrow money but was unable to do so on the security of his house because it was fully mortgaged. The respondent, his mother, agreed to mortgage her house as security for the loan. Her son's usual solicitors declined to act in the transaction. However, the appellant solicitors agreed to act for both mother and son in the mortgage transaction after advising the respondent to seek independent advice, and explaining to her that she would be the principal debtor and not merely the guarantor. When the son's business failed and he became bankrupt, the respondent was left with the liability of repaying the mortgage. She then brought an action against the appellant solicitors alleging *inter alia* that they had breached their fiduciary duty in:

(a) failing to decline to act for her;
(b) failing to adequately advise the respondent of her need for independent advice; and
(c) failing to disclose that the son's usual solicitors had refused to act and that it was not in her interest to sign the mortgage.

However the facts of the case established that the mother was not concerned with the wisdom of the transaction and that she was merely seeking the services of a solicitor to ensure that the mortgage was properly executed. Accordingly, the court held that the solicitors had, by advising her to obtain and by offering to arrange independent advice, done all that was reasonably required of them before accepting her instructions and had therefore not acted in breach of contract or of a fiduciary duty.

Ambit of Attorney's Duty in Cases of Multiple Representation

Where an attorney acts for both parties in a transaction, the general position is that the attorney is obliged to disclose the information which comes into his possession in the course of doing the work the client has instructed him to do. He is not obliged however, to disclose information which has come into his possession independently of any such work, including information which has come into his possession as a result of an earlier transaction in which he was retained.[42] One exception to this general position is where the attorney obtains information of fraudulent dealings from whatever source. In such instances he is under a duty to disclose the information and it is irrelevant that it was not obtained during the course of investigation. The case of *Spector v Ageda*[43] is a case on point. In that case the solicitor acted for the moneylender and borrowers with full knowledge of the illegality of the loan but failed to advise the borrower that the loan was illegal in that it infringed s.7 of the Moneylenders Act. The court held that the solicitor was liable in damages to the borrowers in that he was in breach of his duty towards the borrowers as persons to whom he owed a duty to exercise his skill and knowledge.

The ambit of an attorney's duty in cases of multiple representation was considered in *Mortgage Express Ltd v Bowerman.*[44] In that case the defendant firm of solicitors was instructed to act for both the purchaser and plaintiff mortgage lending company in a conveyancing transaction. In the course of investigating title, on behalf of the plaintiff mortgage company, the solicitor discovered that there was a sub-sale of the property in question, at a substantially lower price than that which was stated in the valuation report upon which the lender was relying.

The court held in that case that the solicitor was liable in negligence to the plaintiff company for failing to report the sub-sale as this information which appeared on the face of the vendor's title came within the scope of the plaintiff's instructions which were to investigate the vendor's title and to deduce it to the mortgagee's solicitor.

In *National Home Loans Corp plc v Giffen Couch & Archer,*[45] a firm of solicitors acted for the borrower and lender, received information relating to arrears on a current mortgage account and the threat of legal proceedings but did not pass this information on to the mortgage lenders.

The court held that the solicitors were not under a duty to report the information which they discovered and which cast doubt on the borrower's ability to repay the loan as their instructions were framed with particularity and specified the matters on which the defendants were required to advise. Accordingly, as the information on arrears and the threat of proceedings did not relate to title or the adequacy of any security, or to any other matter which the defendants were specifically instructed to report on or advise, it followed that the solicitors were not in breach of their fiduciary duty.

It is clear that the main reason for the court arriving at different decisions in the *Bowerman* and *Giffen Couch* cases is essentially because of the differences in the scope and ambit of the client's instructions in the two cases.

In *Bowerman's* case the instructions were framed widely and accordingly the discovery of material bearing on the valuation of the lender's security was held to fall within the ambit of the instructions to investigate title. In *Giffen Couch* the information was available from other sources and more particularly the lendor's express instructions were of a specific and clearly defined scope.

2. CONFLICT OF INTEREST – ATTORNEY ACTING FOR HIMSELF AND CLIENT IN A TRANSACTION

Except with the specific approval of his client, an attorney-at-law is under a duty not to act in any manner in which his professional duties and personal interests are likely to conflict.[46] Circumstances in which an attorney may find himself in such a position is where he acts for himself and for the client in a transaction between them. As Megarry J observed in *Spector v Ageda*, 'in all ordinary circumstances, a solicitor ought to refuse to act for a person in a transaction to which the solicitor is himself a party with an adverse interest; and even if pressed to act after his refusal, he should persist in that refusal'.[47]

Part IV – Other Instances of Disabilities

1. SUIT FOR RECOVERY OF FEES

Eastern Caribbean territories (save St. Lucia and Antigua & Barbuda)
Based on the relevant statutory provision contained in the respective Eastern Caribbean Supreme Court Acts of the various Eastern Caribbean states, (excluding St. Lucia and Antigua & Barbuda), a barrister in the Eastern Caribbean is prohibited from suing for his fees *qua* barrister. However, with the exception of Queen's Counsel, barristers are entitled to practise as solicitors and can therefore recover fees *qua* solicitor.[48]

The relevant section of the Eastern Caribbean Supreme Court Act provides that subject to the exception of Queen's Counsel,

> . . . every person enrolled as a barrister shall be entitled to practise also as a solicitor and to sue for and recover his taxed costs

as such, but if he practises as a solicitor he shall be subject to the liabilities which attach by law to a solicitor.

With respect to St. Lucia, until the passage in November, 2000 of the Legal Profession Act 31/2000, the position on this matter was governed by s.5(2) of the repealed Legal Practitioners Ordinance Ch. 116 which section was essentially the same as the above-mentioned provision.

This prohibition against Queen's Counsel suing for fees is based on a disability, created by statute, which prohibits Queen's Counsel from practising as a solicitor. Indeed as a condition precedent to one's appointment as Queen's Counsel an attorney is required to give an undertaking to that effect which undertaking has the force of law.[49]

In St. Lucia, this statutory prohibition was challenged in the OECS Court of Appeal case of *Husbands v Warefact Ltd*[50] In that case, which was decided prior to fusion, the Court of Appeal held that 'Queen's Counsel cannot sue for fees for any work done as a barrister nor for work normally done by solicitors because he is prohibited from inter alia practising as a solicitor'. In this regard it is to be noted that the appellant has lodged an appeal to the Privy Council and the matter is, to date, pending. However with the passage of the Legal Profession Act 31/2000 which Act fused the legal profession, in St. Lucia, this prohibition against Queen's Counsel suing for his fees is no longer applicable to St. Lucia as of November 2000.

2. ATTORNEY ACTING IN DUAL CAPACITY

(a) Attorney/Trustee

In the absence of an express clause in the trust instrument an attorney is not entitled to receive remuneration in respect of legal business transacted in respect of the trust other than out-of-pocket expenses. This is subject to the exception in the Rule in *Craddock v Piper.*[51]

(b) Attorney/Guardian of Minor or Mental Patient

Where an attorney acts as guardian of a minor, the court is extremely watchful to prevent such persons from being taken advantage of and will hold a very strict hand over all deeds, purchases and conveyances obtained by the attorney soon after the coming of age of the minor.[52]

(c) Attorney/Agent on Sale

It is an established rule of equity that when an attorney is employed by a client as agent for sale, the attorney can neither purchase the property for himself nor make a gain to himself out of the property at the expense of his client, beyond his proper remuneration unless he can prove affirmatively that he furnished the client with all the knowledge he possessed and he disclosed the nature of his interest.[53]

(d) Attorney/Agent for Purchase

The same holds true for an attorney who acts as agent for purchase. Although he is not precluded from buying the property but if he wishes to sell it to his principal, he is bound to give him the fullest possible information both as to the price he paid the vendors and as to the profit, if any, which he would make as a result of the resale.

Accordingly, if an attorney is employed as an agent and secretly buys property for himself and resells it to his client at a profit, the latter may set aside the sale, or he may compel the attorney/agent to account for the profit by repaying the difference in the price with interest.[54]

Reliefs

The client, personal representative of a deceased client or assignee for value of the client, is entitled to obtain, where appropriate, the following reliefs:

a) rescission of the contract. However as a condition precedent to this relief, the *status quo ante* must be capable of being restored.[55]

b) reconveyance of the property by the attorney or purchaser with notice of the impropriety of the purchase by the attorney.

c) recovery of secret commissions/profits with interest. Where an attorney is employed to buy or sell or otherwise act for his client and obtains a secret profit out of the transaction from the other party, the attorney must account for the profits to his client so that the client may recover that part of the sum paid, under the contract which by reason of the contract is in excess of what the attorney should have received. This is unless he obtains a client's permission to keep it.[56]

Any interest accruing in respect of the client's money belongs to the client. By receiving a secret commission an attorney may also render himself liable to criminal and disciplinary proceedings.

Delay and Acquiescence

Any acts of confirmation or acquiescence by the client may effectively debar him from obtaining equitable remedies from the court. In this regard any attempt by the client to rectify any transaction which he is entitled to disaffirm or any long delays in pursuing such remedies may be viewed as acquiescence or confirmation.[57]

ENDNOTES

PART 1

1. [1983] 3 All ER 85 at p. 92 CA revsd [1985] 1 All ER 821 HL. See also *Tufton v Sperni* [1952] 2 TLR 516 at p. 522 CA
2. [1983] 3 All ER 85 CA
3. *Ibid* at p. 91 See also *Edwards v Meyrick* (1842) 2 Hare 60
4. *Ibid.*
5. (1877) 3 App. Cas 254 HL.
6. *Ibid* at p. 266
7. (1923) AC 673 PC. See also *Luddy's Trustee v Peard* (1886) 33 Ch D 500 [1886-90] All ER Rep. 968, *Allicock v Demerara Bauxite Co Ltd* (1968) LRG 140.
8. [1952] All ER Rep. 1362, PC
9. (1907) 97 LT 709.
10. *Ibid* at pp.712 and 713
11. (1870) 22 LT 503
12. [1923] AC 675 PC. See also *Re A Legal Practitioner* (1959) LRBG 13, *Taylor v Salmon* 4 My & Cr 139, *Ex parte James* (1803) 8 Ves 352
13. (1806) 13 Ves 95
14. Antigua & Barbuda - Code of Ethics Part B r.8
    Barbados - Code of Ethics Part VIII r.64
    Eastern Caribbean (save Antigua & Barbuda and St. Lucia) - OECS Code of Ethics Part B r.8
    St. Lucia - Code of Ethics Part B r. 8
    Trinidad & Tobago - Code of Ethics Part B r. 8
15. (1995) 32 WIR 205
16. [1881] 18 Ch D 449 at p.455 CA
17. *Wright v Carter* [1903] 1 Ch 27; [1900-3], All ER Rep 706, 87 LT 624, 19 TLR 29 CA.
18. See *Wintle v Nye* [1959] 1 All ER 552 HL, *Parker v Duncan* (1890) 62 LT 642, *Re Henry* (1898) 7 SCJB 217

PART II

19. *Re a Firm of Solicitors* [1995], 3 All ER 482 at p.488
20. [1912] 1 Ch 831, [1911-13] All ER Rep. 813 CA
21. (1895) 6 SCJB 407
22. (1962) 5 WIR 5
23. [1999] 1 All ER 517 HL
24. *Ibid.*

25. *Ibid* at p. 519
26. *Ibid* at p. 526
27. *Ibid* at p. 527
28. *Re a firm of Solicitors* [1992] 1 All ER 483, [1992] QB 959 CA. See also *Prince Bolkiah v KPMG*, supra at p. 527
29. *Ibid* at pp.527, 528
30. *Re a firm of Solicitors* [1995] supra. See also *Re a firm of Solicitors* [1992] 1 All ER 353 CA
31. [1999] 1 All ER 517 at p. 528 HL
32. [1992] 1 All ER 353CA
33. *Ibid* at p. 369
34. [1999] 1 All ER 517 at p. 531 HL
35. *Saminadhan v Khan* [1992] 1 All ER 963
36. Antigua & Barbuda - Code of Ethics part B r.22
    Barbados - Code of Ethics Part VIII r.78
    Eastern Caribbean (save Antigua & Barbuda and St. Lucia)
    - OECS Code of Ethics Part B r.22
    Jamaica - Canon of Ethics Canon V(f)
    St. Lucia - Code of Ethics Part B r.25
    The Bahamas - Code of Professional Conduct Rule IX, Commentary 6
    Trinidad & Tobago - Code of Ethics Part B r.22

PART III

37. [1917] 2 Ch 71 at p.91. See also *Spector v Ageda* [1973] Ch 30 [1971] 3 All ER 417, *Sahoy v Sahoy* (1967) LRG 240, *Goody v Baring* [1956] 2 All ER 11 at p.12, *Straker v Hansraj Maraj* (1984) 39 WIR22, *Allicock v Demerara Bauxite Ltd* (1968) LRG 140
38. Antigua & Barbuda - Code of Ethics, Part A r.26
    Barbados - Code of Ethics, Part IV r.29
    Eastern Caribbean (save Antigua & Barbuda and St. Lucia)
    - OECS Code of Ethics Part A r.26
    Jamaica - Canon of Ethics, Canon Part IV (1)
    St. Lucia - Code of Ethics, Part A r.29
    The Bahamas - Code of Professional Conduct, Rule V, Commentary 4 & 8
    Trinidad & Tobago - Code of Ethics, Part A r.26
39. Antigua & Barbuda - Code of Ethics, Part B r.11(2)
    Barbados - Code of Ethics, Part VIII r.67(2)
    Eastern Caribbean (save Antigua & Barbuda and St. Lucia)
    - OECS Code of Ethics Part B r.11(2)
    Jamaica - Canon of Ethics, Canon Part IV (c)
    St. Lucia - Code of Ethics, Part B r.14(2)
    The Bahamas - Code of Professional Conduct, Rule V, Commentary 5
    Trinidad & Tobago - Code of Ethics, Part B r.11(2)
40. [1993] 4 All ER 268 PC
41. See The Bahamas Code of Professional Conduct, Rule V, Commentary 5
42. *National Home Loans Corp plc v Giffen Couch & Archer (a firm)* [1997] 3 All ER 808 CA, *Mortgage Express Ltd v Bowerman* [1996] 2 All ER 836 CA
43. [1973] 1 Ch 30

44. [1996] 2 All ER 836 CA
45. [1997] 3 ALL ER 808 CA
46. Antigua & Barbuda - Code of Ethics, Part B r 11(1)
Barbados - Code of Ethics, Part VIII r 67 (1)
Eastern Caribbean (save Antigua & Barbuda and St. Lucia) - OECS Code of Ethics Part B r. 11 (1)
Jamaica - Canon of Ethics, Canon IV (r)
St. Lucia - Code of Ethics, Part B r 14(1)
The Bahamas - Code of Professional Conduct, Rule V, Commentaries 7 & 8
Trinidad & Tobago - Code of Ethics Part B r. 11 (1)
47. [1973] 1 Ch. 30 at p.47

PART IV

48. See chapter 2, endnote 8
49. Anguilla - s.71 Eastern Caribbean Supreme Court (Anguilla) Ordinance 9/1982
Dominica - s.74 Eastern Caribbean Supreme Court (Dominica) Act. Chap 4:02
Grenada - s.80 Eastern Caribbean Supreme Court (Grenada) Act 19/1991
St. Kitts & Nevis - s.74 Eastern Caribbean Supreme Court(St. Christopher & Nevis) Act 1983
St. Vincent & the Grenadines s.74 Eastern Caribbean Supreme Court (St. Vincent & the Grenadines) Act Cap 18
50. CA 7 and 8/1997 St. Lucia (unreported)
51. See chapter 5.
52. *Goddard v Carlisle* (1821) 9 Price 169. See also *Hatch v Hatch* (1804) 9 Ves 292 CA
53. *Regier v Campbell-Stuart* [1939] 3 All ER 235 at pp.239 and 240
54. *Re Haslam v Hier-Evans* [1902] 1 Ch 765
55. *Re Cape Breton Co* [1885] 29 Ch D 795, *Armstrong v Jackson* [1917] 2 KB 822 [1916-17] All ER Rep.
56. *Re Cape Breton Co, supra, Grant v Gold Exploration and Development Syndicate Ltd.* [1900] 1 QB 233 CA, *Brown v IRC* [1964] 3 All ER 119, [1965] AC 244 HL
57. *Re McCallum, McCallum v McCallum* [1901] 1 Ch 143; *Savery v King* (1856) 5 HL Cas 627.

9. CONTEMPT OF COURT AND BREACH OF UNDERTAKINGS

Part I – Contempt of Court

INTRODUCTION

Contempt by attorneys-at-law is but one sphere of a much wider concept of contempt in general. In this regard, the court's jurisdiction to punish an attorney for contempt is not to be confused with its power to punish an attorney for professional misconduct, although the punishment for both, in some instances, is the same. When the court punishes an attorney for professional misconduct, it is in effect exercising its supervisory jurisdiction over an attorney as one of its officers in circumstances where the attorney is guilty of professional misconduct.[1]

However, when the court punishes an attorney-at-law for contempt of court, it is exercising a wider inherent jurisdiction under the general principles which govern the exercise of such power. Although contempt of court is not exclusive to attorneys-at-law, this chapter will focus on the two categories of contempt – criminal contempt and civil contempt, in so far as they relate or apply to attorneys-at-law.

CRIMINAL CONTEMPT

Contempt is of a criminal nature where it consists of conduct or words spoken which obstruct or are calculated to obstruct, prejudice or interfere with the due administration of justice whether in respect of criminal or civil proceedings.[2]

Punishment for Criminal Contempt

Punishment for criminal contempt includes the court's summary power of committal,[3] imposition of a fine,[4] the taking of security for good behaviour or alternatively, the court may take the more lenient course of granting an injunction against a threatened contempt or the repetition of the act of contempt, as the case may be.[5]

Instances of Criminal Contempt

Criminal contempt is not confined to contemptuous or offensive words or conduct in the face of the court or to disturbances of court hearings but extends to any clear and unequivocal interference in the administration of justice so that it affects or is intended to affect the course or outcome of judicial proceedings. It is to be noted that steps preparatory to creating a disturbance in court[6] and which may have amounted to a serious contempt, if completed, does not constitute a contempt of court.[7]

Although as Lord Tucker observed in *Izoura v The Queen*, 'it is not possible to particularise the acts which can or cannot constitute contempt',[8] the following are the various categories of criminal contempt as they relate specifically to an attorney-at-law:

A. Improper Conduct in the Face of the Court

Examples of this include:

(i) accusing a judge or the court of a lack of impartiality or integrity. In *Vidyasagara v The Queen*[9] a case on point the attorney in question was found guilty of contempt by the Superior Court of Ceylon for making an allegation of 'the improbability of impartiality on the court's part';

(ii) willfully insulting a trial judge, using improper or offensive language or remarks to a judge;[10]

(iii) conducting oneself in a violent insolent manner before the court or within the precincts of the court.[11] In *Re Johnson*[12] a solicitor was imprisoned for contempt of court for assaulting the solicitor on the other side with grossly abusive expressions and threatening gestures on his way from the judge's room to the entrance gate of the court;

(iv) trading insults with one's opponent as distinct from trading insults with court. This will not amount to contempt unless counsel persists in his conduct in the face of a ruling by the judge or uses language so offensive or so outrageous and provocative as to lead to a brawl in court.[13]

B. *Scandalising the Court*

Scandalising the court constitutes any act done or writing published which is calculated to bring a court or a judge into contempt or lower his authority or to interfere with the administration of justice. In *Daw v Eley,*[14] a solicitor was held guilty of contempt of court, for writing a publication under an assumed name with the intent of attempting to influence the result of a suit, in which he acted as solicitor for the defendant.

In this regard it is to be noted that criticism of the court or its decisions whether written or oral, even if inaccurate is not a contempt provided that the criticism is not actuated by improper motives or a malicious attempt to impair the administration of justice.

As Atkin LJ observed in *Ambard v AG of Trinidad & Tobago:*

> The path of criticism is a public way; the wrong-headed are permitted to err therein: provided that members of the public abstain from imputing improper motives to those taking part in the administration of justice and are generally exercising a right of criticism and not acting in malice….[15]

Examples of Scandalising the Court include:

- attacks on the personal character of a judge. However publishing a libelous statement made of a judge in his personal capacity does not amount to a contempt of court;[16]
- statements to the effect that the accused in a criminal case will not get a fair trial;
- writing abusive letters to the judge or other court officials.[17] In *Weston v CCC Administrator*[18] a solicitor wrote an offensive letter of protest to the court's administrator. The court held that although the letter was most discourteous it was not a contempt of court as it had not interfered with the administration of justice.[19]

C. *Non-attendance of Attorney at Court*

The cases of *Izoura v The Queen*[20] and *Weston v CCC Administrator*[21] are instructive on this point. In both cases, solicitors were summoned to court to explain their respective absences from court on the dates on which their matters were listed for hearing. In both instances the solicitors were not informed that their attendances were required through official channels, but instead were informed verbally by their clients.

It was held in both cases, that although the conduct of the solicitors in each case was discourteous and might perhaps amount to a dereliction of duty to their clients, (in other words professional misconduct), the solicitors had nevertheless done nothing to interfere with the due administration of justice and their respective failure to attend court, not being a breach of any court order, the solicitors in the court's opinion had not crossed the line between mere discourtesy and contempt of court. However it is to be noted that the outcome would be different had there been an official communication or court order for attendance.

As Lord Denning MR commented in *Weston v CCC Administrator:*

> I have no doubt that if a solicitor deliberately fails to attend with the intent to hinder or delay the hearing... he would be guilty of contempt of court. He would be interfering with the course of justice.[22]

Indeed in *R v Hill*[23] the British Columbia Court of Appeal upheld the lower Court's conviction for contempt by a barrister, for absenting himself from court without justifiable excuse. The court held that the attorney had crossed the boundaries of mere discourtesy.

D. Abuse of Pleading Process

Between the seventeenth and eighteenth centuries, attorneys were punished for contempt for signing prolix and scandalous pleadings. More recently, attorneys have been punished for contempt in respect of pleadings which contain feigned or fictitious allegations of facts or issues. In *Linwood v Andrews and Moore*[24] a barrister was imprisoned for contempt for conspiring with a solicitor to present a false affidavit to the court.

In *Re Eslam,*[25] a solicitor was fined for contempt for instituting proceedings on fictitious facts and in *Re Weisz,*[26] a solicitor was punished for contempt for instituting proceedings containing a fictitious endorsement for the purpose of deceiving the court by concealing that the action was not maintainable in law.

E. Abuse of the Court Process

Instances of abuse of the court's process include the forging or altering of court documents and similar acts of dishonesty or fraud.

In addition, an attorney who institutes proceedings for the sole purpose of delay, quite apart from being guilty of professional misconduct, may well render himself liable in contempt of court. The Jamaican case of *Chamberlain and Edwards v Agard and Superintendent of Prisons of St Catherine District*[27] is instructive. In that case the appellant was sentenced to death. A motion seeking a declaration for a stay of execution was denied on the ground that the application was devoid of merit. On the eve of the execution, another motion seeking precisely the same declaration, supported by the same facts, was lodged. The court held *inter alia* that the lodging of the exact replica of an earlier application amounted to the flouting of the court's decisions and an abuse of the course of justice. Carey JA observed that, 'any further application of a similar nature can only serve to demonstrate wilfull and contumelious conduct and must render all those who take part by lodging and/or appearing in support as being in contempt of court'.

Scope of Summary Power to Punish Contempt by Committal

The court's summary power to punish contempt by committal is a power which the court must of necessity possess. It is given so as to maintain the dignity and authority of the court and to ensure a fair trial. It is to be exercised so as to prevent disorder, to enable witnesses to be free from fear and a judge from being improperly influenced.[28] Its usefulness depends on the wisdom and restraint with which it is exercised and to use it to suppress methods of advocacy which are merely offensive is to use it for a purpose for which it was not intended.[29]

As Atkin LJ observed in *Ambard v AG of Trinidad & Tobago:*

> Justice is not a cloistered virtue. She must be allowed to suffer the scrutiny and respectful, even through outspoken comments of ordinary man.[30]

Order of Committal

Where the court invokes its summary power to punish contempt whether pursuant to committal proceedings or pursuant to an order of committal made by a judge of his own motion, it is usually exercised in instances of contempt in the face of the court, although as Stephenson LJ noted in *Balogh v St Alban's Crown Court* punishment by committal may be invoked in other instances of contempt, other than contempt in the face of the court.[31] However it must never be invoked unless nothing else will do to protect the ends of justice and ensure that a trial in progress or about to start can be brought to a proper and dignified end. Examples of cases where this summary power has been invoked include throwing a brick at a judge, and inciting persons to picket the court by distributing leaflets in the court's gallery.[32]

Committal by Judge of His Own Motion

Where the contempt is committed in the face of the court, the judge may commit the offender on his own motion *instanter* and without notice or formal institution of committal proceedings.

However this jurisdiction should be exercised only in exceptional cases. As Lord Denning MR noted in *Balogh v St Alban's Crown Court:*

> It is to be exercised by a judge of his own motion only when it is urgent and imperative to act immediately so as to maintain the authority of the court to prevent disorder – to enable witnesses to be free from fear – and jurors from being improperly influenced – and the like.[33]

Opportunity to Explain

In the court's exercise of its summary power to punish for contempt in face of the court, an attorney should first be given an opportunity to show cause or explain his conduct before punishment is allowed. The contempt must be stated clearly and distinctly and the alleged offender should be allowed to consult a solicitor or counsel before he is dealt with.[34]

Maharaj v AG of Trinidad & Tobago,[35] is instructive of this point. It was held *inter alia* that the judge had failed to explain to the appellant that the contempt with which he intended to charge him 'was a vicious attack on the integrity of the court'; and that his failure to do so vitiated the appellant's committal for contempt since he had not been afforded the opportunity to explain what he had meant by 'unjudicial conduct'.

CIVIL/PROCEDURAL CONTEMPT

This consists of disobedience to a judgment order or other process of court in a civil action.[36] It is essentially a wrong done to the person who is entitled to the benefit of a judgment or order of the court.[37]

Punishment for Civil Contempt

The punishment for civil contempt is the same as for criminal contempt. More particularly, a judgment or order against an attorney may be enforced by an order of committal or by a writ of sequestration against the attorney's property. As is the case with respect to criminal contempt, the power to order committal for civil contempt is a power which the court is slow to exercise. The court will only do so where it is satisfied that the order itself was clear and unequivocal and where the disobedience to the order involves some impropriety, fault or other misconduct on the part of the attorney. Where disobedience to a court order is unintentional, committal will not be ordered but the attorney will be ordered to pay the cost of the application for committal. In addition, the attorney may also be subject to disciplinary proceedings being instituted against him.

Unlike criminal contempt, civil contempt can be waived by the party for whose benefit the order was made and in such cases the court will not exercise its jurisdiction if the parties have settled their dispute.

Part II – Breach of Undertakings by An Attorney-at-Law

INTRODUCTION

An undertaking is a pledge or promise made by an attorney-at-law in his professional capacity to do or to refrain from doing some act. Although undertakings may be given orally, they should as a general rule be written or confirmed in writing.[38]

In this regard an undertaking must be clear and unambiguous in its terms.[39] As Sir Richard Scott VC observed in the Court of Appeal decision of *Bentley v Gaisford*:

> Solicitors' undertakings cast a heavy burden of observance on the solicitors who give them. A solicitor's undertaking which is not clear in its term and which leaves it uncertain what the solicitor may or may not do is unsatisfactory.[40]

The undertaking must also be capable of being performed *ab initio*. Indeed the respective Code/Canon of Ethics of the various territories provides that 'an attorney-at-law shall not give a professional undertaking he cannot fulfill'.[41] Although the court will not order an attorney to perform an undertaking which is incapable for the attorney to perform, it may nonetheless order the attorney to compensate the person who has suffered in consequence of his failure to implement his undertaking.

In addition, it is to be noted that an undertaking given to the court may be treated as conduct amounting to civil contempt even if the breach is not willful or deliberate.[42]

OPTIONS AVAILABLE

Where an attorney is in breach of a professional undertaking, three options are available to the injured party. He can proceed:

(i) by an action at law;
(ii) by an application to the Law/Bar Association or other competent tribunal to take and/or recommend disciplinary proceedings against the attorney; or
(iii) by an application to the court to exercise its inherent supervisory jurisdiction over attorneys-at-law as one of its officers.[43]

Where compliance or enforcement of an undertaking is sought, the application should be made to the court rather than the Law/Bar Association as the Law/Bar Association has no power to order or recommend compliance; it may only take or recommend disciplinary action as the case may be.[44]

In so far as the disciplinary sanctions for professional misconduct are concerned, the respective Code/Canon of Ethics of the various territories (save The Bahamas) provides that:

> An attorney shall not commit a breach of an undertaking to a Judge, a court other Tribunal or an official thereof, whether such undertaking relates to an expression of intention as to future conduct or is a representation that a particular state of facts exists.[45]

JURISDICTION OF THE COURT TO ENFORCE UNDERTAKINGS

An undertaking given by an attorney to his client or to a third person or to the court in the course of proceedings may be enforced summarily against him. However for an undertaking to be enforceable, it must be given by the attorney in his professional capacity or as an agent of the client.[46]

The jurisdiction of the court to enforce an undertaking by summary process is based on the court's right to require its officers to observe a high standard of professional conduct. As Sir John Donaldson MR observed in *John Fox v Bannister, King & Rigbeys* when speaking of the court's summary jurisdiction over an attorney with respect to undertakings:

> It is in a sense a domestic jurisdiction to which solicitors are only amenable because of their special relationship with the court and it is designed to impose higher standards than the law generally applies.[47]

It is immaterial that there was no misconduct on the part of the attorney or that the undertaking was not enforceable as a contract against the attorney, the attorney's word should be his bond. As was noted in *R v Gray:*

> In enforcing undertakings the court is not guided by considerations of contract but aims at seeking honesty of conduct in its officers[48]

However as a general rule the court will not enforce an undertaking by summary process unless there has been a serious dereliction of duty on the attorney's part.[49]

EXAMPLES OF UNDERTAKINGS

Examples of undertakings include an undertaking to enter an appearance in an action,[50] to repay money lent for benefit of client by another solicitor;[51] to hold a sum of money pending the conclusion of negotiations;[52] to forward documents of title;[53] to pay money to a third party not the attorney's client[54] and to pay another attorney's costs of a loan transaction.[55]

ENDNOTES

PART I

1. *Myers v Elman* [1940] AC 282 at pp.317-319. See also *Weston vCCC Administrator* [1977] 1 QB 32.
2. *Izoura v The Queen* [1953] AC 327 P.C. See also *Balogh v St Alban's Crown Court* [1975] QB 73 CA; *Western v CCC Administrator* [1977] 1 QB 32.
3. *Shipworth and the Defendant's Case* (1873) LR 9 QB 230
4. *R v Odham's Press Ltd, ex parte AG* [1957] 1QB 73; [1956] 3 All ER 494.
5. *Brook v Evans* [1860] 29 LJ Ch. 616.
6. *Izoura v The Queen, supra*; See also *Chamberlain and Edwards v AG and The Superintendent of Prisons, St Catherine District Prison* (1979) 16 JLR 403.
7. *Balogh v St Albans Crown Court, supra.*
8. [1953] 327 at p. 336 PC
9. (1963) AC 589 PC
10. *R v Gray* [1900] 2 QB 36.
11. *Ex p Pater* 122 E.R 841 at pp.846-847; *Kirby v Webb* [1887] 3 TLR 763
12. [1887] 20 QBD 68.
13. *Re Pershadsingh* (1960) 2 WIR 340; See also *Parashuram Detaram Shamdasani v King Emperor* [1945] AC 264 PC
14. [1868] 7 LR Eq 49. See also *R v Gray, supra.*
15. [1936] AC 322 at p.335 PC.
16. *R v Davies* [1906] 1KB 32.
17. *R v Freeman* (1925) Times 18 November
18. [1977] 1 QB 32
19. See also *Shipworth and the Defendant's Case* (1873) LR 9 QB 230
20. [1953] AC 327 PC
21. [1977] 1 QB 32
22. *Ibid* at p.43
23. (1976) 73 DLR 621
24. (1888) 58 L.T. 612
25. (1824) 3 B&C 597.
26. [1951] 2 KB 611
27. (1979) 16 JLR 403; See also *Riley v R* (1801) Rowe 657
28. *Balogh v St Albans Crown Court* [1975] QB 73 CA
29. *Parashuram Deteram Shamdasani v King Emperor* [1945] AC 264 at 270 PC
30. [1936] AC 322 at p.335 PC
31. [1975] QB 73 at p. 89 CA
32. *Ibid* at p.84. See also *Re Pollard* (1868) LR 2PC 106
33. [1975] QB 73 at p.85 CA
34. See the Guyanese case of *Re Pershadsingh* (1960) 2WIR 340. See also the Barbadian case of *Bayley v Blackman* CA 73/1988 (unreported) contrast with the Jamaican case of *Eric Frater v R* (1981) 18 JLR 381
35. (1977) 1 All ER 411 PC. See also the Guyanese case of *Re Pershadsingh, supra* and the Barbadian case of *Bayley v Blackman, supra*
36. *Re Dudley* [1883] 12 QBD 44
37. *AG v Walthanston UDC* [1895] 11 TLR 533; *Stancomb v Trowbridge UDC* [1910] 2 Ch 190.

PART II

38. See on this the Bahamas Code of Professional Conduct Rule XVI Commentary 6
39. See on this the Bahamas Code of Professional Conduct Rule XVI Commentary 6. See also *John Fox v Bannister King* [1987] 1 All ER 737; *Al Kandari v JR Brown & Co. (a firm)* [1988] 1 All ER 65 CA
40. [1997] 1 All ER 842 at p.849 CA
41. Antigua & Barbuda - Code of Ethics Part A r.43
Barbados - Code of Ethics Part VI r.47
Eastern Caribbean (save Antigua & Barbuda and St. Lucia)
- OECS Code of Ethics Part A r.4
Jamaica - Canon of Ethics Canon VI (d)
St. Lucia - Code of Ethics Part A r.42
The Bahamas - Code of Professional Conduct Rule XVI, Commentary 6
Trinidad & Tobago - Code of Ethics Part A r.43
42. *Re Agreement of Mileage Conference; Group of the Tyre Manufacturers Conference Ltd* [1966] 2 All ER 849; See also *Silver (Geoffrey) & Drakes v Baines* [1971] 1 All ER 473 at 476.
43. *Udall v Capri Lighting Ltd* [1987] 3 All ER 262 at pp.268-269; [1988] QB 908 at pp.916-918; See also *Rooks Rider v Steel* [1993] 4 All ER 716
44. *Ibid.*
45. Antigua & Barbuda - Code of Ethics, Part B r.30(1)
Barbados - Code of Ethics Part VIII r.86(1)
Eastern Caribbean (save Antigua & Barbuda and St. Lucia)
- OECS Code of Ethics Part B r.30(1)
Jamaica - Canon of Ethics Canon VI (c)
St. Lucia - Code of Ethics Part B r.33(1)
Trinidad & Tobago - Code of Ethics Part B r.30(1)
46. *Silver (Geoffrey) & Drakes v Baines* [1971] 1 All ER 473 CA; *United Mining and Finance Corp Ltd v Becher* [1910] 2 KB 296, [1908-10] All ER Rep 876 CA; *Re a Solicitor* [1966] 3 All ER 52, [1966] 1 WLR 1604.
47. [1987] 1 All ER 737 at p.743. See also *Re a Solicitor* [1966] 3 All ER 52
48. [1892] 2 QB 440; [1987] 1 All ER 737 CA
49. See *John Fox v Bannister King* [1987] All ER 737, *Silver (Geoffrey) & Drakes v Baines* [1971] 1 All ER 473 CA.
50. *Re Kerly, Son and Verden* [1901] 1 Ch. 467 CA.
51. *Silver (Geoffrey) & Drakes v Baines, supra*
52. *Re A Solicitor* [1966] 3 All ER 52 [1966] 1 WLR 1604.
53. *Wong (Edward) Ltd v Johnson and Stokes* [1984] 2 WLR 1 PC.
54. *United Mining and Finance Corp Ltd v Becher* [1910] 2 KB 296.
55. *Rooks Rider v Steel* [1993] 4 All ER 716.

10. PROFESSIONAL NEGLIGENCE

Part I – Scope of Duty

INTRODUCTION

Professional negligence in the case of the attorney/client relationship involves:

1) a legal duty towards the client to exercise care and skill;
2) breach of that duty by the attorney i.e. failure to attain the standard of care and skill prescribed by law; and
3) actual loss to the client as a direct result of that breach[1]

It should be noted that as an alternative to an action for negligence brought by the client, the court may, in the proper case, make an order as to costs against the attorney personally so as to save the expense of a trial.[2] In addition, where the negligence on the part of the attorney involves inexcusable or deplorable delay or neglect he may also be guilty of professional misconduct.[3]

SCOPE OF DUTY IN GENERAL

In the Guyanese case of *Padmey v Radhia,* the Court observed:

> An attorney holds himself out to his clients as possessing adequate skill, knowledge and learning for the purpose of conducting all business that he undertakes, whether contentious or non-contentious.[4]

Although it is difficult to define the exact scope of his duty, an attorney should at least carry out his client's instructions in the matters to which his retainer relates by all proper means and diligence.[5] He should consult with his client on issues of doubt which do not fall within his express or implied discretion and he should keep his client informed as may be reasonably necessary and should comply with any reasonable request from his client in respect of his affairs and he should respond to his clients' telephone calls, keep appointments unless cancellation is unavoidable.[6]

This duty of care imposed on an attorney is dealt with comprehensively in the respective Code/Canon of Ethics of the various territories. In this regard, the relevant rules in the Code /Canon of Ethics provide subject to some variation in wording that:

(i) an attorney-at-law shall deal with his client's business with all due expedition and should whenever reasonably required by the client provide him with information as to the progress of his clients' business.[7]

(ii) it is improper for an attorney-at-law to accept a case unless he can handle it without undue delay.[8]

(iii) an attorney should always act in the best interest of his client, represent him honestly, competently and zealously and endeavour by all fair and reasonable means to obtain for him the benefit of any and every remedy and defence which is authorised by law;[9] and in all jurisdictions save the Bahamas,

(iv) in the exercise of his duties an attorney at law shall not act with inexcusable delay, negligence or neglect.[10]

Scope of Duty in Contentious Business

With respect to contentious business an attorney is liable for:

a. the consequence of ignorance or non-observance of the rules of practice of the court.[11]

b. the want of care in preparation of a case for trial and of attendance of witnesses;[12] and

c. the general mismanagement of the conduct of a case.[13]

As Bankes LJ observed in *Fletcher and Son v Jubb, Booth and Helliwell*, 'solicitors are under an obligation to bring to the discharge of their duties as solicitors reasonable care and skill and knowledge of the practice of the Court whose process they invoke on behalf of a client'.[14]

Although it is difficult to define the exact limit of skill and diligence which a solicitor undertakes to furnish in the conduct of a case or trace precisely the dividing line, nevertheless as L Cottenham remarked in *Hart v Frame*:

> Solicitors certainly ought not to be liable for errors in judgment whether in matters of law or discretion. [15]

Particular Instances

(i) In matters of procedure

An attorney is guilty of professional negligence for ignorance of familiar points of law. This includes:

(a) failure to observe limitation periods.In the Jamaican case of *Martins Tours Ltd v Senta Gilmore*[16] an attorney was held liable in negligence for failing to file notice of appeal in time. In *Kitchen v Royal Airforces Association & Ors,*[17] the solicitor was held liable in negligence for failing to commence an action under the Fatal Accident Act 1846-1908, England and in *Fletcher & Son v Jubb Booth and Helliwell*[18] a solicitor was liable for failing to inform the client that the relevant period of limitation was running out during which the proposed action could be commenced.

(b) failure to give proper notices. In *Murphy v Abrahams*[19] the solicitor was held liable in negligence for failing to give the requisite notice in respect of an appeal against a magistrate's conviction.

(c) failure to check the relevant legislation so as to determine whether the client's action was maintainable in law.[20]

(ii) In matters of evidence

An attorney is under a duty to adduce with all due diligence all evidence relevant to client's cause of action in so far as the same is reasonable or practicable. As the Court noted in the Guyanese case of *Henderson v Seernaithally:*

> it is not sufficient for him (the legal practitioner) to note the nature and substance of his clients' claim...he must make such proper inquiries as will make him master of his client's case; he must determine what evidence will be needed and so inform his client; he must obtain all necessary documents and information in his client's possession and procure all evidence necessary to support his case.[21]

By way of illustration in *Stokes v Trumper*[22] a solicitor was held liable in negligence for examining in chief, witnesses when he intended cross-examination by interrogatories of other witnesses, as a result of which the case was lost. In addition, an attorney is liable for neglecting to summon witnesses or to see that they are in attendance at the trial.[23]

(iii) Acting as Advocate

An attorney is liable if he fails to attend court.[24] In *Burgoine v Taylor,*[25] the defendant was not represented at the trial of his action because his solicitor was ignorant of the fact that in pursuance of an order of the Lord Chancellor, the action had, with others, been transferred from one judge of the Chancery Division to another and he had therefore only looked at the list before the former judge. It was held *inter alia* that he was guilty of gross negligence.

(iv) Want of Prosecution

An attorney is liable if he abandons a cause or matter without reasonable notice to his client. He is also liable for not prosecuting the judgment of the court with diligence or for not issuing execution. *Allen v Sir Alfred Mc Alpine & Sons Ltd*[26] is instructive on this point . In that case, in three actions in two cases, six years, and in the other, seven years after the issue of the respective writs, all three cases were dismissed for want of prosecution and in each case, the fault was that of the legal advisers. The court held *inter alia* that the delay on the part of the solicitor was prolonged and inexcusable and likely to cause severe prejudice to the defendants.

Scope of Duty in Non-Contentious Business

In general an attorney is liable for loss occasioned by ignorance of ordinary points of law. In addition he is liable for failing to advise his client of the steps which ought to be taken.

Particular Instances

(i) Sale/Purchase of Land

In *Pilkington v Wood*[27] a solicitor was held liable in negligence when he failed to ascertain that the vendor who purported to convey certain property as beneficial owner was in fact trustee of that property and had purchased the property in breach of trust so that when the client/purchaser came to sell a year later, he found that his title was defective.

In respect of the sale and purchase of, or other dealings with land, an attorney is also liable *inter alia* for:

a) failure to inspect or ascertain or make proper inquiries into the validity of the vendor's title;[28]
b) allowing unusual covenants to be inserted in a transaction and failing to explain the effect to a client of clauses in a headlease which restricted use; [29]
c) failing to register an option to purchase in time;[30] and
d) when acting for the sub lessee, failing to inspect the head lease.

(ii) Wills and Settlement

An attorney is liable *inter alia* for:

a) failing to advise his client that a will may be revoked by the marriage of the testator;[31]
b) failing to warn a testator that a gift to a witness or spouse of a witness would be null and void;[32]
c) failing to ensure that the usual clauses were inserted in a deed of settlement.[33]

(iii) Investment of Money

An attorney's liability in respect of investment of the client's money depends on the nature and terms of the retainer and whether the attorney has advised the client to seek expert advice on the soundness of the investment.[34]

Part II – Liability in Tort and Contract

An attorney-at-law may be liable to his client in contract and/or tort for any loss accruing from breach of his professional duty. Until the landmark decision of *Midland Bank Trust Co Ltd v Hett, Stubbs & Kemp*[35] it seemed settled that an attorney-at-law could not be liable to his client in contract and tort for professional negligence. The client was deemed to be confined to his contractual remedies. The thinking of the Court at the time is exemplified in the case of *Groom v Crocker.*[36] In that case the court stated unequivocally that the relationship of solicitor and client is a contractual one and accordingly it was by virtue of that relationship that the duty of care arose. In the court's opinion it had no existence apart from that relationship. The court therefore concluded that a solicitor could not be liable to his client both in contract and tort where this contractual relationship existed.

This decision was not however followed in *Midland Bank*, a case which involved an action commenced against the defendant firm of solicitors in which the client claimed damages for negligence or alternatively breach of contract for the defendants' breach of their professional duties in failing to register an option to purchase and further failing to advise as to the necessity for so doing.

The court held that the duty of care imposed on the defendant solicitors arose by reason of the special relationship between their client and them and accordingly, a solicitor could be liable both in contract and tort for professional negligence arising out of that special relationship.

After tracing the development of the law in this area and reviewing the various authorities Oliver J in his leading judgment based his decision in large measure on two cases: *Hedley Byrne & Co v Heller Partners Ltd*[37] and *Esso Petroleum Co Ltd v Mardon.*[38]

According to Oliver J, *Hedley Bryne,* a case in which it was held that a professional man is liable in tort for negligence if he gives guidance to another who he knows or should know is relying on it and who in fact relies on such guidance, destroyed the reasoning of *Groom v Crocker* which based liability for professional negligence solely on the contractual relationship.

Further, according to Oliver J, the later case of *Esso Petroleum v Mardon* which applied the *Hedley Byrne* principle and which held that the plaintiff company was liable both in contract and tort for professional negligence, established by so doing that the mere existence of a contractual duty did not exclude a similar independent duty which arises in tort by reason of the relationship of proximity between the parties.

However it is to be noted that there are a line of cases which have not adopted the *Midland Bank* position, most notably the Privy Council decision in *Tai Hing Cotton Mill Ltd v Liu Chong Hing Bank Ltd*,[39] a case which involves the banker/client relationship.

In that case Lord Scarman expressed the view that:

> There was no advantage to the law's development in searching for a liability in tort where the parties are in a contractual relationship.

He further observed that:

> It was necessary for the avoidance of confusion that the law adhere to the contractual analysis.[40]

However, in spite of the Privy Council ruling in the *Tai Hing Cotton Mill* case, the line of cases since *Midland Bank* which involve the attorney/client relationship has adopted the *ratio dicendi* of *Midland Bank*. In this regard, in the Jamaican case of *Mason v McClean*[41] the Court of Appeal held that the attorney in question owed the client a duty of care in contract and tort for failing to file suit within the statutory period of limitation. However, it is significant to note that no mention was made in the court's judgment, of the *Midland Bank* decision, although *Mason v McClean* was decided after the *Midland Bank* case.

However in the English case of *Bell v Peter Browne & Co*,[42] the decision in *Midland Bank* was expressly approved. In that case the plaintiff client brought an action in contract and tort against the defendant solicitors for breach of contract and negligence for failing to take any steps to protect the plaintiff's interest, either by arranging for a declaration of trust to be prepared or by registering a caution in the Land Registry. Although the court dismissed the client's case because at the date of issue of the writ, the action in contract as well as in tort was time-barred, Beldam LJ noted in respect of an attorney's duty of care:

> It is now established that an action may be brought for breach of the duty either founded in contract or in tort.[43]

Part III – Liability to Third Parties for Professional Negligence

In general an attorney owes a professional duty of care to his client and no one else. He is subject to professional rules and standards and he owes a duty to the court as one of its officers. But within that framework it is to his client that he owes a duty to exercise a standard of skill and care appropriate to his status as an attorney.[44]

However an attorney who is negligent in carrying out his professional duties may be liable in tort to a third party in cases where a *prima facie* duty of care can be established.

Based on the case law to date, an attorney's liability to a third party seems to be relegated to wills i.e. to cases where a would-be beneficiary suffers financial loss as a direct result of an attorney's negligence in the preparation or lack of preparation of his client's will, and where most significantly, the negligence is only discovered after the testator's death.

It is submitted that this exception as to liability to third parties arises essentially because of the special nature of the will-making process in that:

(i) the main and in some instances, the sole purpose for making a will is to confer a benefit on a third party beneficiary; and
(ii) a will speaks and takes effect only upon the death of the testator.

In addition, since negligence does not of itself automatically constitute professional misconduct, there would be, as a rule, no punitive sanction which could be imposed in respect of the attorney's default. In the words of Sir Donald Nicholls VC in the Court of Appeal decision in *White v Jones*:

> He (the solicitor) would go scot-free. He could commit a breach of his professional duty, with impunity. That cannot be right. That cannot accord with the objectives the law seeks to attain when imposing upon solicitors and other professional advisers a duty to exercise due professional skill and care.[45]

IMPULSE TO DO PRACTICAL JUSTICE

Although the earlier case of *Ross v Caunters*[46] decided that the defendant solicitor was liable to the third party beneficiary in negligence for failing to ensure that the will in question was witnessed in accordance with the statutory requirements, it is significant to note that the *ratio decidendi* in that case was restricted to a consideration of the three-fold elements of the tort of negligence, which on the facts, the court held existed, i.e. that:

(i) that the beneficiary was someone to whom the solicitor owed a duty of care as being a person within his direct contemplation as being likely to be injured by his failure to carry out the testator's instructions;
(ii) breach of that duty of care; and
(iii) loss as a direct result of the breach.

It was not until the Court of Appeal decision in *White v Jones,* that the court included as part of its *ratio decidendi* 'that it was just, fair and reasonable that the solicitor be held liable to compensate the intended beneficiaries in circumstances where there was no remedy in contract and the client's estate had no effective remedy'.[47]

In his leading judgment, Sir Donald Nicholls, VC made it quite clear that it was this ground which he considered the most critical factor. Sir Nicholls observed:

> Instructions to prepare a will are different from other instructions to a solicitor. The failure to carry them out properly results in the client's purpose being thwarted but leaves the client's estate with no effective remedy.[48]

Sir Nichols acknowledged that by so making the solicitor liable to an intended beneficiary, that the court was in effect fashioning a remedy for a solicitor's breach of his professional duty to his client.[49] To this end he noted with approval Bingham LJ's observations in *Simaan General Contracting Co v Pilkington Glass Ltd (No. 2),* where Bingham LJ observed:

> Just as equity remedied the inadequacies of the common law so has the law of torts filled gaps left by other causes of action where the interest of justice so required.[50]

Having been held liable in negligence to the third party beneficiaries, the solicitor appealed the decision of the Court of Appeal contending:

(i) that since the disappointed beneficiaries' claim was for purely financial loss their claim could not be sustained as such claims could lie only in contract and not in tort; and
(ii) that no claim lay in tort for damages in respect of a mere loss of an expectation which fell exclusively within the zone of contractual liability.[51]

In considering and effectively dismissing the grounds of appeal raised by the solicitor, the House of Lords adopted and expanded upon the reasoning advanced by the Court of Appeal, and in particular, by Sir Donald Nichols, VC in his leading judgment.

The House of Lords acknowledged (as previously alluded to by Sir Nichols in the Court of Appeal decision in that case) that the lacuna in the law, more specifically the conceptual difficulties of applying the doctrine of tortious negligence to the facts of the case presented a challenge (a challenge which had not been raised in the earlier case of *Ross v Canters).* Their

Lordships were of the view that filling this lacuna in the law was of cardinal importance and sought to do so by fashioning a specific judicial remedy – what their Lordships referred to as 'an impulse to do practical justice'.[52]

The House of Lords held that the solicitor was liable to the disappointed beneficiary although there was no confidential or fiduciary relationship between them. It based much of its *ratio* on the fact that neither the testator nor his estate had a remedy and accordingly 'an injustice would occur because of a lacuna in the law'.[53]

RATIONALE FOR JUDICIAL REMEDY

It seems clear from the judgments of the majority of their Lordships in *White v Jones*, that this 'impulse to do practical justice' is fueled as much by a desire to give a disappointed beneficiary a remedy as by a desire to ensure that a solicitor is held accountable for breach of his professional duty.

In this regard Goff LJ quoted with approval Cooke J in *Gartside v Sheffield Young and Ellis* where Cooke J observed:

> To deny an effective remedy in a plain case would seem to imply a refusal to acknowledge the solicitor's professional role in society.[54]

Applicability of Impulse to do Practical Justice

This 'impulse to do practical justice' seemed to have informed the court's decision in later cases in which other legal challenges were raised by attorneys in respect of their liability to third party beneficiaries.

The case of *Carr-Glynn v Frearson (a firm)*[55] is a case in point. According to the facts of the *Carr-Glynn* case, the testatrix executed a will drawn up by the defendant solicitors in which she left the plaintiff her share in a property. The solicitors advised the testatrix that there was some doubt as to whether her share in the property was held by her as joint tenant or tenants in common but failed to ensure on what basis the testatrix held her share. When the testatrix died it was discovered that the property was held on a joint tenancy and had passed to the remaining tenant by survivorship. As a result the plaintiff received nothing under the will. She brought an action for negligence against the solicitors contending that they had breached their duty of care to her as an intended beneficiary in failing to ensure on what basis the testatrix held her share in the property, in failing to ensure that the joint tenancy was secured and thereby failing to give effect to the testatrix's wishes.

The court at the chancery level held that the solicitor was not liable to the disappointed beneficiary as the estate theoretically had a remedy, although not enforced, against the solicitor for breach of his duty in preparing the testator's will.

According to the court, it was unacceptable that the solicitor should be at risk of two separate claims for identical loss at the suit of both the personal representatives and the intended beneficiary, when recovery by one would not bar recovery by the other.

The Court of Appeal overturned this decision and held that a duty of care was owed to the intended beneficiary, notwithstanding that the testator's estate might also have a remedy against the solicitor for breach of duty.

The decision to overturn the decision of the Chancery Court was clearly based, in large measure, on the *White v Jones* 'impulse to do practical justice'. This is clear from the leading judgment of Chadwick LJ, where he referred to the House of Lords decision of *White v Jones,* and concluded in similar terms that:

> For my part I would find it equally extraordinary and as much a matter for concern if the only person for whose benefit a valid claim could be pursued (the residuary legate) was a person who suffered no loss . . . and the only person who has suffered a loss has no claim . . . I am satisfied that it would be consistent with the approach of the majority of the House of Lords in White v Jones to fashion a remedy in cases of this nature also if that can be done without imposing a double liability on a solicitor in order to avoid which would otherwise be an injustice.[56]

SCOPE OF DUTY OF CARE TO THIRD PARTIES

(1) Acting in Subsequent Transaction

A solicitor who acts for a testator in preparing his will owes no duty of care to a beneficiary when acting for the testator in a subsequent transaction which *inter alia* adversely affects the value of an asset which formed part of the beneficiary's potential interest under the will. This is so because in the subsequent transaction there is no close proximity between the would be beneficiary and the solicitor as the benefit of the third party is not the object of the transaction. In *Clarke v Bruce Lance & Co (a firm) and Others,*[57] the testator had executed a will which included a specific devise to the plaintiff of an interest in a petrol service station. The will was drawn up by the defendant firm. Later the testator retained the defendant to act for him in relation to granting to a third party, of among other things, an option to purchase the service station on his or his wife's death, whichever was the later, at a fixed price of £28,000. On his death, the station's value had increased substantially beyond that amount. The plaintiff commenced an action alleging that the defendant solicitors owed him a duty of care as a person whose interest under the will would to their knowledge be affected by the granting of the option. The court however held that there was no degree of proximity between the plaintiff and defendant for as Balcombe LJ noted in that case:

> In no way can it be said that the defendant's contemplation of the plaintiff in relation to the grant of the option was actual, nominate and direct.[58]

The court accordingly held the defendant solicitors owed no duty of care to the plaintiff.

(2) Will-Making Process

With respect to the preparation of a testator's will, an attorney's liability extends not only to default or negligence in the actual preparation or non-preparation of the will but also to his general failure to give effect to the testator's testamentary intentions.

The case of *Carr-Glynn v Frearsons* (a *firm*)[59] is instructive. In that case the court held that the solicitor was liable for failing to ensure the testatrix serve notice of severance of a joint tenancy in property disposed of by her in her will. As a consequence, upon the testatrix's death the plaintiff beneficiary received nothing under the will as this failure on the solicitor's part amounted, in the court's view, to a failure to give effect to the testatrix's testamentary intentions. As Chadwick LJ observed in the Court of Appeal decision in that case:

> This is not a case in which the solicitors were instructed to advise in relation to an inter vivos transaction which was independent

of the will making process. On a proper analysis, the service of notice of severance was part of the will-making process.[60]

(3) Liability to Third Parties - is it applicable only to wills?

As a general rule an attorney's liability in negligence to third parties, seems to date, to be restricted to the area of wills. However, according to the authority of the case of *Hemmens v Wilson Browne*[61] there can be circumstances in which a solicitor may owe a duty of care to third parties in carrying out an *inter vivos* transaction. Although these circumstances were not considered in any detail, an attorney clearly would not be liable to a third party in an *inter vivos* transaction where the client is still alive when the default is discovered, and the client is still able to put things right. As Sir Nichols VC noted in the Court of Appeal decision in *White v Jones:*

> If the mistake such as faulty witnessing is discovered, in the testator's lifetime the third party will suffer no loss. The cost of preparing and signing a new will would be recoverable by the client from the solicitor.[62]

However in the appropriate case an attorney may be liable to a third party in an *inter vivos* transaction where the client is dead, or any other circumstances in which an irremediable situation has occurred putting it beyond the client's power to rectify the situation such as the insanity, insolvency or bankruptcy of the client[63] for as Lord Goff noted in the House of Lords decision in *White v Jones*:

> The same liability should logically be imposed in cases where an inter vivos transaction is ineffective and the defect was not discovered until the donor was no longer able to repair it.[64]

(4) Duty to Mitigate

According to the authority of *Walker v Medlicott & Son*[65] a disappointed beneficiary is under a duty to mitigate his damages, in that case, by bringing proceedings for rectification of the testator's will, and more particularly to exhaust this remedy before considering bringing proceedings for negligence against the solicitor for breach of his duty in preparing the testator's will.

LIABILITY TO THE PARTY ON THE OTHER SIDE

Hostile Litigation

Although a solicitor does not normally owe a duty of care to his client's opponent in hostile litigation, he would nevertheless be deemed to owe such a duty if he steps outside his role as attorney for his client and personally accepts responsibilities towards his client's opponents. The case *Al-Kandari v Brown & Co (a firm)*[66] is instructive in this point.

In *Al-Kandari v Brown & Co (a firm,)* a case involving a child custody battle, the defendant firm of solicitors gave an implied undertaking to the plaintiff wife's solicitor to retain the husband/client's passport and not to release it to him. The husband's passport was deposited with the Kuwait Embassy by the defendant's London agent in order to get the children's names removed from it. The Embassy informed the agent that they could not remove the children's name from the passport immediately but would retain the passport until the children's birth certificates were obtained. The husband told the defendant that he would take the necessary documents to the Embassy the next day. The defendant relying on the assurance from the Embassy that the passport would be safe did not send anyone to be present when the husband was at the Embassy and did not inform the plaintiff's solicitors of what had happened. While the passport was in the Embassy's possession the husband persuaded the Embassy to release it to him. The husband then arranged for three persons to kidnap the plaintiff while he abducted the children and took them out of the country to Kuwait, using the passport to do so.

The plaintiff subsequently brought an action against the defendants for breach of undertaking. The court held that when the defendants gave an implied undertaking to retain the husband's passport and not release it to the husband they were not acting as solicitors or agents of the husband but as independent custodians of the passport subject to the direction of the court and the joint direction of the parties. In the circumstances, the court held that the defendant solicitors owed the plaintiff a duty to take reasonable care to keep the passport in their possession (save as the plaintiff might otherwise agree) and to inform the plaintiff if for any reason it ceased to be in their possession.

Non-contentious Business

As a general rule in conveyancing transactions the attorney acting for the vendor does not generally owe the buyer a duty of care when answering inquiries before the contract and the like, because in the context of a contract for sale of land the buyer has a remedy against the seller in respect of any misrepresentation given on his behalf. Furthermore where an agent has acted within the scope of his authority on behalf of a known principal, it is the principal who owes a duty of care to the third party. However where an attorney steps outside his role of solicitor for his client and accepts direct responsibility towards the third party with whom his client was dealing, he is deemed to owe the third party a duty of care.[67]

ENDNOTES

PART I

1. See *Purves v Landell* (1845) 12 Cl & Fin 91, See also the Jamaican case of *Forrester v Francis* CLE 156/1983 (unreported).
2. *Myers v Elman* [1940] AC 282 at 319 HL.
3. See chapter 12 at pp.191-194 post.
4. (1931-37) LRBG 49.
5. *Alexander v Simpson* (1903) 8 SCJB 137.
6. *Godefroy v Dalton* (1830) 6 Bing 460. See also:
   The Bahamas - Code of Professional Conduct Rule II Commentary 6.
7. Antigua & Barbuda - Code of Ethics Part A r.27(1)
   Barbados - Code of Ethics Part III r.30(1)
   Eastern Caribbean (save St. Lucia and Antigua & Barbuda)
   - OECS Code of Ethics Part A r.27(1)
   Jamaica - Canon of Ethics, Canon IV (r)
   St. Lucia - Code of Ethics, Part A r.26(1)
   The Bahamas - Code of Professional Conduct Rule 11 Commentary 6
   Trinidad & Tobago - Code of Ethics Part A r.27(1)
   See also *Alexander v Simpson* (1903) 8 SCJB 137.
8. Antigua & Barbuda - Code of Ethics Part A r.27(2)
   Barbados - Code of Ethics Part III r.30(2)
   Eastern Caribbean (save St. Lucia and Antigua & Barbuda)
   - OECS Code of Ethics Part A r.27(2)
   St. Lucia - Code of Ethics, Part A r.26(2)
   The Bahamas - Code of Professional Conduct Rule 11 Commentary 3
   Trinidad & Tobago - Code of Ethics Part A r.27(2)
9. Antigua & Barbuda - Code of Ethics Part A r.21(1)
   Barbados - Code of Ethics Part III r.24(1)
   Eastern Caribbean (save St. Lucia and Antigua & Barbuda)
   - OECS Code of Ethics Part A r.21
   St. Lucia - Code of Ethics, Part A r.26(2)

The Bahamas - Code of Professional Conduct Rule VIII Commentary 1
Trinidad & Tobago - Code of Ethics Part A r.21 (1)
10. Antigua & Barbuda - Code of Ethics Part B r.18
Barbados - Code of Ethics Part VIII r.74
Eastern Caribbean (save St. Lucia and Antigua & Barbuda)
- OECS, Code of Ethics Part B r.18
Jamaica - Canon of Ethics, Canon IV (s)
St. Lucia - Code of Ethics, Part A r.21
Trinidad & Tobago - Code of Ethics Part A r.27(1)

11. *Godefroy v Dalton* (1830) 6 Bing. 460 at 467; See also *Padmey v Radhia* (1931-37) LRBG 49.
12. *Ibid.* See also *Hawkins v Harwood* (1849) 4 Ex Ch. 503.
13. *Hatch v Lewis* (1861) 2 F&F 467.
14. [1920] 1 KB 275 at p. 279 CA.
15. (1839) 6 Cl & Fin 193 at p.210 HL; See also *Heywood v Wellers (a firm)* [1976] 1 QB 446; *Griffiths v Evans* [1953] 2 All ER 1364, [1953] 1 WLR 1424 CA. See also The Bahamas, Code of Professional Conduct Rule II Commentary 7.
16. (1969) 14 WIR 136.
17. [1958] 2 All ER 241; [1958] 1 WLR 563 CA.
18. [1920] 1 KB 275 CA.
19. (1889) Times 3 April.
20. *Forrester v Francis* CLE 156/1983 Jamaica (unreported).
21. [1938] LRBG 94; See also *Roe v Robert Macgregor and Sons Ltd* [1968] 2 All ER 636, [1968] 1 WLR 925 CA, *Manley v Bailhache* (1893)6 SCJB 205, *Crook v Derbyshire* [1961] 3 All ER 786, [1961] 1 WLR 1360 CA.
22. (1855) 2 K&J 232.
23. *Sander v Prothers & Prothers* (1966) Sol. Jo. 218.
24. *Fergusson v Lewis* (1879) 14 L Jo 348. See also *R v Wilhel and Stewart* (1964) 8 JLR 392
25. (1878) 9 Ch D 1.
26. [1968] 2 QB 229, [1968]1 All ER 543; [1968] 2 WLR 366 CA. See also *Reggentin v Beecholme Bakeries* Ltd [1968] 2 QB 276 CA.
27. [1953] Ch. 770, [1953] 2 All ER 810, [1953] 3 WLR 522.
28. *Wilson v Tucker* (1822) 3 Stark 154.
29. *Sykes v Midland Bank Executor and Trustee Co Ltd* [1971] 1 QB 113, [1970] 2 All ER 471, [1970] 3 WLR 273 CA.
30. *Midland Bank Trust Co Ltd v Hett Stubbs and Kemp* [1979] 1 Ch. 384, [1978] 3 All ER 571, [1978] 3 WLR 167 CA
31. *Hall v Meyrick* [1957] 1 All ER 208, [1957] 2 QB 455 revsd [1957] 2 All ER 722, [1957] 2 QB 472, [1957] 3 WLR 273 CA.
32. *Ross v Caunters* [1980] Ch. 297, [1979] 3 All ER 580.
33. *Sykes v Midland Bank Executor and Trustee Co Ltd, supra.*
34. *Dooby v Watson* (1888) 39 Ch. D 178, 58 LT 943.

PART II

35. [1979] 1 Ch 384, [1978] 3 All ER 571 [1978] 3 WLR 167 CA
36. [1939] 1KB 194, [1938] 2 All ER 394, CA.
37. [1964] AC 465, [1963] 2 All ER 575, [1963] 3 WLR 101 HL.

38. [1976] 2 All ER 5, [1976] QB 801 CA.
39. [1986] AC 80 [1985] 2 All ER 947, [1985] 3 WLR PC.
40. [1986] AC 80 at p.107 PC.
41. [1979] 16 JLR 432. See also C. Dennis Morrison Q.C. *Lawyers Client and The Neighbour Principle* published in the 1980 West Indian Law Journal at p. 30.
42. [1990] 3 All ER 124. See also *Henderson v Merritt Syndicates Ltd* [1994] 3 All ER 506 HL.
43. *Ibid* at p.133.

PART III

44. *White and Another v Jones and Others* [1993] 3 All ER 481 at p. 489 CA.
45. *Ibid* at p.490.
46. [1980] Ch 297, [1979] 3 All ER 580.
47. [1993] 3 All ER 481 CA.
48. *Ibid* at p.490.
49. *Ibid.*
50. [1988] 1 All ER 791 at p. 804, [1988] QB 758 at p. 782, (quoted at p.490 of *White v Jones, supra*).
51. *White v Jones* [1995] 1 All ER 691 HL.
52. *Ibid* at p.701.
53. *Ibid.*
54. [1983] NZLR 37 at p.43 quoted at p.701 of *White v Jones* [1995] 1 All ER 691 HL.
55. [1997] 2 All ER 614 revsd [1998] 4 All ER 225 CA.
56. [1998] 4 All ER 225 at p.234 CA.
57. [1988] 1 All ER 364 CA.
58. *Ibid* at p.370.
59. [1997] 2 All ER 614 revsd [1998] 4 All ER 225 CA.
60. [1998] 4 All ER 225 at p.233 CA.
61. [1993] 4 All ER 826 at p.837.
62. [1993] 3 All ER 481 at p.490 CA.
63. See *Hemmens v Wilson Browne* [1993] 4 All ER 826 at p. 837.
64. [1995] 1 All ER 691 at 700 HL.
65. [1999] 1 All ER 685 CA.
66. [1988] 1 All ER 833 CA
67. *Gran Gelato Ltd v Richcliff (Group) Ltd* [1992] 1 All ER 865

11. IMMUNITY FROM ACTION FOR NEGLIGENCE

INTRODUCTION

As a general rule, an attorney enjoys no special immunity from action for any loss or damage caused by his negligence or lack of skill in the performance of his functions.[1]

However with respect to the conduct and management of a case in court, in accordance with the decision in *Rondel v Worsley*,[2] public policy requires that an attorney remain immune from suit. Further, in accordance with the authority of *Saif Ali v Sydney Mitchell & Co (a firm)*,[3] this immunity extends to pre-trial work so intimately connected with the conduct of a case in court so that it can fairly be said to be a preliminary decision affecting the way the case is to be conducted at the hearing.

With respect to advocate immunity this is governed by statute in Antigua & Barbuda, Barbados, Guyana, St. Lucia, and Trinidad & Tobago[4] and in the case of Jamaica, the Eastern Caribbean territories (save Antigua & Barbuda and St. Lucia) and The Bahamas, by the common law.[5]

In Guyana, St. Lucia and Trinidad & Tobago the *Rondel v Worsley* and *Saif Ali* decisions have been codified.[6] With respect to Antigua & Barbuda and Barbados,[7] these territories have codified the *Rondel v Worsley* decision in their respective Legal Profession Acts, but these territories have not extended, by legislation, the scope of advocate immunity to include pre-trial work. This is despite the fact that the *Saif-Ali* decision in the case of Antigua & Barbuda, pre-dates the passage of the Legal Profession Act of this territory. It is therefore uncertain whether the *Saif Ali* decision is applicable to either of these jurisdictions.

Public Policy Basis of Advocate Immunity

Prior to the House of Lords decision in *Rondel v Worsley*,[8] an advocate's immunity from suit was believed to be based on his contractual incapacity to sue for his fees. But Upjohn J made it clear in *Rondel v Worsley*, that this immunity is not based on an attorney's 'status, his inability to sue or his incapacity to contract'.[9]

Indeed it is submitted that, were this the basis of the immunity, attorneys-at-law in the English speaking Caribbean territories would not be able to claim immunity from actions for negligence, as there is currently either *de jure* or *de facto* fusion of the legal profession in these territories. As a consequence, with the limited exception of Queen's Counsel in the Eastern Caribbean (excluding St. Lucia and Antigua & Barbuda), legal practitioners may sue for and recover fees due and owing to them from their clients.[10]

Scope of Advocate Immunity

The test established for determining the scope of an advocate's immunity was first enunciated by McCarthy P in the New Zealand Court of Appeal case of *Rees v Sinclair*.[11] This test was adopted and applied in the Privy Council decision in *Saif Ali v Sydney Mitchell & Co (a firm)*.[12] According to the *ratio decidendi*, of the *Saif Ali* case, an advocate's immunity extends, as previously stated, to pre-trial work so intimately connected with the conduct of the case so that it can fairly be said to be a preliminary decision affecting the way the case is to be conducted at the hearing.

Meaning of Pre-Trial Work

Although the majority of the members of the House of Lords in *Rondel v Worsley* expressed the view that an advocate's immunity from suit extended to work done in the conduct of litigation in criminal and civil proceedings and could therefore include the drawing and settling of pleadings, these observations,[13] as Lord Wilberforce noted in his judgment in *Saif Ali*, have the status of *obiter dicta*,[14] since the court was not concerned with the matters taking place out of court.

Indeed, according to the authority of *Saif Ali* and the later decisions of *Somasundaram v M Julius Melchior & Co*,[15] and *Acton v Graham Pearce & Co (a firm)*[16] the ambit of an attorney's immunity, although not limited to door of the court proceedings, does not extend to:

(i) an instructing attorney or solicitor, not acting in the capacity of counsel/advocate attorney; or
(ii) failure to act on counsel's advice; or to
(iii) failure to put the relevant issues to counsel; or to
(iv) the settling or drawing of pleadings.

ADVOCATE IMMUNITY – A THING OF THE PAST?

As a consequence of the landmark House of Lords decision of *Hall v Simons*,[17] advocate immunity has been effectively abolished in England.

In its wide-ranging judgment the House of Lords held *inter alia* that public interest in the administration of justice no longer required that an advocate enjoy immunity from suit for alleged negligence in the conduct of civil or criminal proceedings.[18]

In arriving at this ground-breaking decision, the majority of the House of Lords examined exhaustively and comprehensively the public policy reasons for the granting of advocate immunity as enunciated in *Rondel v Worsley* and concluded that not one of these reasons had sufficient weight to sustain or justify its retention.

Core Reasons

In this regard, the following are the core reasons which were considered and effectively dismissed by the majority of the House of Lords in *Hall v Simons*:

(i) The Cab Rank Rule

According to the cab rank rule (which is not applicable to the Caribbean territories considered in this text),[19] an advocate is bound to accept any client desirous of his services in the field in which he practises, once he is disengaged and a proper fee is tendered. But as Lord Steyn noted in his judgment, 'although the rule is a valuable professional rule, its impact on the administration of justice in England is not great'.[20]

In any case as Lord Steyn further observed:

> In real life a barrister could circumvent the rule by raising his fees within limits

(ii) Analogy to Immunity from Action for Defamation in Court Proceedings

The argument that advocate immunity is in conformity with or analogous to the privilege or immunity in an action for defamation enjoyed by all those engaged in the administration of justice whether as a judge, juror, witness, party counsel, or solicitor was rejected by their Lordships.[21]

In this regard, their Lordships drew a distinction between the two immunities and noted that in the case of participants in court proceedings, the protection from an action for defamation was founded on powerful public interest, that is, that the administration of justice requires that participants are able to speak freely without being inhibited by the fear of being sued for what they say whereas in the case of an advocate's immunity from an action for negligence, the majority of their Lordships upon reflection, concluded that no such powerful public interest ground exists.[22] As Lord Steyn observed in reference to the granting of advocate immunity on this basis:

> If the latter immunity has merit it must rest on other grounds . . . it has, on analysis, no or virtually no weight at all.[23]

Lord Hoffmann further observed that 'the advocate immunity cannot be, founded on the general proposition that people doing their best in a difficult job, should not be exposed to vexatious claims', for as he concluded 'this argument could apply to many other persons besides lawyers'.[24]

(iii) The Danger of Relitigation

In their respective judgments, the majority of their Lordships conceded that on public policy grounds, the risk of relitigation provided perhaps the most substantive argument for the retention of an advocate's immunity from suit.[25] In this regard Lord Hoffmann acknowledged that for public policy reasons that it may be against the public interest to retry a case which had been decided by another court.[26] However in this regard, a distinction was drawn between jury cases and cases in which there was no verdict by a jury or no court decision in which public policy considerations would be a factor as the issue much less the risk of relitigation would not arise.[27]

Their Lordships acknowledged that public policy considerations could apply in the case of collateral challenges to criminal or civil decisions but concluded in the case of collateral challenges to such decisions or verdicts, that the abuse of process principle enunciated in *Hunter v Chief Constable of the West Midlands Police*[28] would provide a sufficient check and balance in such instances.[29] According to the principle enunciated in *Hunter*, the court can strike out as an abuse of process, a second action in which the plaintiff seeks to relitigate issues decided in earlier proceedings if such relitigation would be manifestly unfair to the defendant or would bring the administration of justice into disrepute.

Additionally, their Lordships were of the view that the new Civil Procedure Rules 1999 would restrict the ability of clients to bring unmeritous and vexatious claims as the rules confer on the court extensive power to strike out unsustainable claims.[30]

In the case of criminal convictions, the House of Lords was of the opinion that where a criminal conviction was set aside there could be no public policy objections to an action in negligence being brought by the client against his legal representative at a criminal trial.[31]

With respect to collateral challenges to civil decisions, in particular, the principles of *res judicata* issue estoppel and abuse of process would, in the court's view, provided sufficient protection against any risk of abuse by potential litigants.[32]

Lord Steyn summed up the court's position in respect of this core reason. He concluded:

> A barrister's immunity is not needed to deal with collateral attacks on criminal and civil decisions. The public interest is satisfactorily protected by independent principles and powers of the court.[33]

(iv) Duty of the Advocate to the Court and Divided Loyalty

Their Lordships agreed that it was essential to protect and not undermine the overriding duty of an advocate to the court but it doubted whether advocate immunity was necessary to ensure that barristers respect their duty to the court.[34] Indeed, as Lord Steyn observed, in the European Union, advocates have no such immunity.[35]

With respect to the issue of divided loyalty Lord Hoffman expressed the view that the court's power to make a wasted costs order against a solicitor as well as a barrister by reason of their misconduct, default or negligence in the conduct of litigation would act as a sufficient deterrent or check and balance on the advocate attorney.[36] Although the wasted costs order which was introduced by s.4 of the Court and Legal Services Act 1990 was originally thought to be appliable only to solicitors, the Court of Appeal judgment in *Ridehalgh v Horsefield*[37] established unequivocally that it was applicable to both barristers and solicitors.

OTHER REASONS

Having examined and essentially disposed of the core reasons for the retention of an advocate's immunity from suit, the court turned its attention to the development and changes in the law, the legal profession and the wider society, which led it to conclude in the words of Lord Steyn:

> In today's world, the decision (in *Rondel v Worsley*) no longer correctly reflects public policy. The basis of the immunity of barristers has gone.[38]

In arriving at this conclusion, the court considered in particular:

(i) the changes in the legal profession which have resulted in the law becoming more commercial, barristers being permitted to advertise and to enter into contracts for legal services with professional clients,[39]

(ii) the growing awareness of the public of their legal rights coupled with the public perception that the law singles out its own for protection no matter how great the breach of the barrister,[40] and

(iii) developments in the law of negligence, which have incrementally whittled away at the protection from suits in negligence which barristers' immunity has traditionally premised on the inability to contract.[41]

IMPLICATIONS OF THE HALL V SIMONS DECISION FOR THE ENGLISH-SPEAKING CARIBBEAN

The impact of the *Hall v Simons* decision on the question of advocate immunity in the respective Caribbean territories is too early to predict. In the case of Antigua & Barbuda, Barbados, Guyana, St. Lucia and Trinidad & Tobago, an attorney's immunity from suit is specifically governed by the relevant statutory provision contained in the respective Legal Profession Acts of these territories.[42] The statutory provision is clear and unequivocal; an attorney is immune from an action in negligence in the conduct and management of a case in court. Accordingly, unless and until the relevant statutory provision in these territories is repealed, the *Hall v Simons* decision is simply of intellectual relevance or importance.

In the case of Jamaica and The Bahamas advocate immunity is governed by the common law. Although these territories receive the English common law the cut off point for the reception of the English common-law pre-dates the *Hall v Simons* decision.

POSITION IN EASTERN CARIBBEAN (save Antigua & Barbuda and St. Lucia)

In the Eastern Caribbean territories (save Antigua & Barbuda and St. Lucia) the position with respect to advocate attorney is governed (as is the case in England) by the common law. In addition the respective Supreme Court Acts of the Eastern Caribbean territories (with the notable exception of St. Lucia) provide for the incorporation of English law and procedure relating to solicitors; taxation, and bills of costs.[43] However the relevant provision does not provide for the reception of English law relating to barristers. As the issue of immunity from suit is referable to advocates and solicitors acting as advocates, it remains to be seen whether the decision in *Hall v Simons* will be adopted in these territories.

ENDNOTES

1. Antigua & Barbuda - s.10(1) Legal Profession Act 9/1997
   Barbados - s.10(1) Legal Profession Act Cap. 370A
   Guyana - s.9(b) Legal Practitioners (Amendment) Act 3/1980
   St. Lucia - s.22 Legal Profession Act Cap. 31/2000
   Trinidad & Tobago - s.22(1) Legal Profession Act Cap. 21/1986
2. [1967] 3 All ER 993, [1969] 1 AC 191 HL
3. [1978] 3 All ER 1033, [1980] AC 198 HL
4. Antigua & Barbuda - s.10(1) Legal Profession Act 7/1997
   Barbados - s.10(1) Legal Profession Act Cap. 370A
   St. Lucia - s.22(2) and (3) Legal Profession Act 31/2000
   Trinidad & Tobago - s.22(2) and (3) Legal Profession Act 21/1986
5. See *Rondel v Worsley, supra.*
6. Guyana - s.9 (b) Legal Practitioners (Amendment) Act 3/1980
   St. Lucia - s.22(2) and (3) Legal Profession Act 31/2000
   Trinidad & Tobago - s.22(2) and (3) Legal Profession Act 21/1986.
7. Antigua & Barbuda - s.10(1) Legal Profession Act 9/1997.
   Barbados - s.10(1) Legal Profession Act Cap. 370A.
8. [1967] 3 All ER 993, [1969] 1 AC 191 HL.
9. [1967] 3 All ER 999 at p.1033 HL.
10. See chapter 8. With respect to the prior position see also the Guyanese case of *Lopes v Adams and Vanier* (1965) 9 WIR 183.
11. [1974] 1 NZLR 180.

12. [1978] 3 All ER 1033 HL, [1980] AC 198.
13. [1967] 3 All ER 993 at p.1035 HL
14. [1978] 3 All ER 1033 at p. 1037, HL
15. [1989] 1 All ER 129 CA.
16. [1997] 3 All ER 909.
17. [2000] 3 WLR 543 HL
18. *Ibid.*
19. The relevant rule of the Code/Canon of Ethics of the various territories save Barbados provides in effect that an attorney is not obliged to act either as advisor or advocate for every person who may wish to become his client; he has a right to decline employment. However, where a person is charged with a capital offence, except for good reasons he shall not refuse to act. In the case of Barbados, although the attorney may decline a retainer, he may only do this in special circumstances such as conflict of interest. See on this:

Antigua & Barbuda	-	Code of Ethics, Part A rr. 9, 17
Barbados	-	Code of Ethics Part II r.12
Eastern Caribbean (save Antigua & Barbuda and St. Lucia)		
	-	OECS Code of Ethics Part A rr. 9, 17
Jamaica	-	Canon of Ethics III (a)
St. Lucia	-	Canon of Ethics Part A rr. 9, 17
The Bahamas	-	Code of Professional Conduct Rule XIII Commentary 9
Trinidad & Tobago	-	Code of Ethics Part A rr. 9, 17.

20. *Supra* at 550. See also dictum of Lord Hoffmann at p. 558.
21. *Supra* at pp. 585- 586 per Lord Hope of Craighead.
22. See in particular the dicta of Lord Hoffman at p.571; of Lord Hope of Craighead at pp. 585, 586; of Lord Browne-Wilkinson at p.556.
23. *Supra* at p.551.
24. *Supra* at p. 562.
25. *Ibid.* See in particular the dicta of Lord Hoffmann at p.571; of Lord Hope of Craighead at pp.585, 586; and of Lord Browne-Wilkinson at p.556.
26. *Ibid* at p.571. See also the dicta of Lord Hoffmann at pp. 572 to 574; of Lord Steyn; and of Lord Browne-Wilkinson at pp. 556, 557.
27. *Ibid.* See also the dictum of Lord Browne-Wilkinson at pp. 556-557.
28. [1982] AC 529, [1981] 3 WLR 906, [1981] 3 All ER 727 HL
29. See on this the dicta of Lord Steyn at pp. 551-552; of Lord Browne-Wilkinson at pp. 556-557; of Lord Hope of Craighead at p.598; and of Lord Hutton at p.601.
30. See in particular the dicta of Lord Steyn at p.554; Lord Hoffman at pp.562, 562, 565, 566, 567, 577.
31. See in particular the dictum of Lord Browne-Wilkinson at pp.556, 557 and 558.
32. *Supra* at p.552 per Lord Steyn
33. *Ibid.*
34. See in particular the dicta of Lord Steyn at pp.552-554; of Lord Hoofman at pp.558, 563-565; and of Lord Hope of Craighead at pp. =586-588, 596, 597.
35. *Ibid.* p.552.
36. *Ibid.* at p. 565, 566.
37. [1994] Ch. 205 CA, [1994] 3 All ER 848, [1994] 3 WLR 462 CA.
38. *Hall v Simons* [2000] 3 WLR 543 *supra* at p.543.

39. *Ibid* at p.554
40. *Ibid* at p.554
41. *Ibid* at 554
42. See endnote 4 *supra.*
43. See Chapter 1 at pp. 1 & 2 ante

12. PROFESSIONAL MISCONDUCT

INTRODUCTION

Professional misconduct may be defined as conduct which involves a failure on the part of an attorney to fulfill his duty, in promoting in his own sphere of interest, the cause of justice.[1] This duty on the part of the attorney is wide-ranging in its scope. As Deyalsingh J noted in the Trinidad & Tobago case of *In the matter of Gail Robinson and Beverly Scobie, Solicitors and In the Matter of the Inherent Jurisdiction of the Court:*

> Unprofessional conduct is not limited to cases where the misconduct charged amounts to an indictable offence or is professional in character but extends to all cases where the solicitor's conduct is improper i.e. such as to render him unfit to be an officer of the court.[2]

In so far as upholding and maintaining professional standards of conduct, the court in England observed in *Re a Solicitor* [1975][3] that this was primarily a matter for the profession to determine and further that the court should accept the high standards set by the profession as expressed (in so far as England is concerned) through the Disciplinary Committee of the Law Society.

With respect to the Caribbean territories (save Guyana)[4] the respective Code/Canon of Ethics of these territories contains rules which govern and regulate the standards of professional conduct expected of attorneys-at-law. In this regard, although there is some variation in the wording, the Canon/Code of Ethics of the various territories (save The Bahamas) provides in effect that specific breaches of the rules contained therein shall constitute professional misconduct and more specifically an attorney who commits such breaches shall be liable to any of the penalties which the Disciplinary Committee and or the court is empowered to impose.[5]

The Code/Canon of Ethics also provides in effect that certain breaches, while not automatically amounting to punishable professional misconduct, is a derogation from the high standards of conduct expected from an attorney and may, depending on the circumstances of the case amount to such conduct or form a material ingredient thereof.[6]

In the case of The Bahamas, it is to be noted that there are no provisions in The Bahamas Bar (Code of Professional Conduct) Regulations which require mandatory compliance with the rules of professional conduct set out in the Code. In this regard Regulation 3 merely directs that every attorney shall in the pursuit of his profession comply with and be subject to the Rules of Professional Conduct.

Notwithstanding the position in The Bahamas, professional misconduct, on the part of an attorney in effect involves a breach of the Rules set out in the Code/Canon of Ethics of the various territories. Accordingly, this chapter will focus on professional misconduct in so far as it involves breaches of these rules. (The breaches of duty considered in this chapter are by no means exhaustive. For an examination of breaches which are specifically relevant to proceedings in court see chapter 14 post).

BREACHES OF DUTY CONSTITUTING PROFESSIONAL MISCONDUCT

It should be noted at the outset that there is a duty on every attorney to report improper or unprofessional conduct by a colleague to the Law/Bar Association or other appropriate tribunal save where the information relating to improper or unprofessional conduct is received in professional confidence.[7]

(1) Breach of Duty to State and Public

An attorney is under a duty not to advise or assist in the violation of the laws of the state and when he does so, he is guilty of professional misconduct.[8] As the court observed in *Goodenough v Spencer*:

> No solicitor or counsel has a right in the discharge of his professional duties to involve his client, by his advice, in the violation of the laws of the State and when he does so, he becomes implicated in the client's guilt, if when following the advice, a crime against the laws of the State is committed.[9]

All Jurisdictions

In addition, an attorney is guilty of professional misconduct where he enters into a partnership or fee sharing arrangement concerning the practise of law with non-qualified bodies or persons, or where he holds out a person who is not qualified to practise law as a partner, associate, consultant or attorney-at-law.[10]

(2) Breach of Duty to The Court

As an officer of the court, an attorney is under a duty to be 'a helper in the administration of justice'[11] and accordingly, he is under a duty to maintain a respectful attitude towards the court and not engage in undignified or discourteous conduct which is degrading to the court.[12]

As Reid LJ noted in *Rondel v Worsley*:

> Counsel as an officer of the court concerned in the administration of justice has an over-riding duty to the court.[13]

Accordingly an attorney who is in breach of any of his recognised duties to the court as one of its officer is guilty of professional misconduct. Such breaches include:

(i) willfully making false accusation against a judge or magistrate.[14]

(ii) writing abusive, threatening and improper letters to the court, the object of which is to *inter alia* influence the judge to depart from his judicial duty and adopt a cause he would not otherwise pursue.[15]

(iii) willfully acting without authority.[16]

(iv) permitting a client to swear a false affidavit.[17] In the Guyanese case of *Re a Legal Practitioner*,[18] a case in which the attorney's client swore a false affidavit to the effect that all the debts of the estate were fully paid, the court held, that based on the special circumstances of the cases, that the attorney-at-law was not guilty of professional misconduct but that he would however have been found so guilty if he had knowingly and deliberately permitted his client to swear a false affidavit. Indeed in *Re Davies*,[19] a solicitor was suspended for two years because he *inter alia* allowed his client to swear a false affidavit, which both he and his client knew to be false.

(v) attempting to influence the court by e.g. privately discussing a pending case with the presiding judge. The extent to which the court might or might not be influenced by such communications is not the issue rather it is in the interest of justice that no impression of partiality or favouritism on the part of the court be created.

(vi) knowingly producing in court a document which was not properly stamped as provided for by the relevant law.[20]

(vii) knowingly taking a bad point to deceive the court. But as Lord Denning MR observed in *Abraham v Jutson,* 'An attorney is not guilty of misconduct simply because he takes a point, which the tribunal holds to be bad. He only becomes guilty of misconduct if he is dishonest'.[21] An example of taking a bad point includes referring to an authority which shows it clearly to be a bad point.

(viii) knowingly using perjured evidence or testimony or participating in the creation of evidence the attorney knows to be false.[22]

(ix) introducing improper evidence, irrelevant evidence and making unfair remarks to the jury.[23]

(3) Breach of Duty to Client

In General

An attorney is under a duty to always act in the best interest of his client, to represent him honestly, competently and zealously and endeavour to obtain the benefit of any and every remedy and defence which is authorised by law.[24] This general duty on the part of an attorney was considered in the Trinidad & Tobago case of *Sankar v The State*[25] a case in which the Privy Council held that the defence attorney in a murder trial had failed in his duty:

(i) to explain to his client his position with respect to giving or failing to give evidence; and

(ii) to place the options before his client even if he, the attorney, should then feel obliged to withdraw from the trial.

In respect of the attorney's retainer, on acceptance of the retainer the attorney is in breach of his duty if he ventures to advise until he has obtained full knowledge of the facts. He should therefore avoid making bold assurances and beware of rash and confident guarantees especially when his employment depends on these assurances.[26]

In this regard an attorney is under a duty to avoid useless litigation; to advise his client candidly and honesty about his chances of success or failure and not to allow the person who trusts him to embark on useless hopeless litigation or to continue proceedings where the prospects of success are non-existent. However, as Sir Thomas Bingham MR noted in *Ridehalgh v Horsefield*:

> A legal representative is not to be held to have acted improperly simply because he acts for a party who pursues a claim or defence which is plainly doomed to fail...Legal representatives will of course, whether barristers or solicitors, advise the client of the perceived weakness of the case and the risk of failure. But clients are free to reject advice and insist that the case be litigated. [27]

Nevertheless, as was held in the Guyanese case of *Bartrum v Hopkinson*[28] an attorney, should not by reason of misrepresentation, induce his client to settle an action contrary to his wishes.

In Particular

An attorney is *inter alia* guilty of professional misconduct *vis-a-vis* his clients in the following specific instances:

(i) Confidentiality

Where he fails or neglects to preserve the confidentiality of client except if such communication has been made in furtherance of a crime, fraud or other unlawful transaction.[29]

(ii) Conflict of Interest

Where he acts in any manner in which his professional duties and his personal interest conflict or are likely to conflict.[30]

(iii) Multiple Representation

Where in the case of multiple representation, he acts or continues to act where the interest of his respective clients are likely to conflict or his professional judgment is likely to be impaired.[31]

(iv) Fees

Where he charges fees which are unfair and unreasonable or where he charges fees which are either an over or under-estimate of the services rendered.[32]

(v) Duty to Exercise Care and Skill

An attorney is under a general duty to act expeditiously in dealing with his client's matters and to bring to the discharge of his duties thereunder, the necessary degree of skill, competence and knowledge. In failing to exercise due care and skill in the conduct of his duties an attorney may be guilty of professional misconduct. This misconduct may, depending on the facts of the case, be compensatory or punitive in nature.

(a) Professional Misconduct of a Compensatory Nature – Wasted Costs in Proceedings

In proceedings in court where an attorney acts in the capacity of a solicitor or instructing attorney and costs are needlessly incurred or wasted by his failure or default in acting with reasonable expedition and competence, an attorney is deemed to be guilty of professional misconduct. However in such instances of professional misconduct the court does not exercise a punitive jurisdiction over the offending attorney. Its jurisdiction, which is exclusive to the court is compensatory in nature and is limited to the court making an order as to costs against the attorney personally.[33]

(b) Professional Misconduct of a Punitive Nature

Although there is some variation in the actual wording, the respective Code/Canon of Ethics of the various territories, provides that an attorney-at-law shall not act with unreasonable or undue delay, negligence or neglect[34] and in the case of Jamaica, inexcusable or deplorable negligence or neglect.[35] Such neglect or default on an attorney's part not only constitutes professional negligence (as was always the case) but may constitute professional misconduct in respect of which the court or other competent tribunal may properly exercise its punitive jurisdiction.

This rule is mandatory and is especially significant for the Caribbean as prior to the passage of a Code/Canon of Ethics in these territories there was no indigenous legal authority on this issue; reliance was placed on English case law authority.

In this regard, until the English Court of Appeal case of *Re A Solicitor* (1972)[36] the position in England appeared to be that professional negligence did not constitute professional misconduct of a punitive nature unless it involved dishonourable conduct or moral turpitude. However in *Re A Solicitor* (1972), the Court of Appeal held *inter alia* that negligence in a solicitor might amount to professional misconduct if it was inexcusable and such as to be regarded as deplorable by his professional colleagues. The Court also held that professional misconduct was not limited to cases which the solicitor had been guilty of disgraceful or dishonourable conduct.

Until fairly recently, the English position prior to *Re A Solicitor* (1972) seems to have been followed in the various Caribbean territories. This is exemplified by the 1976 Jamaican Court of Appeal case of *Diggs-White v Dawkins.*[37] In that case it was held *inter alia,* that negligence or neglect did not constitute professional misconduct of a punitive nature. In support of its decision the Court of Appeal relied on the English case of *Re Cooke*[38] in which Lord Esher, was quoted with approval. According to Lord Esher, in order for the court to exercise its penal jurisdiction over a solicitor it was not sufficient that his conduct would support an action for negligence or want of skill:

> It must be shown that the solicitor had done something dishonourable to him as a man and dishonourable in his profession.

However, subsequent to the decision in *Diggs-White v Dawkins*, the Legal Profession (Canon of Ethics) Rules were made pursuant to s.12(7) of the Legal Profession Act. In this regard Canon IV (s) of the Canon of Ethics provides in effect that 'in the performance of his duties an attorney-at-law shall not act with inexcusable or deplorable negligence or neglect'.

The effect of the inclusion of this rule based *inter alia* on the authority of the 1986 Jamaican Court of Appeal decision of *Witter v Forbes*[39] is that professional negligence may constitute professional misconduct of a punitive or penal nature although the negligence or neglect does not involve dishonourable conduct or moral turpitude.

In this regard the facts of *Witter v Forbes* are instructive. In that case the attorney's client found himself indebted to Citibank in the sum of JA$15,000. After some negotiations with the attorney on behalf of his client, Citibank proposed a settlement in a letter dated January 27, 1979 and addressed to the client. This proposal was never communicated by the attorney to his client until October, 1980.

In proceedings brought before the General Legal Council for professional misconduct, one of the grounds of complaints was that the attorney was in breach *inter alia* of the above-mentioned Canon IV (s) of the Canon of Ethics.

The appellant attorney argued however that any finding of professional misconduct on his part, must involve an element of wrong doing, deceit or moral turpitude .

However in his leading argument, Carey JA stated that:

- that the Canon of Ethics under which that particular rule in respect of negligence falls, prescribes the standard of professional etiquette and professional conduct for attorneys-at-law *vis-a-vis* their clients; and
- that the Canon of Ethics made pursuant to s.12(7) of the Legal Profession Act provides *inter alia* that the Council may prescribe standards of professional etiquette and professional conduct for attorneys and that most significantly s.12(7) in effect provides that the Council may, by rules made for this purpose, direct that any specified breach of the rules shall constitute misconduct in a professional respect.

Accordingly, the Court held that pursuant to s.12(7) of Legal Profession Act that the attorney had clearly infringed the relevant rules of Canon IV which as Carey JA pointed out do not require that the attorney's negligence involve dishonourable conduct or moral turpitude.

In the 1986 Barbadian case of *In the Matter of Winston Haynes,* and *In The Matter of the Legal Profession Act Cap. 370A*[40] it is significant that the Court of Appeal held that the attorney's gross negligence amounted to professional misconduct.

It seems therefore clear that, quite apart from the English case law,[41] by the inclusion of a specific rule with respect to negligence in the mandatory provisions of the respective Code/Canon of Ethics of the various territories, an attorney may be guilty of professional misconduct of a punitive nature even though the negligence complained of does not involve dishonourable conduct.

(vi) Fraud/Misappropriation of Clients' Funds

As a general rule, any form of fraud or dishonesty committed by an attorney against the interest of his client will be deemed to be professional misconduct. This includes misappropriation of a client's funds,[42] failure to apply a client's funds for the purpose for which it was intended,[43] overcharging,[44] and failing to keep proper accounts.[45]

In this regard, although there is some variation in the wording, the respective Code/Canon of Ethics of the various territories provides in effect that:

(i) an attorney-at-law shall never mingle funds of others with his own and he shall at all times be able to refund money he holds for others; and

(ii) an attorney-at-law shall keep such accounts as clearly and accurately to distinguish the financial position between himself and his clients as and when required.[46]

Apart from the abovementioned rules, the respective Legal Profession Acts of Antigua & Barbuda, Barbados, Jamaica, St. Lucia and Trinidad & Tobago, contain provisions which in effect empower the Law/Bar Association to make Accounts Rules prescribing *inter alia,* the type of clients' accounts to be kept, the manner of operating them, the particulars to be recorded and the manner of recording them. [47]

In this regard, it is to be noted that the Bar Association of Barbados, and most recently the General Legal Council of Jamaica have made Accounts Rules under their respective Legal Profession Acts.[48] These rules are quite detailed and comprehensive and provide guidelines and provisions for the keeping of client accounts, maintaining of books of assets in respect of client's money received, held or paid by the attorney and the payment of interest on client's money.

(4) Breach of Duty to Profession and Fellow Attorneys

In General

In accordance with the relevant Rule in the Code/Canon of Ethics of the various territories, an attorney's conduct to his fellow attorneys 'shall be characterised by courtesy, fairness and good faith and he shall not permit ill-feelings between his clients to affect his relationship with his colleagues'.[49]

In Particular

(i) Undertakings

An attorney is under a duty to fulfill an undertaking not only given to the court but also to his fellow attorneys. Breach of such undertaking not only constitutes in the proper case a contempt of court but also constitutes professional misconduct.[50]

(ii) Touting and Advertising

The Code/Canon of Ethics of the various territories contains extensive provisions and guidelines with respect to advertising and touting and cautions that an attorney should not in carrying out his practice or otherwise permit an act which is likely to attract business unfairly or unreasonably be regarded as touting or advertising.[51]

With respect to advertising, the relevant rule of the Code also cautions attorneys to avoid by direct or indirect means, attracting the client of another attorney; more specifically, that an attorney shall not in any way make use of any form of advertisement 'to attract clients to himself or any firm with which he is associated and he shall not permit, authorise or encourage anyone to do so or reward anyone for doing so on his behalf'.[52]

One of the most common forms of attracting business is cutting fees; another is any arrangement between an attorney and for example, a real estate broker in which the broker makes a practise of suggesting to purchasers that the services of a particular attorney should be retained.

However, although an attorney is not permitted to advertise, he is nevertheless allowed dignified identification of himself as an attorney-at-law. In this regard, calling cards, office signs, letterheads or directory listings or any other form of professional identification may be used provided the same is dignified and restrained and compatible with the attorney's existing practise.[53]

It is to be noted that in the United Kingdom advertising is permitted as of February 1, 1987, provided that the advertisement complies with the Solicitor's Publicity Code, provided *inter alia*:

(a) the solicitor's independence is not undermined, or compromised; and
(b) the solicitor maintains a proper standard of work.

In so far as touting is concerned, touting is defined as soliciting custom fraudulently and it is an offence whether done by an attorney personally or by someone on his behalf. In this regard, the relevant rule of the Code/Canon of Ethics of the various territories provides that an attorney is deemed to be in breach of his professional duty if he pays or rewards any person directly or indirectly for the purpose of procuring the attorney to be retained in his professional capacity.[54] In Guyana, s.12 of the Legal Practitioners Act Cap 4:01 provides that touting is an offence punishable by conviction.[55]

Criminal Offence

In General

Where an attorney commits a criminal offence which in the opinion of the Court or other competent tribunal is of a nature likely to bring the legal profession into disrepute, the commission of the offence shall constitute professional misconduct. In this regard, the offence must be of a personally disgraceful character, the commission of which would make the attorney unfit to be a member of a strictly honourable profession.[56]

If it is such an offence, the contention that the attorney was wrongfully convicted will not be entertained. Further, it is not necessary that the attorney be prosecuted for the offence or where prosecuted, acquitted on a technical defence once the Court, Disciplinary Committee or the other competent tribunal is satisfied of the facts constituting the crime.

In the case of *Re King*[57] an attorney was convicted at first instance of conspiracy to defraud. On appeal the decision was reversed because the indictment was defective. Upon proceedings to strike him off the Roll of the Court, Denman CJ said:

> We must not merely because the indictment is bad in point of law, shut our eyes to the fact that the jury have convicted him of conduct rendering him unfit to be an attorney.

Further, it is not necessary that the offence or crime be of a pecuniary nature nor that the attorney should have been convicted as a practising attorney. All that is necessary is that the offence brings dishonour to the profession generally.[58]

In Particular

(i) Offences involving Fraud Dishonesty

An attorney who has been convicted of an offence involving fraud or dishonesty will *de facto* be deemed guilty of professional misconduct in his capacity as attorney.[59] Such offences include bribery, forgery, making false affidavits, embezzlement, obtaining money by threats, bribery, fraud and conspiracy to pervert the course of justice.[60]

(ii) Offences Involving Immoral Conduct

This is a second class of cases in respect of which disciplinary sanctions may be imposed against an attorney. Examples of such offences include knowingly permitting premises owned by the attorney to be used as a brothel, acts of indecent assault and using threatening or abusive language intended to provoke a breach of peace.

ENDNOTES

1. *Myers v Elman* [1940] AC 282 at p.319 HL
2. HCA No. 2 of 1985 Trinidad & Tobago (unreported) at p.24. See also *Re Hill* (1868) LR 3 QB 543.
3. [1975] 1 QB 475.
4. With respect to Guyana, although there are no prescribed rules of conduct, the Code/Canon of Ethics of the other territories is in effect (as previously stated), a codification of common law principles and as such the guidelines set out of these rules are equally applicable to Guyana.
5. Antigua & Barbuda - Code of Ethics, Part B r.35(1)
   Barbados - Code of Ethics Part VIII r.90(1). See also Part I r.4
   Eastern Caribbean (save Antigua & Barbuda and St. Lucia)
   - OECS Code of Ethics Part B r.35(1)
   Jamaica - Canon of Ethics Canon VIII (d)
   St. Lucia - Code of Ethics Part B r.40
   Trinidad & Tobago - Code of Ethics Part B r.35(1)
6. Antigua & Barbuda - Code of Ethics Part B r.35(2)
   Barbados - Code of Ethics Part VIII r.90(2). See also Part I r.4
   Eastern Caribbean (save Antigua & Barbuda and St. Lucia)
   - OECS Code of Ethics Part B r.35(2)
   Jamaica - Canon of Ethics Canon VIII (2)
   St. Lucia - Code of Ethics Part B r.54
   Trinidad & Tobago - Code of Ethics Part B r.35(2)
7. Antigua & Barbuda - Code of Ethics Part A r.44
   Barbados - Code of Ethics Part VIII r.48
   Eastern Caribbean (save Antigua & Barbuda and St. Lucia)
   - OECS Code of Ethics Part A r.44
   St. Lucia - Code of Ethics Part A r.43
   Trinidad & Tobago - Code of Ethics Part A r.44
8. Antigua & Barbuda - Code of Ethics Part A r.13
   Barbados - Code of Ethics Part II r.17
   Eastern Caribbean (save Antigua & Barbuda and St. Lucia)
   - OECS Code of Ethics Part A r.13
   St. Lucia - Code of Ethics Part A r.13
   The Bahamas - Code of Professional Conduct Canon II Commentary 6
   Trinidad & Tobago - Code of Ethics Part A r.13
   See also *R v Bullivant* [1900] 2 QB 163.
9. (1874) 46 Pr. 347
10. See chapter 3.
11. *Myers v Elman* [1940] AC 282 at 317 HL
12. See chapter 14.
13. [1967] 3 All ER 993 at 998 HL
14. Antigua & Barbuda - Code of Ethics, Part B r.20
    Barbados - Code of Ethics Part VIII r.76
    Eastern Caribbean (save Antigua & Barbuda and St. Lucia)
    - OECS Code of Ethics Part B r.20
    St. Lucia - Code of Ethics Part B r.23
    The Bahamas - Code of Professional Conduct Rule XII Commentary 4

Trinidad & Tobago - Code of Ethics Part B r.20

15. *LeChmere Charleton's Case* (1837) 2 My & Cr 316 per L. Cottingham LC
16. *Re Gray* (1869) 20 LT 730.
17. *Wheatley v Bastow* (1855) 7 De GM & G 558, [1843-60] All ER Rep. 644. See also the Jamaican case of *Re Henry* (1898) 7 SCJB 217.
18. (1959) LRBG 13.
19. (1898) 14 Times LR 332.
20. *DB Persaud v S Persaud and Somaria* (1939) LRBG 143
21. [1963] 2 All ER 402 at 404 CA.
22. See chapter 14.
23. *Ibid.*
24. Antigua & Barbuda - Code of Ethics, Part A r.21
    Barbados - Code of Ethics Part IV r.24
    Eastern Caribbean (save Antigua & Barbuda and St. Lucia)
    - OECS Code of Ethics Part A r.21
    St. Lucia - Code of Ethics Part A r.20
    The Bahamas - Code of Professional Conduct Rule III Commentary 6
    Trinidad & Tobago - Code of Ethics Part A r.21
25. 46 WIR 452. See also *Codrington (Alfred) v R* (1966) 48 WIR 86.
26. *Orchard v SE Electricity Board* [1978] 1 All ER 95, *Edward v Edwards*[1958] 2 All ER 179, *Ottley v Gilberg* (1845) 14 LJ Ch. 177, *Forrester v Francis* CLE 156/1983 Jamaica (unreported)
27. [1994] Ch 205 at pp.233-234. See also *Edwards v Edwards* [1958] 2 All ER 179.
28. (1931-37) LRBG 69.
29. See chapter 7.
30. See chapter 8.
31. See chapter 8. See also *Anderson v Watson* (1876) 2 SCJB 218.
32. See chapter 5.
33. See chapter 13.
34. Antigua & Barbuda - Code of Ethics, Part B r.18; See also Part A r.27
    Barbados - Code of Ethics Part VIII r.74; See also Part IV r.30
    Eastern Caribbean (save Antigua & Barbuda and St. Lucia)
    - OECS Code of Ethics Part B r.18, See also Part A r.27
    St. Lucia - Code of Ethics Part B r.21; See also Part A r.26
    The Bahamas - Code of Professional Conduct Rule II Commentary 6
    Trinidad & Tobago - Code of Ethics Part B r.18; See also Part A r.27
35. Canon of Ethics IV(s). See also Canon IV(r).
36. [1972] 2 All ER 811, [1972] 1 WLR 869 CA.
37. (1976) 23 WIR 102.
38. (1889) 5 TLR 407 CA and quoted at pp. 106, 107 of *Diggs-White v Dawkins, supra.*
39. CA 1/1986 Jamaica (unreported).
40. A number was not assigned to the matter. However the date of the judgment is January 31 of 1986, Barbados (unreported).
41. See on this *Re a Solicitor* [1972] 2 All ER 811, [1972] 1e 9/1982
42. *Re a Solicitor* 3 JLR 130, *Forde v The Law Society* (1986) 40 WIR 361, *SW Ogle & The Legal Practitioner Ordinance* (1931-38) LRBG, 87, *In the Matter of Gail Robinson and Beverly Scobie and In the Matter of the Inherent Jurisdiction of the Court* HCA 2 /1985 Trinidad and Tobago unreported

43. *Re a Solicitor* (1936-40) 3 JLR 95, *Re a Legal Practitioner* (1963) LRBG 331, *Re Browne* 7 Barb. L.R. 62, *Re Niles* (1993) 47 WIR 38.
44. *Re Eastmond* (1995) 50 WIR 76, *Anderson v Watson* (1876) 2 SCJB 218.
45. *Re a Solicitor* [1972] 2 All ER 811 CA, *Patterson v Matthews* (1923-24) Barb. LR 156.
46. Antigua & Barbuda - Code of Ethics, Part B rr.31, 32
Barbados - Code of Ethics Part VIII rr.87, 88
Eastern Caribbean (save Antigua & Barbuda and St. Lucia)
- OECS Code of Ethics Part B rr.31, 32
St. Lucia - Code of Ethics Part B rr.34,35
The Bahamas - Code of Professional Conduct Rule VI
Trinidad & Tobago - Code of Ethics Part B rr.31, 32
47. Antigua & Barbuda - s.17 Legal Profession Act 9/1997
Barbados - s.13 Legal Profession Act Cap. 370A
Jamaica - s.35 Legal Profession Act 1971
St. Lucia - s.33 Legal Profession Act 31/2000
Trinidad & Tobago - s.33 Legal Profession Act 21/1986
48. Barbados - Legal Profession (Accounts) Rules 1973
Jamaica - The Legal Profession (Accounts and Records) Regulations 1999.
49. Antigua & Barbuda - Code of Ethics Part A r.41
Barbados - Code of Ethics Part VI r.45
Eastern Caribbean (save Antigua & Barbuda and St. Lucia)
- OECS Code of Ethics Part A r.41
Jamaica - Canon of Ethics, Canon VI(a)
St. Lucia - Code of Ethics Part A r.40
The Bahamas - Code of Profession Conduct Rule XVI, Commentaries 1 and 2
Trinidad & Tobago - Code of Ethics Part A r.41
50. See chapter 9 at pp. 156-158 ante.
51. Antigua & Barbuda - Code of Ethics Part B r.5
Barbados - Code of Ethics Part VIII r.61
Eastern Caribbean (save Antigua & Barbuda and St. Lucia)
- OECS Code of Ethics Part B r.5
Jamaica - Canon of Ethics, Canon II(b)
St. Lucia - Code of Ethics Part B r. 5
The Bahamas - Code or Professional Conduct Rule X111Commentary 7
Trinidad & Tobago - Code of Ethics Part B r.5
52. Antigua & Barbuda - Code of Ethics Part B r.6(1). See also s.21(2) and (3) Legal Profession Act
Barbados - Code of Ethics Part VIII r.62(1)
Eastern Caribbean (save Antigua & Barbuda and St. Lucia)
- OECS Code of Ethics Part B r.6(1)
Jamaica - Canon of Ethics, Canon II(d)
St. Lucia - Code of Ethics Part B r. 6(1)
The Bahamas - With respect to The Bahamas, the Code of Professional Rule XIII provides guidelines with respect to advertising which, though not identical in the wording to the

Rules in the Code of Conduct of the other jurisdictions are nonetheless effectively the same.
Trinidad & Tobago - Code of Ethics Part B r.6(1)

53. Antigua & Barbuda - Code of Ethics Part B r.5
Barbados - Code of Ethics Part VIII r.61
Eastern Caribbean (save Antigua & Barbuda and St. Lucia)
- OECS Code of Ethics Part B r.5
St. Lucia - Code of Ethics Part B r. 5
The Bahamas - Code of Professional Conduct, Rule XIII Commentaries 5&7
Trinidad & Tobago - Code of Ethics Part B r.5

54. Antigua & Barbuda - Code of Ethics Part B r.6
Barbados - Code of Ethics Part VIII r.62
Eastern Caribbean (save Antigua & Barbuda and St. Lucia)
- OECS Code of EthicsPart B r.6
Jamaica - Canon of Ethics Canon IV(g)
St. Lucia - Code of Ethics Part B r.6
Trinidad & Tobago - Code of Ethics Part B 6
See also *Re Weise* (1915) 9 SCJB 443

55. See ss.13 and 14 Legal Practitioners Act Cap. 4:01. See also *Leonard v Erskine* (1970) 17 WIR 157

56. Antigua & Barbuda - Code of Ethics Part B r.7
Barbados - Code of Ethics Part VIII r 3
Eastern Caribbean (save Antigua & Barbuda and St. Lucia)
- OECS Code of Ethics Part B r.7
Jamaica - Canon of Ethics Canon III(k)
St. Lucia - Code of Ethics Part B r.10
Trinidad & Tobago - Code of Ethics Part B r.7
See also comments of Lord Esher MR in *Re Weare* [1893] 2 QB 439 at p.446. See also *Re Blake* (1860) E & E 34.

57. (1845) 8 QB 129

58. *Re Hill* (1868) LR 3 QB 543.

59. *Re Weare* supra

60. *Re Blake* supra. *Stephens v Hill* (1842) 10 M & W 28; *Re Sinanan* (1964) 7 WIR 93

13. PROFESSIONAL DISCIPLINE

Part I – Punitive Jurisdiction

INTRODUCTION

A lawyer who transgresses accepted standards of professional conduct is subject to the disciplinary jurisdiction of the court and/or other competent tribunal. This disciplinary jurisdiction is both punitive and compensatory in nature.[1] In this regard, it is to be noted that the exercise of the court's punitive jurisdiction over attorneys is separate and distinct from the legal rights and remedies which a client or other aggrieved party may have against such attorney. As Lord Esher MR observed in *Re Grey*[2] (and quoted in approval by Lyttleton Wills J in the St. Lucian case of *Becar v Cooper)*:

> The court has a punitive and disciplinary jurisdiction over solicitors as officers of the court which is not exercised for the purpose of enforcing legal rights but for the purpose of enforcing honourable conduct on the part of the court's own officers. That power of the court is quite distinct from any legal rights or remedies of the parties and cannot therefore, be affected by anything which affects the strict legal rights of the parties.[3]

POSITION IN ENGLAND

It is important in considering this subject, to consider the position in England and contrast it with the position which currently obtains in most of the English-speaking Caribbean for the following reasons:

(i) the very origin and development of legal professional discipline in the English-speaking Caribbean territories is firmly rooted in the British legal disciplinary system; and

(ii) prior to the establishment of the Council of Legal Education of the West Indies, barristers were British-trained and admitted to practice by the Inn at which they attended; in the case of solicitors, the vast majority undertook or completed their training in England and were admitted to by the High Court of England, before returning to their respective home territories.[4]

As the court observed in *AG of the Gambia v N'jie* in accordance with the common law of England, judges have the right to prohibit or suspend both barristers and solicitors from practice.[5]

Barristers

However with respect to barristers, this power had been delegated almost exclusively to the Inns of Court from time immemorial and in more modern times, to the Senate of the Four Inns of Court, by a resolution passed in 1967[6] and then in 1974, to the Senate of the Inns of Court and the Bar. In this regard, the benchers of each Inn has the sole authority to admit students and to call duly qualified students to the Bar. Most significantly, the benchers have traditionally exercised and continue to exercise almost exclusive disciplinary jurisdiction over barristers. Historically the English courts have never purported to exercise any considerable jurisdiction over their conduct. In practice, the extent of this summary jurisdiction has been to refuse the offending barrister audience. However, it is to be noted as was held in *Re Gray's Inn* that:

> any person disbarred by his Inn of Court has always been and is entitled to appeal to the judges to revise the decree of his benchers disbarring him.[7]

The extent to which the Bar operates independently of the court with respect to the discipline of barristers is exemplified by the fact that the Bar formulates and determines its own rules of professional conduct. The Code of Conduct of the Bar for England and Wales is purely self-regulatory and not subject to the approval of the judges of the court.[8]

Solicitors

With respect to solicitors, solicitors are officers of the courts in which they practise and in this regard the position in England is the same in the English-speaking Caribbean in that attorneys-at-law in the various Caribbean territories are officers of the court even in territories where the profession is not fused. This is because as is the case with solicitors in England, attorneys in the Caribbean are admitted to practise by the Court, their names are entered on the Roll of the Court and it follows, as Denning MR remarked in *R & T Thew v Reeves (No 2),* that they should be subject to the disciplinary jurisdiction of the court.[9]

In this regard, the rationale for the court's disciplinary jurisdiction over solicitors was considered in *Stephens v Hill*[10] and quoted with approval by Lord Wright in *Myers v Elman*. Lord Wright observed:

> The underlying principle is that the court has a right and duty to supervise the conduct of its solicitors and to visit with penalties, any conduct of a solicitor which is of such a nature as to tend to defeat justice in the very cause in which he is engaged professionally.[11]

This view was echoed in the Guyanese case of *Re A Legal Practitioner* where the court noted that:

> The courts are the defenders and also the guardians of the honour of the legal profession. The faith and trust reposed by the public in members of the profession must be maintained and the standard of conduct kept at a high level by the court and by the profession itself. If the conduct of a lawyer falls beneath that what is expected of him, the Court has a duty to take appropriate action in the matter.[12]

It is perhaps for the very reasons stated above that it is only within fairly recent times that the courts in England have delegated their punitive powers to the Law Society and even this was effected incrementally.

Indeed, when the Disciplinary Committee of the Law Society in England was first established in 1888, its powers were limited to investigating complaints, to dismissing complaints which had no merit and to making recommendations to the court for the court to take the appropriate disciplinary action. All punitive powers ie. fining, suspending or striking a solicitor off the Roll were exercised exclusively by the Court. However in 1919 the Disciplinary Committee of the Law Society was given full punitive powers, ie. *inter alia,* the power to fine, suspend and strike a solicitor off the Roll of the Court.[13]

The basis for this almost exclusive delegation of punitive powers to the Law Society was considered by Denning MR in *R & T Thew v Reeves (No 2)*. Denning LJ observed:

> Nowadays it would usually be inappropriate for any judge to exercise his punitive jurisdiction of his own motion. The judge would appear to be both prosecutor and judge. This is a role which does not become him well. It should be avoided in all but the most exceptional cases.[14]

POSITION IN THE CARIBBEAN

With the exceptions of The Bahamas and Jamaica and to a limited extent, Trinidad & Tobago and St. Lucia, the punitive jurisdiction of the courts has not been delegated; it is still exercised exclusively by the Court, and it is exercisable over all attorneys-at-law, even in those territories where the profession is not fused. This is because in the Caribbean, as stated above, all attorneys-at-law are admitted to practise by the courts.

The rationale for the retention by the court of its punitive jurisdiction in most of the English-speaking Caribbean was considered by Lord Wynford in *Re Antigua & Barbuda JJ*[15] which was quoted with approval in the Trinidad & Tobago case of *Re Sinanan*.[16] Lord Wynford observed with respect to barristers:

> In the colonies there are no Inns of Court, but it is essential for the due administration of justice that some persons shall have authority to determine who are fit persons to practise as advocates and attorneys there. Now advocates have always been admitted in the colonial courts by the judges and the judges alone. The power of suspending from practise must, we think, be incidental to that of admitting to practise as is the case in England with regard to attorneys. In Antigua & Barbuda, the character of advocates and attorneys are given to one person; the court therefore that confers both characters may, for just cause take both away.

Although the above observation was made in 1830 with respect to Antigua & Barbuda (and prior to fusion of the profession in Antigua), it still holds true not only for Antigua & Barbuda but also for most of the Caribbean territories.

EXTENT AND ABMIT OF THE COURT'S INHERENT DISCIPLINARY JURISDICTION

The extent and ambit of the court's inherent jurisdiction to punish an attorney on its own motion, without reference to the relevant disciplinary tribunal, was considered at length in the Trinidad & Tobago case of *In the matter of Gail Robinson and Beverly Scobie and In the Matter of the Inherent Jurisdiction of the Court.*[170]

In that case which was decided prior to fusion of the profession in Trinidad & Tobago, two solicitors were summoned to appear in the High Court to show cause why they should not be disciplined by way of having their names struck off the Roll of the Court. The facts which led up to the hearing of disciplinary charges by the judge are instructive. A summary judgment application had been made by the National Insurance Board (NIB), a client of the law firm of which the two solicitors were partners, for the payment over to NIB of the balance of three million dollars with interest, which sum NIB had entrusted to the solicitors.

At the conclusion of the summary judgment proceedings, Deyalsingh J, the presiding judge, after ruling in favour of NIB, determined that a *prima facie* case of wrongful conversion had been made out against the two solicitors.

After consideration and examination of the various authorities, Deyalsingh J concluded that in spite of the objections of the legal representative for the Disciplinary Committee of the Law Society, that, as a judge of the High Court, he had a right and duty to exercise the court's inherent jurisdiction to discipline the two solicitors. Indeed Deyalsingh J, emphasized that:

> The court's inherent jurisdiction in respect of solicitors cannot be disputed. It is the guardian of the good conduct of the profession and it is incumbent on the court to see that the conduct of its officers is beyond reproach and punish those whose conduct is unbecoming of the officer.[18]

Although the *Gail Robinson* case was decided prior to the passage of the Legal Profession Act 21/1986, the court's inherent punitive jurisdiction has been expressly retained by s.42 of the Legal Profession Act. In this regard, it is to be noted that the respective Legal Profession Acts of Barbados, Antigua & Barbuda, Jamaica, St. Lucia and Guyana[19] also contain the equivalent statutory provision.

Nevertheless it is submitted that in spite of the inherent right of the court to exercise its punitive jurisdiction on its own motion, the proper course for the court to adopt, except in the most urgent and exceptional cases, is for the judge to make or cause the Registrar to make a report to the relevant Disciplinary Tribunal where evidence of misconduct is brought to its attention at the hearing of matter or other proceedings in court. Indeed the respective Legal Profession Acts of Antigua & Barbuda, Barbados, Trinidad & Tobago, St. Lucia and Jamaica, expressly provide that:

> At the hearing of a matter in which a Judge considers that an act of professional misconduct or criminal offence has been committed by an attorney-at-law, he may make or cause the Registrar to make an application to the Committee in respect of the attorney-at-law.[20]

However, a course which is open and proper for the court to adopt in cases where there is evidence of criminal wrongdoing on the part of the attorney (and which was also adopted by Deyalsingh J in *the Gail Robinson* case) is for the judge to refer the matter to the office of the Director of Public Prosecution (DPP) or equivalent office in the various territories. Indeed in the Barbadian Court of Appeal case of *In the Matter of Jeffrey L Toppin, Attorney-at-law and In the Matter of the Legal Profession Act Cap. 370A,*[21] the Court of Appeal ordered that the attorney's name be removed from the Roll of the Court for gross professional misconduct, *inter alia*, for the misappropriation of funds of his client and failing to account to the client for monies paid to him. The court further ordered that the papers in the matter be referred to the DPP for his consideration with respect to further proceedings.

THE EXERCISE OF THE COURT'S PUNITIVE JURISDICTION IN THE CARIBBEAN

Trinidad & Tobago

Prior to the passage in 1986 of Legal Profession Act 21/1986, (which Act *inter alia* fused the legal profession) the punitive discipline of barristers and solicitors was exercised exclusively by the courts.

Barristers

With respect to barristers, although they were admitted to practise by the local courts, the court as late as 1962 seemed hesitant to exercise its inherent punitive jurisdiction over barristers. This reluctance was mainly because, at that date, most, if not all, barristers practising law in Trinidad & Tobago were trained at one of the Inns of Court in England and were admitted to practise by the Inn of Court at which they had attended prior to returning home. This reluctance on the part of the Trinidad & Tobago court is reflected in the judgment in the landmark case of *Re Sinanan.*[22] In that case the Attorney General moved the court for an order that Mr. Sinanan, a British trained barrister-at-law be struck off the Roll of barristers in Trinidad & Tobago on the ground that he was totally unfit to continue to practise as a barrister by reason of his conviction of the offence of fraudulent conversion.

However it was objected on behalf of Mr. Sinanan that the judges of the Supreme Court they had no jurisdiction to prohibit or suspend a barrister from practice. Indeed the court in its judgment acknowledged that:

> It is common ground that the judges have never themselves sought and that they have not heretofore at any time been invited to exercise any discipline over barristers although occasions have arisen in the past when such a power if exercisable may properly have been exercised.[23]

After consideration of various authorities, in particular the case of the *Attorney General of Gambia v N'jie,* the court concluded that as judges of the Supreme Court admitted barristers to practise in Trinidad & Tobago they also had the power to prohibit or suspend them from practice.[24]

As a direct result of the recommendations made by the court in *Re Sinanan,* the Barristers Disciplinary Rules (1965) were passed pursuant to s.76 and s.77 of the then Supreme Court of Judicature Act 12/1962 and a Barristers Disciplinary Committee established.[25] The Committee was given limited powers, i.e. the power to investigate complaints, dismiss those complaints which in the opinion of the Committee were without merit, and where relevant, make recommendation to the court for the court to take the appropriate disciplinary action.

Solicitors

With respect to solicitors, a Disciplinary Committee was established in 1943 under the Solicitors' Ordinance Ch. 7 No. 4 renamed the Solicitors Act Chap 6:50 under the 1981 Revised Laws of Trinidad & Tobago. This Committee was appointed by the Chief Justice with the concurrence of a puisne judge and comprised seven solicitors. However, as with the case with barristers, the Committee's powers were limited to inquiries into allegations of professional misconduct and where appropriate forwarding complaints to the High Court with their recommendations in instances where the Committee was of the opinion that a case has been made out which might justify the taking of disciplinary action.

Current Position

In 1986, the legal profession was fused by the passage of the Legal Profession Act 21/1986. Under s.36(1) of the Act, a Disciplinary Committee for the newly fused profession was established. Pursuant to s.39(1), the Disciplinary Committee was given limited disciplinary powers, that is the power:

(i) to impose a fine as it thinks proper;
(ii) to reprimand an attorney; and
(iii) to order an attorney to pay to the applicant or person aggrieved such sum into court by way of compensation and reimbursement and such further sum in respect of the expenses incidental to the hearing of the application and consideration of the report as the Committee thinks fit.

In addition, as was the case previously in respect of solicitors and barristers, the Committee retained its power of investigation and dismissal.

However in instances where the Disciplinary Committee is of the opinion that a case has been made out which justifies a more severe punishment, be it suspension or removal from the Roll of the Court, it is required pursuant to s.39(3), to forward to the Chief Justice and Attorney General a copy of the proceedings before it with its recommendation. In accordance with s.41 of the Act, the High Court sitting as a full court consisting of three judges may *inter alia*, make an order for suspension of the attorney or removal of the attorney's name from the Roll of the Court.

Right of Appeal

Pursuant to s.40 of the Legal Profession Act, the attorney has a right of appeal to the Court of Appeal where he is aggrieved by a decision or penalty imposed by the Committee in exercise of the limited powers conferred on it under s.39(1) of the Legal Profession Act.

In addition, in accordance with s.41(3) of the Act an attorney also has a right of appeal to the Court of Appeal from any decision or other determination made by the High Court.

It is noted that where an attorney appeals an order of suspension or removal, the order is not to be entered or published or acted upon until the order is confirmed on appeal. The attorney may therefore continue to practise in the interim.[26]

Barbados and Guyana

The respective disciplinary committees of these territories have been given powers similar to the original punitive jurisdiction of the Law Society in England ie. the power to investigate complaints, dismiss complaints in which no *prima facie* case has been made out, and to report and recommend to the Court, where appropriate, the suspension from practice of an attorney or his removal from the Roll of the Court.

Barbados

Prior to the passage in 1973 of the Legal Profession Act Cap. 370A, (which Act fused the legal profession) all matters of discipline of solicitors and barristers were the exclusive domain of the courts. Unlike the other jurisdictions, a disciplinary committee or tribunal was not established by statute whether under the Solicitors Act Cap. 373 or the Barristers Act Cap. 366.

Current Position

With the passage of the Legal Profession Act a Disciplinary Committee of the Bar Association was established for the first time pursuant to s.18 thereof. However, the Act does not specify the powers of the Committee. In this regard, s.19 merely provides that a client may make an application to the Committee in respect of an allegation concerning professional misconduct. The Act does not specify that the Committee has the power to investigate and to dismiss such complaints. Indeed s.21 simply provides that where the Committee after a hearing, decides that a case of professional misconduct has been made out, the Committee shall forward its finding with the appropriate recommendation to the Court of Appeal. Recommendations which the Committee may make include suspension from practice, removal from the Roll of Court, the imposition of a fine or a simple reprimand.[27]

Guyana

Prior to the passage of the Legal Practitioners Ordinance 68/1952, matters of legal professional discipline were referred exclusively to the Court. However with the passage of the Legal Profession Ordinance 68/1952, a Legal Practitioners Committee was established, consisting of ten members including

(i) the Attorney General, as Chairman of the Committee,
(ii) the Solicitor General and Crown Solicitors as *ex officio* members; and
(iii) seven other members appointed by the Chief Justice.

In so far as the Court's exercise of its inherent punitive jurisdiction over barristers in particular, the courts in Guyana, unlike Trinidad & Tobago at the time, had no difficulty in exercising its punitive powers. Indeed as the court noted in its judgment in the 1958 case of *Re A Legal Practitioner*:

> It is settled that this court has always had the power of depriving a barrister-at-law who had been admitted by it, of his right to practise before the court of the colony Such power being incidental to that of admitting to practise.[28]

Current Position

In 1975, the Legal Practitioners Act Cap. 4:01 was enacted. Pursuant to s.23 thereof, the number of members of the Legal Practitioner's Committee was increased to a maximum of 15. In 1980, the Legal Practitioner Act was amended for the purpose *inter alia* of fusing the legal profession. However the court continues to exercise exclusive punitive jurisdiction over this fused profession.

Eastern Caribbean territories (save Antigua & Barbuda and St. Lucia)

In the Eastern Caribbean, with the exception of Antigua & Barbuda and St. Lucia, there are no committees established for dealing with matters of discipline of barristers or solicitors. Although these territories have functioning bar associations, these associations are incorporated societies with absolutely no statutory disciplinary powers or authority.

The control and discipline of the profession is regulated by a single provision contained in the respective Supreme Court Acts of these territories, which provision empowers any two judges and in the case of Anguilla a single judge[29] of the High Court for reasonable cause to exercise two specific punitive powers; to suspend any barrister or solicitor or order his name to be struck off the Roll of the Court. More particularly, there is no provision for the exercise of any other punitive powers by the Court eg. reprimanding or fining.

Further, there is no statutory provision or regulations in these territories establishing a procedure under which a Committee or other tribunal may determine whether a *prima facie* case has been made out against a practitioner so that an appropriate recommendation may be made to the court.

No arrangements exist under which a complainant is directed to send his complaint to any specific officer eg. the Registrar or for anyone to assist the complainant in the preparation of his case. There are no prescribed forms for making a complaint. Although statute provides for punitive powers to be exercised by two judges (except in Anguilla), there is no provision for a procedure if judicial opinion is divided.

The result of this legislative vagueness is that within recent memory, if at all, not a single lawyer has been disciplined in these territories as provided for under the law.[30]

Antigua & Barbuda

Until the passage in 1997 of the Legal Profession Act 9/1997, the position with respect to the discipline of barristers and solicitors was the same as that which currently obtains in the other Eastern Caribbean territories (save St. Lucia).

It is to be noted that even though the Legal Profession Act of Antigua & Barbuda makes provision for the establishment of a Disciplinary Committee of the Law Council with the same powers as are exercisable by the respective Disciplinary Committees of Barbados and Guyana, to date, the Committee has not been constituted.

St. Lucia

Prior to the passage in November 2000 of the Legal Profession Act 31/2000 (which Act fused the legal profession), the court's punitive jurisdiction over barristers and solicitors was regulated by the Legal Practitioners Ordinance Ch. 116.

Section 18 of the Legal Practitioners Ordinance conferred on the court specific punitive powers of suspension and removal from the Roll of the Court. In addition, s.19(1) conferred summary powers on the court to investigate and decide any question or complaint made with reference to the powers, duties, rights or obligations of a legal practitioner. Pursuant to these summary powers, the court could make such order as the justice may require, including directions for payment of money unlawfully held and/or the payment of costs. In *Becar v Cooper*,[31] the Supreme Court of the then Windward and Leeward islands held that a solicitor was guilty of a breach of his professional duty under s.19(1) of the Legal Practitioners Ordinance in refusing to refund, on demand, the retainer fee of the applicant client. The court accordingly reprimanded the solicitor and made an order against the solicitor for repayment to the applicant client of the retainer fee.

Current Position

With the passage of the Legal Profession Act, provision was made for the establishment of a Disciplinary Committee with the same limited disciplinary powers as are currently exercisable by the Disciplinary Committee of Trinidad & Tobago i.e. the power of dismissal, reprimand, imposition of a fine and the making of an order for costs or compensation as the case may be.[32] (It is to be noted that at the date of writing the members of the Committee have been appointed but no matters have as yet been listed for hearing.)

Where the Committee is of the opinion that a case justifies more severe punishment Such as suspension or removal from the Roll, the Committee in accordance with s.39(3) is required to refer the matter to the High Court for determination by a single Judge in Chambers. The High Court in accordance with s.41(1) of Legal Profession Act may *inter alia* make an order removing the name of the attorney from the Roll or order the suspension of the attorney from practice for such time as the court thinks fit. The attorney pursuant to s.41(2) of the Act, has a right of appeal to the Court of Appeal.

Appeals (Professional Misconduct) Commission

Where an attorney is aggrieved by a decision or penalty imposed by the Disciplinary Committee in accordance with the specific punitive powers conferred on the Committee under s.38(1) of Legal Profession Act, he may appeal against such decision or penalty to the Appeals (Professional Misconduct) Commission established under s.40(1) of Legal Profession Act.[33]

The Commission upon hearing an appeal under this section may affirm, or set aside the decision or penalty imposed or may substitute its own decision or penalty or alternatively remit the matter to the Committee for a rehearing.[34]

In accordance with s.40(9)an attorney has the right to appeal to the Court of Appeal in respect of the decision of the Appeals Commission.

Jamaica

Barristers

Prior to 1960, the Judges of the Supreme Court, exercised exclusive punitive jurisdiction over barristers. However in 1960, The Bar Regulations Law, Cap. 120 was enacted. This law established a Disciplinary Committee of the Bar Association comprising *inter alia* of the Attorney General as an *ex officio* member, and six barristers duly appointed by the Governor on the recommendation of the Bar Association.[35] The Committee was given full punitive powers, including the power to fine, reprimand, suspend and to debar a barrister-at-law from practice.[36]

Solicitors

Pursuant to the Solicitors Law Cap. 363, a Solicitors Disciplinary Committee was established in 1941. In accordance with s.35(2) on the hearing of an application, the Committee was given the power to *inter alia* remove from, or strike off the Roll, the name of the solicitor to whom the application relates and to suspend the solicitor from practice.

Current Position

In 1972, the Legal Profession Act was enacted. This Act *inter alia* fused the legal profession and established the General Legal Council as the disciplinary body for the newly fused profession of attorneys-at-law.[37] The Council was charged with the general duty to uphold the standards of professional conduct of attorneys-at-law and in particular, was given the full punitive powers as previously enjoyed by the respective Solicitors and Barristers Disciplinary Committees.[38]

Right of Appeal

Pursuant to s.16 of the Legal Profession Act, an attorney has a right of appeal to the Court of Appeal against any order made by the Committee. The Court of Appeal:

(i) may dismiss the appeal and confirm the order; or

(ii) may allow the appeal and set aside the order; or
(iii) may vary the order; or
(iv) may allow the appeal and direct that the application be re-heard by the Committee.

Where it makes an order for rehearing of an application, s.17(1) specifically provides that no greater punishment shall be inflicted upon the attorney than was inflicted by the order made on the first hearing.

Where the Court of Appeal confirms the order whether with or without variation, the order takes effect from the date of the Order made by the Court of Appeal confirming it.[39]

The Bahamas

Prior to the passage in 1992 of the Legal Profession Act, 26/1992 the discipline of legal practitioners was exercised by the Disciplinary Committee of the Bar Association and Bar Council. This Committee was established in 1973, pursuant to s.29 of The Bahamas Bar Act Ch. 44. In accordance with s.30 of The Bahamas Bar Act, the Disciplinary Committee was given full punitive powers over counsel and attorney including the power to order the payment of a penalty to strike an attorney and counsel off the Roll of the Court, and to suspend an attorney and counsel from practice for a period not exceeding three years.

Current Position

In 1992 The Bahamas Bar Act was repealed and replaced by the Legal Profession Act 20/1992. Under the Legal Profession Act an Ethics Committee and a Disciplinary Committee was established.

Ethics Committee

The Ethics Committee operates as a hybrid of a disciplinary tribunal and a screening committee. In this regard, it is charged with the following duties and functions:

(i) upholding the standards of the profession;
(ii) receiving complaints in rescpect of attorneys and counsel; and
(iii) determining whether there exists reasonable grounds for making a complaint.[40]

This Committee also has limited punitive powers in that it may reprimand an attorney and counsel. However, if the Committee is of the view that the facts of the complaint warrant a penalty or order other than reprimand, the Committee is required to refer the complaint to the Disciplinary Committee.

Disciplinary Tribunal

The Disciplinary Tribunal's functions and duties include the hearing of complaints referred to it by the Ethics Committee and where appropriate, dismissal of such complaints. In addition, the Tribunal has full punitive powers including the power to suspend an attorney and counsel from practice, to strike an attorney and counsel off the Roll of the Court, and to make an order of compensation against the attorney and counsel.[41]

Orders made by the Disciplinary Tribunal must be prefaced with a statement of the Tribunal's findings and signed by the Chairman of the Tribunal and thereafter filed with the Registrar.[42]

Right of Appeal

Pursuant to s.54 of Legal Profession Act, the attorney and counsel who is aggrieved by the order of the Ethics Committee or the Disciplinary Tribunal as the case may be, may appeal to the Court of Appeal.

It is to be noted that subject to any appeal brought against the order of the Tribunal or Ethics Committee, the order made by either body shall be acted upon and be enforceable in the same manner as a judgment or order of the court. [43]

Compensation Fund

Barbados and Trinidad & Tobago

Apart from the various punitive sanctions which may be imposed against an attorney personally by the court or duly authorised disciplinary tribunal, the respective Legal Profession Acts of Barbados and Trinidad & Tobago provide for the establishment of a Compensation Fund and for the Fund to be maintained and administered by the Council of the Law/Bar Association of these territories.[44]

Each practitioner is a member and required to contribute to the Fund, which the Council holds as trustee for the purpose of giving financial relief to persons, who in the opinion of the Council, have sustained losses as a result of the dishonesty of an attorney.

The financial relief is given by way of a grant to the aggrieved party. The financial award may be made whether or not the attorney in question had a practising certificate in force at or after the commission of the act of dishonesty, or whether the attorney has died or has had his name removed from the Roll or has ceased to practise or has been suspended.

Hardship Grant

In addition, the Council is empowered to make a hardship grant in cases where the Council is satisfied that the attorney has failed to account for any trust property of which he is a trustee.

Compensation Rules

Barbados

In the exercise of the powers conferred on the Bar Association under s.51(6) of Legal Profession Act Cap. 370A, the Bar Association has made Compensation Rules – The Attorney-at-Law Compensation Fund Rules, 1984.[45] These rules set out the procedure to be followed in making an application for a grant from the Compensation Fund including the delivery of a Notice of Hardship in the form prescribed to the Secretary of the Association, together with an application for a grant out of the Compensation Fund.

AMBIT OF PUNITIVE JURISDICTION IN GENERAL – IS IT EXTRA-TERRITORIAL?

The ambit of the court's punitive jurisdiction whether exercised by the Court or a disciplinary tribunal, is not limited to acts of omission or dishonesty committed locally ie. within the jurisdiction in which the attorney is admitted to practise. According to the authority of *McCalla v The Disciplinary Committee of the General Legal Council,*[46] the court's jurisdiction by necessary implication extends to misconduct committed abroad.

The facts of *McCalla* are instructive. In September, 1962 *McCalla* was admitted to practise in Jamaica. Between 1977 to 1985 he lived and worked in Canada. During that period he was admitted to practice by the Ontario Bar. His name remained on the Roll in Jamaica. In March 1985 he returned to Jamaica and resumed practice. Subsequent to his return to Jamaica, the General Legal Council of Jamaica discovered that McCalla had been struck off the Roll of Solicitors by convocation of the Law Society of Upper Canada *inter alia* for:

(i) publishing as his work, research material prepared by other persons without obtaining permission; and
(ii) holding himself out, in his application for employment with the Federal Government, as a Q.C. and former Deputy Minister of Justice in Jamaica.

Based both on the charges which led to McCalla being struck off the Roll in Canada and on the results of the General Council's investigations, disciplinary proceedings were commenced in Jamaica against McCalla by the Chairman of the Council to have him struck of the Roll of the Court of Jamaica. In the judgment delivered by the Court of Appeal, Wright JA addressed the issue of the general entitlement of the Council to uphold standards of professional conduct. Wright JA observed:

> There is no qualification attached thereto. Indeed it would be ludicrous in the extreme if a Jamaican attorney were allowed to roam the world conducting himself in a manner which breaches the rules of conduct which govern the profession of which he is a member and be allowed to maintain that he is not subject to the sanction of those rules because his conduct was outside Jamaica.[47]

PUNITIVE DISCIPLINE OF LAW CLERKS/LEGAL EXECUTIVES

Antigua & Barbuda, Barbados and The Bahamas

The respective Legal Profession Acts of the abovementioned territories, contain specific statutory provisions[48] which empower the Disciplinary Committee/Tribunal of these territories to exercise extensive disciplinary jurisdiction over law clerks in the employ of an attorney-at-law and in the case of The Bahamas, over legal executives in the employ of counsel and attorney.

Antigua & Barbuda and Barbados

According to the relevant provisions of the Legal Profession Act of these territories,[49] the Disciplinary Committee of the Law Council/Bar Association of Antigua & Barbuda and Barbados respectively, may make an order debarring, an attorney except with the written permission of the Bar Association/Law Council, from taking in, retaining, employing or remunerating a law clerk who:

(a) has been convicted by a court of;
  (i) larceny, embezzlement or fraudulent connection; or
  (ii) any other criminal offence in respect of any money belonging to or held or controlled by the attorney by whom he is or was employed or any client of that attorney; or

(b) reasonably suspected by the Bar Association/Law Council of having been a party to any act or default of the attorney of whom he is or was a clerk.

The Bahamas

The disciplinary sanctions imposed by the disciplinary tribunal against a legal executive who is found guilty of improper conduct are spelt out in s.38(1) of the Legal Profession Act. Pursuant to s.38(1), the Disciplinary Tribunal on hearing a complaint of misconduct on the part of a law clerk may *inter alia:*

(i) dismiss the complaint; or

(ii) make such disciplinary order as they think fit including removing the name of the legal executive, imposing a penalty not exceeding one thousand dollars against the legal executive or making an order of compensation for any loss or damage or personal injury resulting from the improper conduct and making an order as to the payment of costs or of such other sum against the legal executive as the tribunal may consider a reasonable contribution towards costs.

Part II – Compensatory Jurisdiction

In so far as the compensatory jurisdiction of the Court is concerned, it is exercised by the court making an order as to costs against an attorney personally; in some instances the costs of the other side or in the proper case the costs of both parties.[50]

This compensatory jurisdiction is retained and exercised exclusively by the courts both in England and in the Caribbean. However it is exercised in restricted circumstances more specifically in cases where an attorney acting in the capacity of a solicitor/instructing attorney in the course of proceedings in court causes costs to be improperly incurred or wasted by undue delay or without reasonable cause or by any other misconduct or default on his part.[514] In such instances it is to be noted that the attorney is also answerable for the default of his employees.[52]

Although the court's exercise of this disciplinary jurisdiction is essentially compensatory in nature, there is, as Lane CJ observed in *Holder v CPS,* a punitive element. Lord Lane noted:

> The costs which the solicitor will have to pay from his own pocket will only be those which his default has caused. There is nothing to be added to that figure to mark the disapproval of the court or by way of deterrence. To that extent the object of the jurisdiction is to compensate. However there is a punitive element in that the solicitor will be ordered to pay a bill which would otherwise be paid by one of the parties to the litigation. There is also an element of deterrence in that an attorney wishes to avoid the expense and adverse publicity, which the exercise of the court's compensatory jurisdiction necessarily entails.[53]

The court's common law compensatory jurisdiction is supplemented by the relevant Rules of the Orders and Rules of the Supreme Court of the various territories, which Rule provides that where in any proceedings before the Supreme Court, costs are incurred improperly or without reasonable cause or are wasted by undue delay or by misconduct or default, on the part of the attorney, the court may exercise its summary power against the attorney whom it considers responsible and may make an order as to costs against the attorney personally.[54]

It is to be noted that the court's compensatory jurisdiction does not come to an end merely because the attorney ceases to be on the record. As the court noted in *Brendon v Spiro,*[55] a judge of the High Court before whom an action has been tried, has an inherent jurisdiction to entertain an application that a solicitor who has acted for a party should on the alleged ground of his professional misconduct pay personally, the costs to be paid by the party notwithstanding that he has ceased to be on record of the action before the verdict is returned or even before the trial begins.

It is to be noted that this summary procedure may be invoked not only in cases where the conduct of the attorney is inexcusable and such as to merit reproof but also to save the expense of an action and in the proper case, takes the place of an action for negligence.[56]

NEGLIGENCE/DEFAULT – WHAT CONDUCT IS SUFFICIENT?

The court's compensatory jurisdiction will be invoked, where the conduct of the attorney involves a serious dereliction of duty to the court, which causes extra costs to be incurred. An improper act or omission which falls short of serious dereliction of duty, gross negligence or gross neglect is not sufficient for an order to be made against an attorney-at-law for personal payment of costs.[57]

However it is to be noted that in England as of April, 1986, a new rule R.S.C. O.62 r.11 was introduced in place of R.S.C. O.62 r.8.

In accordance with R.S.C. O.62 r.11, a solicitor in civil proceedings may be ordered to pay wasted costs personally if they have been incurred unreasonably or improperly or have been thrown away by his incompetence even though the solicitor has not been guilty of serious misconduct or serious dereliction of his duty.[58] As was noted by May LJ in *Sinclair Jones v Kay:*

> The principle requiring gross misconduct laid down in the older authorities are not applicable, where there is an application made to the court under the modern O.62 r.11.[59]

Part III – Disciplinary Committees/ Tribunals

CONSTITUTION AND MEMBERSHIP

The disciplinary committee/tribunal of the various jurisdictions is constituted under the respective Legal Profession Act of these territories.[60]

Antigua & Barbuda

The Disciplinary Committee of the Law Council is yet to be constituted, despite the fact that The Legal Profession Act 9/1997 was enacted in Antigua & Barbuda since 1997. However, pursuant to s.22 of the Legal Profession Act and the First Schedule thereto, the Disciplinary Committee shall consist of five persons, appointed by the Governor General after consultation with the Chief Justice. The membership of the Committee when constituted shall comprise three attorneys of not less than ten years standing, one other attorney, and interestingly and most significantly, one person who is not an attorney-at-law. The Chairman is to be appointed by the Governor General, amongst the attorneys of at least ten years standing in the profession.

Barbados

The membership of the Disciplinary Committee pursuant to the Fourth Schedule to the Legal Profession Act[61] consists of seven persons, of whom at least three are required to be attorneys of not less than ten years standing. The members are nominated by the Bar Association.

Guyana

The Legal Practitioners Committee consists of a maximum of 15 members, including the Attorney General, Solicitor General and State Solicitor as *ex officio* members. The Attorney General is the Chairman of the Committee and in his absence, the Solicitor General acts as Chairman.[62] The other 12 members are appointed by the Chancellor. In addition the Committee may sit in more than one division.[63] It is interesting to note that unlike the other territories:

(i) the Legal Practitioners Committee is not a Committee constituted by or under the authority of the Bar Association; and
(ii) there is no statutory requirement that members of the Committee be in practice for a minimum number of years.

Jamaica

Pursuant to s.11 of the Legal Profession Act, the disciplinary committee consist of a minimum of 15 persons appointed by the General Legal Council. The persons who may be appointed to the committee include members or former members of the Council, current or former holders of high judicial office, attorneys who were members of a former disciplinary body and attorneys who have been in practice for not less than ten years.[64] The Chairman of the Committee is one of the members of the Committee who is appointed by the Council.[65] The Committee usually sit in two or more divisions so as to expedite the investigation and/or the hearing of complaints made against attorneys. Each such committee is required to appoint its own Chairman and to act only while at least three members are present.[66]

St. Lucia

The Disciplinary Committee pursuant to s.36 of The Legal Profession Act and the Fourth Schedule thereto consist of seven members appointed by the Chief Justice after consultation with the Council of the Bar association, three of whom include members of the Council, and the others are attorneys-at-law not less than ten years standing. The Chairperson and Vice Chairperson are appointed by the Chief Justice after consultation with the Council and attorneys who have held high judicial office or are attorneys-at-law of not less than ten years standing. The Committee, pursuant to s.37 of Legal Profession Act may sit in two Districts and the Chairman subject to the direction of the Council shall determine the composition of each District.

Appeals (Professional Misconduct) Commission

The Appeals Commission established under s.40 of the Legal Profession Act consists of the following five members: one arbiter nominated by the Attorney General, one arbiter nominated by the Bar Association; two arbiters nominated by the Governor General and one arbiter who shall be the Chairman, nominated by the Chief Justice and who shall be an attorney-at-law of not less than 15 years standing. It is significant to note that the two arbiters appointed by the Governor General are not attorneys-at-law. Their only qualification is that they be persons of good standing in the community and their appointment is for the express purpose of representing the public interest.

The Bahamas

Ethics Committee – Pursuant to r.1 of the Fifth Schedule made under s.30 of the Legal Profession Act, the Ethics Committee consists of three members of the Bar Association of not less than five years. The members are appointed by the Bar Council. The Chairman of the Ethics Committee is appointed from members of the Committee in accordance with r.5 of the Fifth Schedule.

Disciplinary Tribunal –With respect to the composition of the Discipline Tribunal, pursuant to the Sixth Schedule made under s.31 of the Legal Professional Act 26/1992, the Disciplinary Tribunal consists of two judges appointed by the Chief Justice, seven counsel and attorneys of not less than seven years standing at the Bar, appointed by the Bar Council and most significantly, two persons selected outside of the legal profession and appointed by the Attorney General. In accordance with r.2, the Chairman of the Tribunal is required to be one of the two judges and the Tribunal may sit in two divisions.

Trinidad & Tobago

The Disciplinary Committee of the Council of the Law Association is established under s.36 of the Legal Profession Act. The Committee sits in two divisions. Its membership consists of the President of the Law Association and 15 other members appointed by the Chief Justice after consultation with the Council. The Chairman and Vice Chairman are persons who have held high judicial office or are attorneys of not less than ten years standing. The Chairman, Vice Chairman and the other members of the Committee are appointed by the Chief Justice after consultation with the Council. These members are required to be an attorneys of not less than ten years standing in the legal profession.

DISCIPLINARY POWERS

The disciplinary powers of the respective Committees/Tribunals have already been considered.

PROCEDURE

(All territories save The Bahamas)

The procedure governing the respective Committee's/Tribunal's exercise of its disciplinary powers is set out (with the exception of Guyana)[67] in the relevant schedule to the respective Legal Profession Acts of the various territories. In general, the procedure takes the following form:

A formal application in the prescribed form is made by the complainant to the committee. The application is supported by affidavit(s) deposed to by the applicant setting out the facts in support thereof. It is usually made by a client but may be made, with leave of the court, by any other aggrieved person. The application is submitted to the Secretary of the Committee/Tribunal who thereafter sends it on to the relevant Disciplinary Committee/Tribunal of the respective territories.

The application sets out the grounds of complaints and *inter alia* calls upon the attorney to answer the allegation set out in the supporting affidavit of the complainant.[68] (If the complaint is of a criminal nature the matter is referred to the DPP)[69]

Before fixing a date for hearing of the complaint, the Committee carries out investigations into the allegations. To this end, the Committee may require the applicant to supply such further documents relating to the allegations, as it deems fit.[70] If in the opinion of the Committee, no *prima facie* case has been made out, the Committee dismisses the application without requiring the attorney to appear to answer the allegations and notifies the applicant and the attorney-at-law in writing of the dismissal.[71] However in Guyana, pursuant to s.24(3)of the Legal Profession Act Cap 4:01, the Committee before dismissing the complaint hears the applicant to give him the opportunity to show cause why his application was dismissed.

Where a *prima facie* case has been made out, a date for hearing of the application is fixed by the Committee and the notice of hearing together with a copy of the application and affidavit is then served on the attorney by the Marshall of the Court. The Notice which takes a prescribed form includes a request for a list of documents including affidavit(s) in answer on which the attorney proposes to rely. The date of hearing, depending on the territory, is between 14 to 21 clear days of the date of notice.[72]

Thereafter the attorney is required to file affidavit(s) in answer together with any other supporting documents and serve copies thereof on the Secretary of the Committee and on the applicant. Either party may inspect the documents contained in the list furnished by each other.

In Antigua & Barbuda, Barbados, Guyana, St. Lucia and Trinidad & Tobago, statute provides that the Secretary of the Committee/Tribunal shall be the Registrar of the Supreme Court or a person deputed by the Registrar (usually the Deputy or Assistant Registrar).[73] However, in Barbados as of 1995, the person deputed by the Registrar under s.18(2) of Legal Profession Act Cap. 370A, is no longer the Deputy Registrar but is a non-attorney-at-law. The decision to appoint a non-attorney was taken in large part to address the public perception of a lack of transparency in the conduct of disciplinary proceedings by the Committee particularly as all the members of the Disciplinary Committee (unlike the Bahamas and Antigua & Barbuda) are non attorneys-at-law. As the Court acknowledged in *Haynes Attorney-at-Law and In the Matter of the Legal Profession Act 370A* dated January 3, 1986:[74]

> There is no provision in the Legal Profession Act for the representation of the public interest in the constitution of the disciplinary committee, the entire membership of which is made up of attorneys-at-law.

In Jamaica, there is no requirement that the Secretary to the Committee be an attorney-at-law. Rule 2 of the Disciplinary Proceedings Rules (set out in Fifth Schedule to the Legal Profession Act) simply provides that the Secretary is a person appointed by the Committee to be Secretary thereof and in practice the Secretary is not an attorney-at-law.

The Bahamas

The procedure for the hearing of complaints by the Ethics Committee or the Disciplinary Tribunal, as the case may be, is not set out in any detail. There are no procedural rules nor prescribed forms for making a complaint to the Ethics Committee, to which body all complaints must be first submitted. In practice the complainant submits a letter to the Secretary of the Ethics Committee setting out in the letter, the nature of the complaint. The letter is then forwarded to the Ethics Committee and a copy of the complaint is sent to the attorney in question.

Where the Ethics Committee is of the view that a *prima facie* case has been made out against the attorney, the Committee will either hear the matter, or if the misconduct in the Committee's view warrants a punishment more severe than a reprimand, the complaint is forwarded to the Disciplinary Tribunal.

Pursuant to s.36(4), the hearing of a complaint and every application relating to a complaint by the Disciplinary Tribunal or the Ethics Committee is heard in private. However the attorney may request, by notice delivered to the Secretary to the Tribunal or Committee as the case may be, for the hearing to be in public. The notice which is required to be sent prior to the day fixed for the hearing of the complaint is served personally or by registered post.

HEARING

All jurisdictions

The hearing is conducted in accordance with the ordinary rules of evidence of court. The Committee may proceed and act in whole or in part upon the evidence given by affidavit and may, where required, summon deponents to give oral evidence.[75]

The applications are heard in private.[76] However, in The Bahamas both parties may request that the hearing be conducted in public. In the exercise of the powers conferred on the respective committees, the committee has the powers of a Judge of the High Court, *inter alia* to summon witnesses, call for production of books and documents, to examine witnesses on oath and where necessary, to make an order of committal where any person before a committee conducts himself in such a manner, that were he before the High Court he would have been held in contempt of court.[77]

STANDARD OF PROOF

The evidential burden, although not specifically provided for, is not the civil burden of proof, it goes beyond a balance of probabilities.

This point was considered in *Bhandari v Advocates Case* where it was held:

> that in every allegation of misconduct involving an element of deceit or moral turpitude it is the duty of the professional domestic tribunal investigating the complaint to apply a high standard of proof and not to condemn on a mere balance of probabilities.[78]

Part IV – The Record of Professional Discipline in the English-Speaking Caribbean

INTRODUCTION

An examination of the record of professional discipline in many of the territories reveals that there are few and in some cases, no instances of disciplinary action being taken by the court or other duly authorized committee/tribunal.

Indeed there is a perception, that the profession is somewhat reluctant to enforce, by disciplinary sanction, the high standards of ethical conduct coincidental with and expected of the profession of the law.

In this regard, according to one senior member of the Bar Association of Guyana, and member of the Legal Practitioners Committee:

> The perception is that the indulgent approach springs from a feeling of professional camaraderie. This lack of zeal in taking complaints to their logical conclusion has contributed to a cynical attitude on the part of disgruntled litigants who view the complaint procedure as a classic case of trying the Devil in Hell.

NATURE OF COMPLAINTS

The complaints which are made to the respective Disciplinary Committee or Tribunals of the various territories range from delays on the part of the attorney in responding to queries by the client, overcharging, negligence, and most significantly, misappropriation of the client's funds. In this regard, the observation has been made in respect of Barbados that many of the complainants view the Disciplinary Committee more as a debt collecting agency rather than a disciplinary body.

STATISTICAL RECORD OF PROFESSIONAL DISCIPLINE

When one examines the statistical record of professional discipline in many of the English speaking Caribbean territories, the perception in so far as the public is concerned, is that the profession has in large measure failed to maintain the high standard of ethical conduct expected of the noble profession of the law. Based on the information available, the following is a general record of professional discipline in the various territories within the last five to ten years.

In Barbados

Between 1996-2000, there has been an average of 65 complaints per annum made to the Secretary of the Committee. However in 2000, the figure rose to over 100. On an average seventy per cent of the complaints are heard at a formal hearing. Within the last ten years two attorneys have been disciplined by way of being struck off the Roll.

In the Eastern Caribbean

The position in the Eastern Caribbean has already been considered. Not one single attorney has been disciplined within the last ten years. (It remains to be seen with respect to Antigua & Barbuda and St. Lucia, whether the establishment of a Disciplinary Tribunal in these territories, will have any impact. In Antigua as previously mentioned, the Disciplinary Committee has not yet been constituted.)

In Guyana

In Guyana, of 248 complaints made to the Disciplinary Committee since 1997 to date, approximately 108 of these cases, fees have been refunded to the complainant and the file closed. Of the eight cases, which the Committee recommended that disciplinary action be taken by the Court, no action to date has been taken. There are currently 32 matters pending before the committee.

In Jamaica

Figures for the past nine years were made available and according to the figures supplied by General Legal Council, between 1992-2000, the number of complaints made to G.L.C. averaged 240 per year. For the period 1995-2000, two attorneys have been suspended, seven removed from the Roll, one reprimanded and 24 fined.

In The Bahamas

No figures are available with respect to The Bahamas.

In Trinidad & Tobago

Within the last ten years an average of five attorneys have been disciplined per year by way of reprimand or fine. The numbers of complaints filed have averaged 70 complaints per annum out of which the Committee hears approximately half. However within that same ten-year period not one single attorney has been disciplined by way of suspension or being struck off the Roll. One complaint has been forwarded to the Court.

POSTSCRIPT

Although one must be mindful of making sweeping generalizations nevertheless when the record of legal professional discipline in most of the Caribbean territories is examined, it seems that public cynicism is well grounded in reality.

In this regard the exhortations of Justice Deyalsingh in the case of *In the Matter of Gail Robinson and Beverly Scobie and In the Matter of the Inherent Jurisdiction of the Court* are instructive. Although Deyalsingh J was referring specifically to the Court's role in disciplining, his words of admonition are applicable, irrespective of whether it is the court or a delegated body exercising disciplinary powers.

Deyalsingh J observed:

> The Court must resort to a more frequent use of its inherent jurisdiction to discipline practitioners. The public interest requires no less and the Courts must not shirk its duty in protecting innocent members of the public from the malpractices of practitioners.[79]

To do otherwise according to Bernard CJ, the former Chief Justice of Trinidad & Tobago, in the Court of Appeal case of *Forde v Law Society*, 'is a betrayal of that trust itself and a sad reflection not only on the legal profession but also on the entire administration of justice'.[80]

ENDNOTES

PART I

1. See *Myers v Elman* [1940] 1 AC 282 at pp.318 and 319 HL.
2. [1892] 2 QBD 440 CA.
3. (1958) Judgments of the Supreme Court of the Windward and Leeward Islands 30.
4. See Ch. 2.
5. [1961] AC 617 at p 630 per Lord Denning PC.
6. This Resolution was confirmed by the Court in *Re S (a barrister)* [1970] 1 All ER 949. See also Vol. 3 Halsburys Laws of England, 4th edn. at pp. 589-591.
7. *R v Grays' Inn* 1 Doubl. 354 CA.
8. *Re T (A Barrister)* [1982] 1 QB 430.
9. [1982] 3 All ER 1086 at p 1086 at 1088 CA.
10. (1842) 10 M & W 28.
11. [1940] AC 282 at p 319 HL.
12. (1958) LRBG 25 at p.28.
13. See *In the Matter of Gail Robinson and Beverly Scobie and In the Matter of the Inherent Jurisdiction of the Court* HCA 2/1985 Trinidad & Tobago (unreported) at pp. 16, 17 and 18
14. *Supra* at p.1088.
15. See (1930) 1 Knapp 267 at p.268.
16. (1964) 7 WIR 93
17. HCA No. 2/1985 Trinidad & Tobago (unreported)
18. *Ibid* at p.24.
19. Antigua & Barbuda - s.27(2) Legal Profession Act 9/1997
    Barbados - s.23 Legal Profession Act Cap. 370A
    Guyana - s.33 Legal Profession Act Cap. 4:01 as amended by Legal Profession (Amendment) Act 3/1980
    St. Lucia - s.37(2) Legal Profession Act 31/2000.
20. Antigua & Barbuda - s.23(2) Legal Profession Act 9/1997
    Barbados - s.19(2) Legal Profession Act Cap. 370A
    Jamaica - s.12(2) Legal Profession Act 1971
    St. Lucia - s.37(2) Legal Profession Act 31/2000
    Trinidad & Tobago - s.37(2) Legal Profession Act 11/1986.
21. Judgment dated December 2, 1987. No number was assigned to the proceedings.
22. (1964) 7 WIR 93.
23. *Ibid* at p.94.
24. *Ibid.*
25. See *In the Matter of The Barrister (Disciplinary Proceedings) Rules 1965 and In the Matter of James R. Makhan* HCA No. 7/1965 Trinidad & Tobago (unreported).
26. See s.29(1) Legal Profession Act 21/1986.
27. See The Legal Profession Disciplinary Committee Reference to Court of Appeal Rules (1985) SI 1985 No. 189.
28. (1958) LRBG 25 at p.26. See also s.24(3) and (4) Legal Practitioners Act Cap. 4:01 as amended by Legal Practitioners (Amendment) Act 3/1980.
29. Anguilla - s.73 Eastern Caribbean Supreme Court (Anguilla) Ordinance 9/1982
    Dominica - s.76 Eastern Caribbean Supreme Court (Dominica) Act Chap 4:02

Grenada	-	s.82 Eastern Caribbean Supreme Court (Grenada) Act 19/1991
St. Kitts & Nevis	-	s.76 Eastern Caribbean Supreme Court (St. Christopher & Nevis) Act 1993
St. Vincent & the Grenadines		s.76 Eastern Caribbean Supreme Court (St. Vincent & the The Grenadines) Act Cap 18

30. *The Evolving Legal Profession in the Commonwealth* by Sir Alfred Phillips 1978. See on this Oceana Publications Inc at Ch 6 entitled Admission to the Profession at pp.53-54
31. HCA 46/1957 Judgments of the Supreme Court of the Windward and Leeward Islands 3
32. Pursuant to s.39(1) of Legal Profession Act 31/2000.
33. Pursuant to s.40(9) of Legal Profession Act 31/2000.
34. Pursuant to s.40(8) of Legal Profession Act 31/2000.
35. Section 5 of Bar Regulations Law Cap. 120.
36. Section 6 of Bar Regulations Law Cap. 120.
37. Section 11 Legal Profession Act 1971
38. Section 12(4) Legal Profession Act 1971
39. Section 17(2) Legal Profession Act 1971
40. Section 30(1) Legal Profession Act 26/1992.
41. Section 38 Legal Profession Act 26/1992.
42. Section 40 Legal Profession Act 26/1992.
43. Section 40(2) Legal Profession Act 26/1992.
44. Barbados - s. Legal Profession Cap 370A
    Trinidad & Tobago - s.51 Legal Profesion Act 21/1986
45. By SI 1984 No. 86.
46. (1993) 49 WIR 213. See also *R v The Disciplinary Committee of the General Legal Council Ex p. McCalla* Misc. Suit No. M 75/1992 (unreported).
47. *McCalla v The Disciplinary Committee of the General Legal Council* (1993) 49 WIR 213 at p.235.
48. Antigua & Barbuda - ss.32 and 33 Legal Profession Ordinance 9/1997
    Barbados - ss. 29, 30 and 31 Legal Profession Act Cap. 370A
    The Bahamas - ss. 31, 36, 38 and 40 Legal profession Act, 26/1992
49. Antigua & Barbuda - s.32 Legal Profession Act 26/1992
    Barbados - s.29 Legal Profession Act Cap. 370A

PART II

50. *Fargnoli v Luck and AG* (1965) LRBG 486; *Woods v HG Liquors Ltd and Anor* (1995) 48 WIR 240; *R & T Thews Ltd v Reeves (No. 2)* [1982] 3 All ER 1086 CA.
51. *R & T Thews Ltd v Reeves (No 2) Ibid* at pp. 1088 and 1089 CA See also *Weston v CCC Administrator* [1977] 1 QB 32 at p. 42 CA
52. *Myers v Elman* [1940] AC 282 HL. Contrast with *Habil Kadir v Demerara Mutual Life Assurance Society Ltd* (1968) LRG 312.
53. [1990] 1 All ER 368 at 372 CA.
54. Barbados - RSC O.62 r.8 Rule of the Supreme Court of Judicature, 1982
    Guyana - RSC O.49 r.8 Rules of the Supreme court 1955
    The Bahamas - RSC O.59 r.8 The Rules of the Supreme Court 1978
    Trinidad & Tobago - RSC O.62 r. 8 Orders and Rules of the Supreme Court of Judicature of Trinidad & Tobago, 1975.
55. [1937] 2 All ER 496 CA.

56. *Myers v Elman* [1904] 1 AC 289 at p.319 HL; See also *Newbiggen-by-the-Sea Gas Co v Armstrong* (1879) 13 Ch D 310 CA, *Nelson v Nelson* [1997] 1 All ER 970 CA; *Penn v Bristol and West* [1997] 3 All ER 470 CA.
57. *Orchard v South Eastern Electricity Board* [1987] 1 All ER 95 CA.
58. *Gupta v Comer* [1991] 1 All ER 269 CA; *Langley v Northwest Water Authority* [1991] 3 All ER 610; *Re A Company* (No. 066785 of 1995) [1996] 2 All ER 917.
59. [1988] 2 All ER 611 at p.616 CA.

PART III

60. Antigua & Barbuda	-	s.22 Legal Profession Act 9/1997
Barbados	-	s.18 Legal Profession Act Cap. 370A
Guyana	-	s.23 Legal Profession Act Cap. 4:01 as amended by Legal Profession (Amendment) Act 3/1980
Jamaica	-	s.11 Legal Profession Act. See also Legal Profession (Amendment) Act 19/1994
St. Lucia	-	s.36 Legal Profession Act 31/2000
The Bahamas	-	ss. 30 and 31 Legal Profession Act 26/1992
Trinidad & Tobago	-	s.36 Legal Profession Act 21/1986

61. See s.18 Legal Profession Act Cap. 370A.
62. Pursuant to s.23 Legal Practitioners Act Cap. 4:01.
63. Pursuant to s.25 Legal Practitioners Act Cap. 4:01.
64. See also the Third Schedule made under s.11 of Legal Profession Act 1971
65. See r.2 of the Third Schedule supra.
66. Pursuant to s.13 of the Legal Profession Act 1971

67. Antigua & Barbuda	-	Fifth Schedule pursuant to s.24 of the Legal Profession Act 9/1997
Barbados	-	Fifth Schedule pursuant to s.20 of the Legal Profession Act Cap. 370
Guyana	-	ss.24, 27, 28 Legal Profession Act Cap. 4:01 as amended by Legal Profession (Amendment) Act 3/1980
Jamaica	-	Fourth Schedule pursuant to s.14 of the Legal Profession Act
St. Lucia	-	Fifth Schedule pursuant to s.38 of the Legal Profession Act 31/2000
Trinidad & Tobago	-	Fifth Schedule pursuant to s.38 of the Legal Profession Act 21/1986

68. *Ibid.*
69. *In the Matter of Gail Robinson and Beverley Scobie and In the Matter of the Inherent Jurisdiction of the Court* HCA No. 2/1985 Trinidad & Tobago (unreported). See also *In the Matter of Jeffrey L Toppin, Attorney at Law and In the Matter of the Legal Profession Act Cap 370A* judgment dated Dec. 2, 1987 Barbados (unreported)

70. Antigua & Barbuda	-	r.4 Fifth Schedule made pursuant to s.24 of the Legal Profession Act 9/1997
Barbados	-	r.4 Fifth Schedule made pursuant to s.20 of the Legal Profession Act Cap. 370A
Guyana	-	s.24(3) Legal Profession Act Cap. 4:01 as amended by Legal Profession (Amendment) Act 3/1980
Jamaica	-	r.2 First Schedule made pursuant to the Legal Profession Act 1971

St. Lucia	-	r.3(1) Fifth Schedule of the Legal Profession Act 31/2000
Trinidad & Tobago	-	r.4 Fifth Schedule of the Legal Profession Act 21/1986

71. *Ibid.*

72. Antigua & Barbuda	-	rr.5 and 6 Fifth Schedule made pursuant to s.24 of the Legal Profession Act 9/1997
Barbados	-	s.18(2) Legal Profession Act Cap. 370A
Guyana	-	r. 2 and 3 First Schedule to Legal Profession (Amendment) Act 3/1980
Jamaica	-	r. 5 and 6 Fourth Schedule to the Legal Profession Act 1971
St. Lucia	-	r. 4 and 5 Fifth Schedule to the Legal Profession Act 31/2000
Trinidad & Tobago	-	r. 5 and 6 Fifth Schedule to the Legal Profession Act 21/1986
73. Antigua & Barbuda	-	s.22(1) Legal Profession Act 9/1997
Barbados	-	s.18(2) Legal Profession Act Cap 370A
Guyana	-	s.24(10) Legal Profession Act Cap. 4:01
St. Lucia	-	s.36(2) Legal Profession Act 31/2000
Trinidad & Tobago	-	s.33(2) Legal Profession Act 21/1986

74. No number was assigned to the proceedings.

75. Antigua & Barbuda	-	rr.9 and 10 Fifth Schedule to Legal Profession Act 9/1997
Barbados	-	r.9 Fifth Schedule to Legal Profession Act Cap. 370A
Guyana	-	r.7 of First Schedule to Legal Profession Act Cap. 4:01
Jamaica	-	r.10 Fourth Schedule to Legal Profession Act 1971
St. Lucia	-	rr. 8 and 9 Legal Profession Act 31/2000
Trinidad & Tobago	-	rr. 9 and 10 Legal Profession Act 21/1986
76. Antigua & Barbuda	-	r.13 Fifth Schedule to Legal Profession Act 9/1997
Barbados	-	r.11 Fifth Schedule to Legal Profession Act Cap. 370A
Guyana	-	r.11 First Schedule to Legal Profession Act Cap. 4:01
Jamaica	-	r.14 Fourth Schedule to Legal Profession Act 1971
St. Lucia	-	r.12 Fifth Schedule to Legal Profession Act 31/2000
Trinidad & Tobago	-	r.13 Fifth Schedule to Legal Profession Act 21/1986
77. Antigua & Barbuda	-	r.19 Fifth Schedule to Legal Profession Act 9/1997
Barbados	-	See s.20(3) Legal Profession Act Cap. 370A. See also r.14 Fifth Schedule to Legal Profession Act Cap. 370A
Jamaica	-	r.14 Fourth Schedule to Legal Profession Act 1971
St. Lucia	-	rr.17 and 18 Fifth Schedule to Legal Profession Act 31/2000
Trinidad & Tobago	-	r.19 Fifth Schedule to Legal Profession Act 21/1986

78. [1956] 3 All ER 742 at pp. 744, 745 P.C.

PART IV

79. *In the Matter of Gail Robinson and Beverly Scobie* and *In the Matter of The Inherent Jurisdiction of The Court* HCA 2/1985 Trinidad & Tobago (unreported) at p.4.
80. (1987) 40 WIR 361 at p.374.

14. ROLE AND DUTIES OF ADVOCATE ATTORNEY

INTRODUCTION

The relevant Code/Canon of Ethics of the various territories contains comprehensive guidelines with respect to the role and duties of the advocate attorney, whether as prosecution or defence counsel. These guidelines are both general and specific in nature.

However it is to be noted that with the limited exception of The Bahamas, the Code/Canon of Ethics of the respective territories does not provide specific guidelines or rules with respect to confessions of guilt. Accordingly, The Code of Conduct for the Bar of England and Wales 1990 has been adopted in the absence of such specific provisions.

Secondly, there is substantial overlap between professional misconduct and the role and duties of advocate attorney, as many of the breaches of duty by advocate attorney which are outlined in the respective Code/Canon of Ethics also constitute professional misconduct. As professional misconduct has already been considered in chapter 13, this chapter will focus on the role and duties of advocate attorney as they pertain specifically to the conduct of proceedings in court.

GENERAL DUTIES OF PROSECUTION AND DEFENCE COUNSEL

In so far as prosecution counsel is concerned, his role and duties are somewhat wider in scope than that of defence counsel. Although both defence and prosecution counsel have an overriding duty to the court as one of its officers, defence counsel is expressly obligated to represent his client zealously and to obtain for his client the best remedy and defence authorised by law.[1] Prosecution counsel, on the other hand, has a broader obligation to seek justice, and in a criminal case to employ every legitimate means to bring about a just conviction.[2]

Duty to Court In General

In the discharge of his functions and responsibilities, an advocate attorney whether prosecution or defence, shall maintain a respectful attitude to the court and not engage in undignified or discourteous conduct which is degrading to the court.[3] It should be noted, as was pointed out in Rule VIII Commentary 12 of the Code of Professional Conduct of The Bahamas, a consistent pattern of rude, provocative or disruptive conduct by the attorney, even though unpunished as contempt may well merit discipline.

In this regard, as an advocate attorney, prosecution or defence counsel:

(i) shall not make statements or ask questions which are scandalous or intended only to intimidate or insult a witness or some other person;[4]
(ii) shall, in keeping with his duties as an officer of the court, concerned with the administration of justice, be punctual in attendance before the courts and be concise and direct in the trial and disposition of cases. In addition, when asked by the court, he shall inform the court of the estimated length of the proceedings before the court and of any new developments which might affect the estimated length of the trial or proceedings;[5]
(iii) shall not withhold authorities or documents which may tell against his client but which the law or standards of his profession require him to produce and when referring to any authority in support of his cases it is his duty to ensure that the decision relied upon has not been over-ruled.[6]

Duty to Court In Particular

(i) Judges

In the conduct of proceedings before the court, an attorney shall never seek privately to influence directly or indirectly judges of the court in his favour or in the favour of his client, by giving, lending or promising anything of value to the judge.[7] And conversely, an attorney shall not willfully make false accusations against a judge or other judicial officer.[8]

(ii) Jurors

With respect to jurors, an attorney shall not:

(a) give, lend or promise anything of value to a juror where there is a matter pending in which he is engaged;[9]

(b) make any attempts to curry favour with juries by fawning, flattery or pretended concern for their personal comfort ;[10]

(c) communicate with a juror as to the merits of such proceedings, except where authorized by law or the practise in the court or in the normal course of proceedings with a judge or person exercising judicial functions.[11]

(iii) Witnesses

An attorney is under a duty not to withhold facts or secret witnesses in order to establish the guilt or innocence of the accused.[12] In addition, he shall not, for the purposes of making any person unavailable as a witness, advise or cause that person to secret himself or leave the jurisdiction of the court.[13]

Further, he shall not pay or offer to pay or acquiesce in the payment of compensation to a witness for giving evidence in any cause or matter, save as payment for expenses reasonably incurred and as reasonable compensation for loss of time in attending for preparation of and testifying at the trial. The same also holds true for an expert witness; he shall not be paid other than a reasonable fee for his professional services.[14]

In the conduct of proceedings, advocate attorney is under a duty not to needlessly inconvenience, abuse, intimidate or harass a witness.[15] In so far as the attorney himself is concerned, he shall not appear as a witness for his own client except as to merely formal matters or where such appearance is essential to the ends of justice.[16] As the Jamaican Court of Appeal held in *R v Harris Hoo Shue*[17] it is not desirable that attorneys should unnecessarily import themselves into cases as witnesses. However if an attorney is a necessary witness for his client with respect to matters formal, he should entrust the conduct of the case to another attorney of his client's choice and he should not appear as advocate in any appeal from the decision in those proceedings.

(iv) Perjured Evidence/Fraud/Illegal Conduct

An advocate attorney is under a general duty, as an officer of the court, to never knowingly mislead the court or lend himself to casting aspersions on the other party or witnesses for which there is no sufficient basis in the information in his possession.

In this regard he:

(a) shall not knowingly use perjured testimony or false evidence or participate in the creation or use of evidence which he knows to be false;[18]

(b) shall not knowingly make a false statement of law or fact;

(c) shall not knowingly represent falsely to a judge, a court or other tribunal that a particular state of facts exists.[19] When he becomes aware of false information which has been presented to the court, with the intent of misleading or deceiving the court he cannot sit by passively; he either discloses the inconsistent evidence to the court or promptly calls upon the witness to rectify same;[20] and

(d) shall not counsel or assist his client or a witness in conduct that he knows to be illegal or fraudulent.[21]

DUTIES OF DEFENCE COUNSEL

In General

Every counsel has a duty to his client fearlessly to raise every issue, advance every argument and ask every question, however distasteful, which he thinks will help his client's case. However in carrying out his duty to his client, he also has an over-riding duty to the court as one of its officers concerned in the administration of justice.[22] Although as Lord Diplock observed with reference to defence counsel in *Saif Ali v Sydney Mitchell & Co Ltd*:

> Consistently with the rule that the prosecution must prove its case, he may passively stand by and watch the court being misled by reason of its failure to ascertain facts which are within the barrister's knowledge.[23]

In the conduct of the trial or proceedings, defence counsel shall endeavour to maintain his position of justice as an advocate and shall neither in argument to the court or in the address to the jury, assert his personal belief in his client's innocence or in the justice of his cause or his personal knowledge as to any of the facts involved in the matter under investigation.[24]

In Particular

(i) Defending a Client Accused of a Crime

When defending a client accused of a crime, irrespective of any belief or opinions which he may have formed as to the guilt or innocence of his client, defence counsel must endeavour to protect his client from being convicted except by a competent tribunal upon evidence which is sufficient to support a conviction for the offence with which the client is charged.[25] In so doing, he must not assert that which he knows to be false or set up a case inconsistent with the information given to him by his client.

In this regard, one of the most challenging dilemmas with which defence counsel is faced, is where his client who is accused of a crime, confesses his guilt to him.

As the representative of his client, an attorney's duty is to maintain the client/attorney confidentiality, but on the other hand he also has a duty to the court as one of its officers not to knowingly mislead the court or to assert that which he knows to be untrue.

The course of conduct adopted by defence counsel in the above circumstances depends primarily on two basic factors:

(a) whether the accused client has made a clear and unequivocal confession of guilt; and
(b) the stage at which the confession was made.

Where the confession is made before the commencement of proceedings

If the confession is made before the proceedings have started, the attorney may withdraw forthwith from the client's employment;[26] he may continue to act if the plea is to be one of guilty. However if the client insists on entering a plea of not guilty, the attorney may continue to represent the accused but only after he has explained to the client what the consequences will be and in particular the very strict restrictions which are placed on the conduct of the defence.[27] (*see below*)

Where the confession is made during proceedings

In criminal cases the attorney must seek leave of the court to withdraw and it is a matter of the Court's discretion whether leave will be granted. However, where the confession is made during the proceedings or in circumstances in which he cannot withdraw without compromising his client's position, the attorney should continue to act but within the very strict limitations imposed on him in the conduct of his client's defence.[28] (*see below*).

Limitations Imposed on Client on Conduct of Case

Although defence counsel should not reveal the client's perjury he must at the same time avoid any involvement in the client's perjury. He should therefore seek to avoid direct examination of his client; he shall not argue to the jury the accused' s known false version of the facts; he may not recite or rely upon the client's false testimony in his arguments. In addition he cannot make a plea in mitigation.[29]

In particular, defence counsel may not protest his client's innocence nor set up an affirmative case consistent with the client's confession by e.g. asserting or suggesting that some other person committed the offence charged or by calling any evidence in support of an alibi intended to show that the accused could not have done or in fact had not done, the act of which he is accused.[30]

Although the accused has the right to give evidence in his own defence, defence counsel should properly advise him upon this but the decision must be taken by the client himself.[31] If the accused insists, defence counsel should make a record of the fact that the accused is taking the stand against his advice.

Although defence counsel is severely restricted in the conduct of the accused client's defence in cases where the client has confessed his guilt, the attorney may nevertheless present a technical defence by, *inter alia,* objecting to the competency of the court, the form of the indictment and the admissibility or sufficiency of the evidence.[32] In attacking the evidence for the prosecution, he is entitled to test the evidence of each individual witness for the prosecution by, *inter alia,* cross-examination or in his speech to the tribunal and to argue that the evidence taken as a whole is insufficient to amount to proof that the accused is guilty of the offences charged, but he should go no further than that.[33]

(ii) Disclosure of Previous Conviction of Client

Where the prosecution has led the court to believe that the accused client has no previous conviction, defence counsel is under no duty to disclose facts to the contrary which are known to him.

(iii) Withdrawing From Case

As mentioned above, one of the options open to defence counsel is to decline to act further for an accused client in cases where the client confesses his guilt but insists upon entering a plea of not guilty. However quite apart from this specific instance, the relevant Code/Canon of Ethics of the various territories[34] sets out the general circumstances in which an attorney is entitled to withdraw his services from a matter pending before the court or other tribunal.

Those circumstances are:

(a) where the client insists upon his representing a claim or defence that he cannot conscientiously advance;
(b) where the client seeks to pursue a course of conduct which is illegal or which will result in deliberately deceiving the Court;
(c) where a client has in the course of the proceedings perpetrated a fraud upon a person or tribunal and on request by the attorney-at-law has refused or is unable to rectify the same;
(d) where his continued service will involve him in the violation of the law or a disciplinary rule;
(e) where the client by any other conduct renders it unreasonably difficult for the attorney-at-law to carry out his service as such effectively, or in accordance with the judgment and advice of the attorney-at-law, or the rules of law or professional ethics; and
(f) where for any good and compelling reason it is difficult for him to carry out his services effectively.

Lord Wright remarked in the case of *Myers v Elman*:

> While an attorney owes a duty to his client he is also a helper in the administration of justice. As such if he is asked or required to by his client, to do something inconsistent with his duty to the court it is for him to point out that he cannot do it and if necessary to cease to act.[35]

DUTIES OF PROSECUTION COUNSEL

As was noted in Rule VII, Commentary 3 of the Code of Professional Conduct of The Bahamas, 'the prosecutor exercises a public function involving much discretion and power and must act fairly and dispassionately'. Accordingly, his primary duty is not to represent any party, but to assist the court in the administration of justice and to ensure the efficient speedy and proper conduct of the case. In this regard, prosecution counsel should not endeavour to obtain a conviction by all means at his command.[36]

In addition, it is his duty to present the case fairly and impartially and to this end, to see that the jury is properly instructed in the law applicable to the facts of the case.

In particular, in the conduct of a trial, prosecution counsel is under a duty to make timely disclosure to the accused or his counsel (or to the court if the accused is not represented) of all relevant facts and witnesses known to him, whether tending towards the guilt or innocence of the accused.[37] In this regard prosecution counsel is under a specific duty:

(a) to ensure that the witnesses and all relevant statements in the possession of the prosecution have been promptly made available to the defence; and
(b) to decide what additional evidence is necessary and to set out in writing precisely what is required with a view to sending it on to the defence as soon as possible.[38]

If at any stage he is convinced that there is no evidence against the defendant or so little evidence that it would not be safe to leave the case to the jury, it is the duty of prosecution counsel to acquaint the court of his views and to ask leave to withdraw the prosecution. It is quite wrong of counsel to accept any instructions to go on with a prosecution, once he has formed a view that the prosecution should not continue.[39]

It is also prosecution's duty not to withhold facts tending to prove the innocence or guilt of the accused. With respect to settling of the indictment, prosecution counsel should ensure that he settles the indictment promptly and refrain from over-loading the indictment with too many defenses or too many counts.[40]

With respect to the sentencing of the accused, prosecution counsel should not attempt by advocacy, to influence the court with regard to sentencing. Finally, if the defence is unrepresented it is his duty to inform the court of any mitigating circumstances within his knowledge.[41]

ENDNOTES

1. Antigua & Barbuda - Code of Ethics Part A rr. 20,21
   Barbados - Code of Ethics Part III r.23, Part IV r.24
   Eastern Caribbean (save Antigua & Barbuda and St. Lucia)
   - OECS Code of Ethics Part A rr. 20, 21
   Jamaica - Canon of Ethics, Canon IV

St. Lucia - Code of Ethics, Part A. rr.19,20
The Bahamas - Code of Professional Conduct Rule VIII, Commentaries 1, 8
Trinidad & Tobago - Code of Ethics Part A rr. 20, 21

2. Antigua & Barbuda - Code of Ethics Part A r.14
Barbados - Code of Ethics Part III r.18
Eastern Caribbean (save Antigua & Barbuda and St. Lucia) - OECS Code of Ethics Part A r.14
Jamaica - Canon of Ethics Canon III (h)
St. Lucia - Code of Ethics Part A. r.14
The Bahamas - Code of Professional Conduct, Rule VIII, Commentary 7
Trinidad & Tobago - Code of Ethics Part A r. 14

3. Antigua & Barbuda - Code of Ethics Part A r.36(1) Part B r.19
Barbados - Code of Ethics Part V r.40(1) Part VIII r.75
Eastern Caribbean (save Antigua & Barbuda and St. Lucia) - OECS Code of Ethics Part A r.36(1) Part B r.19
Jamaica - Canon of Ethics Canon V (a)
St. Lucia - Code of Ethics Part A. r.35(1), Part B r.22
The Bahamas - Code of Professional Conduct, Rule VIII, Commentary 12
Trinidad & Tobago - Code of Ethics Part A r.36(1) Part B r.19

4. See on this The Bahamas Code of Professional Conduct Rule VIII Commentary 1(j).

5. Antigua & Barbuda - Code of Ethics Part A r. 39
Barbados - Code of Ethics Part V r.43
Eastern Caribbean (save Antigua & Barbuda and St. Lucia) - OECS Code of Ethics Part A r.39
Jamaica - Canon of Ethics Canon V (q)
St. Lucia - Code of Ethics Part A. r.38
Trinidad & Tobago - Code of Ethics, Part A r. 39

6. *Rondel v Worsley* [1969] 1 AC 191 at p.227, [1967] 3 All ER 993 at p.998, HL. See also *Young v Morales* (1995) 50 WIR 433. See also The Bahamas, Code of Professional Conduct, Rule VIII Commentary 1(g).

7. Antigua & Barbuda - Code of Ethics Part A r.38
Barbados - Code of Ethics Part V r.42
Eastern Caribbean (save Antigua & Barbuda and St. Lucia) - OECS Code of Ethics Part A r.38
Jamaica - Canon of Ethics Canon IV r(e)
St. Lucia - Code of Ethics Part A. r.37
The Bahamas - Code of Professional Conduct Rule VIII, Commentary 1(c)
Trinidad & Tobago - Code of Ethics Part A r.38

8. Antigua & Barbuda - Code of Ethics Part B r.20
Barbados - Code of Ethics Part VIII r.76
Eastern Caribbean (save Antigua & Barbuda and St. Lucia) - OECS Code of Ethics Part B r.20
Jamaica - Canon of Ethics Canon V (c)
St. Lucia - Code of Ethics Part B. r.23

	Trinidad & Tobago	- Code of Ethics Part B r.20
9.	Antigua & Barbuda	- Code of Ethics Part B r.23
	Barbados	- Code of Ethics Part VIII r.79
	Eastern Caribbean (save Antigua & Barbuda and St. Lucia)	- OECS Code of Ethics Part B r.23
	Jamaica	- Canon of Ethics Canon V (b)
	St. Lucia	- Code of Ethics, Part B. r.26
	The Bahamas	- Code of Professional Conduct Part VIII, Commentary 1
	Trinidad & Tobago	- Code of Ethics Part B r. 23
10.	Antigua & Barbuda	- Code of Ethics Part A r.38
	Barbados	- Code of Ethics Part V.42
	Eastern Caribbean (save Antigua & Barbuda and St. Lucia)	- OECS Code of Ethics Part A r.38
	St. Lucia	- Code of Ethics Part A. r.37
	Trinidad & Tobago	- Code of Ethics Part A r.38
11.	Antigua & Barbuda	- Code of Ethics Part B r. 24
	Barbados	- Code of Ethics Part VIII r.80
	Eastern Caribbean (save Antigua & Barbuda and St. Lucia)	- OECS Code of Ethics Part B r.24
	Jamaica	- Canon of Ethics Canon V (i)
	St. Lucia	- Code of Ethics Part B r.27
	Trinidad & Tobago	- Code of Ethics Part B r.24
12.	Antigua & Barbuda	- Code of Ethics Part B r. 2(2)
	Barbados	- Code of Ethics Part VIII r.58(2)
	Eastern Caribbean (save Antigua & Barbuda and St. Lucia)	- OECS Code of Ethics Part B r 2(2)
	St. Lucia	- Code of Ethics Part B. r.2(2)
	The Bahamas	- Code of Professional Conduct Rule VIII, Commentary 1(h)
	Trinidad & Tobago	- Code of Ethics Part B r.2(2)
13.	Antigua & Barbuda	- Code of Ethics Part B r. 25
	Barbados	- Code of Ethics Part VIII r.81
	Eastern Caribbean (save Antigua & Barbuda and St. Lucia)	- OECS Code of Ethics Part B r.25
	Jamaica	- Canon of Ethics, Canon V(k)
	St. Lucia	- Code of Ethics Part B. r28
	The Bahamas	- Code of Professional Conduct Rule VIII Commentary 1(h)
	Trinidad & Tobago	- Code of Ethics Part B r. 25
14.	Antigua & Barbuda	- Code of Ethics Part B r. 26
	Barbados	- Code of Ethics Part VIII r.82
	Eastern Caribbean (save Antigua & Barbuda and St. Lucia)	- OECS Code of Ethics Part B r.26
	Jamaica	- Canon of Ethics Canon IV (l)
	St. Lucia	- Code of Ethics Part B. r.29
	Trinidad & Tobago	- Code of Ethics Part B r. 26
15.	Antigua & Barbuda	- Code of Ethics Part A r.35(1)
	Barbados	- Code of Ethics Part IV r38(1)

Eastern Caribbean (save Antigua & Barbuda and St. Lucia)
- OECS Code of Ethics Part A r.35(1)

Jamaica - Canon of Ethics Canon V (p)
St. Lucia - Code of Ethics Part B. r.34(1)
The Bahamas - Code of Professional Conduct Rule VIII, Commentary I(j)
Trinidad & Tobago - Code of Ethics Part B r.35(1)

16. Antigua & Barbuda - Code of Ethics Part A r.35(2)
Barbados - Code of Ethics Part IV r.39(2)
Eastern Caribbean (save Antigua & Barbuda and St. Lucia)
- OECS Code of Ethics Part A r.35(2)
Jamaica - Canon of Ethics Canon V(p)
St. Lucia - Code of Ethics Part A. r.34(2)
The Bahamas - Code of Professional Conduct, Rule VIII, Commentary 3
Trinidad & Tobago - Code of Ethics Part A r.35(2)

17. (1936-40) 3 JLR 108, see also *R v Jacquith and Emode* [1989] Crim. LR 508 at p.563.

18. Antigua & Barbuda - Code of Ethics Part A r.35(2)
Barbados - Code of Ethics Part IV r.39(2)
Eastern Caribbean (save Antigua & Barbuda and St. Lucia)
- OECS Code of Ethics Part B r.27
Jamaica - Canon of Ethics Canon V (m)
St. Lucia - Code of Ethics Part B. r.30
The Bahamas - Code of Professional Conduct Part VIII Commentary 1
Trinidad & Tobago - Code of Ethics Part B r.27

19. Antigua & Barbuda - Code of Ethics Part A r.30(2)
Barbados - Code of Ethics Part VIII r.86(2)
Eastern Caribbean (save Antigua & Barbuda and St. Lucia)
- OECS Code of Ethics Part B r30(2)
Jamaica - Canon of Ethics Canon VI (cc)
St. Lucia - Code of Ethics Part B. r.33(2)
The Bahamas - Code of Professional Conduct Part VIII, Commentary 1(e)
Trinidad & Tobago - Code of Ethics Part B r.30(2)
See also *Pinder v Blake* CA 5/1985, Bahamas (unreported); *Re James Grey* (1869) 20 LT 730.

20. Antigua & Barbuda - Code of Ethics Part B r. 28
Barbados - Code of Ethics Part VIII r.84
Eastern Caribbean (save Antigua & Barbuda and St. Lucia)
- OECS Code of Ethics Part B r.28
Jamaica - Canon of Ethics Canon V (n)
St. Lucia - Code of Ethics Part B. r.31
The Bahamas - Code of Professional Conduct Part VIII, Commentary 2
Trinidad & Tobago - Code of Ethics Part B r.28
See also *Vernon v Bosley (No 2)* [1997] 3 WLR 683.

21. Antigua & Barbuda - Code of Ethics Part B r. 28
Barbados - Code of Ethics Part VIII r.84

Eastern Caribbean (save Antigua & Barbuda and St. Lucia)
- OECS Code of Ethics Part B r.28

Jamaica	-	Code of Ethics Canon V (n)
St. Lucia	-	Code of Ethics Part B. r.31
The Bahamas	-	Code of Professional Conduct Part VIII Commentary 1(b)
Trinidad & Tobago	-	Code of Ethics Part B r. 28

22. See *Rondel v Worsley* [1967] 3 All ER 993 at p.998, [1969] 1 AC 191 at 227 HL
23. [1980] AC 198 at p.220 PC
24. Antigua & Barbuda - Code of Ethics Part A r. 37
Barbados - Code of Ethics Part V r.41
Eastern Caribbean (save Antigua & Barbuda and St. Lucia)
- OECS Code of Ethics Part A r.37
Jamaica - Canon of Ethics, Canon V(j)
St. Lucia - Code of Ethics Part A. r.36
The Bahamas - Code of Professional Conduct, Rule VIII Commentary 3
Trinidad & Tobago - Code of Ethics Part A r.37
25. Antigua & Barbuda - Code of Ethics Part A r.25
Barbados - Code of Ethics Part IV r.28
Eastern Caribbean (save Antigua & Barbuda and St. Lucia)
- OECS Code of Ethics Part A r.25
Jamaica - Canon of Ethics Canon III (g)
St. Lucia - Code of Ethics Part A. r.24
The Bahamas - Code of Professional Conduct, Rule VIII Commentary
Trinidad & Tobago - Code of Ethics Part A r.25
26. The Code of Conduct for the Bar of England and Wales 1990 para. 12.5.
27. *Ibid.*
28. The Bahamas - Code of Professional Conduct Rule VIII Commentary 9. See also The Code of Conduct for the Bar of England and Wales 1990 para. 13.3 and *R v Lyons* [1978] 68 Cr. App 104.
29. *Ibid.*
30. The Bahamas - Code of Professional Conduct Rule VIII Commentary 9. See also The Code of Conduct for the Bar of England and Wales 1990 para. 13.4.
31. *Sankar v The State* (1996) 46 WIR 452. See also The Code of Professional Conduct of England and Wales 1990 para 12.4. See also Code of Conduct for the Bar of England and Wales 1990 para. 13.4
32. The Bahamas - Code of Professional Conduct Rule VIII Commentary 9. See also The Code of Conduct for the Bar of England and Wales 1990 para. 13.4.
33. The Bahamas - Code of Professional Conduct Rule VIII, Commentary 9.
See also Code of Conduct for the Bar of England and Wales 1990 para. 13.5.
34. Antigua & Barbuda - Code of Ethics Part B r 13.
Barbados - Code of Ethics Part VIII r 69.

Eastern Caribbean (save Antigua & Barbuda and St. Lucia)

	-	OECS Code of Ethics Part B r 13.
Jamaica	-	Canon of Ethics Canon IV (q).
St. Lucia	-	Code of Ethics Part B r 16.
The Bahamas	-	Code of Professional Conduct Rule XI, Commentary 4. See also Rule VIII Cmmentary 2 (b).
Trinidad & Tobago	-	Code of Ethics Part B r 13.

35. [1914] AC 282 at 317 HL

36. The Bahamas - Code of Professional Conduct Rule VIII Commentary 7. See also the Code of Professional Conduct for the Bar of England and Wales para 11.11

37. *Ibid.*

38. See on this the Code of Professional Conduct for the Bar of England and Wales para 11.4(d)

39. *Abbot v Refuge Assurance Ltd* [1961] 1 QB 433 at 451

40. See on this The Code of Professional Conduct for the Bar of England and Wales para 11.4(d)

41. See on the Code of Professional Conduct for the Bar of England and Wales para 11.8.

Appendix 1

Antigua & Barbuda

Code of Ethics

The Legal Profession Act 1997

FOURTH SCHEDULE
PART A (Section 21)

Code of Ethics

General Guidelines

I. In Relation to the Profession and Himself

1. An attorney-at-law shall observe the rules of this Code, maintain his integrity and the honour and dignity of the legal profession and encourage other attorneys-at-law to act similarly both in the practice of his profession and in his private life, shall refrain from conduct which is detrimental to the profession or which may tend to discredit it.
2. An attorney-at-law shall expose without fear or favour before the proper tribunals unprofessional or dishonest conduct by any other attorney-at-law and shall not lightly refuse a retainer against another attorney-at-law who is alleged to have wronged his client or committed any other act of professional misconduct.
3. (1) An attorney-at-law shall scrupulously preserve his independence in the discharge of his professional duties.
   (2) An attorney-at-law practising on his own account or in partnership, shall not engage in any other business or occupation if doing so may cause him to cease to be independent.
4. An attorney-at-law shall protect the profession against the admission thereto of any candidate whose moral character or education render him unfit for such admission.

5. (1) An attorney-at-law shall not endeavour by direct or indirect means to attract the clients of another attorney-at-law and where a client is referred to him by another attorney-at-law the clients remains of all other purposes the client of the referring attorney-at-law to whom the client is referred shall act with due deference to the relationship between the client and the referring attorney-at-law.
   (2) Where a referred client offers other work to the attorney-at-law to whom he is referred and the offer is sufficiently proximate to the referral, that attorney-at-law shall not accept that offer unless it has been brought to the attention of the referring attorney-at-law.
6. An attorney-at-law may speak in public or write for publication on legal topics so long as he does not thereby advertise his own professional competence and is not likely to be regarded as being concerned thereby with the giving of individual advice.
7. The best advertisement for an attorney-at-law is the establishment of a well merited reputation for personal integrity, capacity, dedication to work and fidelity to trust and it is unprofessional —
   (a) to solicit business by circulars or advertisements or interviews not warranted by personal relations;
   (b) to seek retainers through agents or any kind.
8. An attorney-at-law shall defend the interest of his client without fear or judicial disfavour or public unpopularity and without regard to any unpleasant consequences to himself or to any other person.
9. Subject to paragraph 17, no attorney-at-law is obliged to act either as adviser or advocate for every person who may wish to become his client; he has a right to decline employment.
10. No client is entitled to receive nor should any attorney-at-law render, any service or advice involving disrespect for judicial office or the corruption of any persons exercising a public or private trust or deception or betrayal of the public.
11. Every attorney-at-law should bear in mind that the oath of office taken on his admission to practise is not a mere form but is a solemn undertaking to be strictly observed on his part.
12. An attorney-at-law should also bear in mind that he can only maintain the high traditions of his profession by being a person of high integrity and dignity.

II. In Relation to the State and the Public

13. An attorney-at-law owes a duty to the State to maintain its integrity, its constitution and its laws and not to aid, abet, counsel or assist anyone to act in any way contrary to those laws.
14. When engaged as a public prosecutor the primary duty of an attorney-at-law

is not to secure a conviction but to see that justice is done and to that end he shall not withhold facts tending to prove either the guilt or innocence of the accused.

15. An attorney-at-law shall endeavour by lawful means where the needs of society require, to promote and encourage the modernization, simplification and reform of the laws.
16. An attorney-at-law shall not by his actions, stir up strife or litigation by seeking out defects in titles, claims for personal injury or other causes of action for the purpose of securing a retainer to prosecute a claim therefor; or pay or reward any person directly and indirectly for the purpose of procuring him to be retained in his professional capacity, and where it is in the interest of his client he shall seek to obtain reasonable settlements of disputes.
17. An attorney-at-law shall not except for good reasons refuse his services in capital offences.
18. An attorney-at-law shall not be deterred from accepting proffered employment owing to the fear or dislike of incurring disapproval of officials other attorneys-at-law or members of the public.
19. Where an attorney-at-law consents to undertake legal aid and he is requested by the Law Council and consents to undertake the representation of a person unable to afford such representation or to obtain legal aid, the attorney-at-law shall not, except for compelling reasons, seek to be excused from undertaking such representation.
20. An attorney-at-law in undertaking the defence of persons accused of crime shall use all fair and reasonable means to present every defence available at law.

III. In Relation to Clients

21. (1) An attorney-at-law shall always act in the best interest of his client, represent him honestly, competently and zealously and endeavour by all fair and honourable means to obtain for him the benefit of any and every remedy and defence which is authorised by law, steadfastly bearing in mind that the duties and responsibilities of the attorney-at-law are to be carried out within and not without the bounds of the law.
    (2) The interests of his client and the exigencies of the administration of justice should always be the first concern of an attorney-at-law and rank before his right to compensation for his services.
22. (1) Before advising on a client's cause an attorney-at-law should obtain full knowledge thereof and give a candid opinion of the merits or demerits and probable results of pending or contemplated litigation.
    (2) An attorney-at-law should beware of proffering bold and confident assurances to his client (especially where employment may depend on such assurances) always bearing in mind that seldom are all the law and

facts on the side of his client and that audi alteram partem is the safest rule to follow.

(3) Whenever the controversy admits of fair adjustment an attorney-at-law should inform his client accordingly and advise to avoid or settle litigation.

23. (1) An attorney-at-law shall at the time of retainer disclose to his client all the circumstances of his relations to the parties and his interest in or connection with the controversy (if any) which might influence the client in his selection of an attorney-at-law.

(2) An attorney-at-law shall scrupulously guard and never divulge his client's secrets and confidences.

24. An attorney-at-law shall treat adverse witnesses, litigants and other attorney-at-law with fairness and courtesy refraining from all offensive personal references and shall avoid imparting to his professional duties his clients personal feelings and prejudices.

25. It is the right of an attorney-at-law to undertake the defence of a person accused of crime regardless of his own personal opinion as to the guilt of the accused and having undertaken such defence he is bound by all fair and honourable means to present every defence that the law of the land permits so that no person may be deprived of life or liberty except by due process of law.

26. (1) An attorney-at-law may represent multiple clients only if he can adequately represent the interests of each and if each consents to such representation after full disclosure of the possible effects of multiple representation.

(2) In all situations where a possible conflict of interest arises, an attorney-at-law shall resolve all conflict by leaning against multiple representation.

27. (1) An attorney-at-law shall deal with his client's business with all due expedition and shall whenever reasonably so required by the client provide him with full information as to the progress of the client's business.

(2) It is improper for an attorney-at-law to accept a case unless he can handle it without undue delay.

28. Where an attorney-at-law determines that the interest of his client requires it, he may with the specific or general consent of the client refer his business or part of it to another attorney-at-law whether or not a member of his own firm.

29. (1) Queen Counsel shall be entitled to accept instructions, appear or do any work without a junior, except where he would be unable properly to carry out his instructions or conduct his case if he were to do so.

(2) Where more than one attorney-at-law appears as advocate for the same party in the same proceedings, who shall lead the conduct of the party's case shall, subject to the instructions of the client be settled by the attorney-at-law representing that party before they appear in court and shall

not be altered during the course of the proceedings and the leader shall have all authority over the conduct of the case.

30. An attorney-at-law including a Queen Counsel who appears with the leader is entitled to a negotiated fee appropriate for his conduct of the case.

31. (1) An attorney-at-law is entitled to reasonable compensation for his services but should avoid charges which either overestimate or undervalue the service rendered.

(2) The ability of a client to pay cannot justify a charge in excess of the value of the service rendered, though the client's indigence may require a charge that is below such value, or even no charge at all.

(3) An attorney-at-law should avoid controversies with clients regarding compensation for his services as far as is compatible with self-respect and his right to receive reasonable compensation for his services.

32. The right of an attorney-at-law to ask for a deposit or to demand payment of out-of-pocket expenses and commitments failing payment of which he may withdraw from the case or refuse to handle it, shall not be exercised where the client may be unable to find other assistance in time to prevent irreparable damage being done.

33. Where an attorney-at-law engages a foreign colleague to advise on a case or to co-operate in handling it, he is responsible for the payment of the latter's charges except there is express agreement to the contrary, but where an attorney-at-law directs a client to a foreign colleague he is not responsible for the payment of the latter's charges, nor is he entitled to a share of the fee of his foreign colleague.

34. An attorney-at-law may at any time withdraw from employment —

(a) where the client fails, refuses or neglects to carry out an agreement with or his obligation to, the attorney-at-law as regards the expenses or fees payable by the client;

(b) where his inability to work with colleagues indicates that the best interest of the client is likely to be served by his withdrawal;

(c) where his client freely assents to the termination of his employment;

(d) where by reasons of his mental or physical condition or other good and compelling reason it is difficult for him to carry out his employment effectively; or

(e) in cases of conflict as contemplated in Rule 26 of this part or Rule II of Part B hereof.

35. (1) An attorney-at-law should not appear as a witness for his own client except as to merely formal matters or where such appearance is essential to the ends of justice.

(2) If an attomey-at-law is a necessary witness for his client with respect to matters other than such as are merely formal, he should entrust the conduct of the case to another attorney-at-law of his client's choice.

IV. In Relation to the Courts and the Administration of Justice

36. (1) An attorney-at-law shall maintain a respectful attitude towards the court and shall not engage in undignified or discourteous conduct which is degrading to the court.
    (2) An attorney-at-law shall encourage respect for the courts and the judges.
    (3) An attorney-at-law shall support judges and magistrates against unjust criticisms.
    (4) Where there is ground for complaint against a judge or magistrate an attorney-at-law may make representation to the proper authorities and in such cases, the attorney-at-law shall be protected.
37. An attorney-at-law shall endeavour always to maintain his position as an advocate and shall not either in argument to the court or in address to the jury assert his personal belief in his client's innocence or in the justice of his cause or his personal knowledge as to any of the facts involved in the matter under investigation.
38. An attorney-at-law should never seek privately to influence directly or indirectly the Judges of the Court in his favour or in the favour of his client, nor should he attempt to curry favour with juries by fawning, flattery or pretended solicitude for their personal comfort.
39. An attorney-at-law shall be punctual in attendance before the Courts and concise and direct in the trial and disposition of causes.
40. An attorney-at-law appearing before the Court shall at all times be attired in such a manner as prescribed or agreed by the proper authorities and as befits the dignity of the Court.

V. In Relation to his Fellow Attorneys-at-law

41. (1) The conduct of an attorney-at-law towards his fellow attorneys shall be characterized by courtesy, fairness and good faith and he shall not permit ill-feeling between clients to affect his relationship with his colleagues.
    (2) All personal conflicts between attorneys-at-law should be scrupulously avoided as should also colloquies between them which cause delay and promote unseemly wrangling.
42. (1) An attorney-at-law shall reply promptly to letters from other attorneys-at-law making inquiries on behalf of their clients.
    (2) An attorney-at-law shall endeavour as far as reasonable to suit the convenience of the opposing attorney-at-law when the interest of his client or the cause of justice will not be injured by so doing.
43. An attorney-at-law shall not give a professional undertaking that he cannot fulfil, and he shall fulfil every such undertaking that he gives.
44. (1) There is a duty on every attorney-at-law to report improper or unprofes-

sional conduct by a colleague to the Law Council, save where the information relating to the improper or unprofessional conduct is received in professional confidence in which case he must respect the duty of silence imposed in such circumstances.

(2) An attorney-at-law shall expose without fear or favour before the proper tribunal unprofessional of dishonest conduct by another attorney-at-law and shall not lightly refuse a retainer against another attorney-at-law who is alleged to have wronged a client.

45. Where an attorney-at-law has been sent money, documents or other things by a colleague which, at the time of sending, are expressed to be sent only on the basis that the attorney-at-law to whom they are sent will receive them on his undertaking to do or refrain from doing some act, the receiving attorney-at-law shall forthwith return whatever was sent if he is unable to accept them on such undertaking, otherwise he must comply with the undertaking.

46. An attorney-at-law shall not in any way communicate upon a subject in controversy or attempt to negotiate or compromise a matter directly with any party represented by another attorney-at-law except through such other attorney-at-law or with his prior consent.

47. (1) An attorney-at-law shall not ignore the customs or practices of the legal profession even when the law expressly permits it, without giving timely notice to the opposing attorney-at-law.

(2) An attorney-at-law should avoid all sharp practices and should refrain from taking any paltry advantage when his opponent has made or overlooked some technical error or matter, bearing in mind that no client has a right to demand that an attorney-at-law representing him shall be illiberal or shall do anything repugnant to his own sense of honour and propriety.

48. An attorney-at-law shall not accept instructions to act in Court proceedings in which to his knowledge the client has previously been represented by another attorney-at-law, unless he first notifies the other attorney-at-law of the change, and makes reasonable efforts to ensure that attorney has been paid for his services, but shall be deemed to have notified the other attorney-at-law if he has made reasonable efforts to notify him.

49. An attorney-at-law shall not accept instructions to act in proceedings (other than Court proceedings) in which to his knowledge, another attorney-at-law has previously represented the client unless he makes reasonable efforts to ascertain that the retainer of that attorney-at-law has been determined by the client, or that the client wishes both attorneys-at-law to represent him.

50. An attorney-at-law who instructs or employs another attorney-at-law to act on behalf of his client, unless otherwise agreed, shall pay the proper fee of such attorney-at-law whether or not he has received payment from the client.

51. In undertaking to render assistance to a foreign colleague, an attorney-at-law shall remember that his responsibility is much greater both when giving advice and handling a case, than it would be had he undertaken to assist a colleague in Antigua and Barbuda.

VI. General

52. Nothing herein contained shall be construed as derogating from any existing rules of professional conduct and duties of an attorney-at-law which are in keeping with the traditions of the legal profession although not specifically mentioned herein.
53. Where in any particular matter explicit ethical guidance does not exist, an attorney-at-law shall determine his conduct by acting in a manner that promotes public confidence in the integrity and efficiency of the legal system and the legal profession.
54. (1) A person who previously held a substantive appointment as a Judge of the Supreme Court shall not appear as an attorney-at-law in any of the Courts of Antigua and Barbuda for a period of ten years commencing on the date of his retirement, resignation or other termination of such appointment.
    (2) This rule shall not apply to a person who is appointed to act as a Judge in a temporary capacity.

PART B

Mandatory Provisions and Specific Prohibitions

1. An attorney-at-law shall not practise as such unless he has been issued a practising certificate in accordance with the provisions of the Act.
2. (1) An attorney-at-law shall never knowingly mislead the Court.
   (2) An attorney-at-law shall not withhold facts or secrete witnesses in order to establish the guilt or innocence of the accused.
3. An attorney-at-law shall not hold out any person who is not qualified to practise law as a partner associate, consultant or attorney-at-law.
4. An attorney-at-law shall not solicit business or consent to become involved in a matter unless at the request of a party thereto. Provided however that it is proper for an attorney-at-law to become involved in matters referred by the Law Association or by another attorney-at-law or for which he is engaged in any other manner not inconsistent with these Rules.
5. An attorney-at-law shall not in the carrying on of his practice or otherwise permit any act or thing which is likely or is intended to attract business unfairly or can reasonably be regarded as touting or advertising.
6. (l) An attorney-at-law shall not in any way make use of any forms of advertisement calculated to attract clients to himself or any firm with which

he is associated and he shall not permit, authorise or encourage anyone to do so or reward anyone for doing so on his behalf.

(2) An attorney-at-law shall not permit his professional standing to be used for the purpose of advertising any particular product, service or commercial organization.

(3) An attorney-at-law shall not advertise for business indirectly by furnishing or inspiring newspaper comment concerning cases or causes in which an attorney-at-law has been or is connected or concerning the manner of their conduct, the magnitude of the interests involved, the importance of the attorney-at-law's position and any similar self-laudations.

Provided however that —

(a) an attorney-at-law may permit limited and dignified identification of himself as an attorney-at-law —

(i) in political advertisements relevant to the cause of a political campaign or issue;

(ii) in public notices where the announcement of his professional status is required or authorised by law, or is reasonably necessary for a purpose other than the attraction of potential clients;

(iii) in reports and announcements of *bona fide* commercial, civic, professional or political organizations in which he serves as a director or officer;

(iv) in and on legal textbooks, articles, professional journals and other legal publications and in dignified and restrained advertisements thereof;

(v) in announcements of any public address, lecture, or publication by him on legal topics, provided that such announcements do not emphasize his own professional competence and are not likely to be regarded as being concerned with the giving of individual advice by him.

(b) An attorney-at-law may speak in public or write for publication on legal topics so long as he does not thereby emphasize his own professional competence and is not likely to be regarded as being concerned thereby with the giving of individual advice.

(c) The following cards, office signs, letterheads or directory listings may be used by an attorney-at-law but in a restrained and dignified form -

(i) a professional card identifying the attorney-at-law by name and as an attorney-at-law giving his decorations and degrees, legal or otherwise, his addresses, telephone numbers and the name of his law firm or professional associates so however that such cards are not published in the news media and are only handed out on request and for the purposes of identification or address.

(ii) a brief professional announcement card to be delivered only to attorneys-at-law, clients, personal friends and relations and government bodies and stating new or changed associations or addresses, changes of firm name or like professional matters;

(iii) a sign or size and design compatible with the existing practice of the profession, on or near the door of the office and in the building directory identifying the law office;

(iv) a letterhead identifying the attorney-at-law by name and as an attorney-at-law and giving his decorations and degrees, legal or otherwise, his addresses, telephone numbers and name of his law firm and of his associates;

(v) a listing in a telephone directory, a reputable law list, legal directory or biographical reference giving brief biographical or other relevant information; and any such professional card, office sign, letterhead or listing may state the attorney-at-law is also a notary public.

7. Where an attorney-at-law commits any criminal offence which in the opinion of the Law Council is of a nature likely to bring the profession into disrepute, such commission of the offence shall constitute professional misconduct if —

(a) he has been convicted by any Court, including a foreign Court of competent jurisdiction, for the offence; or

(b) although he has not been prosecuted the Law Council is satisfied of the facts constituting the criminal offence; or

(c) he has been prosecuted and has been acquitted by reason of a technical defence or he has been convicted but such conviction is quashed by reason of some technical defence.

8. An attorney-at-law shall not acquire directly or indirectly by purchase, or otherwise a financial or other interest in the subject matter of a case which he is conducting.

9. (1) An attorney-at-law shall not enter into partnership or fee sharing arrangements concerning the practice of law with non-qualified bodies or persons.

(2) An attorney-at-law shall not enter into an arrangement for or charge or collect a fee in contravention of these Rules or any other law.

10. (1) An attorney-at-law shall not charge fees that are unfair or unreasonable. (In determining the fairness and reasonableness of a fee the following factors may be taken into account. —

(a) the time and labour required, the novelty and difficulty of the questions involved and the skill required to perform the legal service properly;

(b) the likelihood that the acceptance of the particular employment

will preclude other employment by the attorney-at-law;
(c) the fee customarily charged in the locality for similar legal services;
(d) the amount, if any involved;
(e) the time limitations imposed by the client or by the circumstances;
(f) the nature and length of the professional relationship with the client;
(g) the experience, reputation and ability of the attorney-at-law concerned;
(h) any scale of fees or recommended guide as to charges prescribed by law or by the Law Council).

(2) An attorney-at-law shall not accept any fee or reward for merely introducing a client or referring a case or client to another attorney-at-law.

(3) An attorney-at-law shall not charge a contingency fee save and except reasonable commissions on collection of liquidated claims with the prior agreement of the client.

11. (1) Except with the specific approval of his client given after full disclosure, an attorney-at-law shall not act in any manner in which his professional duties and personal interests conflict or are likely to conflict.

(2) An attorney-at-law shall not accept or continue his retainer or employment on behalf of two or more clients if their interests are likely to conflict or if his independent professional judgement is likely to be impaired.

12. (1) An attorney-at-law who withdraws from employment under Rule 34 of Part A shall not do so until he has taken reasonable steps to avoid foreseeable prejudice or injury to the position and rights of his client including —
(a) giving due notice;
(b) allowing time for employment of another attorney-at-law;
(c) delivering to the client all documents and property to which he is entitled subject however to any lien which the attorney-at-law may have over the same;
(d) complying with such laws, rules or practice as may be applicable; and
(e) where appropriate, obtaining the permission of the Court where the hearing of the matter has commenced.

(2) An attorney-at-law who withdraws from employment shall refund promptly such part of the fees, if any already paid by his client as may be fair and reasonable having regard to all the circumstances.

13. An attorney-at-law shall withdraw forthwith from employment or from a matter pending before a tribunal —

(a) where the client insists upon his representing a claim of defence that he cannot conscientiously advance;
(b) where the client seeks to pursue a course of conduct which is illegal or which will result in deliberately deceiving the Court;
(c) where a client has in the course of the proceedings perpetrated a fraud upon a person or tribunal and on request by the attorney-at-law has refused or is unable to rectify the same;
(d) where his continued employment will involve him in the violation of the law or a disciplinary rule;
(e) where the client by any other conduct renders it unreasonably difficult for the attorney-at-law to carry out his employment as such effectively, or in accordance with the judgement and advice of the attorney-at-law, or the rules of law or professional ethics;
(f) where for any good and compelling reason it is difficult for him to carry out his employment effectively.

14. An attorney-at-law shall not retain money he received for his client for longer than is absolutely necessary.
15. An attorney-at-law shall never disclose, unless lawfully ordered to do so by the Court or required by statute, what has been communicated to him in his capacity as an attorney-at-law by his clients or his client's attorney-at-law and this duty not to disclose extends to his partners, to junior attorneys-at-law assisting him and to his employees provided however that an attorney-at-law may reveal confidences or secrets necessary to establish or collect his fee or to defend himself or his employees or associates against an accusation of wrongful conduct.
16. An attorney-at-law shall not permit his professional services or his name to be used in any way which would make it possible for persons who are not legally authorised to do so to practise law.
17. An attorney-at-law shall not delegate to a person not legally qualified and not in his employ or under his control, any functions which are by the laws of Antigua and Barbuda only to be performed by a qualified attorney-at-law.
18. In the performance of his duties an attorney-at-law shall not act with inexcusable or undue delay, negligence or neglect.
19. An attorney-at-law shall not engage in undignified or discourteous conduct which is degrading to the Court or his profession.
20. An attorney-at-law shall not willfully make false accusations against a Judge or Magistrate.
21. An attorney-at-law who holds a public office shall not use his public position to influence or attempt to influence a tribunal to act in favour of himself or of his client.
22. An attorney-at-law shall not accept private employment in a matter upon the merits of which he previously acted in a judicial capacity or for which he

had substantial responsibility while he was in public employment.

23. An attorney-at-law shall not give, lend or promise anything of value to a Judge, juror or official of a tribunal before which there is pending matter in which he is engaged.
24. In any proceedings in a Court an attorney-at-law shall not communicate or cause any other person to communicate with a juror as to the merits of such proceedings, and shall only do so with a Judge or person exercising judicial functions —
    (a) in the normal course of the proceedings; or
    (b) where authorised by law, or the practice of the Courts.
25. An attorney-at-law shall not for the purpose of making any person available as a witness, advise or cause that person to secrete himself or leave the jurisdiction of the Court.
26. An attorney-at-law shall not pay or offer to pay or acquiesce in the payment of compensation to a witness for giving evidence in any cause or matter save as reimbursement for expenses reasonably incurred and as reasonable compensation for loss of time in attending for preparation and for testifying, and in the case of an expert witness a reasonable fee for his professional services.
27. An attorney-at-law shall not knowingly use perjured testimony or false evidence or participate in the creation of or use of evidence which he knows to be false.
28. An attorney-at-law shall not counsel or assist his client or a witness, in conduct that the attorney-at-law knows to be illegal or fraudulent, and where he is satisfied that his client has in the course of the particular representation perpetrated a fraud upon a person or tribunal, he shall promptly call upon him to rectify the same.
29. An attorney-at-law shall not knowingly make a false statement of law or fact.
30. (1) An attorney-at-law shall not commit a breach of an undertaking given by him to a Judge, a Court or other Tribunal or an official thereof, whether such undertaking relates to an expression of intention as to future conduct or is a representation that a particular state of facts exists.
    (2) An attorney-at-law shall not knowingly represent falsely to a Judge, a Court or other Tribunal or to an official of a Court or other Tribunal, that a particular state of facts exists.
31. In pecuniary matters an attorney-at-law shall be most punctual and diligent, he shall never mingle funds of others with his own and he shall at all times be able to refund money he holds for others.
32. (1) An attorney-at-law shall keep such accounts as clearly and accurately distinguish the financial position between himself and his client as and when required.
    (2) An attorney-at-law shall comply with such rules as may be made by the

Council under section 27 of the Act.

(3) Nothing contained in Rules 31 and 32 shall deprive an attorney-at-law of any recourse or right whether by way of lien, set-off, counterclaim, charge or otherwise against monies standing to the credit of a client's account maintained by at attorney-at-law.

33. An attorney-at-law shall reply promptly to any letter received from the Law Association relating to his professional conduct.

34. Where no provision is made in these rules in respect of any matter, the rules and practice of the legal profession which formerly governed the particular matter shall apply in so far as is practicable.

35. (1) Breach by an attorney-at-law of any of the Rules contained in this Part shall constitute professional misconduct and an attorney-at-law who commits such a breach shall be liable to any of the penalties which the Law Council and the Court is empowered to impose.

(2) Breach by an attorney-at-law of any of the provisions of Part A of this Code while not automatically amounting to punishable professional misconduct is a derogation from the high standards of conduct expected from an attorney-at-law and may, depending on the circumstances of the particular case, amount to such misconduct or form a material ingredient thereof.

FIFTH SCHEDULE

(Section 24(2)

Disciplinary Proceedings Rules

1. These Rules, may be cited as the Legal Profession (Disciplinary Proceedings) Rules 1995. Short title.

2. For the purposes of these Rules, "Secretary" means the Registrar or the person deputed by him for the time being to perform all or any of the functions of Secretary. Secretary.

3. An application to the Law Council to require an attorney-at-law to answer allegations contained in an affidavit shall be in writing under the hand of the applicant in Form 1 of the Appendix and shall be sent to the Secretary together with an affidavit by the applicant in Form 2 of the Appendix stating the matters of fact on which he relies in support of this application. Application and affidavits.

4. Before fixing a day for the hearing the Law Council may require the applicant to supply such further information and documents relating to all allegations as it thinks fit, and in any case where in the opinion of the Law Council no prima No case to answer.

facie case is shown, the Law Council may, without requiring the attorney-at-law to answer the allegations, dismiss the application and notify the applicant and the attorney-at-law of the dismissal.

5. In any case in which, in the opinion of the Law Council, a *prima facie* case is shown, the Law Council shall fix a day of hearing and the Secretary shall serve notice thereof on the applicant and on the attorney-at-law with a copy of the application and affidavit. The notice shall not be less than a 21 days' notice. **Notice of hearing.**

6. The notice to the applicant shall be in Form 3 and to the attorney Form 4 of the Appendix as the case may be, and shall require the applicant and the attorney-at-law respectively to furnish to the Secretary and to each other a list of all documents on which they respectively propose to rely. Such lists shall, unless otherwise ordered by the Committee, be furnished by the applicant and by the attorney-at-law respectively at least 7 days before the day of hearing.

7. Either party may inspect the documents included in the list furnished by the other party and a copy of any document mentioned in the list of either party shall, on the application of the party requiring it, be furnished to that party by the other within 3 days after the receipt of the application. **Inspection of documents.**

8. If either or both parties fail to appear at the hearing the Law Council may, upon proof of service or the notice of hearing, proceed to hear and determine the application in his or their absence. **Absence of parties.**

9. The Law Council may, in its discretion, either as to the whole case or as to any particular facts, proceed and act upon evidence given by affidavit; but any party to the proceedings may require a deponent to any such affidavit to be summoned to appear before the Law Council, unless the Law Council is satisfied that the affidavit is purely formal and that the requirement of the appearance of the deponent is made frivolously. **Affidavit evidence.**

10. A summons issued by the Law Council under section 34 may be in Form 5 of the Appendix with such variation as the case may require. **Subpoenas.**

11. The Law Council shall hear all applications in private. **Privacy of hearings.**

12. Notes of proceedings shall be taken by the Secretary or other person appointed by the Law Council, and any party who appeared at the proceedings shall be entitled to inspect the **Notes of proceedings.**

original or a copy thereof. Every person entitled to be heard at the hearing upon the consideration of the Report by the Court, shall be entitled to a copy of such notes on payment of the charges (if any) prescribed by the rules of court.

13. Notwithstanding anything to the contrary, the Law Council may extend or abridge the time for doing anything under these Rules. **Power to extend time.**

14. (1) Attorneys-at-law and witnesses shall have the same privileges and immunities in relation to hearings on applications under this Act as in any court of law. **Privileges and immunities.**
    (2) A party to an application is entitled to be represented by an attorney-at-law.

15. No stamp duty shall be paid on any document and no fee shall be exigible by the Registrar in respect of any application alleging professional misconduct by an attorney-at-law. **Exemption from stamp duty.**

16. If after hearing an application the Law Council is satisfied that no case of professional misconduct has been made out, it may dismiss the application. **Dismissal of application after hearing.**

APPENDIX
FORM 1

Form of Application against an attorney-at-law

To the Law Council constituted under the Legal Profession Act 1997.

In the Matter of .... attorney-at-law, and

....

In the Matter of the Legal Profession Act 1997.

I, the undersigned.. hereby make application that* .... of .... attorney-at-law may be required to answer the allegations contained in the affidavit which accompanies this application.

I make this application on the ground that the matters of fact stated in the said affidavit constitute conduct unbecoming his profession on the part of the said .... in his capacity of attorney-at-law.

In witness whereof I have hereunto set my hand this..............................day of ....19......

.... Signature

.... Address

.... Profession business or occupation.

*insert full name and last known place or places of business.

FORM 2

Form of Affidavit by Applicant

(a)	Name of the attorney-at-law	In the matter of *(a)* an attorney-at-law; and In the matter of the Legal Profession Act 1997.
(b)	Name of applicant.	I, *(b)* make oath and say as follows —
(c)	Place of residence.	(1) That I reside at *(c)*
(d)	Parish.	in the Parish of *(d)*
(e)	Occupation	and am a *(e)*
(f)	Postal Address	and my postal address is *(f)*
(g)	Name of attorney-at-law	(2) That *(g)*
(h)	Set out facts complained of	*(h)*
(i)	Set out shortly the ground of complaint	(3) The complaint I make against the attorney-at-law is that he *(i)*

....
Signature or Mark or Applicant

If the person making the affidavit can read and write strike out the words in brackets

Sworn at ....
in the Parish of ....
this .... day of ...., 19.....

(the same having been first read over and explained to deponent when he/she appeared fully to understand the same) before me —

....
Notary Public/Justice of Peace.

FORM 3

Form of Notice by Law Council to Applicant

Complaint No .... of 19.........

In the Matter of .... attorney-at-law

and

In the Matter of the Legal Profession Act 1997.

To...

of..

The .... day of ...., 19......... is the day fixed for the hearing of your application in the matter of .... attorney-at-law by the Law Council constituted under the Legal Profession Act 1997.

The Law Council will sit at .... at .... o'clock in the forenoon. If you fail to appear the Law Council may in accordance with the Rules made under the Legal Profession Act 1997, proceed in your absence.

You are required by the Rules under the Legal Profession Act 1997 to furnish to the said .... and the Secretary of the Law Council at .... at least 14 days before the said .... day of .... 19....... a list of all documents on which you propose to rely.

Either party may inspect the documents included in the list furnished by the other and a copy of any document mentioned in the list of either party must on the application of the party requiring it, be furnished to that party by the other within three days after receipt of the application.

You are requested to acknowledge the receipt of this Notice without delay. Dated the .... day of ...., 19 ....

....

Secretary,
Law Council

FORM 4

(Rule 6)

Form of Notice by Law Council to attorney-at-law

Complaint No .... of 19.........

In the Matter of .... attorney-at-law

and

In the Matter of Legal Profession Act 1997

To .... of .... attorney-at-law.

Application has been made by .... of .... to the Law Council constituted under the Legal Profession Act 1997 that you may be required to answer the allegations contained in the affidavit a copy whereof accompanies this Notice.

The .... day of .... 19......... is the day fixed for the hearing of the application by the Law Council. The Law Council will sit at .... at .... o'clock in the forenoon. If you fail to appear the Law Council may in accordance with the Rules made under the Legal Profession Act 1997 proceed in your absence.

You are required by the Rules made under the Legal Profession Act 1997 to furnish to the applicant and to the Secretary of the Law Council at .... at least 14 days before the day fixed for hearing a list of all the documents on which you propose to rely.

Either party may inspect the documents included in the list furnished by the other and a copy of any documents mentioned in the list of either party must, on application of the party requiring it, be furnished to that party by the other within 3 days after the receipt of the application.

You are requested to acknowledge receipt of this Notice without delay. Dated the .... day of ....19...........

....

Secretary,
Law Council

FORM 5

Form of Summons by Law Council to Witness

(Rule 10)

Complaint No...............of 19..........

In the Matter of..attorney-at-law

and

In the Matter of the Legal Profession Act 1997

To...

You are hereby summoned to appear before the Law Council constituted under the Legal Profession Act 1997 at .... on the .... day of .... at the hour of .... o'clock in the .... noon, and so from day to day until the application in the above matter is heard, to give evidence on behalf of .... (if the person summoned is to produce books or documents add) and you are required to bring with you (specify the books or documents required).

Whereof fail not at your peril.

Dated this .... day of .... 19 ....

....

Chairman,
Law Council.

SIXTH SCHEDULE

(Section 42)

Amendment of Written Laws

	First Column	Second Column
Cap. 72	Registration and Record Act	After section 14 insert the following— "Instruments to be indorsed. 14A (1) Subject to subsection (2), the Registrar shall not record any instrument relating to— (a) real or personal property; or (b) Any legal proceeding, unless it is signed by an attorney-at-law in the manner provided by section 13 (1) of the Legal Profession Act 1997.

First Column	Second Column
Cap. 72 Registration and Record Act	(2) Subsection (1) does not apply to (a) an instrument drawn or prepared by a notary public, a public officer or officer of a statutory board acting in the course of his duty; (b) a will or other testamentary instrument; (c) an agreement under hand only; (d) a letter or power of attorney; or (e) a transfer of stock containing no trust or limitation thereof."
Cap. 143 Eastern Caribbean Supreme Court Act	Repeal Part IV (sections 69 to 78).
Cap. 374 Registered Land Act	After section 106 (3), insert the following subsections — "(4) Subject to subsection (5), the Registrar shall not register any instrument relating to land unless it is signed by an attorney-at-law in the manner provided by section 13 (1) of the Legal Profession Act 1997. (5) Subsection (5) does not apply to- (a) an instrument drawn or prepared by a notary public, a public officer of a statutory board, acting in the course of his duty; or (b) a power of attorney".
Cap. 347 Professions Licensing Act	Schedule, Part I, delete the words "Barrister at Law or Solicitor"

Passed the House of Representatives this 26th day of February, 1997.

B. Harris,
Speaker.

S. Walker,
Clerk to the House of Representatives.

Passed the Senate this 5th day of March, 1997.

M. Percival,
President.

S. Walker,
Clerk to the Senate.

Appendix 2
Barbados

The Legal Profession Code of Ethics, 1988

S.I. 1988 No.113
The Legal Profession Act, Cap. 370A

Part I

PRELIMINARY

1. This Code may be cited as the Legal Profession Code of Ethics, 1988.
2. In this Code
   "tribunal" includes the Disciplinary Committee.
3. Every attorney-at-law shall uphold at all times the standards set out in this Code.
4. A breach of the rules in Parts II, to VII may constitute professional misconduct and in Part VIII shall constitute professional misconduct.

Part II

IN RELATION TO THE PROFESSION AND HIMSELF

5. (1) An attorney-at-law whether in practice or not shall uphold at all times the standards set out in this Code.
   (2) An attorney-at-law shall maintain his integrity and the honour and dignity of the legal profession and of his own standing as a member of it and shall encourage other attorneys-at-law to act similarly both in the

practice of his profession and in his private life and shall refrain from conduct which is detrimental to the profession or which may tend to discredit it.

6. (1) An attorney-at-law shall scrupulously preserve his independence in the discharge of his professional duties.
   (2) An attorney-at-law practising on his own account or in partnership shall not engage in any other business or occupation if doing so may cause him to have a conflict of interest.
7. An attorney-at-law shall protect the profession against the admission thereto of any candidate who is unfit for such admission.
8. (1) An attorney-at-law shall not endeavour by direct or indirect means to attract the clients of another attorney-at-law and where one attorney refers a client to another attorney-at-law, the client remains the client of the referring attorney-at-law and the attorney-at-law to whom the client is referred shall act with due deference to the relationship between the client and the referring attorney-at-law.
   (2) Where a referred client offers other work to the attorney-at-law to whom he was referred and the offer is sufficiently proximate to the referral, that attorney-at-law shall not accept that offer unless it has been brought to the attention of the referring attorney-at-law.
9. An attorney-at-law may speak in public or write for publication on legal topics provided that he does not thereby emphasize his own professional competence.
10. The best advertisement for an attorney-at-law is the establishment of a well merited reputation for personal integrity, capacity, dedication to work and fidelity to trust and it is unprofessional
    (a) to solicit business by circulars or advertisements or interviews not warranted by personal relations;
    (b) to seek retainers through agents of any kind.
11. An attorney-at-law shall defend the interests of his client without fear of judicial disfavour or public unpopularity and without regard to any unpleasant consequences to himself or to any other person.
12. An attorney-at-law is obliged to act, either as adviser or advocate in the field in which he proposes to practise, for every person who may wish to become his client on payment of the proper professional fee charged in accordance with rule 68. Special circumstances such as a conflict of interest or the possession of relevant and confidential information may justify his refusal to accept a particular employment.
13. No client is entitled to receive nor should any attorney-at-law render, any service or advice involving disloyalty to the State or disrespect for judicial office or the corruption of any persons exercising a public or private trust or deception or betrayal of the public.

14. Every attorney-at-law should bear in mind that the oath of office taken on his admission to practise is not a mere form but is a solemn undertaking to be strictly observed on his part.
15. An attorney-at-law should also bear in mind that he can only maintain the high traditions of his profession by being a person of high integrity and dignity.
16. (1) The dress of an attorney-at-law appearing in open Court should be unobstrusive and compatible with the wearing of robes.
    (2) Suits and dresses should be of dark colour. Dresses or blouses should be long sleeved and compatible with the wearing of bands and collarettes. Shirts and blouses should be predominantly white or other unemphatic appearance. Collars should be white and shoes dark.
    (3) No conspicuous jewellery or ornaments should be worn.
    (4) Attorneys should at all times, both in Court and when seeing clients, dress in a manner appropriate to and compatible with the status of their profession.

Part III

IN RELATION TO THE STATE AND THE PUBLIC

17. An attorney-at-law owes a duty to the State to maintain its integrity, its constitution and its laws and not to aid, abet, counsel or assist anyone to act in any way contrary to those laws.
18. When engaged as a public prosecutor the primary duty of an attorney-at-law is not to secure a conviction but to see that justice is done and to that end he shall not withhold facts tending to prove either the guilt or innocence of the accused.
19. An attorney-at-law shall endeavour by lawful means where the needs of society require, to promote and encourage the modernization, simplification and reform of the laws.
20. An attorney-at-law shall not by his actions, stir up strife or litigation by seeking out defects in titles, claims for personal injury or other causes of action for the purpose of securing a retainer to prosecute a claim therefor; or pay or reward any person directly or indirectly for the purpose of procuring him to be retained in his professional capacity, and where it is in the interest of his client, he shall seek to obtain reasonable settlements of disputes.
21. An attorney-at-law shall not be deterred from accepting proffered employment owing to the fear or dislike of incurring disapproval of officials, other attorneys-at-law or members of the public.
22. Where an attorney-at-law consents to undertake the provision of legal services and he is appointed by the Director of Community Legal Services, by

any Legal Aid and Advisory Authority or is requested by the Bar Association and consents to undertake the representation of a person unable to afford such representation or to obtain legal aid, the attorney-at-law shall not, except for compelling reasons, seek to be excused from undertaking such representation.

23. An attorney-at-law in undertaking the defence of persons accused of crime shall use all fair and reasonable means to present every defence available at law.

Part IV

IN RELATION TO CLIENTS

24. (1) An attorney-at-law shall always act in the best interests of his client, represent him honestly, competently and zealously and endeavour by all fair and honourable means to obtain for him the benefit of any and every remedy and defence which is authorised by law, steadfastly bearing in mind that the duties and responsibilities of the attorney-at-law are to be carried out within and not without the bounds of the law.

(2) The interests of his client and the exigencies of the administration of justice should always be the first concern of an attorney-at-law and rank before his right to compensation for his services.

25. (1) Before advising on a client's cause an attorney-at-law should obtain full knowledge thereof and give a candid opinion of the merits or demerits and probable results of pending or contemplated litigation.

(2) An attorney-at-law should beware of proffering bold and confident assurances to his client (especially where employment may depend on such assurances) always bearing in mind that seldom are all the law and facts on the side of his client.

(3) Whenever the controversy admits of fair adjustment, an attorney-at-law should inform his client accordingly and advise to avoid or settle litigation.

26. (1) An attorney-at-law shall at the time of retainer disclose to his client all the circumstances of his relations to the parties and his interest in or connection with the controversy (if any) which might influence the client in his selection of an attorney-at-law.

(2) An attorney-at-law shall scrupulously guard and never divulge his client's secrets and confidences.

27. An attorney-at-law shall treat adverse witnesses, litigants and other attorneys-at-law with fairness and courtesy refraining from all offensive personal references and shall avoid imparting to his professional duties his client's personal feelings and prejudices.

28. It is the right of an attorney-at-law to undertake the defence of a person accused of crime regardless of his own personal opinion as to the guilt of the accused and having undertaken such defence he is bound by all fair and honourable means to present every defence that the law of the land permits, so that no person may be deprived of life or liberty except by due process of the law.

29. (1) An attorney-at-law may represent multiple clients only if he can adequately represent the interests of each and if each consents to such representation after full disclosure of the possible effects of multiple representation.
 (2) In all situations where a possible conflict of interest arises, an attorney-at-law shall resolve all conflicts by leaning against multiple representation.

30. (1) An attorney-at-law shall deal with his client's business with all due expedition and shall, whenever reasonably so required by the client, provide him with full information as to the progress of the client's business.
 (2) It is improper for an attorney-at-law to accept instructions in a matter unless he can handle it without undue delay.

31. Where an attorney-at-law determines that the interest of his client requires it, he may with the specific or general consent of the client, refer his business or part of it to another attorney-at-law whether or not a member of his own firm.

32. (1) An attorney-at-law on the record may instruct one or more attorneys-at-law to appear as advocates, in the same way as a solicitor on the record prior to 31st March, 1973, instructed Counsel.
 (2) Queen's Counsel shall be entitled to accept instructions, appear or do any work without a junior, except where he would be unable properly to carry out his instructions or conduct his case if he were to do so.
 (3) Where more than one attorney-at-law appears as advocate for the same party in the same proceedings, who shall lead the conduct of that party's case shall, subject to the instructions of the client be settled by the attorneys-at-law representing that party before they appear in court and shall not be altered during the course of the proceedings and the leader shall have all authority over the conduct of the case.

33. An attorney-at-law including a Queen's Counsel who appears with the leader is entitled to negotiated fee appropriate for his conduct of the case.

34. (1) An attorney-at-law is entitled to reasonable compensation for his services but should avoid charges which either over estimate or undervalue the service rendered.
 (2) The ability of a client to pay cannot justify a charge in excess of the value of the service rendered, though the client's indigence may require a charge that is below such value, or even no charge at all.

35. An attorney-at-law should avoid controversies with clients regarding compensation for his services as far as is compatible with self-respect and his right to receive reasonable compensation for his services.
36. The right of an attorney-at-law to ask for a retainer or to demand payment of out-of-pocket expenses and commitments, failing payment of which he may withdraw from the case or refuse to handle it, shall not be exercised where the client may be unable to find other assistance in time to prevent irreparable damage being done.
37. Where an attorney-at-law engages a foreign colleague to advise on a case or to co-operate in handling it, he is responsible for the payment of the latter's charges except there is express agreement to the contrary, but where an attorney-at-law directs a client to a foreign colleague he is not responsible for the payment of the latter's charges, nor is he entitled to a share of the fee of his foreign colleague.
38. An attorney-at-law may at any time withdraw his services
    (a) where the client fails, refuses, or neglects to carry out an agreement with, or his obligation to, the attorney-at-law as regards the expenses or fees payable by the client;
    (b) where his inability to work with colleagues indicates that the best interest of the client is likely to be served by his withdrawal;
    (c) where his client freely assents to the termination of his services;
    (d) where by reasons of his mental or physical condition or other good and compelling reason it is difficult for him to carry out his services effectively; or
    (e) in cases of conflict as contemplated in Rule 29 or Rule 68.
39. (1) An attorney-at-law should not appear as a witness for his own client except as to merely formal matters or where such appearance is essential to the ends of justice.
    (2) If an attorney-at-law is a necessary witness for his client with respect to matters other than such as are merely formal, he should entrust the conduct of the case to another attorney-at-law of his client's choice.

Part V

IN RELATION TO THE COURTS AND THE ADMINISTRATION OF JUSTICE

40. (1) An attorney-at-law shall maintain a respectful attitude towards the court and shall not engage in undignified or discourteous conduct which is degrading to the court.
    (2) An attorney-at-law shall encourage respect for the courts and the judges.
    (3) An attorney-at-law shall support judges and magistrates against unjust criticisms.

(4) Where there is ground for complaint against a judge or magistrate an attorney-at-law may make representation to the proper authorities and in such cases, the attorney-at-law shall be protected.

41. An attorney-at-law shall endeavour always to maintain his position as an advocate and shall not either in argument to the court or in address to the jury, assert his personal belief in his client's innocence or in the justice of his cause or his personal knowledge as to any of the facts involved in the matter under investigation.

42. An attorney-at-law should never seek privately to influence directly or indirectly the Judges of the Court in his favour or in the favour of his client, nor should he attempt to curry favour with juries by fawning, flattery or pretended solicitude for their personal comfort.

43. An attorney-at-law shall be punctual in attendance before the Courts and concise and direct in the trial and disposition of causes.

44. An attorney-at-law shall expose without fear or favour before a proper tribunal, unprofessional or dishonest conduct by any other attorneys-at-law and shall not lightly refuse a retainer against another attorney-at-law who is alleged to have wronged his client or committed any other act of professional misconduct.

Part VI

IN RELATION TO HIS FELLOW ATTORNEYS-AT-LAW

45. (1) The conduct of an attorney-at-law towards his fellow attorneys shall be characterized by courtesy, fairness and good faith and he shall not permit ill-feeling between clients to affect his relationship with his colleagues.

(2) All personal conflicts between attorneys-at-law should be scrupulously avoided as should also colloquies between them which cause delay and promote unseemly wrangling.

46. (1) An attorney-at-law shall reply promptly to letters from other attorneys-at-law making inquiries on behalf of their clients.

(2) An attorney-at-law shall endeavour as far as is reasonable to suit the convenience of the opposing attorney-at-law when the interest of his client or the cause of justice will not be injured by so doing.

47. An attorney-at-law shall not give a professional undertaking that he cannot fulfill, and he shall fulfill every such undertaking that he gives.

48. (1) There is a duty on every attorney-at-law to report improper or unprofessional conduct by another attorney-at-law to the Disciplinary Committee, save where the information relating to the improper or unprofessional conduct is received in professional confidence in which case he must respect the duty of silence imposed in such circumstances.

(2) An attorney-at-law shall expose without fear or favour before the proper tribunal unprofessional or dishonest conduct by another attorney-at-law and shall not lightly refuse a retainer against another attorney-at-law who is alleged to have wronged a client.

49. Where an attorney-at-law has been sent money, documents or other things by another attorney-at-law which, at the time of sending, are expressed to be sent only on the basis that the attorney-at-law to whom they are sent will receive them on his undertaking to do or refrain from doing some act, the receiving attorney-at-law shall forthwith return whatever was sent if he is unable to accept them on such undertaking, otherwise he must comply with the undertaking.

50. An attorney-at-law shall not in any way communicate upon a subject in controversy or attempt to negotiate or compromise a matter directly with any party represented by another attorney-at-law except through such other attorney-at-law or with his prior consent.

51. (1) An attorney-at-law shall not ignore the customs or practices of the legal profession even when the law expressly permits it, without giving timely notice to the opposing attorney-at-law.

(2) An attorney-at-law should avoid all sharp practices and should refrain from taking any paltry advantage when his opponent has made or overlooked some technical error or matter, bearing in mind that no client has a right to demand that an attorney-at-law representing him shall be illiberal or shall do anything repugnant to his own sense of honour and propriety.

52. An attorney-at-law shall not accept instructions to act in Court proceedings in which to his knowledge the client has previously been represented by another attorney-at-law, unless he first notifies the other attorney-at-law of the change, and makes reasonable efforts to ensure that attorney has been paid for his services, but shall be deemed to have notified the other attorney-at-law if he has made reasonable efforts to notify him.

53. An attorney-at-law shall not accept instructions to act in proceedings (other than Court proceedings) in which to his knowledge another attorney-at-law has previously represented the client unless he makes reasonable efforts to ascertain that the retainer of that attorney-at-law has been determined by the client, or that the client wishes both attorneys-at-law to represent him.

54. An attorney-at-law who instructs another attorney-at-law to act on behalf of his client, unless otherwise agreed, shall pay the proper fee of such attorney-at-law whether or not he has received payment from his client.

55. In undertaking to render assistance to a foreign colleague, an attorney-at-law shall remember that his responsibility is much greater both when giving advice and handling a case, than it would be had he undertaken to assist a colleague in Barbados.

Part VII

GENERAL

56. Where in any particular matter explicit ethical guidance does not exist, an attorney-at-law shall determine his conduct by acting in a manner that promotes public confidence in the integrity and efficiency of the legal system and the legal profession.

Part VIII

MANDATORY PROVISIONS AND SPECIFIC PROHIBITIONS

57. An attorney-at-law shall not practise as such unless he has been issued a practising certificate in accordance with the Act.

58. (1) An attorney-at-law shall never knowingly mislead the Court.
    (2) An attorney-at-law shall not withhold facts or secrete witnesses in order to establish the guilt or innocence of the accused.

59. An attorney-at-law shall not hold out any person who is not qualified to practise law as a partner associate, consultant or attorney-at-law.

60. An attorney-at-law shall not solicit business or consent to become involved in a matter unless at the request of a party thereto, but it is proper for an attorney-at-law to become involved in matters assigned to him by the Director of Community Legal Services or referred by the Bar Association or by another attorney-at-law or for which he is engaged in any other manner not inconsistent with these Rules.

61. An attorney-at-law shall not in the carrying on of his practice or otherwise permit any act or thing which is likely or is intended to attract business unfairly or can reasonably be regarded as touting or advertising.

62. (1) An attorney-at-law shall not in any way make use of any form of advertisement calculated to attract clients to himself or any firm with which he is associated and he shall not permit, authorise or encourage anyone to do so or reward anyone for doing so on his behalf.
    (2) An attorney-at-law shall not permit his professional standing to be used for the purpose of advertising any particular product, service or commercial organization.
    (3) An attorney-at-law shall not advertise for business indirectly by furnishing or inspiring newspaper comment concerning cases or causes in which an attorney-at-law has been or is connected or concerning the manner of their conduct, the magnitude of the interests involved, the importance of the attorney-at-law's position and any similar self-laudations.

    Provided however that
    (a) an attorney-at-law may permit limited and dignified identification of

himself as an attorney-at-law

(i) in political advertisements relevant to the course of a political campaign or issue;

(ii) in public notices where the announcement of his professional status is required or authorised by law, or is reasonably necessary for a purpose other than the attraction of potential clients;

(iii) in reports and announcements of *bona fide* commercial, civic, professional or political organizations in which he serves as a director or officer;

(iv) in and on legal textbooks, articles, professional journals and other legal publications and in dignified and restrained advertisements thereof;

(v) in announcements of any public address, lecture, or publication by him on legal topics, provided that such announcements do not emphasize his own professional competence and are not likely to be regarded as being concerned with the giving of individual advice by him.

(b) an attorney-at-law may speak in public or write for publication on legal topics so long as he does not thereby emphasize his own professional competence;

(c) the following cards, office signs, letterheads or directory listings may be used by an attorney-at-law but in a restrained and dignified form

(i) a professional card or brochure identifying the attorney-at-law by name and as an attorney-at-law giving his decorations and degrees, legal or otherwise, his legal areas of work, his addresses, telephone numbers and the name of his law firm or professional associates so however that such cards are not published in the news media;

(ii) a brief professional announcement card to be delivered to attorneys-at-law, clients, personal friends and relations and government bodies and stating new or changed associations or addresses, changes of firm name or like professional matters;

(iii) a sign or a size and design compatible with the existing practice of the profession, on or near the door of the office and in the building directory identifying the law office;

(iv) a letterhead identifying the attorney-at-law by name and as an attorney-at-law and giving his decorations and degrees, legal or otherwise, his addresses, telephone numbers and the name of his law firm and of his associates;

(v) a listing in a telephone directory, a reputable law list, legal directory or biographical reference giving brief biographical or other relevant information; and any such professional card, office sign, letterhead or listing may state the attorney-at-law is also a notary public or a Justice of the Peace.

63. Where an attorney-at-law commits any criminal offence which in the opinion of the Disciplinary Committee is of a nature likely to bring the profession into disrepute, such commission of the offence shall constitute professional misconduct if
    (a) he has been convicted by any court, including a foreign Court of competent jurisdiction, for the offence; or
    (b) although he has not been prosecuted the Committee is satisfied of the facts constituting the criminal offence; or
    (c) he has been prosecuted and has been acquitted by reason of a technical defence or he has been convicted but such conviction is quashed by reason of some technical defence.

64. An attorney-at-law shall not acquire directly or indirectly by purchase, or otherwise a financial or other interest in the subject matter of a case which he is conducting.

65. (1) An attorney-at-law shall not enter into partnership or fee sharing arrangements concerning the practice of law with non-qualified bodies or persons.
    (2) An attorney-at-law shall not enter into an agreement for or charge or collect a fee in contravention of this Code or any other law.

66. (1) An attorney-at-law shall not charge fees that are unfair or unreasonable.
    (2) In determining the fairness and reasonableness of a fee the following factors may be taken into account
        (a) the time and labour required, the novelty and difficulty of the questions involved and the skill required to perform the legal service properly;
        (b) the likelihood that the acceptance of the particular employment will preclude other employment by the attorney-at-law;
        (c) the fee customarily charged in the locality for similar legal services;
        (d) the amount, if any involved;
        (e) the time limitations imposed by the client or by the circumstances;
        (f) the nature and length of the professional relationship with the client;
        (g) the experience, reputation and ability of the attorney-at-law concerned;
        (h) any scale of fees or recommended guide as to charges prescribed by law or by the Judicial Advisory Council.
    (3) An attorney-at-law shall not accept any fee or reward for merely introducing a client or referring a case or client to another attorney-at-law.

67. (1) Except with the specific approval of his client given after full disclosure, an attorney-at-law shall not act in any manner in which his professional duties and his personal interest conflict or are likely to conflict.
(2) An attorney-at-law shall not accept or continue his retainer or employment on behalf of two or more clients if their interests are likely to conflict or if his independent professional judgment is likely to be impaired.

68. (1) An attorney-at-law who withdraws his services under Rule 38 shall not do so until he has taken reasonable steps to avoid foreseeable prejudice or injury to the position and rights of his client including
(a) giving due notice;
(b) allowing time for retaining of another attorney-at-law;
(c) delivering to the client all documents and property to which he is entitled subject however to any lien which the attorney-at-law may have over the same;
(d) complying with such laws, rules or practice as may be applicable; and
(e) where appropriate, obtaining the permission of the Court where the hearing of the matter has commenced.
(2) An attorney-at-law who withdraws his services shall refund promptly such part of the fees, if any, already paid by his client as may be fair and reasonable having regard to all the circumstances.

69. An attorney-at-law shall withdraw forthwith his services or from a matter pending before a tribunal
(a) where the client insists upon his representing a claim or defence that he cannot conscientiously advance;
(b) where the client seeks to pursue a course of conduct which is illegal or which will result in deliberately deceiving the Court;
(c) where a client has in the course of the proceedings perpetrated a fraud upon a person or tribunal and on request by the attorney-at-law has refused or is unable to rectify the same;
(d) where his continued service will involve him in the violation of the law or a disciplinary rule;
(e) where the client by any other conduct renders it unreasonably difficult for the attorney-at-law to carry out his service as such effectively, or in accordance with the judgment and advice of the attorney-at law, or the rules of law or professional ethics;
(f) where for any good and compelling reason it is difficult for his to carry out his service effectively.

70. An attorney-at-law shall not retain money he received for his client longer than is absolutely necessary.

71. An attorney-at-law shall never disclose, unless lawfully ordered to do so by the Court or required by statute, what has been communicated to him in his

capacity as an attorney-at-law by his client and this duty not to disclose extends to his partners, to junior attorneys-at-law assisting him and to his employees provided however that an attorney-at-law may reveal confidences or secrets necessary to establish or collect his fee or to defend himself or his employees or associates against an accusation of wrongful conduct.

72. An attorney-at-law shall not permit his professional services or his name to be used in any way which would make it possible for persons who are not legally authorised to do so to practise law.
73. An attorney-at-law shall not delegate to a person not legally qualified and not in his employ or under his control, any functions which are by the laws of Barbados only to be performed by a qualified attorney-at-law.
74. In the performance of his duties an attorney-at-law shall not act with inexcusable or undue delay, negligence or neglect.
75. An attorney-at-law shall not engage in undignified or discourteous conduct which is degrading to the Court or his profession.
76. An attorney-at-law shall not willfully make false accusations against a Judge or Magistrate.
77. An attorney-at-law who holds a public office shall not use his public position to influence or attempt to influence a tribunal to act in favour of himself or of his client.
78. An attorney-at-law shall not accept private employment in a matter upon the merits of which he previously acted in a judicial capacity or for which he had any responsibility while he was in public employment.
79. An attorney-at-law shall not give, lend or promise anything of value to a Judge, juror or official of a tribunal before which there is a pending matter in which he is engaged.
80. In any proceedings in a Court an attorney-at-law shall not communicate or cause any other person to communicate with a juror as to the merits of such proceedings, and shall only do so with a Judge or person exercising judicial functions
    (a) in the normal course of the proceedings; or
    (b) where authorised by law, or the practice of the Courts.
81. An attorney-at-law shall not for the purpose of making any person available as a witness, advise or cause that person to secrete himself or leave the jurisdiction of the Court.
82. An attorney-at-law shall not pay or offer to pay or acquiesce in the payment of compensation to a witness for giving evidence in any cause or matter save as reimbursement for expenses reasonably incurred and as reasonable compensation for loss of time in attending for preparation and for testifying, and in the case of an expert witness a reasonable fee for his professional services.
83. An attorney-at-law shall not knowingly use perjured testimony or false evi-

dence or participate in the creation of or, use of evidence which he knows to be false.

84. An attorney-at-law shall not counsel or assist his client or a witness, in conduct that the attorney-at-law knows to be illegal or fraudulent, and where he is satisfied that his client has in the course of the particular representation perpetrated a fraud upon a person or tribunal, he shall promptly call upon him to rectify the same.

85. An attorney-at-law shall not knowingly make a false statement of law or fact.

86. (1) An attorney-at-law shall not commit a breach of an undertaking given by him, to a Judge, a Court or other Tribunal or an official thereof, whether such undertaking relates to an expression of intention as to future conduct or is a representation that a particular state of facts exists.

(2) An attorney-at-law shall not knowingly represent falsely to a Judge, a Court or other Tribunal or to an official of a Court or other Tribunal, that a particular state of facts exists.

87. In pecuniary matters an attorney-at-law shall be most punctual and diligent, he shall never mingle funds of others with his own and he shall at all times be able to refund money he holds for others.

88. (1) An attorney-at-law shall keep such accounts as clearly and accurately distinguish the financial position between himself and his client as and when required.

(2) An attorney-at-law shall comply with such rules as may be made by the Judicial Advisory Council under section 13 of the Act, but nothing contained in this Rule or Rule 89 shall deprive an attorney-at-law of any recourse or right whether by way of lien, set-off, counterclaim, charge or otherwise against monies standing to the credit of a client's account maintained by that attorney-at-law.

89. An attorney-at-law shall reply promptly to any letter received from the Disciplinary Committee or the Barbados Bar Association relating to his professional conduct.

90. (1) Breach by an attorney-at-law of any Rules contained in this Part shall constitute professional misconduct and an attorney-at-law who commits such a breach shall be liable to any of the penalties which the Disciplinary Committee recommends and which the Court of Appeal is empowered to impose.

(2) Breach by an attorney-at-law of any of the provisions of Parts II to VII of this Code while not automatically amounting to punishable professional misconduct is a derogation from the high standards of conduct expected from an attorney-at-law and may, depending on the circumstances of the particular case, amount to punishable professional misconduct or form a material ingredient thereof.

Made by the Disciplinary Committee under section 18 of the Legal Profession Act, Cap. 370A this 12th day of December, 1988.

Deputy Chairman	Chairman
Attorneys-at-Law	Attorneys-at-Law
....	....
....	....
....	....
	Secretary

Appendix 3
Organisation of Eastern Caribbean States

Bar Association
Code of Ethics

Rules to regulate the professional practice, etiquette,
conduct and discipline of attorneys-at-law

Effective 15th June 1991

PART A

CODE OF ETHICS

General Guidelines

I. *In Relation to the Profession and Himself*

1. A barrister, solicitor or attorney-at-law (hereinafter "attorney-at-law") shall observe the rules of this Code, maintain his integrity and the honour and dignity of the legal profession and encourage other attorneys-at-law to act similarly both in the practice of his profession and in his private life, shall refrain from conduct which is detrimental to the profession or which may tend to discredit it.
2. An attorney-at-law shall expose without fear or favour before the proper tribunals unprofessional or dishonest conduct by any other attotney-at-law and shall not lightly refuse a retainer against another attorney-at-law who is alleged to have wronged his client or committed any other act of professional misconduct.

3. (1) an attorney-at-law shall scrupulously preserve his independence in the discharge of his professional duties.
   (2) an attorney-at-law practising on his own account or in partnership, shall not engage in any other business or occupation if doing so may cause him to cease to be independent.
4. An attorney-at-law shall protect the profession against the admission thereto of any candidate whose moral character or education render him unfit for such admission.
5. (1) An attorney-at-law shall not endeavour by direct or indirect means to attract the clients of another attorney-at-law and where a client is referred to him by another attorney-at-law the client remains for all other purposes the client of the referring attorney-at-law and the attorney-at-law to whom the client is referred shall act with due deference to the relationship between the client and the referring attorney-at-law.
   (2) Where a referred client offers other work to the attorney-at-law to whom he is referred and the offer is sufficiently proximate to the referral, that attorney-at-law shall not accept that offer unless it has been brought to the attention of the referring attorney-at-law.
6. An attorney-at-law may speak in public or write for publication on legal topics so long as he does not thereby advertise his own professional competence and is not likely to be regarded as being concerned thereby with the giving of individual advice.
7. The best advertisement for an attorney-at-law is the establishment of a well merited reputation for personal integrity, capacity, dedication to work and fidelity to trust. Advertising is only permissible to the extent that it meets the standards set by the OECS Bar Council.
8. An attorney-at-law shall defend the interests of his client without fear of judicial disfavour or public unpopularity and without regard to any unpleasant consequences to himself or to any other person.
9. Subject to paragraph 17, no attorney-at-law is obliged to act either as adviser or advocate for every person who may wish to become his client; he has a right to decline employment.
10. No client is entitled to receive nor should any attorney-at-law render any service or advice involving disloyalty to the State or disrespect for judicial office or the corruption of any persons exercising a public or private trust or deception or betrayal of the public.
11. Every attorney-at-law should bear in mind that the oath of office taken on his admission to practice is not a mere form but is a solemn undertaking to be strictly observed on his part.
12. An attorney-at-law should also bear in mind that he can only maintain the high traditions of his profession by being a person of high integrity and dignity.

II. *In relation to the State and the Public*

13. An attorney-at-law owes a duty to the State to maintain its integrity, its constitution and its laws and not to aid, abet, counsel or assist anyone to act in any way contrary to those laws.
14. When engaged as a public prosecutor the primary duty of an attorney-at-law is not to secure a conviction but to see that justice is done and to that end he shall not withhold facts tending to prove either the guilt or innocence of the accused.
15. An attorney-at-law shall endeavour by lawful means where the needs of society require to promote and encourage the modernization, simplification and reform of the laws.
16. An attorney-at-law shall not by his actions stir up strife or litigation by seeking out defects in titles, claims for personal injury or other causes of action for the purpose of securing a retainer to prosecute a claim therefor; or pay or reward any person directly or indirectly for the purpose of procuring him to be retained in his professional capacity, and where it is in the interest of his client he shall seek to obtain reasonable settlements of disputes.
17. An attorney-at-law shall not except for good reasons refuse his services in capital offences.
18. An attorney-at-law shall not be deterred from accepting proffered employment owing to the fear or dislike of incurring disapproval of officials, other attorneys-at-law or members of the public.
19. Where an attorney-at-law consents to undertake legal aid and he is requested by the Association and consents to undertake the representation of a person unable to afford such representation or to obtain legal aid, the attorney-at-law shall not, except for compelling reasons, seek to be excused from undertaking such representation.
20. An attorney-at-law in undertaking the defence of persons accused of crime shall use all fair and reasonable means to present every defence available at law.

III *In Relation to Clients*

21. (1) An attorney-at-law shall always act in the best interests of his client, represent him honestly, competently and zealously and endeavour by all fair and honourable means to obtain for him the benefit of any and every remedy and defence which is authorised by law, steadfastly bearing in mind that the duties and responsibilities of the attorney-at-law are to be carried out within and not without the bounds of the law.
    (2) The interests of his client and the exigencies of the administration of justice should always be the first concern of an attorney-at-law and rank before his right to compensation for his services.

22. (1) Before advising on a client's cause an attorney-at-law should obtain full knowledge thereof and give a candid opinion of the merits or demerits and probable results of pending or contemplated litigation.
    (2) An attorney-at-law should be wary of proffering bold and confident assurances to his client (especially where employment may depend on such assurances) always bearing in mind that seldom are all the law and facts on the side of his client and that ***audi alteram partem*** is the safest rule to follow.
    (3) Whenever the controversy admits of fair adjustment an attorney-at-law should inform his client accordingly and advise to avoid or settle litigation.
23. (1) An attorney-at-law shall at the time of retainer disclose to his client all the circumstances of his relations to the parties and his interest in or connection with the controversy (if any) which might influence the client in his selection of an attorney-at-law.
    (2) An attorney-at-law shall scrupulously guard and never divulge his client's secrets and confidences.
24. An attorney-at-law shall treat adverse witnesses, litigants and other attorneys-at-law with fairness and courtesy refraining from all offensive personal references and shall avoid imparting to his professional duties his clients' personal feelings and prejudices.
25. It is the right of an attorney-at-law to undertake the defence of a person accused of crime regardless of his own personal opinion as to the guilt of the accused and having undertaken such defence he is bound by all fair and honourable means to present every defence that the law of the land permits so that no person may be deprived of life or liberty except by due process of law.
26. (1) An attorney-at-law may represent multiple clients only if he can adequately represent the interests of each and if each consents to such representation after full disclosure of the possible effects of multiple representation.
    (2) In all situations where a possible conflict of interest arises, an attorney-at-law shall resolve all conflict by leaning against multiple representation.
27. (1) An attorney-at-law shall deal with his client's business with all due expedition and shall whenever reasonably so required by the client provide him with full information as to the progress of the client's business.
    (2) it is improper for an attorney-at-law to accept a case unless he can handle it without undue delay.
28. Where an attorney-at-law determines that the interest of his client requires it, he may with the specific or general consent of the client refer his business or part of it to another attorney-at-law whether or not a member of his own firm.

29. (1) Senior Counsel shall be entitled to accept instructions, appear or do any work without a junior, except where he would be unable properly to carry out his instructions or conduct his case if he were to do so.
    (2) Where more than one attorney-at-law appears as advocate for the same party in the same proceedings, who shall lead the conduct of the party's case shall, subject to the instructions of the client, be settled by the attorney-at-law representing that party before they appear in court and shall not be altered during the course of the proceedings and the leader shall have all authority over the conduct of the case.
30. An attorney-at-law including a Senior Counsel who appears with the leader is entitled to negotiate a fee appropriate for his conduct of the case.
31. (1) An attorney-at-law is entitled to reasonable compensation for his services but should avoid charges which either overestimate or undervalue the service rendered.
    (2) The ability of a client to pay cannot justify a charge in excess of the value of the service rendered, though the client's indigence may require a charge that is below such value, or even no charge at all.
    (3) An attorney-at-law should avoid controversies with the clients regarding compensation for his services as far as is compatible with self-respect and his right to receive reasonable compensation for his services.
32. The right of an attorney-at-law to ask for a deposit or to demand payment of out-of-pocket expenses and commitments, failing payment of which he may withdraw from the case or refuse to handle it, shall not be exercised where the client may be unable to find other assistance in time to prevent irreparable damage being done.
33. Where an attorney-at-law engages a foreign colleague to advise on a case or to co-operate in handling it, he is responsible for the payment of the latter's charges except there is express agreement to the contrary, but where an attorney-at-law directs a client to a foreign colleague he is not responsible for the payment of the latter's charges, nor is he entitled to a share of the fee of his foreign colleague.
34. An attorney-at-law may at any time withdraw from employment —
    (a) where the client fails, refuses, or neglects to carry out an agreement with, or his obligation to, the attorney-at-law as regards the expenses or fees payable by the client;
    (b) where his inability to work with colleagues indicates that the best interest of the client is likely to be served by his withdrawal;
    (c) where his client freely assents to the termination of his employment;
    (d) where by reasons of his mental or physical condition or other good and compelling reason it is difficult for him to carry out his employment effectively; or
    (e) in cases of conflict as contemplated in rule 26 of this Part or rule 11 of

Part B hereof.

35. (1) An attorney-at-law should not appear as a witness for his own client except as to merely formal matters or where such appearance is essential to the ends of justice.

(2) If an attorney-at-law is a necessary witness for his client with respect to matters other than such as are merely formal, he should entrust the conduct of the case to another attorney-at-law of his client's choice.

IV. *In Relation to the Courts and the Administration of Justice*

36. (1) An attorney-at-law shall maintain a respectful attitude towards the court and shall not engage in undignified or discourteous conduct which is degrading to the court.

(2) An attorney-at-law shall encourage respect for the courts and the judges.

(3) An attorney-at-law shall support judges and magistrates against unjust criticisms.

(4) Where there is ground for complaint against judge or magistrate an attorney-at-law may make representation to the proper authorities and in such cases, the attorney-at-law shall be protected.

37. An attorney-at-law shall endeavour always to maintain his position as an advocate and shall not either in argument to the court or in address to the jury assert his personal belief in his client's innocence or in the justice of his cause or his personal knowledge as to any of the facts involved in the matter under investigation.

38. An attorney-at-law should never seek privately to influence directly or indirectly the Judges of the Court in his favour or in the favour of his client, nor should he attempt to curry favour with juries by fawning, flattery or pretended solicitude for their personal comfort.

39. An attorney-at-law shall be punctual in attendance before the Courts and concise and direct in the trial and disposition of causes.

40. An attorney-at-law appearing before the Court shall at all times be attired in such a manner as prescribed or agreed by the proper authorities and as befits the dignity of the court.

V. *In Relation to his Fellow Attorneys-at-law*

41. (1) The conduct of an attorney-at-law towards his fellow attorneys-at-law shall be characterized by courtesy fairness and good faith and he shall not permit ill-feeling between clients to affect his relationship with his colleagues.

(2) All personal conflicts between attorneys-at-law should be scrupulously avoided as should also colloquies between them which cause delay and promote unseemly wrangling.

42. (1) An attorney-at-law shall reply promptly to letters from other attorneys-

at-law making inquiries on behalf of their clients.

(2) An attorney-at-law shall endeavour as far as is reasonable to suit the convenience of the opposing attorney-at-law when the interest of his client or the cause of justice will not be injured by so doing.

43. An attorney-at-law shall not give a professional undertaking that he cannot fulfill, and he shall fulfill every such undertaking that he gives.

44. (1) There is a duty on every attorney-at-law to report improper or unprofessional conduct by a colleague to the Disciplinary Committee, save where the information relating to the improper or unprofessional conduct is received in professional confidence in which case he must respect the duty of silence imposed in such circumstances.

(2) An attorney-at-law shall expose without fear or favour before the proper tribunal unprofessional or dishonest conduct by another attorney-at-law and shall not lightly refuse a retainer against another attorney-at-law who is alleged to have wronged a client.

45. Where an attorney-at-law has been sent money, documents or other things by a colleague which, at the time of sending, are expressed to be sent only on the basis that the attorney-at-law to whom they are sent will receive them on his undertaking to do or refrain from doing some act, the receiving attorney-at-law shall forthwith return whatever was sent if he is unable to accept them on such undertaking, otherwise he must comply with the undertaking.

46. An attorney-at-law shall not in any way communicate upon a subject in controversy or attempt to negotiate or compromise a matter directly with any party represented by another attorney-at-law except through such other attorney-at-law or with his prior consent.

47. (1) An attorney-at-law shall not ignore the customs or practices of the legal profession even when the law expressly permits it, without giving timely notice to the opposing attorney-at-law.

(2) An attorney-at-law should avoid all sharp practices and should refrain from taking any paltry advantage when his opponent has made or overlooked some technical error or matter, bearing in mind that no client has a right to demand that an attorney-at-law representing him shall be illiberal or shall do anything repugnant to his own sense of honour and propriety.

48. An attorney-at-law shall not accept instructions to act in Court proceedings in which to his knowledge the client has previously been represented by another attorney-at-law, unless he first notifies the other attorney-at-law of the change, and makes reasonable efforts to ensure that attorney-at-law has been paid for his services, but shall be deemed to have notified the other attorney-at-law if he has made reasonable efforts to notify him.

49. An attorney-at-law shall not accept instructions to act in proceedings (other than Court proceedings) in which to his knowledge another attorney-at-law

has previously represented the client unless he makes reasonable efforts to ascertain that the retainer of that attorney-at-law has been determined by the client, or that the client wishes both attorneys-at-law to represent him.

50. An attorney-at-law who instructs or employs another attorney-at-law to act on behalf of his client, unless otherwise agreed, shall pay the proper fee of such attorney-at-law whether or not he has received payment from the client.

51. In undertaking to render assistance to a foreign colleague, an attorney-at-law shall remember that his responsibility is much greater both when giving advice and handling a case, than would be had he undertaken to assist a colleague in his State.

VI. *General*

52. Nothing herein contained shall be construed as derogating from any existing rules of professional conduct and duties of an attorney-at-law which are in keeping with the traditions of the legal profession although not specifically mentioned herein.

53. Where in any particular matter explicit ethical guidance does not exist, an attorney-at-law shall determine his conduct by acting in a manner that promotes public confidence in the integrity and efficiency of the legal system and the legal profession.

54. (1) A person who previously held a substantive appointment as a Judge of the Supreme Court in the OECS shall not appear as an attorney-at-law in the Supreme Court in the OECS for a period of five years commencing on the date of his retirement, resignation or other termination of such appointment but in any event he shall not appear as an attorney-at-law in any Magistrate's Court in the OECS.

(2) This rule shall not apply to a person who is appointed to act as a Judge in a temporary capacity.

PART B

MANDATORY PROVISIONS AND SPECIFIC PROHIBITIONS

1. An attorney-at-law shall not practice as such in violation of the laws of the State.

2. (1) An attorney-at-law shall never knowingly mislead the Court.

(2) An attorney-at-law shall not withhold facts or secrete witnesses in order to establish the guilt or innocence of the accused.

3. An attorney-at-law shall not hold out any persons who is not qualified to practice law as a partner associate, consultant or attorney-at-law.

4. An attorney-at-law shall not solicit business or consent to become involved in a matter unless at the request of a party thereto. Provided however that it is proper for an attorney-at-law to become involved in matters referred by the Association or by another attorney-at-law or for which he is engaged in any other manner not inconsistent with these Rules.

5. An attorney-at-law shall not in the carrying on of his practice or otherwise permit any act or thing which is likely or is intended to attract business unfairly or can reasonably be regarded as touting or advertising.

6. (1) An attorney-at-law shall not in any way make use of any forms of advertisement calculated to attract clients to himself or any firm with which he is associated and he shall not permit, authorise or encourage anyone to do so or reward anyone for doing so on his behalf.

(2) An attorney-at-law shall not permit his professional standing to be used for the purpose of advertising any particular product, service or commercial organization.

(3) An attorney-at-law shall not advertise for business indirectly by furnishing or inspiring newspaper comment concerning cases or causes in which an attorney-at-law has been or is connected or concerning the manner of their conduct, the magnitude of the interests involved, the importance of the attorney-at-law's position and any similar self-laudations.

Provided however that—

(a) an attorney-at-law may permit limited and dignified identification of himself as an attorney-at-law —

(i) in political advertisements relevant to the course of a political campaign or issue;

(ii) in public notices where the announcement of his professional status is required or authorised by law, or is reasonably necessary for a purpose other than the attraction of potential clients;

(iii) in reports and announcements of *bona fide* commercial, civic, professional or political organisations in which he serves as a director or officer;

(iv) in and on legal textbooks, articles, professional journals and other legal publications and in dignified and restrained advertisements thereof;

(v) in announcements of any public address, lecture or publication by him on legal topics, provided that such announcements do not emphasize his own professional competence and are not likely to be regarded as being concerned with the giving of individual advice by him.

(b) an attorney-at-law may publish in the media a brief professional announcement (the form, manner, contents and frequency to be approved by the Council) stating new or changed associations or addresses, changes of firm name, temporary closures and re-opening of offices and other like professional matters.

(c) an attorney-at-law may speak in public or write for publication on legal topics so long as he does not thereby emphasise his own professional competence and is not likely to be regarded as being concerned thereby with the giving of individual advice.

(d) the following cards, office signs, letterheads or directory listings may be used by an attorney-at-law but in a restrained and dignified form:

(i) a professional card identifying the attorney-at-law by name and as an attorney-at-law giving his decorations and degrees, legal or otherwise, his addresses, telephone, telex and telefax numbers, and the name of his law firm or professional associates so however that such cards are not published in the news media and are only handed out on request and for the purposes of identification or address;

(ii) a brief professional announcement card to be delivered only to attorneys-at-law, clients, personal friends and relations and government bodies and stating new or changed associations or addresses, changes of firm name or like professional matters;

(iii) a sign of size and design compatible with the existing practice of the profession, on or near the door of the office and in the building directory identifying the law office;

(iv) a letterhead identifying the attorney-at-law by name and as an attorney-at-law and giving his decorations and degrees, legal or otherwise, his addresses, telephone numbers, telex and telefax and the name of his law firm and of his associates;

(v) a listing in a telephone directory, a reputable law list, legal directory or biographical reference giving brief biographical or other relevant information; and any such professional card, office sign, letterhead or listing may state that the attorney-at-law is also a notary public.

7. Where an attorney-at-law commits any criminal offence which in the opinion of the Disciplinary Committee of his Bar Association is, in all the circumstances of the case, of a nature likely to bring the profession into disrepute, such commission of the offence shall constitute professional misconduct if —

(a) he has been convicted by any Court, including a foreign Court of competent jurisdiction, for the offence; or

(b) although he has not been prosecuted the Committee is satisfied of the facts constituting the criminal offence; or

(c) he has been prosecuted and has been acquitted by reason of a technical defence or he has been convicted but such conviction is quashed by reason of some technical defence.

8. An attorney-at-law shall not acquire directly or indirectly by purchase, or otherwise, a financial or other interest in the subject matter of a case which he is conducting.

9. (1) An attorney-at-law shall not enter into partnership or fee sharing arrangements concerning the practice of law with non-qualified bodies or persons.

   (2) An attorney-at-law shall not enter in an arrangement for or charge or collect a fee in contravention of these rules or any other law.

10. (1) An attorney-at-law shall not charge fees that are unfair or unreasonable. In determining the fairness and reasonableness of a fee the following factors may be taken into account:

    (a) the time and labour required, the novelty and difficulty of the questions involved and the skill required to perform the legal service properly;

    (b) the likelihood that the acceptance of the particular employment will preclude other employment by the attorney-at-law;

    (c) the fee customarily charged in the locality for similar legal services;

    (d) the amount, if any, concerned;

    (e) the time limitations imposed by the client or by the circumstances;

    (f) the nature and length of the professional relationship with the client;

    (g) the experience, reputation and ability of the attorney-at-law involved;

    (h) any scale of fees or recommended guide as to charges prescribed by law or by the Association.

    (2) An attorney-at-law shall not accept any fee of reward for merely introducing a client or referring a case or client to another attorney-at-law.

    (3) An attorney-at-law may, with the prior agreement of the client, charge a contingency fee not exceeding twenty percent and reasonable commissions on collection of liquidated claims.

11. (1) Except with the specific approval of his client given after full disclosure, an attorney-at-law shall not act in any manner in which his professional duties and personal interests conflict or are likely to conflict.

    (2) An attorney-at-law shall not accept or continue his retainer or employment on behalf of two or more clients if their interests are likely to conflict or if his independent professional judgement is likely to be impaired.

12. (1) An attorney-at-law who withdraws from employment under rule 34 of

Part A shall not do so until he has taken reasonable steps to avoid foreseeable prejudice or injury to the position and rights of his client, including
- (a) giving due notice;
- (b) allowing time for employment of another attorney-at-law;
- (c) delivering to the client all documents and property to which he is entitled subject however to any lien which the attorney-at-law may have over the same;
- (d) complying with such laws, rules or practice as may be applicable; and
- (e) where appropriate, obtaining the permission of the Court where the hearing of the matter has commenced

(2) An attorney-at-law who withdraws from employment shall refund promptly such part of the fees, if any, already paid by his client as may be fair and reasonable having regard to all the circumstances.

13. An attorney-at-law shall withdraw forthwith from employment or from a matter pending before a tribunal —
- (a) where the client insists upon his representing a claim or defence that he cannot conscientiously advance;
- (b) where the client seeks to pursue a course of conduct which is illegal or which will result in deliberately deceiving the Court;
- (c) where the client has in the course of the proceedings perpetrated a fraud upon a person or tribunal and on request by the attorney-at-law has refused or is unable to rectify the same;
- (d) where his continued employment will involve him in the violation of the law or a disciplinary rule;
- (e) where the client by any other conduct renders it unreasonably difficult for the attorney-at-law to carry out his employment as such effectively, or in accordance with the judgement and advice of the attorney-at-law or the rules of law or professional ethics;
- (f) where for any good and compelling reason it is difficult for him to carry out his employment effectively.

14. An attorney-at-law shall not retain money he received for his client for longer than is absolutely necessary.

15. An attorney-at-law shall never disclose, unless lawfully ordered to do so by the Court or required by statute, what has been communicated to him in his capacity as an attorney-at-law by his client's attorney-at-law and this duty not to disclose extends to his partners, to junior attorneys-at-law assisting him, and to his employees provided however that an attorney-at-law may reveal confidences or secrets necessary to establish or collect his fee or to defend himself or his employees or associates against an accusation of wrongful conduct.

16. An attorney-at-law shall not permit his professional services or his name to be used in any way which would make it possible for persons who are not legally authorised to do so to practice law.
17. An attorney-at-law shall not delegate to a person not legally qualified and not in his employ or under his control any functions of the law of his State only to be performed by a qualified attorney-at-law.
18. In the performance of his duties an attorney-at-law shall not act with inexcusable or undue delay, negligence or neglect.
19. An attorney-at-law shall not engage in undignified or discourteous conduct which is degrading to the Court or his profession.
20. An attorney-at-law shall not willfully make false accusations against a Judge or Magistrate.
21. An attorney-at-law who holds a public office shall not use his public position to influence or attempt to influence a tribunal to act in favour of himself or of his client.
22. An attorney-at-law shall not accept private employment in a matter upon the merits of which he previously acted in a judicial capacity or for which he had substantial responsibility while he was in public employment.
23. An attorney-at-law shall not give, lend or promise anything of value to a Judge, Juror or official of a Tribunal before which there is a pending matter in which he is engaged.
24. In any proceedings in a Court an attorney-at-law shall not communicate or cause any other person to communicate with a juror as to the merits of such proceedings, and shall only do so with a Judge or person exercising judicial functions —
    (a) in the normal course of the proceedings; or
    (b) where authorised by law, or the practice of the Courts.
25. An attorney-at-law shall not for the purpose of making any person available as a witness advise or cause that person to secrete himself or leave the jurisdiction of the Court.
26. An attorney-at-law shall not pay or offer to pay or acquiesce in the payment of compensation to a witness for giving evidence in any cause or matter save as reimbursement for expenses reasonably incurred and as reasonable compensation for loss of time in attending for preparation and for testifying, and in the case of an expert witness a reasonable fee for his professional services.
27. An attorney-at-law shall not knowingly use perjured testimony or false evidence or participate in the creation of or use of evidence which he knows to be false.
28. An attorney-at-law shall not counsel or assist his client or a witness in conduct that the attorney-at-law knows to be illegal or fraudulent, and where he is satisfied that his client has in the course of the particular representation perpetrated a fraud upon a person or tribunal, he shall promptly

call upon him to rectify the same.

29. An attorney-at-law shall not knowingly make a false statement of law or fact.

30. (1) An attorney-at-law shall not commit a breach of an undertaking given by him to a Judge, a Court or other Tribunal or an official thereof, whether such undertaking relates to an expression of intention as to future conduct or is a representation that a particular state of facts exists.

(2) An attorney-at-law shall not knowingly represent falsely to a Judge, a Court or other Tribunal or to an official of a Court or other Tribunal, that a particular state of facts exists.

31. In pecuniary matters an attorney-a-law shall be most punctual and diligent; he shall never mingle funds of others with his own and he shall at all times be able to refund money he holds for others.

32. (1) An attorney-at-law shall keep such accounts as clearly and accurately distinguish the financial position between himself and his clients as and when required.

(2) An attorney-at-law shall comply with such rules as may be made by the Council of the OECS Bar.

(3) Nothing contained in rules 31 and 32 of this Part shall deprive an attorney-at-law of any recourse or right whether by way of lien, set-off, counterclaim, charge or otherwise against moneys standing to the credit of a client's account maintained by that attorney-at-law.

33. An attorney-at-law shall reply promptly to any letter received from the Association relating to his professional conduct.

34. Where no provision is made in these Rules in respect of any matter, the rules and practice of the legal profession which formerly governed the particular matter shall apply in so far as is practicable.

35. (1) Breach by an attorney-at-law of any of the rules contained in this Part shall constitute professional misconduct and an attorney-at-law who commits such a breach shall be liable to any of the penalties which the Disciplinary Committee and the Court is empowered to impose.

(2) Breach by an attorney-at-law of any of the provisions of Part A of this Code while not automatically amounting to punishable professional misconduct is a derogation from the high standards of conduct expected from any attorney-at-law and may, depending on the circumstances of the particular case, amount to such misconduct or form a material ingredient thereof.

Accepted in principle by the OECS Bar at its first General Meeting in St Vincent on 2nd March 1991. Adopted by the OECS Bar Council at its second meeting in Anguilla on 15th June 1991.

Appendix 4
Jamaica

Legal Profession (Canons of Professional Ethics) Rules

STANDARDS OF PROFESSIONAL ETIQUETTE
AND PROFESSIONAL CONDUCT
FOR ATTORNEYS-AT-LAW

Prescribed by the General Legal Council
pursuant to the provisions of section 12(7)
of the Legal Profession Act 1971

In exercise of the powers conferred upon the General Legal Council by section 12(7) of the Legal Profession Act and of every other power hereunto enabling the following rules are hereby made:–

1. These rules may be cited as the Legal Profession (Canons of Professional Ethics) Rules and shall be read and construed as one with the Legal Profession Act hereafter referred to as the Principal Act.
2. In these rules unless the context otherwise requires:
   "Attorney" includes a Firm of attorneys

Definitions "Tribunal" includes the Disciplinary Committee as appointed by virtue of section II of the Principal Act.

CANON I

AN ATTORNEY SHALL ASSIST IN MAINTAINING THE DIGNITY AND INTEGRITY OF THE LEGAL PROFESSION AND SHALL AVOID EVEN THE APPEARANCE OF PROFESSIONAL IMPROPRIETY.

(a) An Attorney who gives a certificate of character to any candidate for enrolment as an attorney shall satisfy himself that the candidate is of good character.

(b) An Attorney shall at all times maintain the honour and dignity of the profession and shall abstain from behaviour which may tend to discredit the profession of which he is a member.

(c) An Attorney shall observe these Canons and shall maintain his integrity and encourage other attorneys to act similarly. He shall not counsel or assist anyone to act in any way which is detrimental to the Legal Profession.

(d) An Attorney shall expose without fear or favour before the proper tribunals, unprofessional or dishonest conduct by any other Attorney and shall not lightly refuse a retainer against another Attorney who is alleged to have wronged his client.

CANON II

AN ATTORNEY SHALL NOT INDULGE IN OR ASSIST IN ANY UNAUTHORISED, IMPROPER OR UNPROFESSIONAL PRACTICE.

(a) An Attorney shall not hold out any person (not qualified to practise as a lawyer) as a partner, associate consultant or Attorney.

(b) An Attorney shall not in the carrying on of his practice or otherwise permit any act or thing which is likely or is intended to attract business unfairly or can reasonably be regarded as touting or advertising.

(c) An Attorney shall not endeavour by direct or indirect means to attract the client s of his fellow Attorneys and where one Attorney refers a client to another Attorney, the client remains the client of the referring Attorney and the Attorney to whom the client is referred shall act with due deference to the relationship between the client and the referring attorney.

(cc) Where a referred client offers other work to the Attorney to whom he was referred and the offer is sufficiently proximate to the referral, that attorney shall not accept that offer unless it has been brought to the attention of the referring Attorney.

(d) Except as permitted by clause (e) and (f) of this Canon, an Attorney shall not in any way make use of any form of public advertisement calculated to attract clients to himself or any firm with which he may be associated and he shall not permit, authorise, or encourage anyone to do so, or reward anyone for doing so, on his behalf.

(e) Notwithstanding the provisions of Canon II (d), an Attorney may permit limited and dignified identification of himself as an Attorney as follows:-

(i) in political advertisement relevant to the course of a political campaign or issue;

(ii) in public notices where the announcement of his professional status is required or authorised by Law, or is reasonably necessary for a purpose other than the attraction of potential clients;

(iii) in reports and announcements of *bona fide* commercial, civic, professional or political organizations in which he serves as a Director or officer;

(iv) in and on legal textbooks, articles and other legal publications and in dignified and restrained advertisements thereof;

(v) in announcements of any public address, lecture, or publication by him on legal topics, provided that such announcements do not emphasize his own professional competence and are not likely to be regarded as being concerned with the giving of individual advice by him.

(f) Notwithstanding the provisions of Canon II (d) an Attorney may speak in public or write for publication on legal topics provided that he does not thereby emphasize his own professional competence and is not likely to be regarded as being concerned thereby with the giving of individual advice.

(g) An Attorney shall not permit his professional standing to be used for the purpose of advertising any particular product, service or commercial organization.

(h) Subject to the provisions of Canon II (i) an Attorney shall not use professional cards, office signs, letterheads, or directory listings or like professional notices or devices.

(i) Notwithstanding the provisions of Canon II (h), the following cards, office signs, letter heads or directory listings may be used but in a restrained and dignified form:-

(i) a professional card identifying the Attorney by name and as an Attorney, giving his decorations and degrees (legal or otherwise), his addresses, telephone numbers and the name of his Law firm or professional associates, provided that such cards are not published in the news media and are only handed out on request and for the purposes of identification or address;

(ii) a brief professional announcement card stating new or changed associations or addresses, changes of firm name or like professional matters provided that such cards are delivered only to Attorneys, clients, former clients, personal friends, relations and government bodies;

(iii) a sign on or near the door of the office, and in the building directory identifying the Law office, provided that it is of a size and design compatible with the existing practice of the profession.
(iv) a letterhead identifying the Attorney by name and as an Attorney and giving his decorations and degrees (legal or otherwise), his addresses, telephone numbers and the name of his Law firm and of his associates;
(v) a listing in a telephone directory, a reputable law list, legal directory or biographical reference giving brief biographical or other relevant information and any such professional card, office sign, letterhead or listing may state that the Attorney is also a Notary Public.

(j) Save as provided by Section 7 of the Principal Act, an Attorney shall not practise as a lawyer unless he has paid the prescribed fee in accordance with Section 5(2) of the Principal Act and has been issued with a Practising Certificate by the General Legal Council.

CANON III

AN ATTORNEY OWES A DUTY TO THE PUBLIC TO MAKE HIS COUNSEL AVAILABLE AND A DUTY TO THE STATE TO MAINTAIN ITS CONSTITUTION AND ITS LAWS AND SHALL ASSIST IN IMPROVING THE LEGAL SYSTEM.

(a) An Attorney is under no obligation to act on behalf of every person who may wish to become his client, but in furtherance of the ethics of the profession to make legal services fully available, he shall not lightly decline a proffered retainer.
(b) An Attorney may accept a general or special retainer from a client and the retainer rules hitherto applicable in the case of counsel shall apply *mutatis mutandis*.
(c) An Attorney shall not be deterred from accepting proffered employment owing to the fear or dislike of incurring disapproval of officials, fellow Attorneys or members of the public.
(d) When an Attorney consents to undertake legal aid and he is appointed by the Court or is requested by his professional association to undertake the representation of a person unable to afford such representation or to obtain legal aid such attorney shall not (except for compelling reasons) seek to be excused from undertaking such representation.
(e) An Attorney shall not (except for good reasons) refuse his services in Capital offences.
(f) An Attorney shall not act contrary to the laws of the land, or aid, counsel or assist any man to break those laws.

(g) An Attorney in undertaking the defence of persons accused of crime shall use all fair and reasonable means to present every defence available at law, without regard to any personal views he may hold as to the guilt of the accused.

(h) An Attorney engaged in conducting the prosecution of an accused person has a primary duty to see that justice is done and he shall not withhold facts or secrete witnesses which tend to establish the guilt or innocence of the accused.

(i) An Attorney shall not by his actions stir up strife or litigation, and where it is in the interest of his client he shall seek to obtain reasonable settlements of disputes.

(j) An attorney shall endeavour by lawful means where the needs of society require to promote and encourage the modernization, simplification and reform of laws.

(k) Where an Attorney commits any criminal offence which in the opinion of the Disciplinary Committee is of a nature likely to bring the profession into disrepute, such commission of the offence shall constitute misconduct in a professional respect if:-

   (i) he has been convicted by any court (including a foreign court of competent jurisdiction) for such offence; or

   (ii) although he has not been prosecuted the Committee is satisfied of the facts constituting such criminal offence; or

   (iii) he has been prosecuted and has been acquitted by reason of a technical defence or he has been convicted but such conviction is quashed by reason of some technical defence.

CANON IV

AN ATTORNEY SHALL ACT IN THE BEST INTERESTS OF HIS CLIENT AND REPRESENT HIM HONESTLY, COMPETENTLY AND ZEALOUSLY WITHIN THE BOUNDS OF THE LAW. HE SHALL PRESERVE THE CONFIDENCE OF HIS CLIENT AND AVOID CONFLICTS OF INTEREST.

(a) An Attorney may enter into partnership with one or more Attorneys but he shall not enter into partnership or fee sharing arrangements concerning the practice of law with non-qualified persons or bodies.

(b) An Attorney may employ another Attorney for any purpose and on any terms as may be agreed upon.

(c) An Attorney shall exercise independent judgment within the bounds of the law and the ethics of the profession for the benefit of his client.

(d) Where an Attorney determines that the interest of his client requires it, he may with the specific or general consent of the client refer his business or part of it to another Attorney whether or not a member of his own firm.

(e) An Attorney shall not enter into an agreement for or charge or collect an illegal fee.

(f) The fees that an Attorney my charge shall be fair and reasonable and in determining the fairness and reasonableness of a fee any of the following factors may be taken into account:-

- (i) the time and labour required, the novelty and difficulty of the questions involved and the skill required to perform the legal service properly;
- (ii) the likelihood that the acceptance of the particular employment will preclude other employment by the attorney;
- (iii) the fee customarily charged in the locality for similar legal services;
- (iv) the amount, if any, involved;
- (v) the time limitations imposed by the client or by the circumstances;
- (vi) the nature and length of the professional relationship with the client;
- (vii) the experience reputation and ability of the Attorney concerned;
- (viii) whether the fee is fixed or contingent;
- (ix) any scale of fees or recommended guide as to charges prescribed by the Incorporated Law Society of Jamaica, the Bar Association, the Northern Jamaica Law Society or any other body approved by the General Legal Council for the purpose of prescribing fees.

(g) An Attorney shall not pay or accept any fee or reward for merely introducing a client or referring a case or client to another Attorney.

(h) An Attorney on the record may instruct one or more Attorneys to appear as Advocates, in the same way as a Solicitor on the record has hitherto instructed Counsel.

(i) Where more than one Attorney appear'as Advocates for the same party in the same proceeding, the question of who should lead the conduct of that party's case shall (subject to the instructions of the client) be settled between the Attorneys representing that party, before they appear in Court and shall not be altered during the course of the proceedings and the leader so appointed shall have all the authority over the conduct of the case as was hitherto possessed by the leading counsel.

(j) Except with the specific approval of his client given after full disclosure, an Attorney shall not act in any manner in which his professional duties and his personal interests conflict or are likely to conflict.

(k) Subject to the provisions of Canon IV (l), an Attorney shall not accept or continue his retainer or employment on behalf of two or more clients if their interests are likely to conflict or if the independent professional judgment of the Attorney is likely to be impaired.

(l) Notwithstanding the provisions of Canon IV (k), an Attorney may represent multiple clients if he can adequately represent the interests of each and if each consent to such representation after full disclosure of the possible effects of such multiple representation.

(m) In all situations where a possible conflict of interest arises, an Attorney shall resolve all doubts against the propriety of multiple representation.

(n) An Attorney may at any time withdraw from employment:-

(i) where the client fails, refuses, or neglects to carry out an agreement with, or his obligation to, the Attorney as regards the expenses or fees payable by the client; or

(ii) where his inability to work with co-Attorneys indicates that the best interest of the client is likely to be served by his withdrawal; or

(iii) where his client freely assents to the termination of his employment; or

(iv) where by reasons of his mental or physical condition or other good and compelling reason it is difficult for him to carry out his employment effectively; or

(v) where any of the provisions of Canon IV (j), (k) or (m) apply.

(o) An Attorney who withdraws from employment by virtue of any of the provisions of Canon IV (n) shall not do so until he has taken reasonable steps to avoid foreseeable prejudice or injury to the position and rights of his client including:-

(i) giving due notice;

(ii) allowing time for employment of another Attorney;

(iii) delivering to the client all documents and property to which he is entitled;

(iv) complying with such laws, rules or practice as may be applicable; and

(v) where appropriate obtaining the permission of the Court where the hearing of the matter has commenced.

(p) An Attorney who withdraws from employment in accordance with Canon IV (o) shall refund promptly such part of the fees (if any) paid in advance, as may be fair and reasonable having regard to all the circumstances.

(q) An Attorney shall withdraw forthwith from employment or from a matter pending before a Tribunal:-

(i) where the client insists upon his representing a claim or defence that he cannot conscientiously advance;

(ii) where the client seeks to pursue a course of conduct which is illegal or which will result in deliberately deceiving the Court;

(iii) where a client has in the course of the proceedings perpetrated a fraud upon a person or tribunal and on request by the Attorney has refused or is unable to rectify the same;

(iv) where his continued employment will involve him in the violation of a Rule of Law or a disciplinary rule;

(v) where the client by any other conduct renders it unreasonably difficult for the Attorney to carry out his employment as such effectively, or in accordance with the judgment and advice of the Attorney, or the Canons of professional ethics;

(vi) where for any good and compelling reason it is difficult for him to carry out his employment effectively.

(r) An Attorney shall deal with his client's business with all due expedition and shall whenever reasonably so required by the client provide him with all information as to the progress of the client's business with due expedition.

(s) In the performance of his duties an Attorney shall not act with inexcusable or deplorable negligence or neglect.

(t) An Attorney shall not knowingly:-
   (i) reveal a confidence or secret of his client; or
   (ii) use a confidence or secret of his client:-
      (1) to the client's disadvantage; or
      (2) to his own advantage; or
      (3) to the advantage of any other person unless in any case it is done with the consent of the client after full disclosure.

      Provided however, that an Attorney may reveal confidences or secrets necessary to establish or collect his fee or to defend himself or his employees or associates against an accusation of wrongful conduct.

CANON V

AN ATTORNEY HAS A DUTY TO ASSIST IN MAINTAINING THE DIGNITY OF THE COURTS AND THE INTEGRITY OF THE ADMINISTRATION OF JUSTICE.

(a) An Attorney shall maintain a respectful attitude towards the Court, not for the sake of the holder of any office, but for the maintenance of its supreme importance, and he shall not engage in undignified or discourteous conduct which is degrading to the Court.

(b) An Attorney shall encourage respect for the Courts and Judges.

(c) An Attorney shall not willfully make false accusations against a Judicial officer and shall support such officers against unjust criticisms.

(d) Where there is ground for complaint against a Judicial officer, an Attorney may make representation to the proper authorities and in such cases an Attorney shall be protected.

(e) An Attorney who holds a Public Office shall not use his public position to influence or attempt to influence a Tribunal to act in favour of himself or of his client.

(f) An Attorney shall not accept private employment in a matter upon the merits of which he previously acted in a Judicial capacity or for which he had substantial responsibility while he was in public employment.

(g) An Attorney who previously held a substantive appointment as a Judge of the Supreme Court or the Court of Appeal shall not appear as an Attorney in any of the Courts of the island, after demitting such office.

(h) An Attorney shall not give, lend or promise anything of value to a Judge, juror or official of a tribunal before which there is a pending matter in which he is engaged.

(i) In any proceeding in a Court an Attorney shall not communicate or cause any other person to communicate with a juror as to the merits of such proceedings, and shall only do so with a Judge or person exercising Judicial function:-

(i) in the normal course of the proceedings, or

(iii) where authorised by law, or the practice of the Courts or with the consent of the parties.

(j) Attorney shall endeavour always to maintain his position as an Advocate and shall not either in argument to the Court or in address to the jury assert his personal belief in his client's innocence or in the justice of his cause or his personal knowledge as to any of the facts involved in the matter under investigation.

(k) An Attorney shall not for the purpose of making any person unavailable as a witness, advise or cause that person to secrete himself or leave the jurisdiction of the Court.

(l) An Attorney shall not pay or offer to pay or acquiesce in the payment of compensation to a witness for giving evidence in any cause or matter save as reimbursement for expenses reasonably incurred and as reasonable compensation for loss of time in attending for preparation and for testifying, and in the case of an expert witness a reasonable fee for his professional services.

(m) An Attorney shall not knowingly use perjured testimony or false evidence or participate in the creation or use of evidence which he knows to be false.

(n) An Attorney shall not counsel or assist his client or a witness, in conduct that the Attorney knows to be illegal or fraudulent, and where he is satisfied that his client has in the course of the particular representation perpetrated a fraud upon a person or tribunal, he shall promptly call upon him to rectify the same.

(o) An Attorney shall not knowingly make a false statement of law or fact.

(p) While appearing on behalf of his client, an Attorney shall avoid testifying on behalf of that client, except as to merely formal matters, or when essential to ends of justice and if his testimony is material to the cause he shall, wherever possible, leave the conduct of the case to another Attorney.

(q) An Attorney shall be punctual in attendance before the Courts and concise and direct in the trial and disposition of causes.

(r) An Attorney appearing before the Court shall at all times be attired in such manner as may be prescribed or agreed by the proper Authorities and as may befit the dignity of the Court.

(s) Subject to the provisions of subsection 2 of section 5 of the Principal Act, an Attorney shall not practise as a lawyer except by virtue of and in accordance with the practising certificate issued to him by the General Legal Council.

CANON VI

AN ATTORNEY HAS A DUTY TO MAINTAIN A PROPER PROFESSIONAL ATTITUDE TOWARDS HIS FELLOW ATTORNEYS

(a) An Attorney's conduct towards his fellow Attorneys shall be characterized by courtesy and good faith and he shall not permit ill-feeling between clients to affect his relationship with his fellow Attorneys or his demeanour towards the opposing party.

(b) An Attorney shall endeavour as far as is reasonable to suit the convenience of the opposing Attorney when the interest of his client or the cause of justice will not be injured by so doing.

(c) An Attorney shall not commit a breach of an undertaking given by him to a Judge, a Court or other tribunal or an official thereof, whether such undertaking relates to an expression of intention as to future conduct or is a representation that a particular state of facts exists.

(cc) An Attorney shall not knowingly represent falsely to a Judge, a Court or other tribunal or an official of a Court, or other tribunal, that a particular state of facts exists.

(d) An Attorney shall not give a professional undertaking which he cannot fulfil and shall fulfil every such undertaking which he gives.

(e) Where an Attorney has been sent money, documents or other things by another Attorney which (at the time of sending) are expressed to be sent only on the basis that the Attorney to whom they are sent will receive them on his undertaking to do or refrain from doing some act, the receiving Attorney shall forthwith return such things if he is unable to accept them on such undertaking, but otherwise must comply with such undertaking.

(f) An Attorney shall not in any way communicate upon a subject in controversy or attempt to negotiate or compromise a matter directly with any party represented by another Attorney except through such other Attorney or with his prior consent.

(g) An Attorney shall not ignore the customs or practices of the Profession even when the law expressly permits it, without giving timely notice to the opposing Attorney.

(h) An Attorney shall not accept instructions to act in Court proceedings in which to his knowledge the client has previously been represented by another Attorney, unless he first notifies the other Attorney of the change.

Provided that an Attorney shall be deemed to have notified the other Attorney if he has made reasonable efforts to notify him.

(i) An Attorney shall not accept instructions to act in proceedings (other than Court proceedings) in which to his knowledge, another Attorney has previously represented the client unless he makes reasonable efforts to ascertain that the retainer of that Attorney has been determined by the client, or that the client wishes both Attorneys to represent him.

(j) An Attorney who instructs or employs another Attorney to act on behalf of his client, unless otherwise agreed, shall pay the proper fee of such Attorney whether or not he has received payment from his client.

CANON VII

AN ATTORNEY SHALL MAINTAIN PROPER ACCOUNTS AND OBSERVE PROPER ACCOUNTING PRINCIPLES IN THE CONDUCT OF HIS ACCOUNTS ESPECIALLY AS REGARDS ACCOUNTING FOR THE FUNDS OF HIS CLIENTS.

(a) An Attorney shall comply with rules as may from time to time be prescribed by the General Legal Council relating to the keeping in separate accounts:-
   (i) the funds of himself or any firm with which he is associated; and
   (ii) those of his clients.

(b) An Attorney shall:-
   (i) keep such accounts as shall clearly and accurately distinguish the financial position between himself and his client as and when required; and
   (ii) account to his client for all monies in the hands of the Attorney for the account or credit of the client, whenever reasonably required to do so

   and he shall for these purposes keep the said accounts in conformity with the regulations which may from time to time be prescribed by the General Legal Council.

(c) Nothing in these Canons shall deprive an Attorney of any recourse or right whether by way of lien, set-off, counterclaim, charge or other wise against monies standing to the credit of a client's account maintained by that Attorney.

CANON VIII

GENERAL

(a) Nothing herein contained shall be construed as derogating from any existing rules of professional conduct and duties of an Attorney which are in keeping with the traditions of the legal profession, although not specifically mentioned herein.

(b) Where in any particular matter explicit ethical guidance does not exist, an Attorney shall determine his conduct by acting in a manner that promotes public confidence in the integrity and efficiency of the legal system and the legal profession.

(c) Where no provision is made herein in respect of any matter, the rules and practice of the legal profession which formerly governed the particular matter shall apply in so far as is practicable, and a breach of such rules and practice (depending on the gravity of such breach) may constitute misconduct in a professional respect.

(d) Breach by an Attorney of any of the provisions of Canons I(b), II(a), (b), (d), (g), (h), (j), III(d), (e), (h), (k), IV(a), (e), (g), (j), (o), (p), (r), (s), (t), V(e), (f), (g), (h), (i), (m), (n), (s), VI (c), (cc), (d), (e), (h), (i), (j), VII(a), (b), VIII(b) shall constitute misconduct in a professional respect and an Attorney who commits such a breach shall be subject to any of the orders contained in section 12(4) of the Principal Act.

(e) The Canons of Professional Etiquette for Attorneys-at-Law published in the Jamaica Gazette Extraordinary of the 6th January, 1972 are hereby repealed but nothing contained herein shall be construed as derogating from the right of the Disciplinary Committee of the General Legal Council to hear and determine complaints relating to acts of misconduct alleged to have been committed before the coming into effect of these rules.

Dated this 12th day of December, 1978.

DAVID M. MUIRHEAD,
Chairman, General Legal Council

DOROTHY C. LIGHTBOURNE,
Secretary, General Legal Council
Supreme Court Building, Kingston.

Appendix 5
St. Lucia

Code of Ethics

Form 3

(section26 (3))

THE LEGAL PROFESSION ACT, 2000

Law Officers Certificate

It is hereby certified that is a law officer holding the office of in the Public Service and appointed by the Judicial and Legal Service Commission.

Dated this day of

Attorney General

THIRD SCHEDULE

(Section 35)

PART A

Code of Ethics

GENERAL GUIDELINES

I. In Relation to the profession and oneself

1. An attorney-at-law shall observe the rules of this Code, maintain his integrity and the honour and dignity of the legal profession and encourage other attorneys-at-law to act similarly both in the practice ot his profession and in his private life, shall refrain from conduct which is detrimental to the profession or which may tend to discredit it.

2. An attorney-at-law shall expose without fear or favour before the proper tribunals unprofessional or dishonest conduct by any other attorneys-at-law and shall not lightly refuse a retainer against another attorney-at-law who is alleged to have wronged his client or committed any other act of professional misconduct.
3. (1) An attorney-at-law shall scrupulously preserve his independence in the discharge of his professional duties.
   (2) An attorney-at-law practising on his own account or in partnership shall not engage in any other business or occupation if doing so may cause him to cease to be independent.
4. An attorney-at-law shall protect the profession against the admission into it of any candidate whose moral character or education renders him unfit for such admission.
5. (1) An attorney-at-law shall not endeavour by direct or indirect means to attract the clients of another attorney-at-law and where a client is referred to him by another attorney-at-law the client remains for all other purposes the client of the referring attorney-at-law and the attorney-at-law to whom the client is referred shall act with due deference to the relationship between the client and the referring attorney-at-law.
   (2) Where a referred client offers other work to the attorney-at-law to whom he is referred and the offer is sufficiently proximate to the referral, that attorney-at-law shall not accept that offer unless it has been brought to the attention of the referring attorney-at-law.
6. An attorney-at-law may speak in public or write for publication on legal topics so long as he does not thereby advertise his own professional competence and is not likely to be regarded as being concerned thereby with the giving of the individual advice.
7. The best advertisement for an attorney-at-law is the establishment of a well merited reputation for personal integrity, capacity, dedication to work fidelity and trust and it is unprofessional —
   (a) to solicit business by circulars or advertisements or interviews not warranted by personal relations; or
   (b) seek retainers through agents of any kind.
8. An attorney-at-law shall defend the interests of his client without fear of judicial disfavour or public unpopularity and without regard to unpleasant consequences to himself or to any other person.
9. Subject to paragraph 17, no attorney-at-law is obliged to act either as adviser or advocate for every person who may wish to become his client he has a right to decline employment.
10. No client is entitled to receive nor should any attorney-at-law render, any service or advice involving disloyalty to the State or disrespect for judicial office or the corruption of any persons exercising a public or private trust or

deception or betrayal of the public.

11. Every attorney-at-law should bear in mind that the oath of office taken on his admission to practise is not a mere form but is a solemn undertaking to be strictly observed on his part.
12. An attorney-at-law should also bear in mind that he can only maintain the high traditions of his profession by being a person of high integrity and dignity.

II. In Relation to the Slate and the Public

13. An attorney-at-law owes a duty to the State to maintain its integrity, its Constitution and its laws and not to aid, abet, counsel or assist anyone to act in any way contrary to those laws.
14. When engaged as a public prosecutor the primary duty of an attorney-at-law is not to secure a conviction but to see that justice is done and to that end he shall not withhold facts tending to prove either the guilt or innocence of the accused.
15. An attorney-at-law shall endeavour by lawful means where the needs of society require, to promote and encourage the modernization, simplification and reform of the laws.
16. An attorney-at-law shall not by his actions, stir up strife or litigation by seeking out defects in titles, claims for personal injury or other causes of action for the purpose of securing a retainer to prosecute a claim therefor; or pay or reward any person directly or indirectly for the purpose of procuring him to be retained in his professional capacity, and where it is in the interest of his client he shall seek to obtain reasonable settlements of disputes.
17. An attorney-at-law shall not except for good reasons refuse his services in capital offences.
18. An attorney-at-law shall not be deterred from accepting proffered employment owing to the fear or dislike or incurring disapproval of officials, other attorneys-at-law or members of the public.
19. An attorney-at-law in undertaking the defense of persons accused of crime shall use all fair and reasonable means to present every defense available at law.

III. In Relation to Clients

20. (1) An attorney-at-law shall always act in the best interests of his clients, represent him honestly, competently and zealously and endeavour by all fair and honourable means to obtain for the client any and every remedy and defence which is authorised by law steadfastly bearing in mind that the duties and responsibilities of the attorney-at-law are to be carried out within and not without the bounds of the law.

(2) The interests of his client and the exigencies of the administration of justice should always be the first concern of an attorney-at-law and rank before his right to compensation for his services.

21. (1) Before advising on a client's cause an attorney-at-law should obtain full knowledge thereof and give a candid opinion of the merits or demerits and probable results of pending or contemplated litigation.

(2) An attorney-at-law should beware of proffering bold and confident assurances to his client (especially where employment may depend on such assurances) always bearing in mind that seldom are all the law and facts on the side of his client and that "*audi alteram partem*" is the safest rule to follow.

(3) Whenever the controversy admits of fair adjustment an attorney-at-law should inform his client accordingly and advise him to avoid or settle litigation.

22. (1) An attorney-at-law shall at the time of retainer disclose to his client all the circumstances of his relations to the parties and his interest in or connection with the controversy (if any) which might influence the client in his selection of an attorney-at-law.

(2) An attorney-at-law shall scrupulously guard and never divulge his client's secrets and confidences.

23. An Attorney-at-law shall treat adverse witnesses, litigants and other attorneys-at-law with fairness and courtesy refraining from all offensive personal references and shall avoid imparting to his professional duties his client's personal feelings and prejudices.

24. It is the right of an attorney-at-law to undertake the defense of a person accused of crime regardless of his own personal opinion as to the guilt of the accused and having undertaken such defense he is bound by all fair and honourable means to present every defense that the law of the land permits so that no person may be deprived of life or liberty except by due process of law.

25. (1) An attorney-at-law may represent multiple clients only if he can adequately represent the interests of each and if each consents to such representation after full disclosure of the possible effects of multiple representation.

(2) In all situations where a possible conflict of interest arises, an attorney-at-law shall resolve all conflicts by leaning against multiple representation.

26. (1) An attorney-at-law shall deal with his client's business with all due expedition and shall whenever reasonably so required by the client provide him with full information as to the progress of the client's business.

(2) It is improper for an attorney-at-law to accept a case unless he can handle it without undue delay.

27. Where an attorney-at-law determines that the interest of his client requires

it, he may with the specific or general consent of the client refer his business or part of it to another attorney-at-law whether or not a member of his own firm.

28. (1) A Queen's Counsel shall be entitled to accept instructions, appear or do any work without a junior, except where he would be unable properly to carry out his instructions or conduct his case if he were to do so.
    (2) Where more than one attorney-at-law appears as advocate for the same party in the same proceedings, who shall lead the conduct of that party's case shall, subject to the instructions of the client be settled by the attorneys-at-law representing that party before they appear in court and shall not be altered during the course of the proceedings and the leader shall have all authority over the conduct of the case.
29. An attorney-at-law including a Queen's Counsel who appears with the leader is entitled to negotiate a fee appropriate for his conduct of the case.
30. (1) An attorney-at-law is entitled to reasonable compensation for his services but should avoid charges which either overestimate or undervalue the service rendered.
    (2) The ability of a client to pay cannot justify a charge in excess of the value of the service rendered, though the client's indigence may require a charge that is below such value, or even no charge at all.
    (3) An attorney-at-law should avoid controversies with clients regarding compensation for his services as far as is compatible with self-respect and his right to receive reasonable compensation for his services.
31. The right of an attorney-at-law to ask for a deposit or to demand payment of out-of-pocket expenses and commitments, failing payment of which he may withdraw from the case or refuse to handle it, shall not be exercised where the client may be unable to find other assistance in time to prevent irreparable damage being done.
32. Where an attorney-at-law engages a foreign colleague to advise on a case or to co-operate in handling it he is responsible for the payment of the latter's charges except there is express agreement to the contrary, but where an attorney-at-law directs a client to a foreign colleague he is not responsible for the payment of the latter's charges, nor is he entitled to a share of the fee of his foreign colleague.
33. Subject to paragraph 15 of Part B, an attorney-at-law may at any time withdraw from employment —
    (a) where the client fails, refuses, or neglects to carry out an agreement with, or his obligation to the attorney-at-law as regards the expenses or fees payable by the client;
    (b) where his inability to work with colleagues indicates that the best interest of the client is likely to be served by his withdrawal;
    (c) where his client freely assents to the termination of his employment;

(d) where by reasons of his mental or physical condition or other good and compelling reason it is difficult for him to carry out his employment effectively; or

(e) in cases of conflict as contemplated in paragraph 25 of this Part or paragraph 11 of Part B hereof.

34. (1) An attorney-at-law should not appear as a witness for his own client except as to merely formal matters or where such appearance is essential to the ends of justice.

(2) If an attorney-at-law is a necessary witness for his client with respect to matters other than such as are merely formal, he should entrust the conduct of the case to another attorney-at-law of his client's choice.

IV. In Relation to the Courts and the administration of justice

35. (1) An attorney-at-law shall maintain a respectful attitude towards the Court and shall not engage in undignified or discourteous conduct which is degrading to the Court.

(2) An attorney-at-law shall encourage respect for the courts and the judges.

(3) An attorney-at-law shall support judges and magistrates against unjust criticisms.

(4) Where there is ground for complaint against a judge or magistrate an attorney-at-law may make representation to the proper authorities and in such cases, the attorney-at-law shall be protected.

36. An Attorney-at-law shall endeavour always to maintain his position as an advocate and shall not either in argument to the court or in address to the jury assert his personal belief in his client's innocence or in the justice of his cause or his personal knowledge as to any of the facts involved in the matter under investigation.

37. An attorney-at-law should never ask privately to influence directly or indirectly the Judges of the Court in his favour or in the favour of his client, nor should he attempt to curry favour with juries by fawning, flattery or pretended solicitude for their personal comfort.

38. An attorney-at-law shall be punctual in attendance before the Court and concise and direct in the trial and disposition of causes.

39. An attorney-at-law appearing before the Court shall at all times be attired in such a manner as prescribed or agreed by the proper authorities and as befits the dignity of the Court.

V. In Relation to his fellow Attorneys-at-law

40. (1) The conduct of an attorney-at-law towards his fellow attorneys shall be characterized by courtesy, fairness and good faith and he shall not permit ill-feeling between clients to affect his relationship with his colleagues.

(2) All personal conflicts between attorneys-at-law should be scrupulously avoided as should also colloquies between them which cause delay and promote unseemly wrangling.

41. (1) An attorney-at-law shall reply promptly to letters from other attorneys-at-law making inquiries on behalf of their clients.

(2) An attorney-at-law shall endeavour as far as is reasonable to suit the convenience of the opposing attorney-at-law when the interest of his or her client or the cause of justice will not be injured by so doing.

42. An attorney-at-law shall not give a professional undertaking that he cannot fulfil, and he shall fulfil every such undertaking that he gives.

43. (1) There is a duty on every attorney-at-law to report improper or unprofessional conduct by a colleague to the Committee, except where the information relating to the improper or unprofessional conduct is received in professional confidence in which case he must respect the duty of silence imposed in such circumstances.

(2) An attorney-at-law shall expose without fear or favour before the proper tribunal unprofessional or dishonest conduct by another attorney-at-law and shall not lightly refuse a retainer against another attorney-at-law who is alleged to have wronged a client.

44. Where an attorney-at-law has been sent money, documents or other things by a colleague which, at the time of sending, are expressed to be sent only on the basis that the attorney-at-law to whom they are sent will receive them on his undertaking to do or refrain from doing some act, the receiving attorney-at-law shall forthwith return whatever was sent if he is unable to accept them on such undertaking, otherwise he must comply with the undertaking.

45. An attorney-at-law shall not in any way communicate upon a subject in controversy or attempt to negotiate or compromise a matter directly with any party represented by another attorney-at-law except through such other attorney-at-law or with his proper consent.

46. (1) An attorney-at-law shall not ignore the customs or practices of the legal profession even when the law expressly permits it, without giving timely notice to the opposing attorney-at-law.

(2) An attorney-at-law should avoid all sharp practices and should refrain from taking any paltry advantage when his opponent has made or overlooked some technical error or matter, bearing in mind that no client has a right to demand that an attorney-at-law representing him shall be illiberal or shall do anything repugnant to his own sense of honour and propriety.

47. An attorney-at-law shall not accept instructions to act in Court proceedings in which to his knowledge the client has previously been represented by another attorney-at-law, unless he first notifies the other attorney-at-law of the change, and makes reasonable efforts to ensure that attorney has been

paid for his services, but shall be deemed to have notified the other attorney-at-law if he has made reasonable efforts to notify him.

48. An attorney-at-law shall not accept instructions to act in proceedings (other than Court proceedings) in which to his knowledge, another attorney-at-law has previously represented the client unless he makes reasonable efforts to ascertain that the retainer of that attorney-at-law has been determined by the client, or that the client wishes both attorneys-at-law to represent him.

49. An attorney-at-law who instructs or employs another attorney-at-law to act on behalf of his client, unless otherwise agreed, shall pay the proper fee for such attorney-at-law whether or not he has received payment from his client.

50. In undertaking to render assistance to a foreign colleague, an attorney-at-law shall remember that his responsibility is much greater both when giving advice and handling a case, than it would be had he undertaken to assist a colleague in Saint Lucia.

VI. General

51. Nothing in this Schedule shall be construed as derogating from any existing rules of professional conduct and duties of an attorney-at-law which are in keeping with the traditions of the legal profession although not specifically mentioned here.

52. Where in any particular matter explicit ethical guidance does not exist, an attorney-at-law shall determine his conduct by acting in a manner that promotes public confidence in the integrity and efficiency of the legal system and the legal profession.

53. (1) A person who previously held a substantive appointment as a Judge of the Supreme Court shall not appear as an attorney-at-law in any court in Saint Lucia for a period of ten years commencing on the date of his retirement, resignation or other termination of such appointment.

(2) This rule shall not apply to a person who is appointed to act as a Judge in a temporary capacity.

54. Breach by an attorney-at-law of any of the provisions of this Part while not automatically amounting to punishable professional misconduct is a derogation from the high standards of conduct expected from an attorney-at-law and may, depending on the circumstances of the particular case, amount to such misconduct or form a material ingredient of it.

PART B

Mandatory Provisions and Specific Prohibitions

1. An attorney-at-law shall not practise as such unless he has been issued a practising certificate in accordance with the provisions of this Act.

2. (1) An attorney-at-law shall never knowingly mislead the Court.
   (2) An attorney-at-law shall not withhold facts or secrete witnesses in order to establish the guilt or innocence of the accused.
3. An attorney-at-law shall not hold out any person who is not qualified to practise law as a partner, associate, consultant or attorney-at-law.
4. An attorney-at-law shall not solicit business or consent to become involved in a matter unless at the request of a party to the matter.
5. An attorney-at-law shall not in the carrying on of his practice or otherwise permit any act or thing which is likely or is intended to attract business unfairly or can reasonably be regarded as touting or advertising.
6. (1) An attorney-at-law shall not in any way make use of any form of advertisement calculated to attract clients to himself or any firm with which he is associated and he shall not permit, authorise or encourage anyone to do so or reward anyone for doing so on his behalf.
   (2) An attorney-at-law shall not permit his professional standing to be used for the purpose of advertising any particular product, service or commercial organization.
   (3) An attorney-at-law shall not advertise for business indirectly by furnishing or inspiring newspaper comment concerning cases or causes in which an attorney-at-law has been or is connected or concerning the manner of their conduct, the magnitude of the interests involved, the importance of the attorney-at-law's position and any similar self-laudations.
7. Notwithstanding subparagraph (3) of paragraph 6 an attorney-at-law may permit limited and dignified identification of himself as an attorney-at-law —
   (a) in political advertisements relevant to the course of a political campaign or issue;
   (b) in public notices where the announcement of his professional status is required or authorised by law, or is reasonably necessary for a purpose other than the attraction of potential clients;
   (c) in reports and announcements of *bona fide* commercial, civic, professional or political organisations in which he serves as a director or officer;
   (d) in and on legal textbooks, articles, professional journals and other legal publications and in dignified and restrained advertisements thereof;
   (e) in announcements of any public address, lecture, or publication by him on legal topics, provided that such announcements do not emphasize his own professional competence and are not likely to be regarded as being concerned with the giving of individual advice by him.
8. An attorney-at-law may speak in public or write for publication on legal topics so long as he does not thereby emphasize his own professional competence and is not likely to be regarded as being concerned thereby with the giving of individual advice.

9. The following cards, office signs, letterheads or directory listings may be used by an attorney-at-law but in a restrained and dignified form —
   (a) a professional card identifying the attorney-at-law by name and as an attorney-at-law giving his decorations and degrees, legal or otherwise, his addresses, telephone numbers and the name of his law firm or professional associates so however that such cards are not published in the news media and are only handed out on request and for the purposes of identification or address;
   (b) a brief professional announcement card to be delivered only to attorneys-at-law, clients, personal friends and relations and government bodies and stating new or changed associations or addresses, changes of firm name or like professional matters;
   (c) a sign of a size and design compatible with the existing practice of the profession, on or near the door of the office and in the building directory identifying the law office;
   (d) a letterhead identifying the attorney-at-law by name and as an attorney-at-law and giving his decorations and degrees, legal or otherwise, his addresses, telephone numbers and the name of his law firm and of his associates;
   (e) a listing in a telephone directory, a reputable law list, legal directory or biographical reference giving brief biographical or other relevant information; and any such professional card, office sign, letterhead or listing may state the attorney-at-law is also a notary public.
10. Where an attorney-at-law commits any criminal offence which in the opinion of the Committee is of a nature likely to bring the profession into disrepute, such commission of the offence shall constitute professional misconduct if —
   (a) he has been convicted by any Court, including a foreign Court of competent jurisdiction, for the offence; or
   (b) although he has not been prosecuted the Committee is satisfied of the facts constituting the criminal offence; or
   (c) he has been prosecuted and has been acquitted by reason of a technical defense or he has been convicted but such conviction is quashed by reason of some technical defense.
11. An attorney-at-law shall not acquire directly or indirectly by purchase, or otherwise a financial or other interest in the subject matter of a case which he is conducting.
12. (1) An attorney-at-law shall not enter into partnership or fee sharing arrange- ments concerning the practice of law with non-qualified bodies or persons.
   (2) An attorney-at-law shall not enter into an agreement for or charge or collect a fee in contravention of these Rules or any other law.

13. (1) An attorney-at-law shall not charge fees that are unfair or unreasonable.

(2) In determining the fairness and reasonableness of a fee the following factors may be taken into account —

(a) the time and labour required, the novelty and difficulty of the questions involved and the skill required to perform the legal service properly;

(b) the likelihood that the acceptance of the particular employment will preclude other employment by the attorney-at-law;

(c) the fee customarily charged in the locality for similar legal services;

(d) the amount, if any involved;

(e) the time limitations imposed by the client or by the circumstances;

(f) the nature and length of the professional relationship with the client;

(g) the experience, reputation and ability of the attorney-at-law concerned;

(h) any scale of fees or recommended guide as to charges prescribed by law or by the Bar Association.

(3) An attorney-at-law shall not accept any fee or reward for merely introducing a client or referring a case or client to another attorney-at-law.

(4) An attorney-at-law shall not charge a contingency fee except reasonable commissions on collection of liquidated claims with the prior agreement of the client.

14. (1) Except with the specific approval of his client given after full disclosure, an attorney-at-law shall not act in any manner in which his professional duties and his personal interests conflict or are likely to conflict.

(2) An attorney-at-law shall not accept or continue his retainer or employment on behalf of two or more clients if their interests are likely to conflict or if his independent professional judgment is likely to be impaired.

15. (1) An attorney-at-law who withdraws from employment under paragraph 33 of Part A shall not do so until he has taken reasonable steps to avoid foreseeable prejudice or injury to the position and rights of his client including —

(a) giving due notice in writing;

(b) allowing time for employment of another attorney-at-law;

(c) delivering to the client all documents and property to which he is entitled subject however to any lien which the attorney-at-law may have over the same;

(d) complying with such laws, rules or practice as may be applicable; and

(e) where appropriate, obtaining the permission of the Court where the hearing of the matter has commenced.

(2) An attorney-at-law who withdraws from employment shall refund promptly such part of the fees, if any, already paid by his client as may be fair and reasonable having regard to all the circumstances.

16. An attorney-at-law shall withdraw forthwith from employment or from a matter pending before a tribunal —
   (a) where the client insists upon his representing a claim or defense that he cannot conscientiously advance;
   (b) where the client seeks to pursue a course of conduct which is illegal or which will result in deliberately deceiving the Court;
   (c) where a client has in the course of the proceedings perpetrated a fraud upon a person or tribunal and on request by the attorney-at-law has refused or is unable to rectify the same;
   (d) where his continued employment will involve him in the violation of the law or a disciplinary rule;
   (e) where the client by any other conduct renders it unreasonably difficult for the attorney-at-law to carry out his employment as such effectively, or in accordance with the judgment and advice of the attorney-at-law, or the rules of law or professional ethics;
   (f) where for any good and compelling reason it is difficult for him to carry out his employment effectively.

17. An attorney-at-law shall not retain money he received for his client for longer than is absolutely necessary.

18. An attorney-at-law shall never disclose, unless lawfully ordered to do so by the Court or required by statute, what has been communicated to him in his capacity as an attorney-at-law by his client and this duty not to disclose extends to his partners, to junior attorneys-at-law assisting him and to his employees provided however that an attorney-at-law may reveal confidences or secrets necessary to establish or collect his fee or to defend himself or his employees or associates against an accusation of wrongful conduct.

19. An attorney-at-law shall not permit his professional services or his name to be used in any way which would make it possible for persons who are not legally authorised to do so to practise law.

20. An attorney-at-law shall not delegate to a person not legally qualified and not in his employment or under his control, any functions which are by the Laws of Saint Lucia only to be performed by a qualified attorney-at-law.

21. In the performance of his duties an attorney-at-law shall not act with inexcusable or undue delay, negligence or neglect.

22. An attorney-at-law shall not engage in undignified or discourteous conduct which is degrading to the Court or his profession.

23. An attorney-at-law shall not willfully make false accusations against a Judge or a Magistrate.

24. An attorney-at-law who holds a public office shall not use his public position to influence or attempt to influence a tribunal to act in favour of himself or of his client.
25. An attorney-at-law shall not accept private employment in a matter upon the merits of which he previously acted in a judicial capacity or for which he had substantial responsibility while he was in public employment.
26. An attorney-at-law shall not give, lend or promise anything of value to a Judge, juror or official of a tribunal before which there is a pending matter in which he is engaged.
27. In any proceedings in a Court an attorney-at-law shall not communicate or cause any other person to communicate with a juror as to the merits of such proceedings, and shall only do so with a Judge or person exercising judicial functions —
    (a) in the normal course of the proceedings; or
    (b) where authorised by law, or the practice of the Courts.
28. An attorney-at-law shall not for the purpose of making any person available as a witness, advise or cause that person to secrete himself or leave the jurisdiction of the Court.
29. An attorney-at-law shall not pay or offer to pay or acquiesce in the payment of compensation to a witness for giving evidence in any cause or matter save as reimbursement for expenses reasonably incurred and as reasonable compensation for loss of time in attending for preparation and for testifying, and in the case of an expert witness a reasonable fee for his professional services.
30. An attorney-at-law shall not knowingly use perjured testimony or false evidence or participate in the creation of or use of evidence which he knows to be false.
31. An attorney-at-law shall not counsel or assist his client or a witness, in conduct that the attorney-at-law knows to be illegal or fraudulent, and where he is satisfied that his client has in the course of the particular representation perpetrated a fraud upon a person or tribunal, he shall promptly call to rectify the same.
32. An attorney-at-law shall not knowingly make a false statement of law or fact.
33. (1) An attorney-at-law shall not commit a breach of an undertaking given by him to a judge, a Court or other Tribunal or an official thereof, whether such undertaking relates to an expression of intention as to future conduct or is a representation that a particular slate of facts exists.
    (2) An attorney-at-law shall not knowingly represent falsely to a Judge, a Court or other Tribunal or to an official of a Court or other Tribunal, that a particular state of facts exists.
34. In pecuniary matters an attorney-at-law shall be most punctual and diligent, he shall never mingle funds of others with his own and he shall at all times be able to refund money he holds for others.

35. (1) An attorney-at-law shall keep such accounts as clearly and accurately distinguish the financial position between himself and his client as and when required.
 (2) An attorney-at-law shall comply with such rules as may be made by the Council under section 33 of the Act.
 (3) Nothing contained in paragraphs 30 and 31 shall deprive an attorney-at-law of any recourse or right whether by way of lien, set-off, counter-claim, charge or otherwise against monies standing to the credit of a client's account maintained by that attorney-at-law.

36. An attorney-at-law shall reply promptly to any letter received from the Bar Association relating to his professional conduct.

37. An attorney-at-law shall not act as an attorney, litigator, agent, legal adviser, conveyancer or Notary Royal where the actions of the attorney-at-law would by virtue of his employment amount to a conflict of interest on his part.

38. Where no provision is made in these rules in respect of any matter, the rules and practice of the legal profession which formerly governed the particular matter shall apply in so far as is practicable.

39. An attorney-at-law shall not act on behalf of any person unless the attorney-at-law is authorised in a document evidenced by the signature or mark of that person to act on that person's behalf.

40. An Attorney-at-law shall not execute an instrument which is required to be in notarial form for it to be an authentic writing unless —
 (a) the instrument is signed by all parties in the presence of the attorney-at-law, or
 (b) where a party signs in the absence of the attorney-at-law —
  (i) that party is the manager of a bank or the chairman of the Housing and Urban Development Corporation or a successor body and is effecting a disposition of land, a hypothec or lease pursuant to his or her duties;
  (ii) the Attorney-General, when acting in his/her capacity as Attorney-General, is the attorney-at-law.

41. Breach by an attorney-at-law of any of the provisions contained in this Part shall constitute professional misconduct and an attorney-at-law who commits such a breach shall be liable to any of the penalties which the Committee or the Court is empowered to impose.

FOURTH SCHEDULE

(Section 36(3))

THE DISCIPLINARY COMMITTEE

Constitution and membership

1. (1) The Committee shall consist of seven members appointed by the Chief Justice after consultation with the Council.
   (2) The appointed members of the Committee shall include three members of the Council.
   (3) Subject to subparagraph (4) the other appointed members of the Committee shall be attorneys-at-law of not less than ten years standing.
   (4) The Chairperson and Vice Chairperson of the Committee shall be appointed by the Chief Justice after consultation with the Council and shall be members who have held high judicial office or, are attorneys-at-law of not less than ten years standing.

Term of office

2. Subject to this Schedule the members of the Committee shall hold office for a period not exceeding three years, and are eligible for re-appointment.

Power of Disciplinary Committee to sit in Districts

3. (1) For the purposes of hearing applications made pursuant to section 37 of this Act, the Committee may sit in the two Districts.
   (2) Subject to the directions of the Council, the Chairman of the Committee shall determine the composition of each District.
   (3) Each division is entitled to hear and determine any application and is entitled to exercise all powers of the Committee; and any hearing by or determination or order of such division shall be deemed to be a hearing by or a determination or order of the Committee.

Resignation

4. A member of the Committee may at any time resign his office by letter addressed to the Chief Justice and to the Chairman of the Committee.

Revocation of appointment

5. The Council may, if it thinks it expedient so to do and with the approval of the Chief Justice, at any time revoke the appointment of any member of the Committee.

Appendix 6
The Bahamas

The Bahamas Bar Association Code of Professional Conduct

THE BAR PRACTICE REGULATIONS

S.I. 36/1973.

(SECTION 40)
[Commencement 1st June, 1973.]

1. These Regulations may be cited as the Bar Practice Regulations. Citation.
2. Until other provision is made by law, the practice followed immediately before the commencement of these Regulations governing the matters for which regulations may be made under paragraphs (a) and (b) of section 40 of the Bahamas Bar Act, shall continue in full force and effect. Existing arrangements for practice and accounts of the Bar to remain in force.

THE BAHAMAS BAR (CODE OF PROFESSIONAL CONDUCT) REGULATIONS.

S.I 22/1901.

(SECTION 40)
[Commencement 8th April, 1981.]

1. These Regulations may be cited as the Bahamas Bar (Code of Professional Conduct) Regulations. Citation.
2. In these Regulations — Interpretation.
   (a) a reference to an attorney is a reference to a counsel and attorney as defined in the Act;
   (b) the notes appended as a Commentary to each Rule set out in the Schedule are only intended as general guidelines as to the meaning, scope, requirements and purpose of the respective Rule and do not form part of the Rule.
3. Every attorney shall in the pursuit of the practice of his profession comply with, and be subject to, the Rules of Professional Conduct set out in the Schedule. Code of Conduct.

SCHEDULE

THE BAHAMAS BAR ASSOCIATION CODE *of* PROFESSIONAL CONDUCT

Rule I. INTEGRITY

The attorney must discharge his duties to the Court, his client, members of the public and his fellow members of the profession with integrity.

Commentary

1. Integrity is the fundamental quality of any person who seeks to practise as a member of the legal profession. If the client is in any doubt as to his attorney's trustworthiness the essential element in the true lawyer-client relationship will be missing. If the attorney is lacking in personal integrity his usefulness to his client and his reputation within the profession will be destroyed, regardless of how competent an attorney may be.
2. Dishonourable or questionable conduct on the part of the attorney in either his private life or his professional activities will reflect adversely to a greater or lesser degree upon the integrity of the profession and the administration of law and justice as a whole. If the conduct, whether within or outside the professional sphere, is such that knowledge of it would be likely to impair a client's trust in the attorney as a professional consultant, disciplinary action may be justified.
3. Generally speaking, however, the Bar Council will not be concerned with the purely private or extra-professional activities of an attorney which do not bring his professional integrity or competence into question.

Rule II. COMPETENCE

The attorney must perform all the work and services which he undertakes on behalf of his client in a competent manner, providing a quality of service at least equal to that which attorneys generally would expect of a competent attorney in a like situation.

Commentary

1. Competence in the context of the first branch of this Rule goes beyond formal qualification of the attorney to practise law. It has to do with the sufficiency of the attorney's qualification to deal with the matter in question and includes knowledge and skill and the ability to use them effectively in the interests of the client.

2. As a member of the legal profession, the attorney holds himself out as knowledgeable, skilled and capable in the practice of law. Accordingly his client is entitled to assume that he has the ability and capacity to deal adequately with the legal matters which he undertakes on the client's behalf.
3. It follows that the attorney should not undertake a matter unless he honestly believes that he is competent to handle it or that he can become competent without undue delay, risk or expense to his client. If the attorney proceeds on any other basis he is not being honest with his client. This is an ethical consideration and is to be distinguished from the standard of care which a court would invoke for purposes of determining negligence.
4. Competence in a particular matter involves more than an understanding of the relevant legal principles: it involves an adequate knowledge of the practices and procedures by which such principles can be effectively applied.
5. The attorney must be alert to recognize his lack of competence for a particular task and the disservice he would do his client if he undertook that task. If he is consulted in such circumstances he should either decline to act or obtain his client's instructions to retain, consult or collaborate with an attorney who is competent in that field. The attorney should also recognize that competence for a particular task may require that he seek advice from or collaborate with experts in scientific, accounting or other non-legal fields, and he should not hesitate to seek his client's instructions to consult experts in such a situation.
6. Numerous examples could be given of conduct which does not meet the quality of service required by the second branch of the Rule. The list which follows is illustrative but not by any means exhaustive:
   (a) failure to keep the client reasonably informed;
   (b) failure to answer reasonable requests from the client for information;
   (c) unexplained failure to respond to the client's telephone calls;
   (d) failure to keep appointments with clients without explanation or apology;
   (e) informing the client that something will happen or that some step will be taken by a certain date, then letting the date pass without follow-up information or explanation;
   (f) failure to answer within a reasonable time a communication that requires a reply;
   (g) doing the work in hand but doing it so belatedly that its value to the client is diminished or lost;
   (h) slipshod work, such as mistakes or omissions in statements or documents prepared on behalf of the client;
   (i) failure to inform the client or to explain properly proposals of settlement;
   (j) withholding information from the client or misleading the client as to

the position of the matter to cover up the fact of neglect or mistakes;

(k) self-induced disability, for example, from intoxicants or drugs, which interferes with or prejudices the attorney's services to the client.

7. It will be noted that the Rule does not provide a standard of perfection. A mistake even though it might be actionable for damages in negligence would not necessarily constitute a failure to maintain the standard set by the Rule, but evidence of gross neglect in a particular matter or a pattern of neglect or mistake in different matters may be evidence of such a failure regardless of tortuous liability. In the result, where both negligence and incompetence are established damages may be awarded for the former and the latter can give rise to the additional sanction of disciplinary action.
8. The attorney who is incompetent does his client a disservice, brings discredit on his profession and may bring the administration of justice into disrepute. In addition, he damages his own reputation and practice and may injure those who are associated with or dependent upon him.

Rule III. ADVISING CLIENTS

The Attorney must be both candid and honest when advising his client, acting in the discharge of his responsibilities with the utmost good faith.

Commentary

1. The attorney's duty to the client who seeks legal advice from him is to give the client a competent opinion based on a sufficient knowledge of the relevant facts, an adequate consideration of the applicable law and the attorney's own experience and expertise. The advice must be open and undisguised and must clearly disclose what the attorney honestly thinks as to the merits and probable results.
2. Whenever it becomes apparent that the client has misunderstood or misconceived his position or what is really involved, the attorney should explain as well as advise, so that the client is apprised of his true position and fairly advised with respect to the real issues or questions involved.
3. The attorney should clearly indicate upon what facts, circumstances and assumptions his opinion or advice is based, e.g. in cases where the circumstances do not justify an exhaustive investigation with the consequent expense to the client. However, unless the client instructs him otherwise, the attorney should investigate the matter in sufficient detail to enable him to express an opinion rather than mere comments with many qualifications.
4. The attorney should be wary of bold and confident assurances to his client, especially when his employment may depend upon his advising in a particular way.

5. The attorney should advise and encourage his client to compromise or settle a dispute whenever it is possible to do so on a reasonable basis and he should discourage his client from commencing useless legal proceedings.
6. When advising his client the attorney must never knowingly assist or encourage any dishonesty, fraud, crime or illegal conduct or instruct his client as to how to violate the law and avoid punishment. He should be on his guard against becoming the tool or dupe of an unscrupulous client or those who are associated with that client.
7. A *bona fide* test case is not necessarily precluded by the preceding paragraph and so long as no injury to the person or violence is involved it is not improper for the attorney to advise and represent a client who in good faith and on reasonable grounds desires to challenge or test a law and the test can most effectively be made by means of a technical breach giving rise to a test case.
8. Apart altogether from the substantive law on the subject, it is improper for the attorney to advise, threaten or bring a criminal or quasi-criminal prosecution in order to secure some civil advantage for his client or to advise, seek or procure the withdrawal of a prosecution in consideration of the payment of money or transfer of property to or for the benefit of his client.
9. In addition to his opinion as to the legal questions, the attorney may be asked for or may be expected to give his views as to non-legal matters such as the business, policy or social implications involved in the question or as to the course the client should choose. In many instances the attorney's experience will be such that his views on non-legal matters will be of real benefit to his client. If the attorney does express views on such matters, he should, where and to the extent necessary, point out that he lacks experience or other qualification in the particular field and he should clearly distinguish his legal advice from such other advice.
10. The duty to give honest and candid advice requires the attorney to inform the client promptly when the attorney discovers that a mistake, which is or may be damaging to the client and which cannot readily be rectified, has been made in connection with a mailer for which he is responsible. The attorney should expeditiously deal with any claim which may be made against him and he must not, under any circumstances, take any unfair advantage that would defeat or impair his client's claim. At the same time the attorney should advise his client that the client may obtain legal advice elsewhere as to any rights he may have arising from such mistakes.

Rule IV. CONFIDENTIALITY

The attorney has a duty to hold in strict confidence all information received in the course of the professional relationship from or concerning his client or his client's affairs which information should not be divulged by the attorney unless he is expressly or impliedly authorized by his client or required by the laws of the Commonwealth of The Bahamas so to do.

Commentary

1. The attorney cannot render effective professional service unless there is full and unreserved communication between him and his client. At the same time the client must feel completely secure and he is entitled to proceed on the basis that without any express request or stipulation on his part matters disclosed to or discussed with his attorney will be held secret and confidential.
2. This ethical rule must be distinguished from the evidentiary rule of lawyer and client privilege with respect to oral or documentary communications passing between the client and his attorney. The ethical rule is wider and applies without regard to the nature or source of the information or the fact that others may share the knowledge.
3. As a general rule the attorney should not disclose that a particular person has consulted or retained him, unless the nature of the matter requires it.
4. The attorney owes the duty of secrecy to every client without exception, regardless of whether he is a continuing or casual client. The duty survives the professional relationship and continues indefinitely after the attorney has ceased to act for the client whether or not differences may have arisen between them.
5. The fiduciary relationship between the attorney and his client forbids that the attorney use any confidential information covered by the ethical rule for the benefit of himself or a third person or to the disadvantage of his client. Should the attorney engage in literary works such as his autobiography, memoirs and the like he should avoid disclosure of confidential information.
6. The attorney should take care to avoid disclosure to one client of confidential information concerning or received from another and he should decline employment which might require him to do so.
7. The attorney should avoid indiscreet conversations even with his spouse or family, about a client or his affairs and he should shun any gossip about such things even though the client is not named or otherwise identified. Likewise the attorney should not repeat any gossip or information about his client's business or affairs that he overhears or that is recounted to him. Apart altogether from ethical considerations or questions of good taste indiscreet shop-talk between attorneys, if overheard by third parties able to identify matter being discussed can result in prejudice to the client. Moreover the respect of the listener for the attorneys and the legal professional will probably be lessened.
8. The rule may not apply to facts which are public knowledge but nevertheless

the attorney should guard against participating in or commenting upon speculation concerning his client's affairs or business.

9. Confidential information may be divulged with the express authority of the client or clients concerned, and, in some situations, the authority of the client to divulge may be implied. For example, some disclosure may be necessary in a pleading or other document delivered in litigation being conducted for the client. Again the attorney may disclose the client's affairs to partners or associates in his firm and, to the extent necessary, to this non-legal staff such as secretaries and filing clerks. But this implied authority to disclose places the attorney under a duty to impress upon his employees, students and associates the importance of non-disclosure (both during their employment and thereafter) and requires him to take reasonable care to prevent their disclosing or using any information which he himself is bound to keep in confidence.
10. Disclosure by the attorney may also be justified in order to establish or collect his fee, or to defend himself or his associates or employees against an allegation of malpractice or misconduct, but only to the extent necessary for such purpose.
11. Disclosure of information necessary to prevent a crime will be justified if the attorney has reasonable grounds for believing that a crime is likely to be committed.
12. When disclosure is required by law or by order of a court of competent jurisdiction, the attorney should always be careful not to divulge more information than is required of him.

Rule V. IMPARTIALITY AND CONFLICT OF INTEREST

While it is not desirable that an attorney represent more than one interest in any matter, the Bar recognizes that the choice should be that of the parties after due disclosure by the attorney to the client. Therefore, save after adequate disclosure in writing to and with the consent of the client or prospective client concerned, the attorney must not advise or represent more than one interest in a matter nor shall he act or continue to act in a matter when there is or is likely to be a conflicting interest. A conflicting interest is one which would be likely to affect adversely the judgment of the attorney on behalf of or his loyalty to a client or prospective client or which the attorney might be prompted to prefer to the interest of a client or prospective client.

Commentary

1. The reason for the Rule is self-evident; the client or his affairs may be seriously prejudiced unless the attorney's judgment and freedom of action on his client's behalf are as free as possible from compromising influences.
2. Conflicting interests include but are not limited to the financial interest of

the attorney or an associate of the attorney and the duties and loyalties of the attorney to any other client, including the obligation to communicate information.

3. Associates of the attorney within the meaning of the Rule include his spouse, son or daughter, any relative of the attorney (or of his spouse) who lives under the same roof, any partner or associate of the attorney in the practice of law, a trust or estate in which the attorney has a substantial beneficial interest or for which he acts as a trustee or in a similar capacity, and a corporation of which the attorney is a director or in which he or an associate of his owns or controls, directly or indirectly, a significant number of shares.
4. The Rule requires adequate disclosure to the client so that he may make an informed decision as to whether he wishes the attorney to act for him despite the presence or possibility of the conflicting interest. As important as it is to the client that his attorney's judgment and freedom of action on his behalf should not be subject to other interests, duties or obligations, in practice this factor may not always be decisive. Instead it may be only one of several factors which the client will weigh when deciding whether or not he will give the consent referred to in the Rule. Other factors might include, for example, the availability of another attorney of comparable expertise and experience, the extra cost, delay and inconvenience involved in engaging another attorney and the latter's unfamiliarity with the client and his affairs. In the result, in the judgment of the client his interests may sometimes be better served by not engaging another attorney. An example of this sort of situation is when the client and the other party in commercial transaction are continuing clients of the same law firm but are regularly represented by different attorneys in that firm.
5. Before the attorney accepts employment for more than one client in a matter or transaction the attorney must advise the clients concerned that he has been asked to act for both or all of them, that no information received in connection with the matter from one can be treated as confidential so far as any of the others are concerned, and that if a conflict develops which cannot be resolved, he cannot continue to act for both or all of them and may have to withdraw completely. If one of such clients is a person with whom the attorney has a continuing relationship and for whom he acts regularly, this fact should be revealed to the other or others with a recommendation that they obtain independent representation. If, following such disclosure, all parties are content that the attorney act, he should obtain their written consent, or record their consent in a separate letter to each. He should, however, guard against acting for both sides where, despite the fact that all parties concerned consent, it is reasonably obvious that an issue contentious between them may arise or their interests, rights or obligations will diverge as the matter progresses.

6. If, after the clients involved have consented an issue contentious between them or some of them arises, the attorney although not necessarily precluded from advising them on other noncontentious matters, would be in breach of the rule if he attempted to advise them on the contentious issue. In such circumstances he should ordinarily refer the clients to other lawyers. However, if the issue is one which involves little or no legal advice, for example, a business rather than a legal question in a proposed business transaction, and the clients are sophisticated, he may let them settle it by direct negotiation in which he does not participate. Alternatively, he may refer one client to another attorney and continue to advise the other if it was agreed at the outset that this course would be followed in the event of a conflict arising.
7. The same basic considerations apply, where the conflicting interest arises not by reason of the attorney's duties or obligations to another client but by reason of his own financial or other interest or that of an associate. For example, the attorney or one of his family or his partners might have a personal financial interest in the client or in the matter in which the attorney is requested to act for the client, such as a partnership interest in some joint business venture with the client. Another example is when a debtor-creditor relationship exists between the attorney or his firm and the client. This however is a relationship which should be avoided and save in exceptional circumstances, the attorney should not borrow money from a client who is not in the business attending money and it is undesirable that he lend money to his client except by way of advancing necessary expenses in a legal matter which he is handling for that client.
8. In such a case, when the attorney is asked to act, he must, before accepting the employment, disclose and explain the nature of his conflicting interest to the client, or in the case of a potential conflict, how and why it might develop later. If the attorney does not choose to make such disclosure or cannot do so without breaching a confidence he must decline the employment. If, following such disclosure, the client requests him to act, he should obtain the client's written consent or record such consent in a letter to the client. However, the client's decision that he wants the attorney to act in such circumstances should not be accepted uncritically by the attorney. He should bear in mind that, if he accepts the employment, his first duty will be to his client, and if he has any misgivings about this ability to place his client's interests first, he should decline the employment.
9. The Rule will not prevent an attorney from arbitrating or settling, or attempting to arbitrate or settle, a dispute between two or more clients or former clients who are *sui juris* and who wish to submit the dispute to him.
10. The Rule does not purport to apply to situations in which the attorney is holding funds or property of his client in trust. In all such cases the attorney should abide by the applicable rules of the law and of the Bar Council. For

example, if funds of the client entrusted to the attorney for investment are to be invested in a security in which the attorney or his associate has an interest the attorney should insist that the client be represented by an independent attorney. In such circumstances disclosure to and the consent of the client will not normally suffice.

11. An attorney who has acted for a client in a matter should not thereafter act against him (or against persons who were involved in or associated with him in that matter) in the same or any related matter, or place himself in a position where he might be tempted or appear to be tempted to breach the Rule relating to Confidential Information. It is not, however, improper for the attorney to act against a former client in a fresh and independent matter wholly unrelated to any work he has previously done for that person.
12. For the sake of clarity the foregoing paragraphs are expressed in terms of the individual attorney and his client. However it will be appreciated that the term "client" includes a client of the law firm of which the attorney is a partner or associate whether or not he handles the client's work.
13. Generally speaking in disciplinary proceedings under this Rule the burden of showing good faith and that adequate disclosure was made in the matter and the client's consent obtained, will rest upon the attorney.

Rule VI. OUTSIDE INTERESTS AND THE PRACTICE OF LAW

The attorney who engages in another profession, business occupation concurrently with the practice of law must not allow such outside interests to jeopardize his professional integrity, independence or competence.

Commentary

1. The term "outside interest" covers the widest possible range and includes activities which may overlap or be connected with the practice of law, such as engaging in the mortgage business, acting as a director for a client corporation, writing on legal subjects, etc., as well as activities not so connected, such as careers in business, politics, broadcasting, the performing arts, etc.
2. The attorney must not allow his involvement in an outside interest to impair the exercise of his independent professional judgment on behalf of his clients. Whenever an overriding social, political, economic or other consideration arising from the outside interest might influence the attorney's judgment he should be governed by the considerations declared in the Rule relating to Impartiality and Conflict of Interest and in particular, paragraph 8 thereof.
3. Where the attorney's outside interest is in no way related to the legal services that he performs for clients, ethical considerations will usually not arise

unless his conduct brings him or the profession into disrepute, or his activities impair his competence as, for example, where the outside interest so occupies his time that his clients suffer from inattention or unpreparedness.

4. The attorney must make it clear whether he is acting in his professional capacity as a lawyer or otherwise.

Rule VII. PRESERVATION OF CLIENTS PROPERTY

The attorney owes a duty to his client to observe all laws and rules regarding the preservation and safekeeping of the property of the client entrusted to him and in the absence of any such laws and rules or where the attorney is in doubt he should take the same care of such property as a careful and prudent man would take of his own similar property.

Commentary

1. "Property" apart from clients, moneys, includes securities such as mortgages, negotiable instruments, stocks, bonds, etc., original documents such as wills, titles, deeds, minute books, licences, certificates, etc., other paper such as a client's correspondence files, reports, invoices, etc. and chattles such as jewellery, silver etc.
2. The attorney should promptly notify his client of the receipt of any property of or relating to the client unless he is satisfied that the client is aware that it has come into his custody.
3. The attorney should clearly label and identify his client's property and place it in safekeeping separate and apart from his own property.
4. The attorney should maintain adequate records of client's property in his custody so that he may promptly account for or deliver it to or to the order of the client upon request. He should ensure that it is delivered to the right person, and in case of dispute as to the person entitled he may have recourse to the courts.
5. The duties here expressed are closely related to those regarding confidential information. The attorney should keep his clients' papers and other property out of sight as well as out of reach of those not entitled to see them and should, subject to any rights of lien, promptly return them to the client upon request or on the conclusion of his mandate.
6. The attorney should be alert to claim on behalf of his clients any privilege in respect of their property seized or attempted to be seized by an external authority.

Rule VIII. THE ATTORNEY AS ADVOCATE

When acting as an advocate the attorney must, while treating the tribunal with courtesy and respect, represent his client resolutely, honourably and within the limits of the law.

Commentary

1. The advocate's duty to his client "fearlessly to raise every issue, advance every argument and ask every question, however distasteful, which he thinks will help his client's case" and to endeavour to obtain for his client the benefit of any and every remedy and defence which is authorized by law must always be discharged by fair and honourable means, without illegality and in a manner consistent with the attorney's duty to treat the court with candour, fairness, courtesy and respect. (Note: The words in quotation marks come from the speech of Lord Reid in *Rondel v Worsley* (1969) 1 A.C. (H.I.) 191 at 227).
   - (a) abuse the process of the tribunal by instituting or prosecuting proceedings which, although legal in themselves, are clearly motivated by malice on the part of his client and are brought solely for the purpose of injuring the other party.
   - (b) knowingly assist or permit his client to do anything which the attorney considers to be dishonest or dishonourable.
   - (c) endeavour or allow anyone else to endeavour, directly or indirectly, to influence the decision or action of a tribunal or any of its officials in any case or matter, whether by bribery, personal approach or any means other than open persuasion as an advocate.
   - (d) knowingly attempt to deceive a tribunal or influence the course of justice by offering false evidence, mis-state facts or law, presenting or relying upon a false or deceptive affidavit, suppressing what ought to be disclosed, or assisting in any fraud, crime or illegal conduct.
   - (e) knowingly mis-state the contents of a document the testimony of a witness, the substance of an argument or the provisions of a statute or like authority.
   - (f) knowingly assert that for which there is no reasonable basis in evidence or the admissibility of which must first be established.
   - (g) deliberately refrain from informing the tribunal of any law or jurisprudence which he considers to be directly in point and binding on the tribunal and which has not been mentioned by his opponent.
   - (h) dissuade a material witness from giving evidence or advise such a witness to absent himself.
   - (i) knowingly assist a witness to misrepresent himself or impersonate another.
   - (j) needlessly abuse, intimidate, or harass a witness.
   - (k) needlessly inconvenience a witness
2. (a) Where the attorney discovers that he has unknowingly done or failed to do something which, if done or omitted knowingly, would have been in breach of this Rule his duty to the court requires him, subject to the

Rule on Confidential Information, to disclose the error or omission and do what he reasonable can in the circumstances to rectify it.

(b) If the client desires that a course be taken which would involve a breach of this Rule, the attorney must refuse and do everything reasonably possible to prevent it. If he cannot do so he should, subject to the Rule on Withdrawal, withdraw or seek leave to withdraw.

3. The attorney should not express his personal opinions or beliefs, or assert as fact anything that is properly subject to legal proof, cross examination or challenge. He must not make himself in effect an unsworn witness or put his own credibility in issue. If the attorney is a necessary witness he should testify and the conduct of the case should be entrusted to another attorney. The attorney who was a witness in the proceedings should not appear as advocate in any appeal from the decision in those proceedings. There are no restrictions upon the advocate's right to cross-examine a fellow attorney and the attorney who does appear as a witness should not expect to receive special treatment by reason of his professional status.

4. The attorney may properly seek information from any potential witness (whether under subpoena or not) but he should disclose his interest and take care not to subvert or suppress any evidence or procure the witness to stay out of the way. An opposite party who is professionally represented should not be approached or dealt with save through or with the consent of his attorney.

5. The attorney should never waive or abandon his client's legal rights (for example an available defence under the statute of limitations) without his client's informed consent, but in civil matters it is desirable that the attorney should avoid and discourage his client from resorting to frivolous or vexatious objections or attempts to gain advantage from slips or oversights not going to the real merits, or tactics which will merely delay or harass the other side. Such practices can readily bring the administration of justice and the legal profession into disrepute.

6. Whenever the client's case can be fairly settled the attorney should advise and encourage his client to do so rather than commence or continue legal proceedings.

7. When engaged as a prosecutor the attorney's prime duty is not to seek to convict but to see that justice is done through a fair trial upon the merits. The prosecutor exercises a public function involving much discretion and power, and must act fairly and dispassionately. He should not do anything which might prevent the accused from being represented by counsel or communicating with counsel and to the extent required by law and accepted practice, he should make timely disclosure to the accused or his counsel (or to the court if the accused is not represented) of all relevant facts and witnesses known to him, whether tending towards guilt or innocence.

8. When defending an accused person the attorney's duty is to protect his client as far as possible from being convicted except by a tribunal of competent jurisdiction and upon legal evidence sufficient to support a conviction for the offence with which he is charged. Accordingly, notwithstanding the attorney's private opinions as to credibility or merits, the attorney may properly rely upon any evidence or defences including "technicalities" not known to be false or fraudulent.
9. Admissions made by the accused to his attorney may impose strict limitations on the conduct of the defence, and the accused should be made aware of this. For example, if the accused clearly admits to his attorney the factual and mental elements necessary to constitute the offence, the attorney, if convinced that the admissions are true and voluntary, may properly take objection to the jurisdiction of the court, or to the form of the indictment, or to the admissibility or sufficiency of the evidence, but he must not suggest that some other person committed the offence or call any evidence which, by reason of the admissions, he believes to be false. Nor may he set up an affirmative case inconsistent with such admissions, e.g. by calling evidence in support of an alibi intended to show that the accused could not have done, or in fact had not done, the act. Such admissions will also impose a limit upon the extent to which the attorney may attack the evidence for the prosecution. He is entitled to test the evidence given by each individual witness for the prosecution and to argue that the evidence taken as a whole is insufficient to amount to proof that the accused is guilty of the offence charged, but he should go no further than that.
10. Where, following investigation,
    (a) a defence attorney *bona fide* concludes and advises his accused client that an acquittal of the offence charged is uncertain or unlikely,
    (b) the client is prepared to admit the necessary factual and mental elements,
    (c) the attorney fully advises the client of the implications and possible consequences, and particularly of the detachment of the court, and
    (d) the client so instructs him,

    it is proper for the attorney to discuss with the prosecutor and for them tentatively to agree on the entry of a plea of "guilty" to the offence charged or to a lesser or included offence appropriate to the admissions, and also on a disposition or sentence to be proposed to the court. The public interest must not be or appear to be sacrificed in the pursuit of an apparently expedient means of disposing of doubtful cases, and all pertinent circumstances surrounding any tentative agreements, if proceeded with, must be fully and fairly disclosed to the court. The judge must not be involved, in any such discussions or tentative agreements, save to be informed thereof.
11. An undertaking given by the attorney to the court or to another attorney in the course of litigation must be strictly and scrupulously carried out. Unless

clearly qualified, the attorney's undertaking is his personal promise and responsibility.

12. At all times the attorney should be courteous and civil to court and to those engaged on the other side. Legal contempt of court and the professional obligation are not identical, and a consistent pattern of rude, provocative or disruptive conduct by the attorney, even though unpunished as contempt, might well merit discipline.
13. In adversary proceedings the attorney's function as advocate is openly and necessarily partisan. Accordingly, he is not obliged (save as required by law or under paragraph 1 (h) above) to assist his adversary or advance matters derogatory to his own client's case. When opposing interests are not represented, for example, in *ex parte* or uncontested matters, or in other situations where the full proof and argument inherent in the adversary system cannot obtain, the attorney must take particular care to be accurate, candid and comprehensive in presenting his client's case so as to ensure that the court is not misled.
14. The principles of the present Rule apply generally to the attorney in his capacity as advocate and therefore extend not only to court proceedings but also to appearances and proceedings before boards, administrative tribunals and other bodies, regardless of their function or the informality of their procedures.

Rule IX. THE ATTORNEY IN PUBLIC OFFICE

The attorney should bring to the discharge of his duties in any public office which he holds the same high standards of conduct which he is required to observe as a practising attorney.

Commentary

1. The Rule applies to an attorney who is elected or appointed to a legislative or administrative office at any level of government regardless of whether or not he attained such office because of his professional qualifications. He must bear in mind that he is in the public eye and therefore the legal profession can more readily be brought into disrepute by failure on his part to observe its ethical standards of conduct.
2. The attorney who holds public office must not allow his personal or other interests to conflict with the proper discharge of his official duties. If he holds a part-time public office he must not accept any private legal business in which his duty to his client will or may conflict with his official duties, and if some unforeseen conflict arises he should terminate the professional relationship, explaining to his client that his official duties must prevail. The

attorney who holds a full-time public office will not be faced with this sort of conflict, but he must nevertheless guard against allowing his independent judgment in the discharge of his official duties to be influenced by his own interest, that of some person closely related to or associated with him, that of his former or prospective partners or associates.

3. In the context of the foregoing paragraph, persons closely related to or associated with the attorney include his spouse, son or daughter, any relative of the attorney (or of his spouse) who lives under the same roof, a trust or estate in which the attorney has a substantial beneficial interest or for which he acts as a trustee or in a similar capacity, and a corporation of which the attorney is a director or in which he or some person closely related to or associated with him holds or controls, directly or indirectly, a significant number of shares.
4. Subject to any special rules applicable to the particular public office, the attorney holding such office should, when he sees that there is a possibility of a conflict of interest, disqualify himself by declaring his interest at the earliest opportunity, and he should not take part in any consideration or discussion of or vote with respect to the matter in question.
5. When the attorney or any of his partners or associates is a member of an official body he should not appear professionally before that body. However subject to the rules of the official body it would not be improper for him to appear professionally before a committee of such body if such partner or associate is not a member of that committee.
6. The attorney should not represent in the same or any related matter any persons or interests with whom he has been concerned in an official capacity. Likewise, he should avoid advising upon a ruling of an official body of which he is a member or of which he was a member at the time the ruling was made.
7. By way of corollary to the Rule, relating to Confidential Information, confidential information acquired by the attorney by virtue of his holding public office should be kept confidential and should not be divulged or used by him merely because he has ceased to hold such office.
8. Generally speaking, the Bar Council will not be concerned with the execution of the official responsibilities of a lawyer holding public office, but if his conduct in office reflects adversely upon his integrity or his professional competence, he may be subject to disciplinary action.

Rule X. FEES

The attorney should not

(a) stipulate for, charge or accept any fee which is not fully disclosed, fair and reasonable;

(b) appropriate any funds of his client held in trust or otherwise under his control for or on account of his fees without the express authority of his client, except in accordance with the custom or accepted practice of the profession;

(c) enter into any agreement or stipulate payment only in the event of success in any suit, action or other contentious proceedings for which he is retained or employed to prosecute.

Commentary

1. A fair and reasonable fee will depend upon and reflect such factors as
   (a) the time and effort required and spent;
   (b) the difficulty and importance of the matter;
   (c) whether special skill or service has been required and provided;
   (d) the customary charges of other attorneys of equal standing in like matters and circumstances;
   (e) the amount involved or the value of the subject matter;
   (f) the results obtained;
   (g) scales advised by the Bar Association;
   (h) such special circumstances as loss of other employment, uncertainty of reward, and urgency.

   A fee will not be fair and reasonable if it is one which cannot be justified in the light of all pertinent circumstances, including the factors mentioned, or is so disproportionate to the services rendered as to introduce an element of fraud or dishonesty.

2. It is in keeping with the best traditions of the legal profession to reduce or waive a fee in a situation where there is hardship or poverty, or the client or prospective client would otherwise effectively be deprived of legal advice or representation.

3. Breach of this Rule and misunderstandings respecting fees and financial matters bring the legal profession into disrepute and reflect adversely upon the general administration of justice. The attorney should try to avoid controversy with his client with respect to fees, and he should be ready to explain the basis for his charges (especially if the client is unsophisticated or uninformed as to the proper basis and measurements for fees). He should give the client a fair estimate of fees and disbursements, pointing out any uncertainties involved, so that the client may be able to make informed decisions. When something unusual or unforeseen occurs which may substantially affect the amount of the fee, the attorney should forestall misunderstandings or disputes by explanations to his client.

   Whilst there may be special circumstances in particular cases which justify the quotation or acceptance of a fee less than the minimum scale as advised from time to time by the Bahamas Bar Association it is generally considered improper deliberately to undercut fees by quoting or accepting a reduced fee from any prospective new client and especially if it is known or there are reasonable grounds to believe that such person is or has been represented by another attorney in The Bahamas.

4. The attorney should not charge his client interest on an overdue account unless permitted by law, and then only after adequate notice to the client.
5. In matters where the attorney is acting for two or more clients on the same side it is his duty to divide his fees and disbursements equitably between them in the absence of agreement otherwise.
6. A fee will not be a fair one within the meaning of the Rule if it is divided with another attorney who is not a partner or associate unless (a) the client consents, either expressly or impliedly to the employment of the other attorney, and (b) the fees are divided in proportion to the work done and responsibilities assumed.
7. The fiduciary relationship between the attorney and his client requires full disclosure in all financial matters between them and prohibits the acceptance by the attorney of any hidden fees. No fee, reward, costs, commission, interests, rebate, agency or forwarding allowance or other compensation whatsoever related to professional employment may be taken by the attorney from anyone other than the client without full disclosure to and the consent of the client or, where the attorney's fees are being paid by someone other than the client such as a borrower, or a personal representative, the consent of such other. So far as disbursements are concerned, only *bona fide* and specified payments to others may be included, and if the attorney is financially interested in the person to whom the disbursements are made, such as an investigating, brokerage or copying agency, he must expressly disclose this fact to his client.
8. It is the generally accepted practice in real estate transactions and collection matters for the attorney to deduct his fees and disbursements from moneys paid to him on behalf of his client.

Rule XI. WITHDRAWAL

The attorney owes a duty to his client not to withdraw his services except for good cause and upon notice appropriate in the circumstances.

Commentary

1. Although the client has the right to terminate the lawyer-client relationship at will, the attorney has no such freedom of action. Having accepted professional employment he should complete the task to the best of his ability unless there is justifiable cause for his terminating the relationship.

2. In all situations where the attorney withdraws from employment he should act so as to minimize expense and avoid prejudice to his client, and do all that he reasonably can to facilitate the orderly transfer of the matter to the attorney who succeeds him.
3. Where withdrawal by the attorney is required or permitted by this Rule he must comply with all applicable rules of the court, and, where required by rules or practice, obtain the court's permission to withdraw.
4. In some circumstances the attorney will be under a positive duty to withdraw. The obvious case is where he is discharged by the client. Other examples are (a) if he is instructed by his client to do something inconsistent with his duty to the court and if, following explanation, the client persists in his instructions; (b) if the client is guilty of dishonourable conduct in the proceedings or is taking a position solely to harass or maliciously injure another; (c) if it becomes clear that the attorney's continued employment will involve him in a breach of this Code, such as for example a breach of the Rule relating to Impartiality and Conflict of Interest; or (d) if the attorney discovers that he is not competent to handle the matter. In these situations it will be the attorney's duty to inform his client that he must withdraw.
5. Situations where an attorney would be entitled to withdraw, although not under a positive duty to do so, will usually only arise where there has been a serious loss of confidence between the attorney and the client. Such a loss of confidence goes to the very basis of the relationship. Thus, if the attorney is deceived by his client he will have justifiable cause for withdrawal. Again, the refusal of the client to accept and act upon the attorney's advice on a significant point might indicate such a loss of confidence. However, the attorney should not use the threat of withdrawal as a device to force a hasty decision by his client on a difficult question.
6. Failure on the part of the client after reasonable notice to provide funds on account of disbursements or fees would also justify withdrawal by the attorney, if no serious prejudice to the client would result.
7. No hard and fast rules can be laid down as to what will constitute reasonable notice prior to withdrawal. Where the point is covered by statutory provisions or rules of court, these will govern. In other situations the attorney must be governed by the basic principle that he should protect his client's interests to the best of his ability and that he should not desert his client at a critical stage of a matter or at a time when his withdrawal would put the client in a position of disadvantage or peril.
8. Upon his discharge or withdrawal the attorney should
   (a) deliver to or to the order of the client all papers and property to which the client is entitled;
   (b) give the client all information he may require in connection with the case or matter;

(c) account for all funds of the client then held or previously dealt with, including the refunding of any remuneration not earned during his employment;
(d) promptly render his account for outstanding fees and disbursements;
(e) co-operate with the attorney who succeeds him for the purposes outlined in paragraph 2.

The obligation in clause (a) to deliver papers and property is subject to the lawyer's right of lien referred to in paragraph 10. In the event of conflicting claims to such papers or property the attorney should use his best efforts to have the claimants settle the dispute.

9. Co-operation with the successor attorney will normally include providing him with memoranda of facts and law which have been prepared by the attorney in connection with the matter, but confidential information which is not clearly related to the matter should not be divulged without the express consent of the client.

10. Where upon the discharge or withdrawal of the attorney the question of his right of lien for unpaid fees and disbursements arises, he should have due regard to the effect of its enforcement upon the client's position. Generally speaking the attorney should not enforce his lien if the result would be to materially prejudice the client's position in any uncompleted matter.

11. Before accepting employment, the successor attorney should be satisfied that the other approves or has withdrawn or has been discharged by the client. It is quite proper for the successor attorney to urge the client to settle or take reasonable steps towards settling or securing any outstanding account of the other attorney, especially if the latter withdrew for good cause or was capriciously discharged. But if a trial or hearing is in progress or imminent, or if the client would otherwise be prejudiced, the successor attorney should not allow any outstanding account to interfere with his acting for the client.

12. Where an attorney acting for several clients in a case or matter ceases to act for one or more of them, he should co-operate with his successor attorney or attorneys to the extent permitted by his Code, and seek to avoid any unseemly rivalry or appearance of

13. When a law firm is dissolved it will usually result in the termination of the lawyer-client relationship as between a particular client and one or more of the attorneys involved. In such cases most clients will prefer to retain the services of the attorney whom they regarded as being in charge of their business prior to the dissolution. However, the final decision rests with the client, and the attorneys who are no longer retained by that client should act in accordance with the principles here set out, and in particular paragraph 2.

Rule XII. THE ATTORNEY AND THE ADMINISTRATION OF JUSTICE

The attorney should encourage public respect for and strive to improve the administration of justice.

Commentary

1. The admission to and continuance in the practice of law implies on the part of the attorney a basic commitment to the concept of equal justice for all within an open, ordered and impartial system. However, judicial institutions will not function effectively unless they command the respect of the public and, because of changes in human affairs and imperfections in human institutions, constant efforts must be made to improve the administration of justice and thereby maintain public respect for it.
2. The attorney's training, opportunities and experience enable him to observe the workings and to discover the strengths and weaknesses of laws, legal institutions and authorities. He should therefore lead in seeking improvements in the legal system, but his criticisms and proposals should be *bona fide* and reasoned.
3. The obligation outlined in the Rule is not restricted to the attorney's professional activities but is a broad general responsibility resulting from his position in the community. His responsibilities are greater than those of a private citizen. He must not subvert the law by counselling or assisting in activities which are in defiance of it, and he must do nothing to lessen the respect and confidence of the public in the legal system of which he is a part. He should take care not to weaken or destroy public confidence in legal institutions or authorities by broad irresponsible allegations of corruption or partiality. The attorney in public life must be particularly careful in this regard because the mere fact that he is an attorney will lend weight and credibility to his statements. But for the same reason he should not hesitate to speak out where he sees an injustice.
4. Although proceedings and decisions of tribunals are properly subject to scrutiny and criticism by all members of the public, including attorneys, members of tribunals are often prohibited by custom or by law from defending themselves. Their inability to do so imposes special responsibilities upon attorneys. First, the attorney should avoid criticism which is petty, intemperate or unsupported by his *bona fide* belief in its real merit, bearing in mind that in the eyes of the public his professional knowledge lends weight to his judgments or criticisms. Secondly, if he himself has been involved in the proceedings, there is the risk that his criticism may be, or may appear to be, partisan rather than objective. Thirdly, where the tribunal is the target of unjust criticism, the attorney as a participant in the administration of justice, is uniquely able to and should support the tribunal, both because its

members cannot defend themselves and because the attorney is thereby contributing to greater public understanding of and thus respect for the legal system.

5. Whenever the attorney seeks legislative or administrative changes, he should disclose whether he is pursuing his own interest, or that of a client or whether he is acting in the public interest. The attorney may advocate such changes on behalf of a client even though he does not agree with them, but when he purports to act in the public interest, he should espouse only those changes which he conscientiously believes to be in the public interest.

Rule XIII. AVAILABILITY OF LEGAL SERVICES.

Whereas limited publication of an attorney's name or firm name for information purposes is a useful adjunct to the overall availability of legal services to the public, unregulated competitive advertising is incompatible with the integrity of the profession and may be detrimental to the public interest. The following categories of limited advertising are considered acceptable, subject, in any particular case, to disallowance by the Bar Council:—

(a) Listings in professional legal directories, telephone directories, professional journals or other similar publications.

(b) Publication of names on legal aid panels and referral services sponsored or approved by the Bar Council, including those of foreign diplomatic missions, professional and community oriented bodies.

(c) The use of name plates on law offices and the publication of professional cards and announcements.

(d) Any other category or mode of limited advertising which the Bar Council in its discretion may from time to time allow.

Commentary

1. It is essential that a person requiring legal services be able to find, with a minimum of difficulty or delay, an attorney who is qualified to provide such services. In a relatively small community, where attorneys are well known, the person will usually be able to make an informed choice and select a qualified lawyer in whom he has confidence. However in larger centres these conditions may not obtain and as the practice of law becomes increasingly complex and the practice of the individual attorney tends to become restricted to particular fields of law, the reputations of attorneys and their competence or qualification in particular fields may not be sufficiently well known to enable a person to make an informed choice. Thus one who has had little or no contact with attorneys or who is a stranger in the community may have difficulty in finding an attorney who has the special skill required for the particular task. Telephone directories, legal directories and

referral services will help him find a lawyer, but not necessarily the right one for the work involved.

2. The individual attorney when consulted by a prospective client in such circumstances should be ready to assist in finding the right attorney for the problem to be dealt with. If, for some reason, he cannot agree to act (e.g. he may not consider himself well qualified in the particular field), he should assist in finding an attorney who is qualified and able to act. Such assistance should be willingly given and, except in very special circumstances, should be given without charge.
3. The individual attorney may also assist in making legal services available by participating in legal aid plans and referral services, by engaging in programmes of public information, education or advice concerning legal matters, and by being considerate of those who seek his advice but who are inexperienced in legal matters or cannot readily explain their problems.
4. The means by which it is sought to make legal services more readily available to the public must be consistent with the public interest and must not be such as would primarily advance the economic interests of any individual attorney or law firm, or detract from the integrity, independence or effectiveness of the legal profession. Unregulated advertising is not in the interest of the public or the profession. Such advertising has for good reason been prohibited by professional bodies. It would be apt to encourage self-aggrandizement at the expense of truth and could mislead the uninformed and arouse unattainable hopes and expectations resulting in the distrust of legal institutions and attorneys. Moreover, there are sound economic reasons for not allowing unregulated advertising, quite apart from the traditional reasons for which the professions have rejected it. There is the risk that such advertising would tend to increase the cost of legal services and in the course of time would tend to bring about a concentration of legal services in large firms that could afford to advertise freely to the detriment of the medium size and small firm, thereby unduly limiting the choice of persons seeking independent legal representation.
5. Limited advertising (as opposed to unregulated advertising) can be of much assistance to persons seeking legal services for example (a) advertising on behalf of the profession by the Bar Council and by the groups authorized by them; (b) publication of names on legal aid panels and referral services sponsored or approved by the Bar Council; (c) the use of name plates on law offices and the publication of professional cards and announcements, including, where permissible, a reference to the fact that an attorney is an accredited specialist or that his practice is restricted to a particular field. The overriding considerations are that the content of such advertising should be true and should not be capable of misleading those to whom it is addressed.
6. When considering whether or not limited advertising in a particular area

meets the public need, consideration must be given to the clientele to be served. Thus the Bar Council must have freedom of action in determining the nature and content of the limited advertising that will best meet the community need.

7. The attorney must not directly or indirectly apply for or seek instructions for professional business or do or permit in the carrying on of his practice any act or thing which may be regarded as touting, or engage in competitive advertising calculated to attract business unfairly. It is competitive and unfair advertising for the attorney to use an ostentatious name plate or display a name plate elsewhere than at his place of business; to put the names of clients on his own letterhead; to allow his name to be put on the note paper of clients or third persons; to circularise former clients on any resumption of practice; or, generally, to circularise non-clients, or to allow his name or description to appear on client's circulars.

   The attorney must not, directly or indirectly, do or permit any act or thing to be done which can reasonably be regarded as professional touting or as designed primarily to attract legal business. The attorney should not offer generally to provide legal services at reduced rates for the sole purpose of attracting clients. However, he may properly assist in making legal services available by charging a reduced fee or no fee at all to a person who would have difficulty in paying the fee usually charged for such service or by accepting a salary, flat fee or retainer from or under a scheme established by Government or the Bar Council or a community service group in order to provide legal services to a defined or identifiable section of the public. For this purpose a community service group means a group established for purposes which are charitable or educational or which involve self-improvement of its members through mutual aid and assistance and includes a group formed for the express purpose of providing legal services to persons who cannot afford normal or fixed or any fees.

8. The attorney should not solicit appearances on radio, television or any other public forum in his professional capacity as an attorney or attempt to use any such appearance as a means of professional advertisement. Nor should he engage in his capacity as an attorney in any public appearance that might discredit the legal profession. It is quite proper for the attorney to appear in his private or personal capacity as a speaker, actor or otherwise on a non-legal programme where his professional activity as an attorney is not the reason for his appearance and in such cases he may be described as an attorney. If his professional capacity is the reason for his appearance, any introduction or description of him should be limited to his name, professional designation and a reasonable amount of biographical detail.

9. The attorney has a general right to decline particular employment (except when he has been assigned as counsel by a court), but it is a right he should

be slow to exercise if the probable result would be to make it very difficult for a person to obtain legal advice or representation. Generally speaking he should not exercise the right merely because a person seeking his services, or that person's cause, is unpopular or notorious, or because powerful interests or allegations of misconduct or malfeasance are involved, or because of his private opinion as to the guilt of the accused. As stated in paragraph 2, the attorney declining employment should assist in obtaining the services of another attorney competent in the particular field and able to act.

10. The attorney should adhere to rules made by the Bar Council with respect to making legal services available and with respect to advertising, but rigid adherence to restrictive rules should be enforced with discretion where an attorney, who may have infringed such rules, acted in good faith in making legal services available more efficiently, economically, and conveniently than they would otherwise have been and where he was not primarily advancing his own economic interests.

Rule XIV. RESPONSIBILITY TO THE PROFESSION

As a member of an honourable profession the attorney should assist in maintaining the integrity of the profession and should participate in its activities.

Commentary

1. Unless an attorney who tends to depart from proper professional conduct is checked at an early stage, loss or damage to his clients or others may ensue. Evidence of minor breaches may on investigation disclose a more serious situation or may indicate the commencement of a course of conduct which would lead to serious breaches in the future. It is therefore proper (unless it is privileged or otherwise unlawful) for an attorney to report to the Bar Council any instance involving or appearing to involve breach of this Code. Where, however, there is a reasonable likelihood that someone will suffer serious damage as a consequence of an apparent breach, for example, where a shortage of trust funds is involved, the attorney has an obligation to the profession to report the matter unless it is privileged or otherwise unlawful for him to do so. In all cases the report must be made *bona fide* without malice or ulterior motive
2. An attorney should not refuse without good and sufficient reason a retainer against another attorney who is alleged to have wronged his client.
3. The attorney has a duty to reply promptly to any communication from the Bar Council.
4. The attorney should not write, in the course of his practice, letters, whether to his client, another attorney or any other person, which are abusive, offen-

sive or otherwise totally inconsistent with the proper tone of a professional communication from an attorney.

5. There should be no discrimination by the attorney on the grounds of race, creed, colour, national origin or sex in the employment of other attorneys or articled students or in other relations between him or her and other members of the profession.
6. In order to enable the profession to discharge its public responsibility to provide independent and competent legal services, the individual attorney should do his part in assisting the profession to function properly and effectively. In this regard, participation in such activities, as law reform, continuing legal education, tutorials, legal aid programmes, community legal service, professional conduct and discipline, liaison with other professions, and other activities of the Bahamas Bar Association, although often time-consuming and without tangible reward, are essential to the maintenance of a strong, independent and useful profession.

Rule XV. PRACTICE BY UNAUTHORIZED PERSONS

The attorney should assist in preventing the unauthorized practice of law.

Commentary

1. Statutory prohibitions against the practice of law by unauthorized persons are for the protection of the public. Unauthorized persons may have technical or personal abilities, but they are immune from control, regulation and, in the case of misconduct, from discipline, and their competence and integrity have not been vouched for by an independent body representative of the legal profession. Moreover, the client of an attorney who is authorized to practice has the protection and benefit of the lawyer-client privilege, the attorney's duty of secrecy, the professional standards of care which the law requires of attorneys, the authority which the courts exercise over them, and of other safeguards such as professional liability insurance, rights with respect to the taxation of bills and rules respecting trust money.
2. The attorney should not employ in any capacity having to do with the practice of law (a) an attorney who is under suspension as a result of disciplinary proceedings, or (b) a person who has been disbarred as an attorney or has been permitted to resign while facing disciplinary proceedings and who has not been reinstated.
3. The attorney must assume complete professional responsibility for all business entrusted to him. He must maintain direct supervision over his staff and over assistants such as students and clerks to whom he delegates particular tasks and functions. For example, if he practises alone or operates a

branch or part-time office, he should ensure that all matters requiring an attorney's professional skill and judgment are dealt with by an attorney qualified to do the work, and that legal advice is not given by unauthorized persons, whether in his name or otherwise. Furthermore, the amount of any fee to be charged to a client should be approved by the attorney.

4. Sections 19 to 23 of the Bahamas Bar Act specifically preclude unqualified persons from (i) acting as counsel and attorney in any case civil or criminal to be heard or determined in any court (ii) using any name, title, addition or description implying that he is qualified or recognised by law as qualified to act as counsel and attorney and (iii) in expectation of any fee, gain or reward, directly or indirectly drawing or preparing any memorandum or articles of association of a company or any instrument relating to real or personal property or to any legal proceedings. Contravention of these sections is a criminal offence punishable by fine and, in some instances, also by imprisonment.

   Where these practices occur and are condoned or acquiesced in by Bahamian attorneys, they should be regarded as examples of improper conduct by the Bahamian attorneys so concerned in addition to being breaches of the law by the outside attorney and they should be reported to the Bar Council for appropriate action.

   For the avoidance of doubt, it is declared that there is nothing improper in a Bahamian attorney consulting with or instructing outside attorneys to draw pleadings or other documents whenever the Bahamian attorney is so instructed by his client and provided that the control of the conduct of the matter rests in the Bahamian attorney.

Rule XVI. RESPONSIBILITY TO LAWYERS INDIVIDUALLY

The attorney's conduct towards other attorneys should be characterized by courtesy and good faith.

Commentary

1. Public interest demands that matters entrusted to an attorney be dealt with effectively and expeditiously, and fair and courteous dealing on the part of each attorney engaged in a matter will contribute materially to this end. The attorney who conducts himself otherwise does a disservice to his client and neglect of the Rule will impair the ability of attorneys to perform their function properly.
2. Any ill feeling which may exist or be engendered between clients, particularly during litigation, should never be allowed to influence attorneys in their conduct and demeanour toward each other or the parties. The presence of personal animosity between attorneys involved in a matter may cause their judgment to be clouded by emotional factors and hinder the proper

resolution of the matter. Personal remarks or references between them should be voided, and haranguing or offensive tactics interfere with the orderly administration of justice and have no place in our legal stem.

3. The attorney should accede to reasonable requests concerning trial dates, adjournments, waiver or procedural formalities and similar matters which do not prejudice the rights of his client. Where the attorney knows that another attorney has been consulted in a matter he should not proceed by default in such matter without inquiry and warning.
4. The attorney should avoid sharp practice. He should not take advantage of or act without fair warning upon slips, irregularities or mistakes on the part of other attorneys not going to the merits or involving the sacrifice of the client's rights.
5. The attorney should answer with reasonable promptness all professional letters and communications from other attorneys which require an answer and he should be punctual in fulfilling all commitments.
6. The attorney should give no undertaking he cannot fulfill and he should fulfill every undertaking he gives. Undertakings should be written or confirmed in writing and they should be absolutely unambiguous in their terms. If the lawyer giving an undertaking does not intend to accept personal responsibility, he should state this quite clearly in the undertaking itself. In the essence of such a statement, the person to whom the undertaking is given is entitled to expect that the attorney giving it will honour it personally.
7. The attorney should not communicate upon or attempt to negotiate or compromise a matter directly with any party who is represented by an attorney except through or with the consent of that attorney.
8. The attorney should avoid ill-considered or uninformed criticism of the competence, conduct, advice or charges of other attorneys but he should be prepared, when requested, to advise and represent a client in a complaint involving another attorney.
9. The same courtesy and good faith should characterize the attorney's conduct toward lay persons lawfully representing others or themselves.

Rule XVII. OBSERVANCE OF CODE

1. The foregoing Rules should not be construed as a denial of the existence of other duties and rules of professional conduct which are in keeping with the traditions of the Legal Profession, though not specifically mentioned therein.
2. Where in any particular matter explicit ethical guidance does not exist, an attorney should determine his conduct by acting in a manner that promotes public confidence in the integrity and efficiency of the legal system and the legal profession.

Commentary

1. Public confidence in the administration of justice and in the legal profession may be eroded by irresponsible conduct on the part of the individual attorney and he should strive to avoid even the appearance of impropriety.
2. Our system of administering justice provides procedures whereby issues can be tried in an impartial manner to the end that such issues may be decided upon the merits. Statements or suggestions by the attorney that he could or would attempt to circumvent those procedures should therefore be avoided because they would tend to bring both him and the legal profession into disrepute.
3. Without express instructions from the client, it is improper for the attorney to insert in the client's will a clause directing the executor to retain the services of the attorney in the administration of the estate.
4. The attorney has a professional duty, quite apart from any legal liability, to meet financial obligations incurred in his practice such as agency accounts, obligations to members of the profession and fees or charges of witnesses, special examiners, registrars, reporters and public officials. Where the attorney incurs an obligation on behalf of a client which the attorney is not prepared to pay personally, he should make his position clear in writing at the time the obligation is incurred.
5. The attorney should not undertake to advise an unrepresented person but should urge him to obtain independent legal advice and if the unrepresented person does not do so, the attorney must take care to see that such person is not proceeding under the impression that his interests will be protected by the attorney. If the unrepresented person requests the attorney to advise or act for him in the matter, the attorney should be governed by the considerations outlined in the Rule relating to Impartiality and Conflict of Interest.
6. The attorney should endeavour to conduct himself at all times so as to reflect credit on the legal profession and to inspire the confidence, respect and trust of his clients and the community.

Rule XVIII. RELATIONSHIP WITH COUNCIL

1. An attorney shall as far as possible respond to a request from the Council or a committee thereof for comments or information on any aspect of a complaint being considered by the Council or the committee.
2. An attorney shall ensure his attendance at disciplinary committee proceedings where so requested by or on behalf of the Council or committee.

THE BAR (DISCIPLINARY PROCEEDINGS) REGULATIONS

(SECTION 40.)
[Commencement 8th April, 1981.]

1. These Regulations may be cited as the Bar (Disciplinary Proceedings) Regulations.

PRELIMINARY

2. In these Regulations —

"complaint" means a complaint under section 28 of the Act of improper conduct against a counsel and attorney or a registered associate;
"hearing" means a hearing by a committee under Part I of these Regulations or, by the Council under Part II thereof, as the case may be;
"party" means a party to proceedings;
"proceedings" means proceedings of a committee.

PART I

COMPLAINTS AGAINST COUNSEL AND ATTORNEYS AND REGISTERED ASSOCIATES

3. (1) Subject to paragraph (2), a complaint shall be in writing under the hand of the complainant in Form 1 and shall be sent to the Secretary of the Council together with an affidavit by the complainant in Form 2 stating the matters of fact on which the complainant relies in support of his complaint.
(2) Where the complaint is by the Registrar and is based on disclosures made in judicial proceedings, the complaint may in lieu of an affidavit by the complainant be accompanied by a certified record of the proceedings.
4. (1) Before determining whether the complaint is one which should be referred to a disciplinary committee under section 28(2) of the Act, the Council may require the complainant to supply to the Council such further information and documents relating to the complaint as the Council considers requisite.
(2) The Council shall transmit to the disciplinary committee all documents received by the Council pursuant to paragraph (1) and regulation 3.
5. Where, in the opinion of the Council, a *prima facie* case is not made out in favour of the complaint, or the complaint if proved would not call for the exercise by a disciplinary committee of any of the disciplinary powers conferred by section 30 of the Act, the Council shall dismiss the complaint and inform the complainant accordingly.

6. In relation to a complaint against a registered associate, the parties to the proceedings for the purpose of these regulations shall be —
   (a) the complainant;
   (b) the registered associate; and
   (c) if the Committee so direct, the counsel and attorney or firm by whom the registered associate was employed at the time of the conduct complained of.

7. (1) A committee, as soon as may be after their appointment under the Act, shall fix a day for the hearing of the complaint, and, subject to paragraph (2), shall cause to be served upon each party notice in writing of the day so fixed, which day shall not be less than twenty-one days from the date of such service, together with a copy of the complaint and of the affidavit or other document in support of the complaint.
   (2) Notice given pursuant to paragraph (1) shall be in such one of Forms 3 to 5 as is appropriate to the circumstances of the case or in such other form as the committee may direct.

8. (1) Every party to whom a notice mentioned in regulation 6(2) is addressed shall serve upon the chairman of the committee and on every other party not less than fourteen days before the day fixed for hearing a list of all the documents on which he intends to rely and a document not in that list shall not be used at the hearing unless the committee otherwise direct.
   (2) Any party shall have the right to inspect the documents included in the list furnished under paragraph (1).
   (3) Four sets of documents each comprising every document mentioned in a list furnished by a party under paragraph (1), shall be supplied by that party to the chairman of the committee, the pages of each set being numbered, consecutively and uniform in size.
   (4) A copy of any document mentioned in any such list shall, on application and on tender of a reasonable charge therefore by the party requiring it, be furnished to that party by the party having possession of the document within three days after the receipt of the application.

9. (1) Any party may by notice in writing at any time not later than nine days before the day fixed for a hearing, call upon any other party (hereinafter in this regulation referred to as "the other party") to admit any document, saving all just exceptions.
   (2) If the other party desires to challenge the authenticity of a document of which notice has been given pursuant to paragraph (1), he shall within six days after receipt of the notice himself give notice that he does not admit the document and requires it to be proved at the hearing; and if he refuses or neglects to give such notice, he shall be deemed to have admitted the document unless the committee otherwise order.

(3) Where a party gives notice of non-admission of a document pursuant to paragraph (2) and the document is proved at the hearing, the costs of proving the document shall be paid by the party that challenged the document, whatever the decision of the committee, unless in the opinion of the committee there were reasonable grounds for not admitting the authenticity of the document.

(4) Where a party proves a document without having given notice to admit under paragraph (1), the costs of proving the document shall not be allowed unless the committee so direct.

10. If any party fails to appear at the hearing, the committee may, upon proof of service upon him of the notice of the hearing, proceed to hear and determine the complaint in his absence.

11. (1) A committee may, in their discretion, either as to the whole case or as to any particular fact or facts, proceed and act upon evidence given by affidavit, but any party to the proceedings may require the attendance upon subpoena of any deponent to any such affidavit for the purpose of giving evidence in person, unless the committee are satisfied that the affidavit is purely formal and that the requirement that the deponent should attend is made with the sole object of causing delay.

(2) If in the opinion of a committee the justice of the case so requires, they may allow an affidavit to be amended or added to, to such extent and on such terms as to costs or otherwise as the committee think fit.

12. A committee may at any stage of the proceedings determine that there is need for a legal officer of the Crown or a counsel and attorney either to assist the committee as *amicus curiae*, or to assist any party, to such extent as the committee think fit, then the committee may enlist the aid of a legal officer of the Crown (subject to the approval of the Attorney General) or a counsel and attorney for the purpose of rendering such assistance and where a legal officer of the Crown or a counsel and attorney appears pursuant to the request of the committee, these Regulations shall have effect *mutatis mutandis.*

13. Every complaint and every application relating to a complaint shall be heard in private, but the findings and any disciplinary order of a committee shall be pronounced in public.

14. (1) Notes of the proceedings shall be taken by the chairman of the committee or with his approval by such other person whose services have been made available to the committee; and any party to the proceedings shall be entitled to inspect the notes.

(2) A copy of such notes shall be supplied to the Council and, if requested, to any other party to the proceedings, but to no other person, on payment to the supplier of such fee as may be fixed by the Council.

15. Service of any notice or other document may be effected under these Regulations by prepaid registered post addressed —

(a) in the case of a counsel and attorney, to the address of his Chambers appearing in the records of the Council; and

(b) in any other case, to the last-known postal address or to the post office box number of the person to be served,

and unless the contrary is proved, such service shall be deemed to have been effected ninety-six hours after posting.

16. A committee may dispense with any requirements of these Regulations respecting the making of affidavits, the supply of documents, the giving of notices, the effecting of service or the time within which anything shall be done, in any case where it appears to the committee to be just to do so.

17. The provisions of the Evidence Act shall apply in relation to proceedings of a committee in the same way as those provisions apply in relation to court proceedings.

18. A subpoena issued under section 29(2) of the Act shall be in Form 6 or Form 7 as the circumstances require.

19. If the decision of a committee is not pronounced at a hearing, the committee shall give notice to the parties of the date on which the decision will be pronounced.

20. The Chairman of the committee shall, within four days after the date on which the decision of a committee has been pronounced, send to each party a copy of the decision free of charge.

21. Subject to the provisions of these Regulations, a committee may regulate their own procedure.

22. All affidavits, books, papers or other documents and all exhibits or other things produced or used at or for the purposes of a hearing shall, after the conclusion of the proceedings, be kept in the custody of the Secretary of the Council and, except as may be required for the purposes of any appeal under section 39 of the Act, shall be subject to the disposition of the Council.

PART II

RESTORATION TO THE ROLL OF FORMER COUNSEL AND ATTORNEYS

23. An application to the Council by a former counsel and attorney, whose name has been struck off the Roll, to have his name restored to the Roll pursuant to section 33 of the Act shall be by way of affidavit in Form 8 addressed to the Council.

24. Every affidavit made pursuant to regulation 23 shall, unless the Council otherwise directs, be supported by letters from two counsel and attorneys in actual practice in The Bahamas to whom the applicant is known.

Appendix 7
Trinidad & Tobago

Code of Ethics

PART B

Constitution of First Council

1. Until the First Council is constituted and a person is appointed to perform the functions of Secretary of the Association, the Registrar shall perform these functions and shall be responsible for making arrangements for constituting the first Council and for holding elections for this purpose.
2. If any difficulties arise in applying any of the provisions of Part A of this Schedule to the constituting of the first Council, the Minister may issue directions modifying these provisions so far as may appear to him necessary or expedient for removing the difficulty, and the Registrar shall for the purpose of constituting the first Council apply these provisions as modified by the Minister.
3. Without prejudice to the generality of subparagraph (1), paragraph 4 of Part A of the First Schedule shall, for the purpose of constituting the first Council, apply as if —
   (a) the words "President of either the Bar Association or the Law Society" were substituted for "President of the Association" in paragraph (a); and
   (b) the words "of the Bar Association and of the Law Society" were substituted for the words "of the Association".

SECOND SCHEDULE

Form 1 (SECTION 19(1))

THE LEGAL PROFESSION ACT, 1986

Certificate of Enrolment

It is hereby certified that is registered on the Roll of attorneys-at-law under section 14 of the Legal Profession Act, 1986, his name having been entered on the Roll.

Dated this day of , 19 .

Registrar of the Supreme Court

Form 2 (Section 23(3))

THE LEGAL PROFESSION ACT, 1986

Practising Certificate

Pursuant to the Legal Profession Act, 1986, it is hereby certified that whose name is registered on the Roll of the attorneys-at-law is entitled to practise as an attorney-at-law.

Dated this day of , 1986.

Registrar of the Supreme Court

Form 3 (Section 26(3))

THE LEGAL PROFESSION ACT, 1986

Law Officer's Certificate

It is hereby certified that is a law officer holding the office of in the Judicial and Legal Service established under the Judicial and Legal Service Act, Chap. 6:01.

Dated this day of 19

Minister/Chief Legal Officer

THIRD SCHEDULE

(Section 35)

PART A

Code of Ethics

General Guidelines

I. In Relation to the Profession and Himself

1. An attorney-at-law shall observe the rules of this Code, maintain his integrity and the honour and dignity of the legal profession and encourage other attorneys-at-law to act similarly both in the practice of his profession and in his private life, shall refrain from conduct which is detrimental to the profession or which may tend to discredit it.
2. An attorney-at-law shall expose without fear or favour before the proper tribunals unprofessional or dishonest conduct by any other attorneys-at-law and shall not lightly refuse a retainer against another attorney-at-law who is alleged to have wronged his client or committed any other act of professional misconduct.
3. (1) An attorney-at-law shall scrupulously preserve his independence in the discharge of his professional duties.
   (2) An attorney-at-law practising on his own account or in partnership, shall not engage in any other business or occupation if doing so may cause him to cease to be independent.
4. An attorney-at-law shall protect the profession against the admission thereto of any candidate whose moral character or education render him unfit for such admission.
5. (1) An attorney-at-law shall not endeavour by direct or indirect means to attract the clients of another attorney-at-law and where a client is referred to him by another attorney-at-law the client remains for all other purposes the client of the referring attorney-at-law and the attorney-at-law to whom the client is referred shall act with due deference to the relationship between the client and the referring attorney-at-law.
   (2) Where a referred client offers other work to the attorney-at-law to whom he is referred and the offer is sufficiently proximate to the referral, that attorney-at-law shall not accept that offer unless it has been brought to the attention of the referring attorney-at-law.
6. An attorney-at-law may speak in public or write for publication on legal topics so long as he does not thereby advertise his own professional competence and is not likely to be regarded as being concerned thereby with the giving of individual advice.

7. The best advertisement for an attorney-at-law is the establishment of a well merited reputation for personal integrity, capacity, dedication to work and fidelity to trust and it is unprofessional —
   (a) to solicit business by circulars or advertisements or interviews not warranted by personal relations;
   (b) to seek retainers through agents of any kind.
8. An attorney-at-law shall defend the interests of his client without fear of judicial disfavour or public unpopularity and without regard to any unpleasant consequences to himself or to any other person.
9. Subject to paragraph 17, no attorney-at-law is obliged to act either as adviser or advocate for every person who may wish to become his client; he has a right to decline employment.
10. No client is entitled to receive nor should any attorney-at-law render, any service or advice involving disloyalty to the State or disrespect for judicial office or the corruption of any persons exercising a public or private trust or deception or betrayal of the public.
11. Every attorney-at-law should bear in mind that the oath of office taken on his admission, to practise is not a mere form but is a solemn undertaking to be strictly observed on his part.
12. An attorney-at-law should also bear in mind that be can only maintain the high traditions of his profession by being a person of high integrity and dignity.

II. In Relation to the State and the Public

13. An attorney-at-law owes a duty to the State to maintain its integrity, its constitution and its laws and not to aid, abet, counsel or assist anyone to act in any way contrary to those laws.
14. When engaged as a public prosecutor the primary duty of an attorney-at-law is not to secure a conviction but to see that justice is done and to that end he shall not withhold facts tending to prove either the guilt or innocence of the accused.
15. An attorney-at-law shall endeavour by lawful means where the needs of society require, to promote and encourage the modernization, simplification and reform of the laws.
16. An attorney-at-law shall not by his actions, stir up strife or litigation by seeking out defects in titles, claims for personal injury or other causes of action for the purpose of securing a retainer to prosecute a claim therefor; or pay or reward any person directly or indirectly for the purpose of procuring him to be retained in his professional capacity, and where it is in the interest of his client he shall seek to obtain reasonable settlements of disputes.
17. An attorney-at-law shall not except for good reasons refuse his services in capital offences.

18. An attorney-at-law shall not be deterred from accepting proferred employment owing to the fear or dislike of incurring disapproval of officials other attorneys-at-law or members of the public.
19. Where an attorney-at-law consents to undertake legal aid and he is appointed by the Legal Aid and Advisory Authority or is requested by the Law Association and consents to undertake the representation of a person unable to afford such representation or to obtain legal aid, the attorney-at-law shall not, except for compelling reasons, seek to be excused from undertaking such representation.
20. An attorney-at-law in undertaking the defence of persons accused of crime shall use all fair and reasonable means to present every defence available at law.

III. In Relation to Clients

21. (1) An attorney-at-law shall always act in the best interests of his client, represent him honestly, competently and zealously and endeavour by all fair and honourable means to obtain for him the benefit of any and every remedy and defence which is authorised by law, steadfastly bearing in mind that the duties and responsibilities of the attorney-at-law are to be carried out within and not without the bounds of the law.
    (2) The interests of his client and the exigencies of the administration of justice should always be the first concern of an attorney-at-law and rank before his right to compensation for his services.
22. (1) Before advising on a client's cause an attorney-at-law should obtain full knowledge thereof and give a candid opinion of the merits or demerits and probable results of pending or contemplated litigation.
    (2) An attorney-at-law should beware of proffering bold and confident assurances to his client (especially where employment may depend on such assurances) always bearing in mind that seldom are all the law and facts on the side of his client and that "audi alteram partem" is the safest rule to follow.
    (3) Whenever the controversy admits of fair adjustment an attorney-at-law should inform his client accordingly and advise to avoid or settle litigation.
23. (l) An attorney-at-law shall at the time of retainer disclose to his client all the circumstances of his relations to the parties and his interest in or connection with the controversy (if any) which might influence the client in his selection of an attorney-at-law.
    (2) An attorney-at-law shall scrupulously guard and never divulge his client's secrets and confidences.
24. An attorney-at-law shall treat adverse witnesses, litigants and other attorneys-at-law with fairness and courtesy refraining from all offensive personal refer-

ences and shall avoid imparting to his professional duties his client's personal feelings and prejudices.

25. It is the right of an attorney-at-law to undertake the defence of a person accused of crime regardless of his own personal opinion as to the guilt of the accused and having undertaken such defence he is bound by all fair and honourable means to present every defence that the law of the land permits so that no person may be deprived of life or liberty except by due process of law.

26. (1) An attorney-at-law may represent multiple clients only if he can adequately represent the interests of each and if each consents to such representation after full disclosure of the possible effects of multiple representation.

(2) In all situations where a possible conflict of interest arises, an attorney-at-law shall resolve all conflicts by leaning against multiple representation.

27. (1) An attorney-at-law shall deal with his client's business with all due expedition and shall whenever reasonably so required by the client provide him with full information as to the progress of the client's business.

(2) It is improper for an attorney-at-law to accept a case unless he can handle it without undue delay.

28. Where an attorney-at-law determines that the interest of his client requires it, he may with the specific or general consent of the client refer his business or part of it to another attorney-at-law whether or not a member of his own firm.

29. (1) An attorney-at-law on the record may instruct one or more attorneys-at-law to appear as advocates, in the same way as a solicitor on the record prior to the commencement of the Act, instructed Counsel.

(2) Senior Counsel shall be entitled to accept instructions, appear or do any work without a junior, except where he would be unable properly to carry out his instructions or conduct his case if he were to do so.

(3) Where more than one attorney-at-law appears as advocate for the same party in the same proceedings, who shall lead the conduct of that party's case shall, subject to the instructions of the client be settled by the attorneys-at-law representing that party before they appear in court and shall not be altered during the course of the proceedings and the leader shall have all authority over the conduct of the case.

30. An attorney-at-law including a Senior Counsel who appears with the leader is entitled to a negotiated fee appropriate for his conduct of the case.

31. (1) An attorney-at-law is entitled to reasonable compensation for his services but should avoid charges which either overestimate or undervalue the service rendered.

(2) The ability of a client to pay cannot justify a charge in excess of the

value of the service rendered, though the client's indigence may require a charge that is below such value, or even no charge at all.

(3) An attorney-at-law should avoid controversies with clients regarding compensation for his services as far as is compatible with self-respect and his right to receive reasonable compensation for his services.

32. The right of an attorney-at-law to ask for a deposit or to demand payment of out-of-pocket expenses and commitments, failing payment of which he may withdraw from the case or refuse to handle it, shall not be exercised where the client may be unable to find other assistance in time to prevent irreparable damage being done.

33. Where an attorney-at-law engages a foreign colleague to advise on a case or to co-operate in handling it, he is responsible for the payment of the latter's charges except there is express agreement to the contrary, but where an attorney-at-law directs a client to a foreign colleague he is not responsible for the payment of the latter's charges, nor is he entitled to a share of the fee of his foreign colleague.

34. An attorney-at-law may at any time withdraw from employment —

(a) where the client fails, refuses, or neglects to carry out an agreement with, or his obligation to, the attorney-at-law as regards the expenses or fees payable by the client;

(b) where his inability to work with colleagues indicates that the best interest of the client is likely to be served by his withdrawal;

(c) where his client freely assents to the termination of his employment;

(d) where by reasons of his mental or physical condition or other good and compelling reason it is difficult for him to carry out his employment effectively; or

(e) in cases of conflict as contemplated in Rule 26 of this part or Rule 11 of Part B hereof.

35. (1) An attorney-at-law should not appear as a witness for his own client except as to merely formal matters or where such appearance is essential to the ends of justice.

(2) If an attorney-at-law is a necessary witness for his client with respect to matters other than such as are merely formal, he should entrust the conduct of the case to another attorney-at-law of his client's choice.

IV. In Relation to the Courts and the Administration of Justice

36. (1) An attorney-at-law shall maintain a respectful attitude towards the court and shall not engage in undignified or discourteous conduct which is degrading to the court.

(2) An attorney-at-law shall encourage respect for the courts and the judges.

(3) An attorney-at-law shall support judges and magistrates against unjust criticisms.

(4) Where there is ground for complaint against a judge or magistrate an attorney-at-law may make representation to the proper authorities and in such cases, the attorney-at-law shall be protected.

37. An attorney-at-law shall endeavour always to maintain his position as an advocate and shall not either in argument to the court or in address to the jury assert his personal belief in his client's innocence or in the justice of his cause or his personal knowledge as to any of the facts involved in the matter under investigation.

38. An attorney-at-law should never seek privately to influence directly or indirectly the Judges of the Court in his favour or in the favour of his client, nor should he attempt to curry favour with juries by fawning, flattery or pretended solicitude for their personal comfort.

39. An attorney-at-law shall be punctual in attendance before the Courts and concise and direct in the trial and disposition of causes.

40. An attorney-at-law appearing before the Court shall at all times be attired in such a manner as prescribed or agreed by the proper authorities and as befits the dignity of the Court.

V. *In Relation to his Fellow Attorneys-at-Law*

41. (1) The conduct of an attorney-at-law towards his fellow attorneys shall be characterized by courtesy fairness and good faith and he shall not permit ill-feeling between clients to affect his relationship with his colleagues.

(2) All personal conflicts between attorneys-at-law should be scrupulously avoided as should also colloquies between them, which cause delay and promote unseemly wrangling.

42. (1) An attorney-at-law shall reply promptly to letters from other attorneys-at-law making inquiries on behalf of their clients.

(2) An attorney-at-law shall endeavour as far as is reasonable to suit the convenience of the opposing attorney-at-law when the interest of his client or the cause of justice will not be injured by so doing.

43. An attorney-at-law shall not give a professional undertaking that he cannot fulfil, and he shall fulfil every such undertaking that he gives.

44. (1) There is a duty on every attorney-at-law to report improper or unprofessional conduct by a colleague to the Disciplinary Committee, save where the information relating to the improper or unprofessional conduct is received in professional confidence in which case he must respect the duty of silence imposed in such circumstances.

(2) An attorney-at-law shall expose without fear or favour before the proper tribunal unprofessional or dishonest conduct by another attorney-at-law and shall not lightly refuse a retainer against another attorney-at-law who is alleged to have wronged a client.

45. Where an attorney-at-law has been sent money, documents or other things

by a colleague which, at the time of sending, are expressed to be sent only on the basis that the attorney-at-law to whom they are sent will receive them on his undertaking to do or refrain from doing some act, the receiving attorney-at-law shall forthwith return whatever was lent if he is unable to accept them on such undertaking, otherwise he must comply with the undertaking.

46. An attorney-at-law shall not in any way communicate upon a subject in controversy or attempt to negotiate or compromise a matter directly with any party represented by another attomey-at-law except through such other attorney-at-law or with his prior consent.

47. (1) An attorney-at-law shall not ignore the customs or practices of the legal profession even when the law expressly permits it, without giving timely notice to the opposing attorney-at-law.

    (2) An attorney-at-law should avoid all sharp practices and should refrain from taking any paltry advantage when his opponent has made or overlooked some technical error or matter, bearing in mind that no client has a right to demand that an attorney-at-law representing him shall be illiberal or shall do anything repugnant to his own sense of honour and propriety.

48. An attorney-at-law shall not accept instructions to act in Court proceedings in which to his knowledge the client has previously been represented by another attorney-at-law, unless he first notifies the other attorney-at-law of the change, and makes reasonable efforts to ensure that attorney has been paid for his services, but shall be deemed to have notified the other attorney-at-law if he has made reasonable efforts to notify him.

49. An attorney-at-law shall not accept instructions to act in proceedings (other than Court proceedings) in which to his knowledge, another attorney-at-law has previously represented the client unless he makes reasonable efforts to ascertain that the retainer of that attorney-at-law has been determined by the client, or that the client wishes both attorneys-at-law to represent him.

50. An attorney-at-law who instructs or employs another attorney-at-law to act on behalf of his client, unless otherwise agreed, shall pay the proper fee of such attorney-at-law whether or not he has received payment from his client.

51. In undertaking to render assistance to a foreign colleague, an attorney-at-law shall remember that his responsibility is much greater both when giving advice and handling a case, that it would be had he undertaken to assist a colleague in Trinidad and Tobago.

VI. General

52. Nothing herein contained shall be construed as derogating from any existing rules of professional conduct and duties of an attorney-at-law which are in keeping with the traditions of the legal profession although not specifically mentioned herein.

53. Where in any particular matter explicit ethical guidance does not exist, an attorney-at-law shall determine his conduct by acting in a manner that promotes public confidence in the integrity and efficiency of the legal system and the legal profession.

54. (1) A person who previously held a substantive appointment as a Judge of the Supreme Court shall not appear as an attorney-at-law in any of the Courts of Trinidad and Tobago for a period of ten years commencing on the date of his retirement, resignation or other termination of such appointment.

(2) This rule shall not apply to a person who is appointed to act as a Judge in a temporary capacity.

PART B

Mandatory Provisions and Specific Prohibitions

1. An attorney-at-law shall not practise as such unless he has been issued a practising certificate in accordance with the provisions of the Act.

2. (1) An attorney-at-law shall never knowingly mislead the Court.

(2) An attorney-at-law shall not withhold facts or secrete witnesses in order to establish the guilt or innocence of the accused.

3. An attorney-at-law shall not hold out any person who is not qualified to practise law as a partner associate, consultant or attorney-at-law.

4. An attorney-at-law shall not solicit business or consent to become involved in a matter unless at the request of a party thereto. Provided however that it is proper for an attorney-at-law to become involved in matters assigned to him by the Legal Aid and Advisory Authority or referred by the Law Association or by another attorney-at-law or for which he is engaged in any other manner not inconsistent with these Rules.

5. An attorney-at-law shall not in the carrying on of his practice or otherwise permit any act or thing which is likely or is intended to attract business unfairly or can reasonably be regarded as touting or advertising.

6. (1) An attorney-at-law shall not in any way make use of any form of advertisement calculated to attract clients to himself or any firm with which he is associated and he shall not permit, authorise or encourage anyone to do so or reward anyone for doing so on his behalf.

(2) An attorney-at-law shall not permit his professional standing to be used for the purpose of advertising any particular product, service or commercial organization.

(3) An attorney-at-law shall not advertise for business indirectly by furnishing or inspiring newspaper comment concerning cases or causes in which an attorney-at-law has been or is connected or concerning the

manner of their conduct, the magnitude of the interests involved, the importance of the attorney-at-law's position and any similar self-laudations.

Provided however that —

(a) an attorney-at-law may permit limited and dignified identification of himself as an attorney-at-law —
   (i) in political advertisements relevant to the course of a political campaign or issue;
   (ii) in public notices where the announcement of his professional status is required or authorised by law, or is reasonably necessary for a purpose other than the attraction of potential clients;
   (iii) in reports and announcements of *bona fide* commercial, civic, professional or political organizations in which he serves as a director or officer;
   (iv) in and on legal textbooks, articles, professional journals and other legal publications and in dignified and restrained advertisements thereof;
   (v) in announcements of any public address, lecture, or publication by him on legal topics, provided that such announcements do not emphasize his own professional competence and are not likely to be regarded as being concerned with the giving of individual advice by him.

(b) An attorney-at-law may speak in public or write for publication on legal topics so long as he does not thereby emphasize his own professional competence and is not likely to be regarded as being concerned thereby with the giving of individual advice.

(c) The following cards, office signs, letterheads or directory listings may be used by an attorney-at-law but in a restrained and dignified form —
   (i) a professional card identifying the attorney-at-law by name and as an attorney-at-law giving his decorations and degrees, legal or otherwise, his addresses, telephone numbers and the name of his law firm or professional associates so however that such cards are not published in the news media and are only handed out on request and for the purposes of identification or address;
   (ii) a brief professional announcement card to be delivered only to attorneys-at-law, clients, personal friends and relations and government bodies and stating new or changed associations or addresses, changes of firm name or like professional matters;
   (iii) a sign or a size and design compatible with the existing practice of the profession, on or near the door of the office and in the building directory identifying the law office;
   (iv) a letterhead identifying the attorney-at-law by name and as an

attorney-at-law and giving his decorations and degrees, legal or otherwise, his addresses, telephone numbers and the name of his law firm and of his associates;

(v) a listing in a telephone directory, a reputable law list, legal directory or biographical reference giving brief biographical or other relevant information; and any such professional card, office sign, letterhead or listing may state the attorney-at-law is also a notary public.

7. Where an attorney-at-law commits any criminal offence which in the opinion of the Disciplinary Committee is of a nature likely to bring the profession into disrepute, such commission of the offence shall constitute professional misconduct if —

(a) he has been convicted by any Court, including a foreign Court of competent jurisdiction, for the offence; or

(b) although he has not been prosecuted the Committee is satisfied of the facts constituting the criminal offence; or

(c) he has been prosecuted and has been acquitted by reason of a technical defence or he has been convicted but such conviction is quashed by reason of some technical defence.

8. An attorney-at-law shall not acquire directly or indirectly by purchase, or otherwise a financial or other interest in the subject matter of a case which he is conducting.

9. (1) An attorney-at-law shall not enter into partnership or fee sharing arrangements concerning the practice of law with non-qualified bodies or persons.

(2) An attorney-at-law shall not enter into an agreement for or charge or collect a fee in contravention of those Rules or any other law.

10. (1) An attorney-at-law shall not charge fees that are unfair or unreasonable. (In determining the fairness and reasonableness of a fee the following factors may be taken into account —

(a) the time and labour required, the novelty and difficulty of the questions involved and the skill required to perform the legal service properly;

(b) the likelihood that the acceptance of the particular employment will preclude other employment by the attorney-at-law;

(c) the fee customarily charged in the locality for similar legal services;

(d) the amount, if any involved;

(e) the time limitations imposed by the client or by the circumstances;

(f) the nature and length of the professional relationship with the client;

(g) the experience, reputation and ability of the attorney-at-law concerned;

(h) any scale of fees or recommended guide as to charges prescribed by law or by the Law Association).

(2) An attorney-at-law shall not accept any fee or reward for merely introducing a client or referring a case or client to another attorney-at-law.

(3) An attorney-at-law shall not charge a contingency fee save and except reasonable commissions on collection of liquidated claims with the prior agreement of the client.

11. (1) Except with the specific approval of his client given after full disclosure, an attorney-at-law shall not act in any manner in which his professional duties and his personal interests conflict or are likely to conflict.

(2) An attorney-at-law shall not accept or continue his retainer or employment on behalf of two or more clients if their interests are likely to conflict or if his independent professional judgment is likely to be impaired.

12. (1) An attorney-at-law who withdraws from employment under Rule 34 of Part A shall not do so until he has taken reasonable steps to avoid foreseeable prejudice or injury to the position and rights of his client including —

(a) giving due notice;

(b) allowing time for employment of another attorney-at-law;

(c) delivering to the client all documents and property to which he is entitled subject however to any lien which the attorney-at-law may have over the same;

(d) complying with such laws, rules or practice as may be applicable; and

(e) where appropriate, obtaining the permission of the Court where the hearing of the matter has commenced.

(2) An attorney-at-law who withdraws from employment shall refund promptly such part of the fees, if any, already paid by his client as may be fair and reasonable having regard to all the circumstances.

13. An attomey-at-law shall withdraw forthwith from employment or from a matter pending before a tribunal —

(a) where the client insists upon his representing a claim or defence that he cannot conscientiously advance;

(b) where the client seeks to pursue a course of conduct which is illegal or which will result in deliberately deceiving the Court;

(c) where a client has in the course of the proceedings perpetrated a fraud upon a person or tribunal and on request by the attorney-at-law has refused or is unable to rectify the same;

(d) where his continued employment will involve him in the violation of the law or a disciplinary rule;

(e) where the client by any other conduct renders it unreasonably difficult for the attorney-at-law to carry out his employment as such effectively, or in accordance with the judgment and advice of the attorney-at-law, or the rules of law or professional ethics;

(f) where for any good and compelling reason it is difficult for him to carry out his employment effectively.

14. An attorney-at-law shall not retain money he received for his client for longer than is absolutely necessary.

15. An attorney-at-law shall never disclose, unless lawfully ordered to do so by the Court or required by statute, what has been communicated to him in his capacity as an attorney-at-law by his client's attorney-at-law and this duty not to disclose extends to his partners, to junior attorneys-at-law assisting him and to his employees provided however that an attorney-at-law may reveal confidences or secrets necessary to establish or collect his fee or to defend himself or his employees or associates against an accusation of wrongful conduct.

16. An attorney-at-law shall not permit his professional services or his name to be used in any way which would make it possible for persons who are not legally authorised to do so to practise law.

17. An attorney-at-law shall not delegate to a person not legally qualified and not in his employ or under his control, any functions which are by the laws of Trinidad and Tobago only to be performed by a qualified attorney-at-law.

18. In the performance of his duties an attorney-at-law shall not act with inexcusable or undue delay, negligence or neglect.

19. An attorney-at-law shall not engage in undignified or discourteous conduct which is degrading to the Court or his profession.

20. An attorney-at-law shall not willfully make false accusations against a Judge or Magistrate.

21. An attorney-at-law who holds a public office shall not use his public position to influence or attempt to influence a tribunal to act in favour of himself or of his client.

22. An attorney-at-law shall not accept private employment in a matter upon the merits of which he previously acted in a judicial capacity or for which he had substantial responsibility while he was in public employment.

23. An attorney-at-law shall not give, lend or promise anything of value to a Judge, juror or official of a tribunal before which there is a pending matter in which he is engaged.

24. In any proceedings in a Court an attorney-at-law shall not communicate or cause any other person to communicate with a juror as to the merits of such proceedings, and shall only do so with a Judge or person exercising judicial functions —

(a) in the normal course of the proceedings; or

(b) where authorised by law, or the practice of the Courts.

25. An attorney-at-law shall not for the purpose of making any person available as a witness, advise or cause that person to secrete himself or leave the jurisdiction of the Court.

26. An attorney-at-law shall not pay or offer to pay or acquiesce in the payment of compensation to a witness for giving evidence in any cause or matter save as reimbursement for expenses reasonably incurred and as reasonable compensation for loss of time in attending for preparation and for testifying, and in the case of an expert witness a reasonable fee for his professional services.

27. An attorney-at-law shall not knowingly use perjured testimony or false evidence or participate in the creation of or use of evidence which he knows to be false.

28. An attorney-at-law shall not counsel or assist his client or a witness, in conduct that the attorney-at-law knows to be illegal or fraudulent, and where he is satisfied that his client has in the course of the particular representation perpetrated a fraud upon a person or tribunal, he shall promptly call upon him to rectify the same.

29. An attorney-at-law shall not knowingly make a false statement of law or fact.

30. (1) An attorney-at-law shall not commit a breach of an undertaking given by him to a Judge, a Court or other Tribunal or an official thereof, whether such undertaking relates to an expression of intention as to future conduct or is a representation that a particular state of facts exists.

    (2) An attorney-at-law shall not knowingly represent falsely to a Judge, a Court or other Tribunal or to an official of a Court or other Tribunal, that a particular state of facts exists.

31. In pecuniary matters an attorney-at-law shall be most punctual and diligent, he shall never mingle funds of others with his own and he shall at all times be able to refund money he holds for others.

32. (1) An attorney-at-law shall keep such accounts as clearly and accurately distinguish the financial position between himself and his client as and when required.

    (2) An attorney-at-law shall comply with such rules as may be made by the Council under section 33 of the Act.

    Provided that nothing contained in Rules 31 and 32 shall deprive an attorney-at-law of any recourse or right whether by way of lien, set-off, counterclaim, charge or otherwise against monies standing to the credit of a client's account maintained by that attorney-at-law.

33. An attorney-at-law shall reply promptly to any letter received from the Law Association relating to his professional conduct.

34. Where no provision is made in these rules in respect of any matter, the rules and practice of the legal profession which formerly governed the particular

matter shall apply in so far as is practicable.

35. (1) Breach by an attorney-at-law of any of the Rules contained in this Part shall constitute professional misconduct and an attorney-at-law who commits such a breach shall be liable to any of the penalties which the Disciplinary Committee and/or the Court is empowered to impose.

(2) Breach by an attorney-at-law of any of the provisions of Part A of this Code while not automatically amounting to punishable professional misconduct is a derogation from the high standards of conduct expected from an attorney-at-law and may, depending on the circumstances of the particular case, amount to such misconduct or form a material ingredient thereof.

FOURTH SCHEDULE

(Section 36)

THE DISCIPLINARY COMMITTEE

Constitution and membership

1. (1) The Disciplinary Committee shall consist of the President of the Association and fifteen other persons appointed by the Chief Justice after consultation with the Council.

(2) The appointed members shall include three members of the Council.

(3) Subject to subparagraph (4) the other appointed members shall be attorneys-at-law of not less than ten years standing.

(4) The Chairman and Vice-Chairman of the Committee shall be appointed by the Chief Justice after consultation with the Council and shall be members who have held high judicial office or, are attorneys-at-law of not less than ten years standing.

Term of office

2. Subject to the provisions of this Schedule the members of the Committee shall hold office for a period not exceeding three years, and are eligible for re-appointment.

Power of Disciplinary Committee to sit in divisions

3. (1) For the purposes of hearing applications made pursuant to section 37 of the Act, the Disciplinary Committee may sit in two divisions.

(2) Subject to the directions of the Council, the Chairman of the Committee shall determine the composition of each division.

(3) Each division shall be entitled to hear and determine any application and shall be entitled to exercise all

powers of the Disciplinary Committee; and any hearing by or determination or order of such division shall be deemed to be a hearing by or determination or order of the Disciplinary Committee.

4. A member of the Committee may at any time resign his office by letter addressed to the Chief Justice and to the Chairman of the Committee. Resignation

5. The Council may, if it thinks it expedient so to do and with the approval of the Chief Justice, at any time revoke the appointment of any member of the Committee. Revocation of appointment

6. Where an appointed member of the Council vacates his seat before the expiration of his term of office a person similarly qualified to him shall be appointed in a similar manner to fill the vacancy for the remainder of that term of office. Filling of vacancies

7. The names of all members of the Committee as first constituted and every change in membership thereof shall be published in the *Gazette*. Publication of membership

8. No member of the Committee shall be personally liable for any act or default of the Committee done or omitted to be done in good faith in the performance of its functions of this Act. Liability for default of Committee

9. Proceedings at meetings
   (1) The Committee shall meet in private at such times as may be expedient for the transaction of business and such meeting shall be held in such places and times and on such days as the Committee shall determine.
   (2) The Chairman or, in his absence, the Vice-Chairman shall preside at meetings of the Committee.
   (3) If, at any meeting of the Committee, the Chairman or Vice-Chairman is for any reason unable to act as such, the members present may elect one of their members to preside at that meeting.
   (4) The quorum of the Committee shall, subject to paragraph 3, be three.
   (5) The validity of any proceedings of the Committee shall not be affected by any vacancy among the members thereof or by any defect in the appointment of a member thereof.
   (6) Subject to this Schedule and the Fifth Schedule, the Committee shall have power to regulate its own proceedings.

FIFTH SCHEDULE

(Section 38)

THE LEGAL PROFESSION (DISCIPLINARY PROCEEDINGS) RULES, 1986

1. These Rules may be cited as the Legal Profession (Disciplinary Proceedings) Rules, 1986. — Short title

2. For the purposes of these Rules, "Secretary" means the Registrar or the person deputed by him for the time being to perform all or any of the functions of the Secretary. — Secretary of the Committee

3. An application to the Committee to require an attorney-at-law to answer allegations contained in an affidavit shall be in writing under the hand of the applicant in Form 1 of the Appendix and shall be sent to the Secretary together with an affidavit by the applicant in Form 2 of the Appendix stating the matters of fact on which he relies in support of his application. — Application and Affidavits Form 1, Form 2

4. Before fixing a day for the hearing, the Committee may require applicant to supply such further information and documents relating to the allegations as it thinks fit, and in any case where in the opinion of the Committee, no *prima facie* case is shown, the Committee may, without requiring the attorney-at-law to answer the allegations, dismiss the application and notify the applicant and the attorney-at-law of the dismissal. — Further information and document no case to answer

5. In any case in which, in the opinion of the Committee, a *prima facie* case is shown, the Committee shall fix a day of hearing and the Secretary shall serve notice thereof on the applicant and on the attorney-at-law, and shall also serve on the attorney-at-law a copy of the application and affidavit. The notice shall not be less than a twenty-one days' notice. — Notice of hearing

6. The notice shall be in Form 3 and Form 4 of the Appendix, at the case may be, and shall require the applicant and the attorney-at-law respectively to furnish to the Secretary and to each other a list of all documents on which they respectively propose to rely. Such lists shall, unless otherwise ordered by the Committee, be furnished by the applicant and by the attorney-at-law respectively at least fourteen days before the day of hearing. — List of documents for hearing Form 3, Form 4

7. Either party may inspect the documents included in the list furnished by the other, and a copy of any document — Inspection of document

mentioned in the list of either party shall, on the application of the party requiring it, be furnished to that party by the other within three days after the receipt of the application.

8. If either or both parties fail to appear at the hearing the Committee may, upon proof of service of the notice of hearing, proceed to hear and determine the application in his or their absence. Proceedings in absence of parties

9. The Committee may in its discretion, either as to the whole case or as to any particular facts, proceed and act upon evidence given by affidavits. Affidavit evidence

10. Where the Committee proceeds to act upon evidence given by affidavit in accordance with rule 9, any party to the proceedings may require any deponent to any such affidavit to be summoned to appear before the Committee, unless the Committee is satisfied that the affidavit is purely formal and the requirement of the appearance of the deponent is made with the sole object of causing delay. Committee may summon deponent to give oral evidence

11. A summons issued by the Committee under section 38 of this Act may be in Form 5 of the Appendix with such variations as the case may require. Subpoena Form 5

12. If the findings and order of the Committee are not pronounced on the date of hearing, notice shall be given to the parties of the date when the findings and order will be pronounced. Notice to parties of date of findings

13. The Committee shall hear all applications in private. Applications to be heard in private

14. The Committee may of their own motion, or upon the application of either party, adjourn the hearing upon such terms as to file Committee may appear just. Adjournment of hearing

15. Notes of proceedings shall be taken by the Secretary or other person appointed by the Committee, and any party who appeared at the proceedings shall be entitled to inspect the original or a copy thereof. Every person entitled to be heard upon an appeal against an order of the Committee shall be entitled to a copy of such notes on the payment of the charges presented by the Committee. Notes of proceedings

16. Service of any notice or document required by these Rules may be effected by registered letter addressed to the last Service of notice of documents

known place of abode or business of the person to be served, and proof that such letter was so addressed and posted shall be proof of service. Any notice or document required to be given or signed by the Secretary may be given or signed by him or by any person duly authorised by the Committee in that behalf.

17. Notwithstanding anything to the contrary the Committee may extend or abridge the time for doing anything under these Rules. Power to extend time

18. All affidavits shall be filed and kept by the Secretary. The Committee may order that any books, papers or other exhibits produced or used at a hearing shall be retained by the Secretary until the time for appealing has expired, and, if notice of the appeal be given, until appeal is heard or otherwise disposed of. Secretary to retain affidavits

19. (1) Attorneys-at-law and witnesses shall have the same privileges and immunities in relation to hearings on applications under this Act as in any court of law. Privileges and immunities

(2) A party to an application is entitled to be represented by an attorney-at-law.

20. If after hearing an application the Committee is satisfied that no case of professional misconduct has been made out, it may dismiss the application Dismissal of application after hearing

APPENDIX

Form 1

(Paragraph 3)

Form of Application against an attorney-at-law

To the Committee constituted under the Legal Profession Act, 1986
In the matter of   an attorney-at-law

and

In the matter of the Legal Profession Act, 1986

I, the undersigned   hereby make application that* of   attorney-at-law, may be required to answer the allegations contained in the affidavit which accompanies this application.

I make this application on the ground that the matters of fact stated in the said affidavit constitute conduct unbecoming his profession on the part of the said   in his capacity of attorney-at-law.

In witness whereof I have hereunto set my hand this   day of   , 19

....
Signature

....
Address

....
Profession, business or occupation

Form 2

(Paragraph 3)

Form of Affidavit by Applicant

(a) Name of attorney-at-law	In the matter of *(a)* an attorney-at-law and In the matter of the Legal Profession Act, 1986
(b) Name of Applicant	I, *(b)* make oath and say as follows:
(c) Place of residence	(1) That I reside at *(c)*
(d) County	in the County of *(d)*
(e) Occupation	and am a (e)
(f) Postal Address	and my postal address is *(f)*
(g) Name of attorney-at-law	(2) That *(g)*
(h) Set out facts complained of	*(h)*
(i) Set out shortly the ground of complaint	(3) The complaint I made against the attorney-at-law is that he (i)
	Sworn at this day of , 19
If the person making the Affidavit can read and write, strike out the words in bracket.	(The same having first read over and explained to the deponent when he/she appeared fully to understand the same)
	Before me:
	....
	Justice of the Peace

Form 3

(Paragraph 6)

Form of Notice by Committee to Applicant

Complaint No. of 19

In the matter of attorney-at-law

and

In the matter of the Legal Profession Act, 1986 (Act 1986)

To

of

The day of , 19 is the day fixed for the hearing of your application in the matter of attorney-at-law by the Disciplinary Committee constituted under the Legal Profession Act, 1986.

The Committee will sit at at o'clock in the forenoon.

If you fail to appear the Committee may in accordance with the Rules made under the Legal Profession Act, 1986 proceed in your absence.

You are requested by the Rules under the Legal Profession Act, 1986, to furnish to the said and the Secretary of the Committee at at least fourteen days before the said day of 19 a list of all documents on which you propose to rely.

Either party may inspect the documents included in the list furnished by the other and a copy of any document mentioned in the list of either party must, on the application of the party requiring it, be furnished to that party by the other within three days after receipt of the application.

You are requested to acknowledge the receipt of this Notice without delay.

Dated the day of , 19

....

Secretary, Disciplinary Committee

Form 4

(Paragraph 6)

Form of Notice by Committee to attorney-at-law

Complaint No. of 19

In the matter of attorney-at-law

and

In the matter of the Legal Profession Act, 1986

To

of attorney-at-law

Application has been made by

of to the Disciplinary Committee constituted under the Legal Profession Act, 1986 that you may be required to answer the allegations contained in the affidavit a copy whereof accompanies this Notice.

The day of , 19 is the day fixed for the hearing of the application by the Committee. The Committee will sit at o'clock in the forenoon. If you fail to appear the Committee may in accordance with the Rules made under the Legal Profession Act, 1986, proceed in your absence.

You are required by the Rules made under the Legal Profession Act, 1986, to furnish to the applicant and to the Secretary of the Committee at least fourteen days before the day fixed for hearing a list of all the documents on which you propose to rely.

Either party may inspect the documents included in the list furnished by the other and a copy of any document mentioned in the list of either party must, on application of the party requiring it, be furnished to that party by the other within three days after receipt of the application.

You are requested to acknowledge receipt of this Notice without delay.

Dated the day of , 19

....

Secretary, Disciplinary Committee

Form 5

(Paragraph 11)

Form of Summons by Committee to Witness

Complaint No. of 19
In the matter of attorney-at-law

and

In the matter of the Legal Profession Act, 1986

To

You are hereby summoned to appear before the Disciplinary Committee constituted under the Legal Profession Act, 1986 at on the day of at the hour of o'clock in the noon, and so from day to day until the application in the above matter is heard, to give evidence on behalf of (if the person summoned is to produce books or documents add) and you are required to bring with you (specify the books or documents required).

Whereof fail not at your peril.

Dated this day of , 19

....
Chairman

SIXTH SCHEDULE

(Sections 55, 57 and 58)

The Compensation Fund

PART A

Compensation of Fund

The Fund shall consist of —

(a) all annual contribution paid under section 59;
(b) all interest, dividends and other income and accretions of the capital arising from the investment of the Fund;
(c) the proceeds of any realisation of any investments of the Fund;
(d) all moneys borrowed for the purposes of the Fund;
(e) all sums received by the Council under any insurance effected by the Council under Paragraph 4 of Part B of this Schedule;
(f) all sums received by the Council under section 57(3); and
(g) any other moneys which may belong or accrue to the Fund or be received by the Council in respect thereof

PART B

1. All moneys from time to time forming part, of the Fund shall applicable— Purposes of Fund
   (a) for payment of any costs, charges and expenses of establishing, maintaining, administering and applying the Fund;
   (b) for payment of any premiums on insurances effected by the Council under paragraph 4;
   (c) for repayment of any moneys borrowed by the Council for the purposes of the Fund and for payment of interest on any moneys so borrowed;
   (d) for payment of any grants which the Council may make under section 57 or 58;
   (e) for payment of any other sums properly payable out of the Fund by virtue of section 57 or this Schedule.
2. The Council may invest, in securities in which trustees are authorised by law to invest trust funds in their hands, any moneys which form part of the Fund and are not immediately required for any of the purposes provided for in this Act. Investment of moneys
3. (1) The Council may borrow for the purposes of the Fund from any Lender and may charge any investments of the Fund by way of security for any such loan. Power to borrow
   (2) The aggregate sum owing at any one time in respect of any loans made under sub-paragraph. (1) shall not exceed one hundred thousand dollars.
4. The Council may insure with any person authorised by law to carry on insurance business in Trinidad and Tobago for such purposes and on such terms as the Council may deem expedient in relation to the Fund. Power to insure
5. The accounts of the Fund shall be audited annually by an accountant appointed for the purpose by the Council. Annual Audit

SEVENTH SCHEDULE

[Section 66(2)]

AMENDMENTS TO WRITTEN LAWS

First Column	*Second Column*
The Supreme Court of Judicature Act, Chap. 4:01	1. In section 2, delete the definition of "roll".

First Column	*Second Column*
	2. In section 7(1) substitute for the words "of the Bar of Trinidad and Tobago" occurring in lines two and three, the words "is an attorney-at-law within the meaning of the Legal Profession Act".
	3. In section 77, substitute for paragraphs (e) and (f), the following — "(e)two practitioner members of the Law Association nominated by the Council of the Law Association and who shall hold office for three years".
	4. Substitute for section 78(1)(l) the following — "(1) for regulating and prescribing the procedure in disciplinary proceedings against attorneys-at-law".
	5. Repeal sections 85 to 95 and the Schedule.
The Judicial and Legal Service Act, Chap. 6:01	Repeal section 5 and the Third Schedule.
The Solicitors Act Chap. 6:50	Repeal the whole Act.
Rules of the Supreme Court 1975 L.N. No. 121 of 1980	In order 58A — (a) revoke and replace rule 1 by the following — "Interpretation 1. In this Order — "the Act" means the Legal Profession Act, 1986; "the Committee" means the Disciplinary Committee established by section 36 of the Act; "the Court" means the High Court sitting as a full court consisting of three judges; "the Roll" means the list of attorneys-at-law kept by the Registrar in accordance with section 13 of the Act; "the Rules" means the Legal Profession (Disciplinary Proceedings) Rules, 1986";

First Column	*Second Column*
	(b) in rule 2(1), substitute the words "section 39(2) of the Act" for the words "rule 17 of the Rules", and in rules 2(1) and (5), substitute the words "section 41 of the Act" for the words "section 81(3) of the Act"; (c) in rules 2(5) and 3(1), substitute the words "attorney-at-law" for the word "barrister"; (d) in rule 5, substitute the word "Roll" for the words "Roll of Barristers".

Passed in the House of Representatives this 31st day of July, 1986.

R. L. GRIFFITH
Acting Clerk of the House

It is hereby certified that this Act is one the Bill for which has been passed by the House of Representatives and at the final vote thereon in the House has been supported by the votes of not less than three-fifths of all the members of the House that is to say by the votes of 33 members of the House.

R. L. GRIFFITH
Acting Clerk of the House

Passed in the Senate this 26th day of August, 1986.

M. CARRINGTON
Acting Clerk of the Senate

It is hereby certified that this Act is one the Bill for which has been passed by the Senate and at the final vote thereon in the Senate has been supported by the votes of not less than three-fifths of all the members of the Senate, that is to say by the votes of 21 Senators.

M. CARRINGTON
Acting Clerk of the Senate

INDEX